LIGHTNING WARRIOR

THE LINDA SCHELE SERIES
IN MAYA AND PRE-COLUMBIAN STUDIES

Lightning Warrior

MAYA ART AND KINGSHIP AT QUIRIGUA

Matthew G. Looper

University of Texas Press

Austin

This series was made possible through the generosity
of William C. Nowlin, Jr., and Bettye H. Nowlin.

Library of Congress Cataloging-in-Publication Data
Looper, Matthew George, 1966–
    Lightning warrior : Maya art and kingship at Quirigua / Matthew G.
Looper.—1st ed.
    p. cm. — (Linda Schele series in Maya and pre-Columbian studies)
Includes bibliographical references and index.
    ISBN 0-292-70556-5 (cloth : alk. paper)
    1. Quirigua Site (Guatemala) 2. Maya sculpture—Guatemala—
Motagua River Valley. 3. Stele (Archaeology)—Guatemala—Motagua
River Valley. 4. Mayas—Kings and rulers. 5. Mayas—Guatemala—
Motagua River Valley—Antiquities. 6. Motagua River Valley (Guate-
mala)—Antiquities. I. Title. II. Series.
    F1435.1.Q8 L66 2003
    972.81′31—dc21   2003010416

Contents

Preface

IN 1990 (the year I began my studies of ancient Maya art in graduate school) my dissertation advisor, the late Linda Schele, and anthropologist David Freidel released their book *A Forest of Kings: The Untold Story of the Ancient Maya*. Using hieroglyphic texts as a foundation, this book endeavored to pave the way for a distinctly humanistic understanding of the ancient Maya, in which the achievements of this civilization are attributed not to impersonal economic trends but rather to individual historical agents. Thus, texts and their associated images are situated within contexts of political struggle, in which elites competed against each other to achieve or maintain ascendancy.

Inspired by this pioneering book, my dissertation (completed in 1995) explored the history of one of the most astonishing of these actors known, whose name was probably K'ak' Tiliw Chan Yo'at/Yo'pat, high king of Quirigua, a relatively small ceremonial city located in southeastern Guatemala (Fig. P.1). This ruler, whose name I have taken the liberty of shortening in the present book to K'ak' Tiliw, first became known to the modern world through the work of David Kelley (1962).[1] The outline biography of this ruler was worked out in various subsequent studies.[2] Reigning from 725 to 785, K'ak' Tiliw was by far the most important ruler of Quirigua. Indeed, his remarkable history and associated monuments mark him as one of the most prominent figures in all of Maya history. Until my dissertation, however, the monuments commissioned during his reign had never been studied in detail or as a unit.

Although Kelley referred to K'ak' Tiliw as "Ruler I," we now know that he was actually designated the fourteenth successor of his dynasty (Riese 1982). Of the rulers who preceded him, only four are named in inscriptions. Peter Mathews identified the name of the first or second Quirigua king, associated with a date in the year 455 (Jones and Sharer 1980). Third and fourth successors may be documented from near the end of the fifth century (Jones 1983a). Another ruler is known to have been active at 653, but his position in the dynasty is not clear (Schele 1989d). K'ak' Tiliw himself was succeeded by a ruler known by the nickname "Sky Xul," who ruled for only about ten years, 785–ca. 795 (Jones and Sharer 1980; Kelley 1962). After 795 the dynastic sequence becomes uncertain, with possibly two rulers following in quick succession. The last known ruler, nicknamed Jade Sky, appears in association with dates in 805 and 810 (Grube, Schele, and Fahsen 1991; Kelley 1962).[3]

While one goal of my dissertation was documentation, another was to attempt a synthesis of what I saw at the time as divergent emphases on esoteric, political, or stylistic aspects of Maya art. Few studies, in my view, utilized style together with iconography to reveal the integrated politico-religious meanings of these works. Among the many insights provided by this holistic approach was the clarification of the relationship between the political identity of the king of Quirigua and the various supernatural entities with whom he was associated through ritual performance and other techniques. In particular, although he is named consistently, the identity of K'ak' Tiliw is not stable but develops within a complex historical discourse, articulated through what I call personae or historically specific conventional identities. My goal in the present book is to chart this discourse on both local and regional scales, as expressed in the design of ceremonial cities, particularly Quirigua and its principal rival, Copan. It suggests a shift of attention from the monumental commissions of a single ruler toward a history of interwoven and inherently unstable identities.

One of the distinct tendencies of the recent monographs on Classic Maya sites is to separate hieroglyphic texts from iconography and/or to privilege one or the other (Houston 1993; Newsome 2001; Tate 1992). The texts and images work together, however, to convey the specific meanings of the monument. The result of this scholarly treatment is to lessen the impact of the monuments' rhetoric. In contrast, this book seeks to reconstruct the politico-religious history of Quirigua, through an approach which gives equal weight to textual and pictorial data, firmly grounded in the archaeological record. It should be noted that this approach diverges somewhat from traditional art history (especially Mesoamerican art history), in that it does not privilege the "masterpieces" but gives equal consideration to small, poorly carved, or eroded monuments. In fact, some of the most battered and crudely executed sculptures at Quirigua are of the greatest historical significance—such as Stela H. In general, my intention is to create a fresh understanding of Maya art history through an exploration of the historical foundations and relationships of monumental rhetoric at Quirigua. This involves detailed and comprehensive comparisons of iconography, style, and rhetorical strategies not only within Quirigua itself but also with other sites with which Quirigua was in contact. These include especially Copan but also other lowland centers. Such an analysis allows for a richer historical perspective on Maya art than has generally been achieved in previous studies. In addition, my historical focus motivates a critique of some of the interpretations that have been made of Maya art in the past, including the existence of a master narrative that underlies iconography as well as the concepts of normative "Maya style" and "southeastern Maya style."

Documentation

The center from which K'ak' Tiliw presided during the eighth century is today called Quirigua, after a nearby village. Discovered in 1840 by the English artist Frederick Catherwood and made famous through American traveler John Lloyd Stephens's book *Incidents of Travel in Central America, Chiapas, and Yucatan* (1841), this archaeological site is located on the floodplain of the Motagua River, which originates in the Guatemalan highlands and flows northeast into the Caribbean. This study focuses primarily on the eleven freestanding monuments attributed to K'ak' Tiliw—in chronological order: Altars M and N,

Stelae S, H, J, F, D, E, C, and A, and Zoomorph B.[4] The monumental texts and images of the two (or three) kings who succeeded K'ak' Tiliw also contain useful information for interpreting the history of his reign.

Supplementary information is embodied in architecture, ceramics, and other archaeological data, which have been well established through the efforts of a number of archaeological projects. These began with some clearing and test pitting by Alfred P. Maudslay in 1883, followed by more substantial excavations sponsored by the School of American Archaeology and the Archaeological Institute of America under the direction of Edgar Lee Hewett between 1910 and 1914 (Maudslay 1889–1902; Saville 1919). Although a number of the publications relating to these expeditions were by Hewett himself, the assistant director of the project, Sylvanus G. Morley, reported many of the results in his monumental study *The Inscriptions of Petén* (1937–1938) and in a guidebook to the site published in 1935.[5] Morley also published short articles on the expedition, of which his 1913 article is the most important (Morley 1912, 1913). The full results of these expeditions, however, were never published. Morley's *Inscriptions of Petén* also includes research he conducted at Quirigua under the auspices of the Carnegie Institution of Washington in 1919 and 1923. The Carnegie Institution sponsored brief projects at Quirigua in 1933 and 1934 (Ricketson 1933, 1935; Strömsvik 1941, 1952). However, the most comprehensive excavations at Quirigua were those conducted under the auspices of the University of Pennsylvania Quirigua Project of 1974–1979, which were designed to provide a more complete archaeological picture of the ancient site. This project included not only extensive excavations and reconstructions of the acropolis and surrounding site core but mapping and excavations in outlying areas of the Motagua valley. The results of these investigations have been published in the Quirigua Reports series.[6] A number of summary articles relating to this research have also appeared (Ashmore 1984, 1987; Jones and Sharer 1980, 1986; Sharer 1978, 1980).

While Maudslay made some excavations of structures at Quirigua, his most important contribution is clearly in the area of documentation of the sculptures at the site. It was he who discovered most of the major sculptures and provided the alphabetical designations used in this

Facing page

P.1. Map of the Maya region, showing sites discussed in this book. Drawing by Thomas Tolles and the author.

Yucatan

Gulf of Mexico

Dzibilchaltun

Chichen Itza

Uxmal

Quintana Roo

Campeche

Calakmul

Altun Ha

Tortuguero

El Mirador
Nakbe
Río Azul

Peten

Uaxactun

Palenque

Tikal
Naranjo

Motul de San José

Piedras Negras

L. Peten-Itza

Gulf of Honduras

El Cayo
Yaxchilan

Caracol

Tonina

Bonampak

Belize

Chiapas

Altar de Sacrificios
Dos Pilas

Nim Li Punit
Lubaantun
Uxbenka
Pusilha

Cancuen

Salinas de los Nueve Cerros

L. de Izabal

Guatemala

Cawinal

Quirigua

Honduras

San Agustín Acasaguastlan

Izapa

Guaytan

Río Amarillo
Copan

Abaj Takalik

Kaminaljuyu

Ixtepeque

El Baúl

Chalchuapa

El Salvador

Pacific Ocean

study. In 1883 he commissioned a set of papier-mâché molds of many of the sculptures. The plaster casts made from these molds are conserved in the British Museum and constitute an important record of the sculptures. Maudslay also photographed most of the monuments and had drawings of many of the inscriptions made by the artist Annie Hunter. These excellent photographs and drawings were published in Maudslay's lavish *Biologia Centrali-Americana: Archaeology* (1889–1902). In 1900 the Peabody Museum of Harvard University also made a series of molds and photographs, which have never been published (Gordon 1913). The photographer associated with the School of American Archaeology expeditions to Quirigua, Jesse L. Nusbaum, created an invaluable corpus of detailed photographs of the Quirigua sculptures, most of which were never published and now reside in the History Library of the Museum of New Mexico in Santa Fe. Morley also made useful photographs of Quirigua monuments during his work at the site, many of which were published (Morley 1913, 1937–1938). Casts were also made from molds taken at the site and are presently displayed in the San Diego Museum of Man. Andrea Stone (1983: Appendix B) prepared a list of casts in museum collections.

In recent decades there has been an attempt to produce a complete record of the Quirigua sculptures in drawings. Monument 26, discovered by the University of Pennsylvania project in 1979, was promptly published (Jones 1983a). Drawings of Altars O' and P', which had been discovered by Earl H. Morris and Gustav Strömsvik in 1934, were made by William Coe and published in the Quirigua Reports (Jones 1983b). In 1980 Andrea Stone (1983, 1985) executed an important set of drawings of the altars and zoomorphs not included in Maudslay's work. My own fieldwork at Quirigua between 1993 and 1996 attempted to produce a complete corpus of drawings of the Quirigua monuments. These drawings were based on photographs taken at the site by Thomas Tolles and were checked against the original monuments, archival photographs, and the surviving casts in museum collections (Looper n.d.). The accumulation of documentary and archaeological data allows us to achieve a rich understanding of the history of Quirigua, which has been summarized in a number of works.[7] These interpretations take on even greater significance, however, in light of the data from Copan, which has witnessed over a century of continuous excavations by numerous institutions.[8] The sculptures of Copan are likewise well documented and have been subjected to detailed iconographic and historical analyses, which provide a wealth of comparative data that can aid in examining Quirigua's history.[9] The present study draws frequently on these sources and is a testament to the dedication of previous investigators.

Acknowledgments

CONTRIBUTING more directly to the present study were a number of friends and colleagues, whose assistance I am pleased to acknowledge. First, my dissertation committee members, John Clarke, Terence Grieder, Joan Holladay, and Brian Stross, offered valuable comments and suggestions for improvement. Andrea Stone was especially generous in this regard, furnishing her comments on several early manuscripts relating to my research in addition to the dissertation draft. Many colleagues in Guatemala also provided assistance. I thank the directorship of the Instituto de Antropología e Historia (IDAEH) for permission to carry out fieldwork at the site and the staff, especially Aura Rosa de Flores and Lic. Erick Ponciano, for use of resources in Guatemala City. The IDAEH staff members at Quirigua deserve special recognition for their congeniality and assistance at the site itself. The director of the Museo de Arqueología e Etnología in Guatemala City, Lic. Dora Guerra de González, generously allowed access to the collection. This project was aided immensely by Carmen Matute de Foncea of the U.S. Embassy and by the support and facilities provided by the Centro de Investigaciones Regionales en Mesoamérica in Antigua, its staff, and its directors, Steven Elliot and Tani Adams.

In the United States, the History Library of the Museum of New Mexico, Santa Fe, and the San Diego Museum of Man (SDMM) graciously allowed access to their collections and archives. I am especially grateful to Paul Johnson for his work preparing photographs from the SDMM archive for publication. The members of the "glyph group" of the SDMM, especially Judith Strupp Green, Janis Indrikis, and Margaret Thomas, provided a critical forum for the development of many ideas presented here. I also wish to thank Elizabeth Carmichael of the Museum of Mankind in London for granting access to the Maudslay casts. This study was enhanced by conversations with many scholars, including Wendy Ashmore, Maricela Ayala F., Erik Boot, Magdiel Castillo, Federico Fahsen, William Fash, David Freidel, Nikolai Grube, Christopher Jones, Rosemary Joyce, Julia Guernsey Kappelman, Rex Koontz, Ruth Krochock, Barbara MacLeod, Martha Macri, Simon Martin, Alfonso Morales, Elizabeth Newsome, Sofía Paredes Maury, Dorie Reents-Budet, Kathryn Reese-Taylor, F. Kent Reilly III, Robert Sharer, David Stuart, Carolyn Tate, Patricia Urban, and Elisabeth Wagner. I wish to acknowledge my advisor Linda Schele, for sharing ideas and resources in the best spirit of collegiality. I could not have completed this project without the efforts of Thomas Tolles, who served as photographer, computer consultant, and editor. I am especially grateful for the many hours he spent preparing the final copies of illustrations.

The fieldwork for this project was supported by grants from the National Science Foundation (DBS 9307752), the William J. Fulbright Scholarship Board of the Institute for International Education, a fellowship from the University of Texas at Austin, the Cornelia and Meredith Long Scholarship, and the Center for Excellence in Learning and Teaching of the California State University, Chico Foundation (Summer Scholars grant). Travel funds were provided in part by the John D. Murchison Professorship in Art, formerly held by Linda Schele, and the Department of Art and Art History at California State University, Chico. The Foundation for the Advancement of Mesoamerican Studies provided funding for travel to London.

INTRODUCTION

Quirigua in the Maya World

I was naturally anxious and expectant on this my first visit to a Central-American ruin, but it seemed as though my curiosity would be ill satisfied, for all I could see on arrival was what appeared to be three moss-grown stumps of dead trees covered over with a tangle of creepers and parasitic plants, around which the undergrowth had been cleared away for the space of a few feet. However, a closer inspection showed that these were no tree-stumps but undoubtedly stone monuments. . . . We soon pulled off the creepers, and with rough brushes, made by tying together the midribs of the leaflets of the corosa palm, we set to work to clear away the coating of moss.

As the curious outlines of the carved ornament gathered shape it began to dawn upon me how much more important were these monuments, upon which I had stumbled almost by chance, than any account I had heard of them had led me to expect. This day's work induced me to take a permanent interest in Central-American Archaeology, and a journey which was undertaken merely to escape the rigours of an English winter has been followed by seven expeditions from England for the purpose of further exploration and archaeological research.

ALFRED P. MAUDSLAY (1889–1902, vol. 5: 2), recalling his first days at Quirigua

When the first European and American explorers penetrated the dense jungles surrounding Quirigua more than 150 years ago, the ruins of this ancient Maya ceremonial center fired the Romantic imagination in search of "lost" civilizations. To the pioneer archaeologist of the ancient Maya, Alfred P. Maudslay, the extraordinary carved monuments at Quirigua were an important inspiration. Today we remain impressed by the grandeur and artistic excellence of Quirigua's sculptures, many of which are justifiably considered masterpieces of Maya art. Carved with stone tools, the sandstone monoliths are varied in form and proportion, from short and squat to extremely tall and slender. Many of the sculptures feature idealized portraits of kings dressed in lavish ceremonial regalia. The hieroglyphic texts that accompany these figures reveal that they were erected in honor of local rulers near the end of the Classic period of Maya civilization (A.D. 250–900).

Now thoroughly excavated and converted into an archaeological park, the monuments of Quirigua stand where they were originally erected, in low-lying plazas adjacent to a palace compound that served as the residence of its rulers about A.D. 450–850. (The names of the Quirigua kings are listed in Appendix A.) Unlike other centers, such as Tikal, Caracol, or Calakmul, Quirigua was never a large urban complex but rather served as the ceremonial and market center for a dispersed rural population, in which ethnic Maya were a minority. Quirigua was established on the north bank of the Motagua, a river originating in the highlands of western Guatemala near the ancient trading center of Chichicastenango. Winding its way between the Chuacús range, which lies to the north, and the great line of volcanoes which loom over the Pacific coast to the south, the river gradually drops into the Motagua valley, one of the prominent geological features of Central America (Fig. I.1). Bordered by the Sierra de las Minas and Montañas del Mico to the north and the Sierra del Merendón and Sierra del Espíritu Santo on the south, the broad valley guides the river's meandering course through hot, moist bottomlands toward the northeast and the Gulf of Honduras. Today the Motagua valley is still the primary artery for travel between the western highlands of Guatemala and the Gulf of Honduras.

The geographical location of Quirigua was undoubtedly selected not only because of the access to the highlands but also because it marked a point where the river crossed the route between the city of Copan and the major centers of the Peten. Heading almost directly north from Copan, the mountain trails passed the Copan satellite Río Amarillo and then connected with the headwaters of the Jubuco and Morjá Rivers, which empty into the Motagua just southeast of Quirigua. Travelers to the Peten could then continue northward from Quirigua over a low pass which placed them on the banks of Lake Izabal. Prehispanic settlements have been documented along this route and at its terminus on Lake Izabal, at modern Mariscos (La Ruta Maya Conservation Foundation n.d.; Orozco et al. n.d.). From there, they could follow the tides of the lake via the Río Dulce to the Gulf of Honduras, which provided access to the numerous sites situated on the coastal rivers of southern Belize, such as Pusilha, Uxbenka, Lubaantun, and Nim Li Punit (Fig. P.1). Alternatively, disembarking at the northeastern end of the lake, they could begin overland treks into the southeastern Peten.

The location of Quirigua at a crossroads between the highlands, the southeastern Maya zone centered on Copan, and the Peten heartland suggests the importance of trade in its economy (Ashmore 1984; Sharer 1978, 1990; Sharer et al. 1983: 48; Sheets 1983). Although excavations suggest that Quirigua was unusually poor in jade compared to other Maya centers, there is archaeological evidence for the city's trade in obsidian, derived primarily from the Ixtepeque source located near the upper Motagua. In addition, the highly fertile bottomlands of the valley no doubt supported agriculture, and there is some evidence for cacao as a local cash crop in the Classic period (Ashmore 1984). The vast forest resources of the lower Motagua valley also probably contributed significantly to the local economy. Despite all these advantages in location and natural resources, however, Quirigua grew slowly and even collapsed for a time, before achieving a period of growth in the eighth century A.D. At its height, Quirigua consisted of a settlement center of only about four square kilometers with a population of no more than two thousand persons (Ashmore 1980a: 23, 1987: 221). Even including the many outlying groups that surrounded the floodplain center in the eighth century, Quirigua was very small, especially compared to its neighbor, Copan, where fifteen to twenty thousand persons occupied a small mountain valley during the Late Classic period (Fash 2001; Webster, Sanders, and van Rossum 1992).

Maya Kingship

While Copan appears to have been settled far earlier than Quirigua and grew much larger, kings ruled both cities during the Classic period. (Lists of events at the two centers appear in Appendices B and C.) Like the kings of many other centers, the Late Classic rulers of Quirigua were considered both political and spiritual leaders. One of the royal roles emphasized in hieroglyphic texts and monumental art is that of a medium between the social and supernatural worlds. Rulers could serve as mediums for supernatural entities during ecstatic ritual (Freidel and Schele 1988a; Freidel, Schele, and Parker 1993; Schele and Freidel 1990). Conjured using ritual implements, represented in figural art, or embodied in sacred masks and costume, deities were manifested in diverse forms so that the kings could communicate with and direct them. Such acts of supernatural communication were closely connected with the sacrifice of blood and other precious substances. Astronomy constituted an important aspect of supernatural contact, for through this knowledge rulers were able to anticipate auspicious moments for activities such as warfare or political ceremonies. Astronomy, numerology, and other sacred knowledge became the basis for the chronology of official histories, as recorded in hieroglyphic codices, painted ceramics, and inscribed monuments. Such knowledge had to be publicly affirmed through performance, however. In this sense, Classic kingship emphasized power through personal charisma.

For about a millennium, beginning around A.D. 100, rulers of ancient Maya sites generally conceived of the transfer of power as dynastic or carried through lineage that was reckoned to a deified ancestor. Rulership was patrilineal and often determined by primogeniture, although occasionally it could pass through brothers. Following the death of the previous ruler, a lord underwent a series of complex accession rituals that associated the ruler with certain distinctive supernatural entities. Their culmination was a ritual death and rebirth, signaled by coronation with a white headband (sak hunal) made of bark paper, which might include jade ornaments that revealed their living spiritual essence. Additional personified headdresses were sometimes presented, and the ruler displayed a snake-footed deity (God K) scepter, called k'awil. As a sign of his new identity, the ruler also assumed a new name, usually derived from a (typically celestial) deity. Frequently, this name was identical to that of a prominent ancestor, and in a real sense the king became the present manifestation of that former personality.

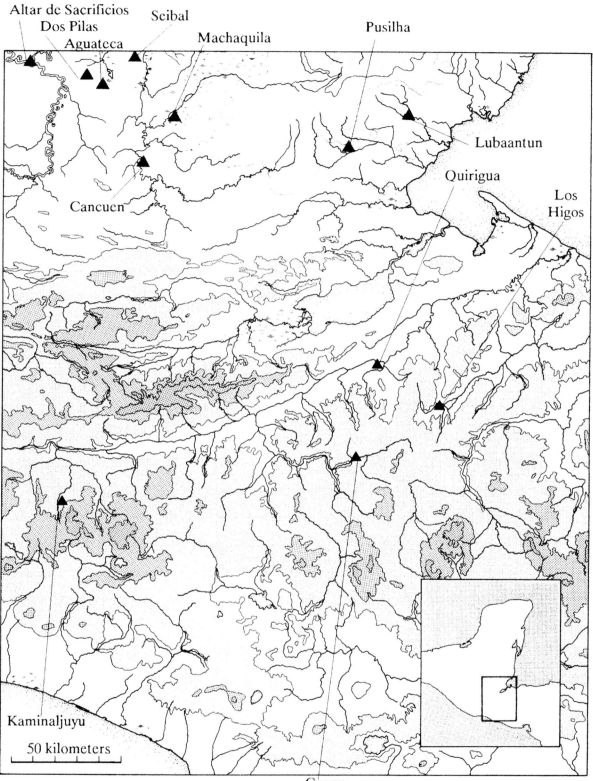

Altar de Sacrificios Seibal   Pusilha
    Dos Pilas
       Aguateca   Machaquila

                                                        Lubaantun
                                        Quirigua
                                                        Los
                                                        Higos
Cancuen

Kaminaljuyu

50 kilometers

Copan

I.1. Map of the Maya southeastern region. Drawing by Karim
Sadr, courtesy Foundation for the Advancement of Mesoamerican Studies, Inc.

An ancient Maya king was entitled to a certain political status, embodied in the emblem glyph title that he usually bore.[1] The emblem glyph is a title naming a person a supreme *ajaw* "lord" of a certain polity, ideally, of equal status with other emblem glyph-bearing rulers. For example, the Quirigua emblem glyph (Fig. I.2) consists of a dotted element reading *k'uhul* "divine," prefixed to a sign depicting a gourd, which was the ancient name for the site. The small sign above the gourd reads *ajaw*. In general, the polity referenced by the emblem glyph signified a city and probably a certain amount of the surrounding land. In many cases, small sites were established at strategic locations within larger polities, such as El Cayo, built on an island near Piedras Negras. The rulers of some subordinate centers were merely called *ajaw* or had specialized titles such as *sajal* instead of the full emblem glyph. Many of these sublords acknowledged the dominance of their overlord in the texts they commissioned. In some rare instances, lords of subordinate centers used the same emblem glyph title as their overlords. An example is B'alam Ajaw of Tortuguero, who was a war leader under K'inich Janab' Pakal I of Palenque during the seventh century. Many of these political hierarchies were expressed through complex references to "overkingship" in hieroglyphic texts.[2] Thus, some lords are stated to be *yajaw* "the *ajaw* of" another. Others conducted actions that are said to have taken place *ukab'jiy* (or *uchab'jiy*) "under the supervision of" an overlord. Political expansion, therefore, was not defined in terms of territorial acquisition per se but by subordination of rulers and their dynastic centers.

Of further importance in maintaining the hierarchy of different polities was the intense rivalry between Tikal and Calakmul, the largest urban settlements in the Classic Maya lowlands.[3] Recent evidence suggests that the economic success and growth of many Classic-period polities were closely tied to a site's political relationship with these two great powers. Although the precise mechanism of these interactions is still being investigated, in-

tersite marriages, elite visits, presentation of gifts, and military intervention have all been suggested as factors. Most of the larger Classic centers had political relationships with either Tikal or Calakmul that sometimes extended over a long period. Accordingly, intersite relationships often developed into enduring rivalries and alliances. Occasionally, however, sites profited through a change of alliance coupled with military victory.[4] The most famous example of this strategy is probably Caracol: beginning as a client of Tikal, Caracol switched sides in A.D. 562 and, aided by Calakmul, witnessed the defeat of its former overlord (Grube 1994; Martin and Grube 2000). Although Tikal and Calakmul did attack each other and each other's allies directly, sometimes an ally of Tikal would attack an ally of Calakmul or vice versa. As will be seen, neither Quirigua nor Copan was isolated from the tension between Tikal and Calakmul. In fact, Quirigua's explosive growth in the eighth century may be explained by reference to these external political relationships, apparently affording its most famous ruler a new route to power through warfare and sacrifice rather than dynastic inheritance.

The focus of this book is the history of this ruler, who led Quirigua into its period of maximum political power during the eighth century, reigning from A.D. 725 to 785. According to the hieroglyphic inscriptions, his name was K'ak' Tiliw Chan Yo'at/Yo'pat, or K'ak' Tiliw for short (Fig. I.3a).[5] Like many elite names of the Classic period, this name derives from that of a deity, thereby evoking both his superhuman power and divine ancestry. The first part of the name includes the words for "fire" (*k'ak'*) and *tiliw*, which is probably a derived form of the root *til*, meaning "burn," followed by *chan* "sky." The last element of this name, *yo'at/yo'pat*, alternates with a glyph that depicts a lightning deity who holds a lobed stone object, often in a quatrefoil shape (Fig. I.3b).[6] This object symbolizes the caves in which the Classic Maya considered many deities, especially the lightning spirits, to reside. It is also utilized by the Yo'at/Yo'pat lightning spirit to crack the carapace of the cosmic turtle, resulting in the rebirth of maize, as discussed below (Fig. I.4). The approximate translation of this ruler's name as "fire-burning celestial lightning god" is truly awesome, representing a significant claim to divine identity.

By 725, when this ruler assumed the title of divine lord of Quirigua, many of the sites in the Maya lowlands were experiencing growth and concomitant political tensions. The neighboring site of Copan in particular was undergoing a population explosion that had begun to stress the valley's carrying capacity. Its ruler, Waxaklajun Ub'ah

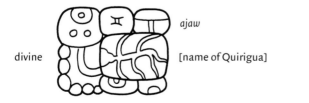

I.2. The Quirigua emblem glyph, from Stela C, D8. Drawing by author.

divine   ajaw   [name of Quirigua]

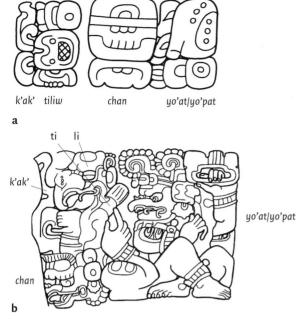

k'ak' tiliw   chan   yo'at/yo'pat

a

ti li

k'ak'

yo'at/yo'pat

chan

b

I.3. Variants of the name of K'ak' Tiliw Chan Yo'at/Yo'pat: *a*, QRG Stela I, D3b–C4; *b*, QRG Zoomorph B, glyph 16. Drawings by author.

K'awil (formerly known to scholars as "18-Rabbit"), witnessed the expansion of Copan during the reign of his predecessor and probable father, Smoke Imix, who had reigned for most of the seventh century, from A.D. 628 to 695. Even so, the end came sooner than Waxaklajun Ub'ah K'awil could have anticipated, when he was captured and sacrificed under the auspices of K'ak' Tiliw in 738.

In this regard Copan was not alone, for this was a time of ruthless conflict and power struggles among elite centers, many of which witnessed the humiliation of defeat in war and the capture of their rulers. Calakmul, for example, suffered the loss of its ruler, Jaguar Paw, in 695. In 711 Palenque also lost its king, K'an Xul, to its enemy Tonina. The victors in these struggles often commissioned major art programs. Tikal, for instance, was enjoying a renaissance under Jasaw Chan K'awil; and master artists at Yaxchilan, under the auspices of Shield Jaguar, were working on Temple 23 and its great lintels featuring his wife, Lady Xok. The ruler of Naranjo, K'ak' Tiliw Chan Chaak, had just completed a series of successful raids in the Yaxha region and commissioned a number of exquisite stelae to commemorate himself and

maize deity   **Yo'at/Yo'pat**

I.4. Resurrection of the maize deity by the actions of a lightning deity (Yo'at/Yo'pat). Classic polychrome vessel, Museum of Fine Arts, Boston (K731). Drawing by author.

his redoubtable mother, Lady Six Sky. One of the most astonishing success stories of the times, however, was that of Dos Pilas, a renegade dynasty that split from Tikal in the mid-seventh century. Led by a series of aggressive rulers who had allied themselves with Calakmul, this polity expanded rapidly, conquering several sites in the region. Ruler 2 of Dos Pilas, who acceded in 698, oversaw the translation of his polity's new wealth and status into massive architectural programs, such as the El Duende group. Quirigua's political strategies bear comparison to those of Dos Pilas in some respects. It seems likely that those in power remained well informed concerning developments in polities both near and far and adjusted policy accordingly, waiting for the perfect moment to strike at those in their path.

What is particularly significant about the history of K'ak' Tiliw is the singular role of monumental texts and images in celebrating the ruler's exploits, by presenting these acts in certain supernatural contexts. During his long reign, Quirigua was embellished with eight known stelae, one large zoomorph, and two smaller zoomorphic sculptures. The monuments are of intrinsic significance to archaeology and art history for their massive scale, elaborate carving, and excellent state of preservation (Fig. I.5). In view of their colossal size, their high sculptural quality, and the eloquent poetics of their hieroglyphic texts, the sculptures of Quirigua stand out as some of the greatest achievements of Classic Maya civilization. They are also nearly all *in situ*, which locks them into a precise spatial and temporal context. But even more important is the survival of the Quirigua monuments as a complete series between the dates of A.D. 746 and 810, spanning the reigns of at least three kings. Few Maya sites provide such a comprehensive record of artistic development over time. In spite of these qualities, previous studies have not adequately contextualized the art or politics of Quirigua within the greater Maya or Mesoamerican traditions. In Maya studies, Quirigua is usually considered of secondary importance, owing to its marginal location and relatively unassuming architecture. This study highlights the importance of the sculptures of Quirigua as a major source of information concerning ancient Maya spirituality and political theory that can be related to a specific historical context.

Sculptural Formats and Practices at Quirigua

Artistic traditions clearly express the political and spiritual ties between Quirigua and other Classic Maya centers. These practices drew indirectly upon traditions that had been developed by one of the most ancient civ-

I.5. QRG Stela F, north face. From Maudslay 1889–1902, *Archaeology*, vol. 2, Plate 35. From the facsimile edition of *Biologia Centrali-Americana* by Alfred Percival Maudslay. Published 1974 by Milpatron Publishing Corp., Stamford, Conn. Further reproduction prohibited.

ilizations of Mesoamerica, the Olmec of the Gulf Coast of Mexico (de la Fuente 1973; Drucker 1952; Milbrath 1979). One of the major centers associated with this culture, La Venta, flourished between 1000 and 600 B.C. Sculptural technique at La Venta was varied, with execution in both high and low relief. Among the Olmec innovations seen at La Venta were some of Mesoamerica's first upright stone monoliths or stelae as well as rectangular thrones and volumetric sculptures in the forms of humans, colossal human heads, animals, and supernatural beings. The Olmec also sometimes associated altars with stelae, as at the highland site of Chalcatzingo (Grove 1984: 62–64). The stela form may have evolved from the Olmec celt or ceremonial axe, which was identified with maize (Porter 1996; Taube 1996). This symbolism is expressed in a set of celtiform stelae set up at the foot of La Venta Mound C (Fig. I.6). These monuments depict supernatural beings wearing elaborate head-

I.7. La Venta Stela 2. Drawing by author.

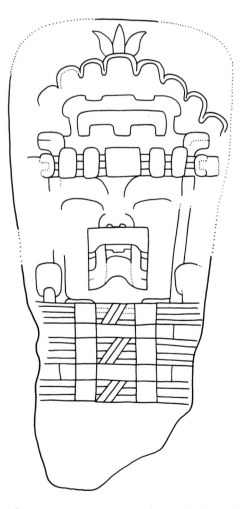

I.6. La Venta Monument 25/26. Drawing by author.

dresses crowned with a trefoil maize icon.[7] Together with the upright form of the stela, such botanical imagery has led some researchers to associate these monuments with concept of a "world tree," a symbolic axis of communication between levels of the universe (Freidel, Schele, and Parker 1993: 134–135; Reilly 1994). But the Olmec stela was not exclusively a supernatural effigy; it could also portray historical personages. The La Venta stelae sometimes show rulers in a narrative mode portraying ritual action (e.g., Stela 5), but these rulers can also be represented iconically, bearing the implements of office and/or placed in cosmological or supernatural settings (e.g., Stelae 1 and 2; Fig. I.7).

As the Olmec culture at La Venta waned, numerous centers elsewhere in Mesoamerica preserved and elaborated these sculptural forms, including thrones or supports as well as stelae. Upright carved slabs appeared for the first time in the Maya lowlands in the Middle to Late Formative period, at sites such as Nakbe and El Mirador

(Hansen 1989; Matheny 1987). Although these monuments were the direct ancestors of Classic stelae, also participating in the development of the stela were centers in Chiapas, the Guatemalan highlands, and the Pacific slope, particularly Izapa, Abaj Takalik, El Baúl, and Kaminaljuyu, all of which thrived in the Late Formative period (300 B.C.–A.D. 250). At these centers, the stela format was exploited even more than it had been among the Olmec. At most of these centers and especially at Izapa, stelae were placed at the base of mounds in a manner reminiscent of La Venta.

Although each of these major Late Formative centers featured stelae bearing varied iconography, one image is common to all four centers: the ruler shown in the ritual of conjuring spirit beings, who appear above him, as on Izapa Stela 4, Kaminaljuyu Stela 11, and El Baúl Stela 1 (Fig. I.8). When they adopted the stela form in the second and third centuries, lowland Maya rulers preferred

this type of scene, the antecedents of which can be traced to Middle Formative Olmec stelae such as La Venta Stela 2. Although iconographic and epigraphic similarities suggest that the early lowland Maya stela was more closely related iconographically and stylistically to the sculptures of El Baúl and Kaminaljuyu than to those of Izapa, the importance of Izapa in promulgating the stela form should not be discounted. As the stela spread throughout the Maya lowlands in the Early Classic period, it retained a number of its Late Formative features. It passed from kingdom to kingdom as a unified conception, replicating the low-relief style and primary function as an expression of the political and religious institution of kingship.

As a defining feature of Classic Maya civilization, the stela has been subjected to intensive study; and several interpretations have been put forth to explain the symbolism of this class of monuments. One of the most important of these is the suggestion that stelae may symbolize the "world tree." According to Mircea Eliade (1964: 120, 194, 269–274), this concept refers to a cosmic tree located at the center of the world that serves to connect the three cosmic realms of the heavens, earth, and underworld and is a source of life. Part of the original support for the association of stelae with the world tree was an erroneous decipherment of the glyph for "stela" as te' tun or "stone tree." We now know that the Maya termed these monuments lakam tun, possibly translated as "huge stone" or "banner stone."[8] Nevertheless, there is ample support for identifying "world trees" both in the Maya ethnographic record and in ancient Maya art.[9] In fact, most of K'ak' Tiliw's portraits show him wearing the "God-C" apron, which Linda Schele and Mary Ellen Miller (1986: 77) convincingly identify as a representation of the trunk and branches of a sacred tree (Fig. I.9).

This costume element appears in diverse contexts (such as figurines and carved panels), however, and is not specific to stelae; thus it cannot be taken as proof that the stela itself symbolizes a tree, like the apron. There is in fact no costume element or other icon that specifically marks stelae as symbolic trees. As an alternative to this generic symbolic equation, it seems more productive to look for specific evidence on how the Maya conceived of individual monuments or programs and thereby gain a sense of the complex history of religious meanings conveyed by the monuments. In the context of such an analysis, it is not only the similarities but also the differences between monumental symbolisms that are significant.

I.8. El Baúl Stela 1. Drawing by Linda Schele, © David Schele, courtesy Foundation for the Advancement of Mesoamerican Studies, Inc.

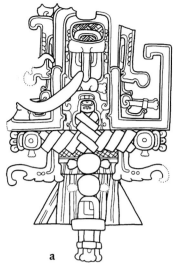

a

b

I.9. Comparison of: *a*, "God-C" apron from royal portrait of QRG Stela F, north; and *b*, central icon from Palenque Temple of the Cross main panel. Drawings by author and Linda Schele, © David Schele, courtesy Foundation for the Advancement of Mesoamerican Studies, Inc.

While the general status of Classic Maya stelae as arboreal effigies is open to question, there is ample evidence to associate them (in addition to zoomorphs, altars, and other types of monuments) with rituals of cosmic renewal (see Christie 1995; Newsome 2001). Stone monuments were incorporated into elaborate cosmological rituals that established the shape and quality of both time and space. To the ancient as well as the contemporary Maya, time does not unfold in an entirely linear sequence but rather as a perpetual cycle of repeating events, initiated by cosmic reordering or Creation. Monuments and architectural programs reproduced aspects of this cosmic order through their conformation to sacred prototypes and their dedication according to the precise schedule dictated by a complex calendrical system.

The connection between monuments and cosmogenesis was articulated through the use of the Long Count calendar, a system for recording time that emerged during the Late Formative period and later spread through the southern Maya lowlands, appearing first at Tikal in A.D. 292. The Long Count calendar explicitly referenced Creation mythology, as it was used in hieroglyphic texts to count the number of days elapsed since the date of Creation, which was August 13, 3114 B.C., according to the Classic-period sources. In fact, Long Count records on stelae are featured information, usually occurring first in the text and sometimes even written larger than other glyphs.

As exemplified by the west text of Quirigua Stela C (Fig. I.10), the Long Count begins with an oversized initial series introductory glyph (ISIG) which may read *tzik hab'* "count of years," into which is infixed a glyph or "patron" associated with the appropriate month in the 365-day *hab'* or "vague year." Following the ISIG are five units of time, each with a numerical coefficient. The highest unit, which scholars designate the *b'aktun* (144,000 days or about 400 solar years), is followed by the *k'atun* (7,200 days or about 20 years), then the *tun* (360 days), *winal* (20 days), and finally *k'in* (single day).[10] On Stela C west, the date is written with the numeral nine (a bar representing five units and four dots representing single units) in the *b'aktun* position. A single dot (framed by two space-filling curls) precedes the *k'atun* glyph, while glyphs for "zero" accompany each of the smaller temporal units. Combining the units with their coefficients, this date can be calculated in the following manner: [9 x 144,000] + [1 x 7200] + [0 x 360] + [0 x 20] + [0] days after the beginning of the current cycle. Traditionally, scholars represent the date on Stela C west in an abbreviated form, listing the coefficients only, in descending or-

der and separated by periods: 9.1.0.0.0. In our calendar, this date corresponds to August 28, 455. On this date, Stela C records that an early king of Quirigua set up a stela. In fact, stelae were usually erected to commemorate such whole *k'atun* endings. Often, however, monuments were also dedicated on quarter-*k'atuns*, which Mayanists term *hotuns*. At Quirigua, for example, the known stelae of K'ak' Tiliw were set up on 9.15.15.0.0, 9.16.0.0.0, 9.16.5.0.0, and so on. Mayanists refer to such anniversaries of the Creation as "period endings" (see Thompson 1950: 181).

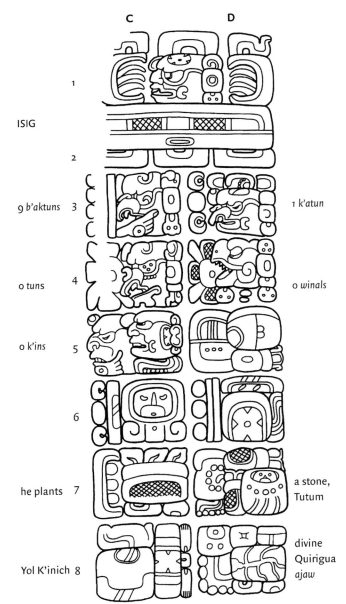

I.10. QRG Stela C, west text, C1–D8. Drawing by author.

Carved on the opposite (east) face of Quirigua Stela C is an inscription that clarifies the connection between the monument dedication and the events of Creation (Fig. I.11). This text is one of the most detailed accounts of these events that survives from the Classic period, containing many unique elements. It begins with a Long Count record of the "zero" date of Creation, rendered as 13.0.0.0.0. Following this are the corresponding positions in the *tzolk'in* or 260-day calendar, 4 Ajaw, and the *hab'*, 8 Kumk'u.[11] Together, these notations are referred to as the Calendar Round. Several events are associated with this date, including a list of sacred platforms or thrones set up by supernatural beings. The first of these objects is dedicated by two deities known as the "Paddlers," aged beings who in ceramic scenes are often shown paddling a canoe. This stone is set up at a place called *nah ho' chan* "First Five Sky" and is identified as a "jaguar platform/throne stone." The second stone dedication is performed by an unknown deity at a location that may read *lakam kah* "Large Town." The second stone is referred to as a "snake platform/throne stone." Finally, the third stone is bundled by Itzamnah, a prominent patron of rulership. The stone set by Itzamnah is stated to be a "water platform/throne stone," and its place of dedication is "??-Sky, First Three-Stone place." The entire process is overseen by an entity called "Six Sky *ajaw*," which David Freidel, Linda Schele, and Joy Parker (1993: 73–74) identify as the "Maize God," but for which I offer a different interpretation (see Chapter 5). The narrative of Stela C is a metaphor for monument dedication by the ruler. His rituals reenact the ordering of the cosmos and compare him to the supernatural beings associated with each of the three stone platforms or thrones.

As discussed in subsequent chapters, specific details of this text were elaborated in order to emphasize the meaning of certain monumental art programs at Quirigua. In particular, boulder sculptures in the form of composite animals were conceived as effigies of these thrones or platforms of Creation (Fig. I.12; Looper 1995b, 2002b). For example, Zoomorph G is named with a logograph (T150) which depicts a bundle of bones (Fig. I.13a).[12] Elsewhere in Maya art, the bone bundle is employed as a throne for supernatural beings (Fig. I.13b) or a support for sacred objects (Fig. I.13c). A polychrome vase shows a spirit seated on the T150 glyph, which is placed atop a round personified stone that is similar to the zoomorphs of Quirigua (Fig. I.13d). There are unfortunately no archaeological data from Quirigua to prove exactly how these monuments were used in ceremony. What is clear is that the unusual elaboration of zoo-morphic sculpture at Quirigua was related to a local interpretation of the lore of cosmogenesis.

It is noteworthy that while the Quirigua account is extremely detailed, parts of its content are consistent with texts from other Maya sites. For example, both the Tablet of the Cross at Palenque and Piedras Negras Altar 1 mention the events of Creation at the First Three-Stone place, which is named in the same manner as on Quirigua Stela C (Fig. I.14a, b). The Creation text of the badly damaged Dos Pilas Panel 18 also mentions the First Three-Stone place (Fig. I.14c). Usually, local elite traditions embroidered the narrative of cosmogenesis by incorporating dynastic ancestors as observers of the events. The key motif of the erection of sacred stones, however, was a widely accepted component of Classic-period lore. Its codification in the inscriptional record may have been historically linked to the spread of period-ending ceremonies involving stelae and other monuments.

The setting of primordial stones was both a principal structuring concept for space and time and a metaphor for social order. As promulgated by the Classic kings, the lore of Creation took on a decidedly elitist tone, implying that the paradigms established by the gods were the inheritance of rulers. As such, cosmogenesis became a royal prerogative that was periodically enacted through ceremonial performance. Through various techniques, rulers drew upon the aesthetic and symbolic significance of popular technologies, such as domestic architecture and agriculture, transforming them into statements of dynastic legitimacy and esoteric power. In the Classic period, the stela gained widespread popularity due to its suitability as a vehicle for political expression. A king's ritual action of stela erection replicated the actions of the creator gods. Further, the workings of the Maya calendar placed each period ending on a day with the same name as the king's political office, Ajaw. Thus, when a king commissioned a stela in his own image, his identity became conflated with the cycle of 360 days. In this way, the religious significance of the anniversary of Creation was appropriated. The stela allowed the king to be linked to the most fundamental definitions of space and time, thereby asserting his supernatural nature.

Beyond its inherent symbolic value, the stela had other ritual functions as a supernatural interface. Since their invention, stelae had been physically associated with mounds and pyramids. The universal Mesoamerican conception of mounds as effigy mountains and of mountains as the abode of spirits and ancestors suggests a function of stelae as portals to the supernatural world. As Evon Vogt (1970: 14–16) notes, the function of the mod-

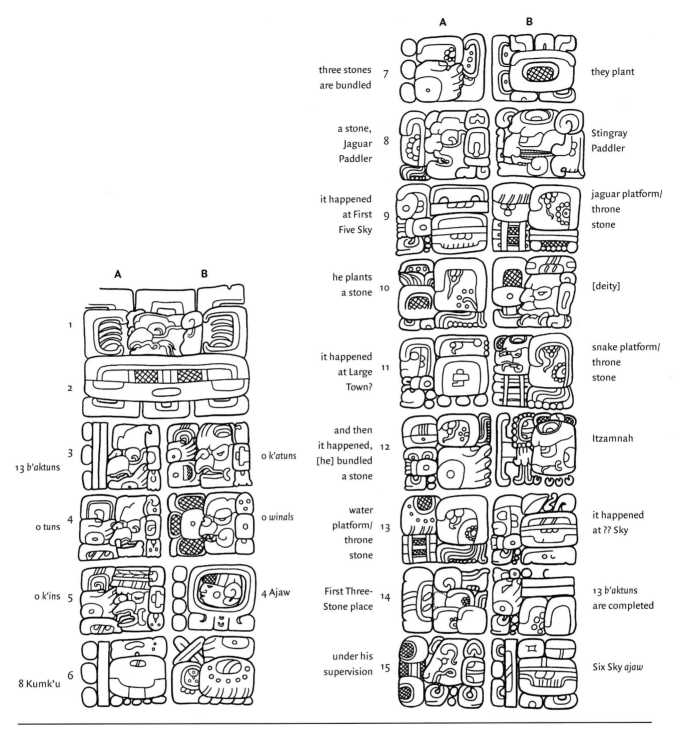

I.11. QRG Stela C, east text. Drawing by author.

ern cross shrines of the Tzotzil Maya of Zinacantan as supernatural "doorways" may be close to that of Classic stelae. There are numerous parallels between the uses of such crosses and ancient stelae, including the practice of "dressing" the object. Postconquest Maya crosses are adorned with flowers and vegetation as well as actual clothing, not only to make the object ready for ritual but

also in recognition of the nature of the cross as a living being (Bricker 1981: 102–109; Vogt 1970: 14–16). Similar wrapping or binding ceremonies were central to the use of stelae in the Classic period, recorded prominently in the inscriptions (Stuart 1996). In one of the rare depictions of a Classic stela, the monument is shown wrapped with a cloth sash (Fig. I.15). In the New Year's pages of the Postclassic Dresden Codex (pp. 26d–28d), upright wooden posts are also adorned with capes and sashes (Fig. I.16). It has been argued that these posts are analogous to Classic stelae (Grube and Schele 1988; Schele and Stuart 1985). The dressing or wrapping of these posts suggests that they, and perhaps Classic stelae as well, were considered to have been vessels for living spirits.[13]

The Dresden Codex images and Classic vase scene noted above also suggest that stelae served as loci for sacrifice. While the codical image shows an offering plate and incense burner placed before the wooden post, the vase depicts a flat stone in front of the stela, upon which is shown a sacrificed child. This image relates to the scenes of bound captives that adorn many actual altars, such as Tikal Altar 8 (Fig. I.17). Here the carved image preserves the sacrificial offering. The Dresden Codex scenes show blood offerings before the post, a ritual implied by the form of actual altars such as that of Copan Stela 4, which has a shallow depression on its upper surface and drainage channels. In fact, many altars are carved in the image of the quatrefoil portal to the under-

world, implying the specialized function of the altar as the point at which energies of sacrifice are magically transferred to the spiritual beings that wait behind or alight upon a stela, such as the jaguar shown on the vase in Figure I.15.

Hieroglyphic texts also contain references to sacrifices performed upon or in front of stelae in the context of their dedication. The text of Quirigua Stela F (Fig. I.18a) records the commonest of these events, a "scattering," which in this case is performed on the monument itself. Here, as elsewhere, the substance scattered is *ch'ah* "drops (of incense)" (Love 1987).[14] A common Classic title, *ch'ahom(a)* (Fig. I.18b), refers to the king as "one who offers drops (of incense)." The interpretation of *ch'ah* as "incense" is convincing, as a *ch'ahom(a)* glyph from Copan depicts a figure depositing a glyph which reads *pom* "copal incense" into a censer (Fig. I.18c; W. Fash, in Schele 1989c). Nevertheless, it is likely that blood and other precious substances were burned along with the incense, providing a rich feast for the spirits.[15] The scattering ceremony may relate to planting practices of Maya

I.12. QRG Zoomorph B, east face. From Maudslay 1889–1902, *Archaeology*, vol. 2, Plate 9. From the facsimile edition of *Biologia Centrali-Americana* by Alfred Percival Maudslay. Published 1974 by Milpatron Publishing Corp., Stamford, Conn. Further reproduction prohibited.

a

b

c

I.13. Glyphs and associations for "thrones" or "supports": a, glyph for "support" or "throne" (T150), depicting a bundle of bones; b, deity seated on a bone bundle, Dresden Codex, p. 53a; c, assemblage of sacred objects placed on a bone bundle, Chinos Black-on-Cream sherd excavated at Buenavista, Belize, MSBX76 (drawn after Reents-Budet et al. 2000: Fig. 6a); d, deity seated on a bone bundle, placed atop a zoomorphic stone, detail of a Classic polychrome vessel. Drawings by author.

d

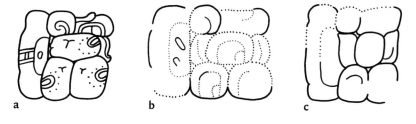

a

b

c

I.14. References to "Three-Stone places" in inscriptions from various sites: a, Palenque Temple of the Cross, main panel, C7; b, Piedras Negras Altar 1, N2; c, Dos Pilas Panel 18, B6. Drawings by author.

I.15. Supernatural beings in association with a stela: Classic polychrome vessel (K718). Drawing by author.

farmers, in which liquid offerings are poured into the ground. In this sense, royal ritual structurally reproduced popular practices, establishing connections with common people but at the same time veiling rulers in an aura of awesome spiritual power.

Several stela scenes which include burning incensarios, such as Nim Li Punit Stela 15 (Fig. I.19), demonstrate that the burning of these offerings was essential to the proper ritual use of the stela. This image shows the scattering ritual in progress, in which standing figures cast drops toward an incense burner placed on the ground. The burning of offerings before a Classic stela strongly recalls the rituals carried out before adorned crosses of modern Zinacantan, in which the cross is readied for supernatural communication by the burning of incense and candles, the "souls" of which provide nourishment for the supernatural beings assembled behind the cruciform "doorway" (Vogt 1970: 14–16).

Even though some sculptors signed their works, there is little additional information about the profession from the Classic period (Montgomery 1995; Stuart 1989b, 1989c). An unprovenanced panel in the museum at Emiliano Zapata in Chiapas, Mexico, displays what appears at first glance to be the sole Classic-period image of a carver at work (Fig. I.20). He is shown seated with crossed legs, touching a zoomorphic carved stone with what appears to be a bone stylus. The text above the sculptor's hand contains the "*lu-bat*" compound which introduces sculptors' signatures, thus identifying the nature of the event depicted (Stuart 1989b, 1990).[16]

I.16. Itzamnah sacrificing a turkey before a *yax itzamnah te'*. Dresden Codex, p. 28c. Drawing by author.

The depiction of a bone stylus on this panel, however, suggests that this is no scene of actual carving, as bone would be suitable for carving only the softest stone. For the sophisticated relief sculpture of sites such as Copan and Quirigua, the sculptor would probably have begun by pecking out the rough form with rough tools of flint, followed by work with a wooden mallet and small chisels of varying sizes made of flint or quartz. Drills were employed as well, and much of the undercutting seen at Copan was probably begun by drilling at an angle to the surface of the block. Glyphic portions of monuments were first roughed out into blocks, as demonstrated by several

I.17. Tikal Altar 8. Drawing by Linda Schele, © David Schele, courtesy Foundation for the Advancement of Mesoamerican Studies, Inc.

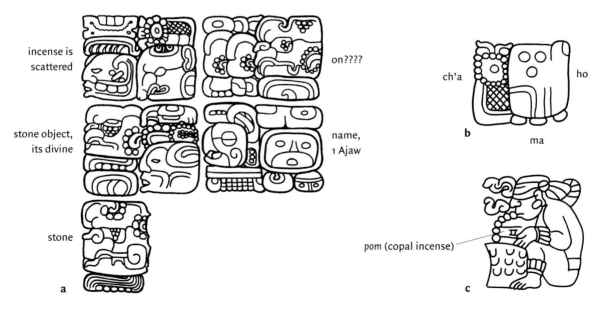

incense is scattered

on????

stone object, its divine

name, 1 Ajaw

stone

ch'a

ho

ma

b

pom (copal incense)

c

a

I.18. Ritual scattering of incense and the *ch'ahom(a)* title: *a*, QRG Stela F, C9–C11a; *b*, QRG Stela C, D14; *c*, CPN Structure 9N-82 bench, detail. Drawings by author.

examples of unfinished texts at Dos Pilas, and then finished as the rest of the monument (Schele and Miller 1986: 39). Rubbing with an abrasive stone such as sandstone would have provided the smooth finish desired for most sculptures and was probably a technique used to sculpt sandstone at Quirigua. The Madrid Codex shows gods carving deity heads or masks using the axe, awl, and drill; however, the heads being fashioned in these scenes are probably made of materials other than stone (Fig. I.21).[17] At Quirigua, K'ak' Tiliw's sculptors employed primarily sandstone, which—when freshly quarried and moistened—would likely have yielded fairly easily to stone tools and is amenable to either deep or shallow relief.[18]

As a final step, most Maya monuments were probably painted. While evidence for polychrome painting exists at some sites such as Yaxchilan and Piedras Negras, the Quirigua monuments preserve only traces of red pigment (for example, on Zoomorphs B and P). It is possible that the Quirigua sculptures were uniformly coated with red paint, a color symbolic of powers of birth, sacrifice, and cosmic renewal. There is no evidence for a naturalistic use of color at the site, nor for the use of color to differentiate sculptural details.

In general, our knowledge of the details of the sculpting process in the Classic period is limited. Nevertheless, Diego de Landa's account of the carving of deity images

I.19. Nim Li Punit Stela 15, detail. Drawing by author.

in wood among the sixteenth-century Yukatek suggests that the activity was accompanied by penitential rituals (Tozzer 1941: 159–161; see also Tate 1992: 30–31, 2001a, 2001b). He observed that when new images of gods were desired, the (male) artisans were shut inside a specially constructed hut and performed their work accompanied by periodic incense-burning and bloodletting. In sixteenth-century Tzotzil, the association between sculpting and bloodletting may be suggested by the term *'an*, which means both "to carve" and "to let blood" (Laughlin 1988: 136). Even in the twentieth century, Ch'orti' Maya sculptors who make sacred crosses practice sexual abstinence, fasting, and work in isolation in the forest, in order to remain "in constant spiritual communication with God" (Girard 1995: 279–280). Such a relationship between the roles of artist and penitent may also have been extant in the Classic period, appearing in the context of the lordly office of *itz'at* "artist, sage, wise man." The supernatural prototypes of the *itz'at* are the deity pair known as the Paddlers, who are called *chan itz'at* "sky artists," possibly in reference to their role as the primordial artists who painted the sky (Barbara MacLeod, cited in Schele 1992b: 257–259). The relationship between the Paddlers and bloodletting is clear from numerous images and texts (Stuart 1984). In addition, a noble bearing the *itz'at* title is shown in charge of the bloodletting ritual depicted on Dos Pilas Panel 19 (Houston 1993: Fig. 4-19).

Even though the letting of blood during sculpting mentioned by Landa has not been conclusively documented in the Classic period, the collectivity of the art production indicated in his report parallels Classic practices. Where the tradition of signing sculptures existed, larger objects such as stelae often bear the signatures of multiple artists, indicating that large commissions were likely collective undertakings. Piedras Negras Stela 12 alone has the signatures of eight different sculptors. Nevertheless, the execution was evidently carefully controlled, so that multiple artists' hands can rarely be securely identified on large monuments, including most of those at Quirigua.

Although a few sculptors' signatures include titles which suggest that they were also painters, Classic Maya elites seem to have placed a higher value on the arts of writing and painting than on sculpture.[19] Not only are there many more images of scribes than of sculptors in Maya art, but writing and painting are often shown as being of divine origin. On a bone from Burial 116 at Tikal, an artist's hand holding the Classic calligraphy brush emerges from the maw to the underworld (Fig. I.22). Even the supernatural patrons of artists, the Pawatuns,

I.20. Emiliano Zapata panel. Drawing by David Stuart.

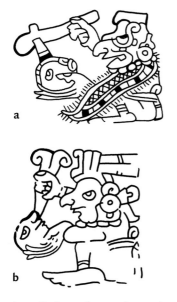

I.21. Gods carving masks, as shown in the Madrid Codex: *a*, p. 96d; *b*, p. 99d. Drawings by author.

are never represented with the tools of sculpture—only the paint pot and brush of the scribe (see Fash 2001: Fig. 74).[20] Such profound elevation and deification of the scribal arts may explain in part why large-scale Classic Maya sculpture designed for public display is so overwhelmingly graphic in style, as the planar nature of relief technique requires thinking in graphic terms. With the few exceptions of certain periods at Copan, Tonina, and perhaps very late Piedras Negras, Classic Maya sculptors conformed closely to the aesthetics of the graphic arts, usually treating monumental sculpture as little more than enriched paintings and often retaining the hairlike, fluid lines characteristic of the calligraphy brush and stylus.[21] In contrast to these norms, sculptors at Copan often moved beyond the realm of the graphic, sometimes creating truly volumetric ("in-the-round") altars and thrones in the forms of animals and composite creatures.

At Quirigua the earliest stelae are clearly subordinate to architecture, being located on or adjacent to platforms in the typical Classic Maya manner. During the reign of K'ak' Tiliw, however, sculptures achieved an elevated status, becoming nearly independent objects. The vast open space of the Quirigua Great Plaza served as the setting for these monuments, which were arranged according to cosmological patterns (Fig. I.23). Although it was based on a design that originated in Copan, K'ak' Tiliw's Great Plaza is so immense that the sense of surrounding architecture which is always present at Copan is greatly reduced at Quirigua. Among all Maya sites, it was Quirigua that came closest to severing the traditional association between stela and mound/pyramid, which had endured since the time of the Olmec. When standing near them, K'ak' Tiliw's stelae convey the sense of being completely self-supporting, demanding equal viewing from all four sides. Further enhancing the impact of these monuments is their huge size, which completely dwarfs the audience. Given that the original plaza floor was about a meter below its current level, the viewer's head originally would not have reached the level of the ruler's feet on some of the stelae. Such effects of scale and setting maximize the presence of the monuments and suggest the central importance of stone sculpture in the artistic program.

Several other features of K'ak' Tiliw's sculptures set them apart from general aesthetic trends in the Classic period, but these are shared to an extent with nearby Copan. Frequently evident at the two sites is a sense that artists were highly experimental, working within a milieu that favored technical virtuosity. At Copan the sculptors during the reigns of the twelfth, thirteenth, and fifteenth rulers explored the dramatic and dynamic effects achieved through deeply undercut and broken stone surfaces (Fig. I.24). At Quirigua the best artists manipulated layered parallel planes in moderately low relief to define shapes and create shadows from the intense sunlight of the Great Plaza (Fig. I.25). There is also an awareness at both sites of the variety in types of cuts and surface treatments possible in stone sculpture, a broad spectrum of which were used at one point or another in

the history of Quirigua and Copan. Such sculptural diversity casts a considerable doubt on the concept of a unified "Quirigua style" or "Copan style," which appears frequently in the literature on Maya art. Although the preference for certain basic sculptural formats at each site may certainly be documented, careful formal comparisons over periods of twenty or even five years at either site reveal the relatively dynamic nature of sculptural traditions in the Maya Southeast. By the eighth century, when the monuments of K'ak' Tiliw were created, the history of forms and techniques utilized at the two nearby sites was rich indeed, immersing the sculptors in a complex artistic culture and resulting in spectacular sculptural achievements.

One purpose of this study is to explore the nature of the transformations within this extraordinary sculptural tradition. In particular, how may we reconstruct the factors which fostered the changes in the style and iconography of eighth-century sculptures at Quirigua during the reign of K'ak' Tiliw? Such a question has been asked of Quirigua sculpture previously, although it has never been fully explored. In nearly all discussions of Quirigua sculpture, the approach has been largely formal, with only recent speculation on the relationship of art to religious and political history. In the earliest of these studies, Herbert Spinden (1913: 175–177) attempted to support an erroneous theory that Quirigua was colonized following the abandonment of Copan by noting many similarities in iconography and representational mode between the two centers.[22] In Spinden's (1913: 175) view, stylistic development proceeded automatically, disconnected from politics, the details of which were unknown at the time: "The course of development of the stelae and altars may be said to begin at Quirigua where it leaves off at Copan." Tatiana Proskouriakoff's (1950: 131) brief but more sensitive discussion of Quirigua sculpture likewise avoids political speculations, focusing exclusively on formal developments. The discovery of the historical identities of the rulers of Quirigua by David Kelley in 1962 had little effect on the study of their monuments, which was largely confined to the identification of the subjects of the portraits (Kubler 1969: 15–18; Miller 1983). The only major study of iconography at Quirigua is Andrea Stone's (1983) unpublished dissertation on the zoomorphs, which related their imagery to concepts of cosmology and creation. Generally, scholars have avoided discussing the political dimensions of style and iconography. Clearly, a study of the nature proposed here necessitates the development of a theoretical framework for such art historical interpretations.

I.22. Bone from Tikal, showing a scribe's hand and brush emerging from the spirit world. Drawing by author.

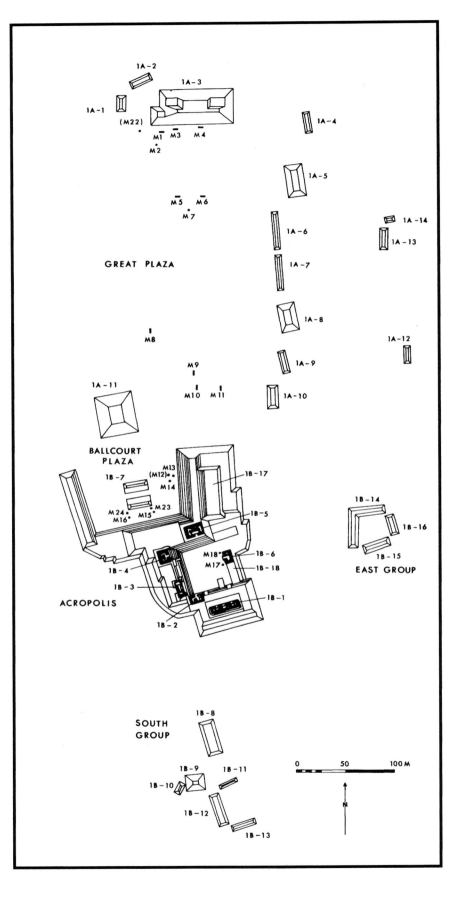

1A-2
1A-3
1A-1
(M22)
M1 M3 M4
M2
1A-4

1A-5

M5 M6
M7
1A-14
1A-6
1A-13
GREAT PLAZA

1A-7

1A-8

M8
1A-12

M9
1A-9

1A-11
M10 M11
1A-10

BALLCOURT
PLAZA
M13
(M12)
1B-7
M14
1B-17
1B-14
1B-5
1B-16
M24 M23
M16 M15
1B-15
M18
1B-6
EAST GROUP
M17
1B-4
1B-18
1B-3
ACROPOLIS
1B-1
1B-2

SOUTH
GROUP
1B-8

1B-9 1B-11
1B-10
1B-12
1B-13

0   50   100 M

N

Facing page

I.23. Map of the Quirigua site core. After Coe and Sharer 1979: Fig. 1. Courtesy of University of Pennsylvania Museum of Archaeology and Anthropology. Key: M1. Stela A; M2. Zoomorph B; M3. Stela C; M4. Stela D; M5. Stela E; M6. Stela F; M7. Zoomorph G; M8. Stela H; M9. Stela I; M10. Stela J; M11. Stela K; M12. Altar L; M13. Altar M; M14. Altar N; M15. Zoomorph O; M16. Zoomorph P; M17. Altar Q; M18. Altar R; M23. Altar O'; M24. Altar P'.

I.24. CPN Stela H, northwest, detail. Photo by author.

I.25. QRG Stela E, north face, detail. Photo by Thomas Tolles.

Art and Ritual

The problem of the relationship between Maya visual culture and politics is itself dependent on the definition of rulership in this society. In this study, two concepts are utilized to interpret the nature of royal power: ritual and persona. The first of these has received less attention in art history than in anthropology, despite its relevance to the field. While ritual is often understood within the context of "religious performance," to which the "secular ceremony" bears little resemblance, this distinction is not useful for the ancient Maya. A working definition of ritual as a "prescribed system of proceeding" (Blier 1996: 189) is useful, not only because it encompasses a variety of performances but because it recognizes the role of political intervention through the regulation of ritual (see also Rappaport 1999: 24). Far from being irrational, meaningless rote ceremony, as it is sometimes popularly conceptualized, ritual is a fundamental mode through which humans create "reality" and bring order to the world. As Suzanne Preston Blier (1996: 189) states: "Rituals . . . offer through their formality and relative fixity a means of measuring, mastering, and making sense of the world at large."

Recent scholarship has sustained a vigorous debate concerning the social functions of ritual (Bell 1992). According to one school of thought, rituals are essentially a symbolic language through which cultural meanings may be grounded in individual experience (Turner 1967). As one of the proponents of this approach, Sherry Ortner (1978: 8), states, "As actors participate in or employ symbolic constructs, their attitudes and actions become oriented in the directions embodied in the form and content of the construction itself; the construct—the model if you will—makes it difficult for them to 'see' and respond to the situation in a different way."

The limitations of this approach are clear. For one thing, it is based on the ethnocentric assumption of a fundamental opposition between the individual and the collective, in which individual difference is a "problem" that is "solved" through ritual. Further, it overemphasizes the cognitive, propositional aspects of ritual.[23] It does not deal with the fundamental nature of rituals as performances, in which nonpropositional, nonsemantic formal elements play a key role in forging social relations. In fact, numerous studies have explored these aspects of ritual. For example, Bruce Kapferer's (1979b) analysis of an exorcism rite in Sri Lanka demonstrated that changes in the relationships of ritual participants were effected through the manipulation of media, space, and audience/participant focus. Rather than merely providing a passive dramatic backdrop for a communicative act, performance may be understood as a medium in which social relations are transformed (see Geertz 1966: 7). An analysis of ritual must consider not only its semantic content, conveyed through verbal texts, but also the way in which the performance reveals experiential truths through bodily praxis.

While this conclusion contributes to an anthropological theory of ritual, it does not constitute a historical model. In order to understand the history of ritual, we must find ways to connect one performance to another, documenting continuities and changes as they are enacted by specific human agents. In Maya archaeology, significant steps in this direction have already been taken, and it is now argued that ancient Maya political history cannot be separated from ritual. The work of Linda Schele and David Freidel in particular has been dedicated to understanding how numerous aspects of ancient Maya political interaction were articulated within a framework of ritual performances. In two studies these authors argued that the origin of Classic-period culture was marked by an abrupt change in ritual (Freidel and Schele 1988a, 1988b). In their view, this took place in the Late Formative period across the Maya lowlands of the Peten and Belize, when monumental architectural structures bearing images of supernatural beings were built as theatrical stages by an emerging nobility. The conduct of rituals in this context provided a basis for these rulers' claims to supernatural ancestry. Eventually, the deity images of the facades were replaced by portraits of rulers, thereby fixing divine identities in a more permanent form.

These interpretations stand in dramatic contrast to previous reconstructions of ancient Maya culture, especially those promulgated by the eminent scholar J. Eric S. Thompson, who saw political (sometimes called "historical") interpretations in direct opposition to ritual (Thompson 1950: 63–65). In Freidel and Schele's view, public performance and charismatic ritual were crucial to the power of Maya rulers, through which they could sway the loyalties of people who viewed and participated in these ceremonies. Performances that displayed differences in regalia, spatial position, and access to sacred materials and objects maintained hierarchical distinction between nobility and commoners. According to Schele and Freidel, the rituals of the ancient Maya elite were carried out principally in order to effect cosmological changes. This definition of ancient Maya power acknowledges the transformational role of ritual and suggests that power is meaningful not in an abstract symbolic sense but to the extent that it is invoked ritually.

While power among the ancient Maya was exerted in the social world, its principal source was perceived as the normally invisible "otherworld," manifested in the form of various spirit forces which together composed the living cosmos.[24] Perhaps the most potent of these was k'uh, roughly translated as "holiness," which was identified with royal blood. Another distinct spiritual force recognized by the Maya translates roughly as "white flower spirit." This essence was thought to reside in the breath but was also profoundly associated with procreation and particularly with umbilical cords. Interestingly, each of these concepts associates spiritual power with substances that emerge from the interior of the body. Accordingly, a fundamental ritual pattern involved the opening of the body so that its immanent forces could be manifested. For example, through the perforation of the body and drawing of royal blood, the power inherent in this substance was revealed and put to use. Likewise, the sacrifice of a captive's intestines magically manifested the powers of the umbilicus. A less violent context for the deployment of spiritual essences was the formal speech and song of the elites, which released the forces of breath and the particular powers of sex and procreation.

Ancient Maya power, then, could be accessed through ritual procedures that centered on the manipulation of the body. Such a focus may imply that Classic Maya political ritual derives from or was otherwise historically related to traditions of shamanistic curing and midwifery. In fact, glyphic texts that accompany such scenes of deity conjuration occasionally refer to the event as the "birth" of the deity. Another expression used in the context of bloodletting is the same as that which relates a child to its mother.[25] Such metaphors may exemplify the elite appropriation of popular ceremonies that existed in Mesoamerica before the advent of kingship.[26]

Rituals designed to release the power of the other-world required a sophisticated means for channeling these tremendous forces. Such was the function of artifacts that we designate as "art," such as bloodletters, bowls for sacrifice, altars, ceramic burners, and stelae. Many of these objects served as implements or tools, including the stingray spines and obsidian lancets that were used to puncture the flesh. Ritual objects also contained and stored these energies, much like a battery. The dedication sequence of a stela, in which cloth or rope bindings fixed the energy of sacrifices in the monument, illustrates this well. The creation of a work of art may itself have been conceived as the infusion of matter with spiritual power, while ritual use enhanced that power. The intentional breakage or destruction of a work of art was also an essential part of the life history of the object, as its power was thereby released to be put to some other use. This belief, for example, probably lay behind the deposit of fragments of monuments in the foundations of stelae at Copan. Works of art were used to manipulate space and create a sacred landscape for ritual. Accordingly, three or four objects placed in a triangle or square constituted a magical diagram, creating a liminal space appropriate to ritual. In sum, Maya artworks may be conceptualized as technology of ritual transformation, which extended the potential of the human agent to manage sacred energies inherent in certain materials, idealized geometric forms, and chronological symmetries.

In addition to its functions as ritual implement, container, and tool for spatial modeling, visual art served as a communicative medium, a site of ritual inscription through which performances were documented and committed to collective memory. Many monuments, such as the stelae of Quirigua, were relatively accessible to the general populace and featured images of what were likely public dance performances by rulers (Looper 2001). Others, such as Yaxchilan Lintel 24 (Fig. I.26), bear texts and images that may have been intended for a more restricted audience consisting of elites and their ancestors. This monument was installed in a temple doorway so that it could only be viewed just inside or outside the doorway, depending on the light. The image features a Yaxchilan ruler holding a burning torch over his kneeling wife, who draws a thorn-studded rope through her punctured tongue. Blood scrolls on her face stand as memorials of this ritual, as do the blood-spattered paper strips in the basket before her. The two main framed texts, located at the top and at the middle left margin of the panel, complement the two figures, labeling them as "images in penance."[27] These inscribed images thus awaken thoughts and feelings in the viewer through their sculptural forms, iconography (images), and spatial relations with architecture and landscape and (in ancient times) through interpretation and display in ritual performance. Because the lintel was installed in a manner that made viewing by living humans difficult, its primary intended audience may have been ancestral. Its specifically penitential subject matter may also suggest this, as such an image might have been considered particularly moving to the ancestors.

A similar propitiatory function is suggested by other lintels and wall panels at Yaxchilan and Copan, which feature texts written in mirror image. While this could be an example of scribal virtuosity, such an arrangement may imply that the texts were meant to be read through the walls or from the sky, that is, by a divine audience. One stela at Piedras Negras even has an inscription on its upper surface, invisible to the earthbound human viewer. Similarly, many beautifully carved monuments, such as the sarcophagus of the king K'inich Janab' Pakal I of Palenque, never saw the light of day, being entombed deep beneath massive architectural structures. These examples serve as reminders that artworks were meant to be viewed and cherished not only by a community of living humans but also by the ancestors. As an activity that was sanctioned by traditional convention, the carving of a text or image had the effect of a magical formula, making the inscribed event happen, regardless of whether it was seen by human eyes.

The making of art was not only the creation of reality through ritual but a fulfillment of the ceremonial obligation of the elite. Texts and representational art actualized the rituals that the elites were required to perform, through their control of sacred materials and knowledge. Further, because ancestors are reborn through their descendants, what the living memorialized through art was in a real sense also remembered by the dead. The value of monumental art, and in turn the spiritual power of the elite, lay in its capacity to incarnate memory and to stimulate reflection and emotion in a diverse and yet interrelated audience. Even public monuments may be considered to be primarily offerings, transactional objects intended to restructure social relations among the living and the dead.

The function of Maya art as offerings or gifts was also crucial in negotiating social status. Trade and exchange networks kept Maya courts supplied with luxurious and exotic materials from which art was made. These materials were worked and combined with local materials in

special ways to produce other commodities, such as painted pottery (Reents-Budet 1994). Monumental sculpture, for instance, required not only locally quarried stone but also specialized tools made from rare imported stone. The technical and esoteric knowledge implied by the production of art objects enhanced the prestige of the elite. But such objects and knowledge had no social value if hoarded. Like the potlatch celebration of the native peoples of the Northwest Coast of North America, which must be witnessed in order to generate prestige, ritual knowledge embodied in art had to be selectively shared with others. In this way, rituals and art objects participated in a network of social and exchange relationships that bound people to the ruler (Clark and Blake 1994). But while they forged social ties, art objects also masked social and political inequalities both within and between cohesive communities (Earle 1990).

Large sculpted stones erected in a public space could embody social exchange too, as their creation and manipulation implied a massive investment in resources, even to those who had not actually witnessed the process of moving them. (This aspect of the monuments still inspires awe today.) Nevertheless, the fixity and the massive scale of monuments permanently withhold them from free economic circulation. At Quirigua restriction of access was further implied by the impassive, unapproachable features of the royal portraits that stare over the heads of the viewer, as well as perimeter foundations, which functioned rather like a velvet rope at a museum. The sculptures were thus kept from the general populace, even though they were given as a public offering.[28] As such, monumental sculptures exemplify the paradoxical nature of certain gifts, which—as discussed by Annette Weiner (1992)—are retained as much as given. This is especially true for objects of great sacred or cosmological significance, such as monumental images. Their monumentality served as a means of governing their social circulation, of preventing the separation of the objects and the cosmological meanings they embodied from the persons who commissioned them.

In the same way that the monumental object functions as a paradoxical gift, so the information that it communicated was both given and withheld. The formalized genres of text and image simultaneously disclosed and concealed the knowledge of its (elite) designer(s). The great abundance and complexity of the pictorial images, obscured and revealed through overlapping of sculpted forms, suggest the wealth of esoteric knowledge claimed by the rulers and partially manifested for the uninitiated.

Hieroglyphic inscriptions are also of critical importance in this regard, in their selectivity and even through the practice of literacy itself. As discussed by Stephen Houston, the standardization of Maya writing and its high degree of elaboration imply that it was probably not fully readable by much of the population (Houston 1994; Houston and Taube 2000). This would have been especially relevant at ancient Quirigua, where most of the local populace was non-Maya. Although evidence is slim for the Classic period, written texts were performed through song or other oral presentation during the colonial period (Thompson 1972: 13; Tozzer 1941: 153). If such practices of "recitation literacy" were extant in the Classic period, then the public display of written texts may have emphasized the knowledge that could only be accessed through ritual performances. In such a manner, valuable information was selectively distributed to the people, with the implication that additional wealth lay behind the inscriptions. Monumentality, for the ancient Maya, thus provided the elite "owners" of the monuments the potential for retaining their identity and perpetuating it into the future. In the words of Weiner (1992: 8), such objects "bring a vision of permanence into a social world that is always in the process of change."

Art and Personae

The importance of art in stabilizing identities prompts a consideration of the specific ways in which ancient Maya monumental portraiture embodies the social person. Indeed, one of the remarkable aspects of Classic Maya art and one that distinguishes it from other areas of the Americas is its "personalized" quality. Specific persons are represented, sometimes on more than one monument, and histories relate momentous events in the lives of kings. In addition, the relatively naturalistic proportions of Maya art, together with an abundance of incidental physiognomic detail such as fingernails and strands of hair, convey a strong sense of immediacy and physical presence of the subject. A few Maya representational traditions, such as that of Palenque, encouraged highly naturalistic royal portraiture, with particular emphasis on distinctive facial characteristics (Griffin 1976).

Accordingly, in recent decades some scholars have written Maya art history in terms of human actors, even

Facing page

I.26. Yaxchilan Lintel 24. From Maudslay 1889–1902, *Archaeology*, vol. 2, Plate 86. From the facsimile edition of *Biologia Centrali-Americana* by Alfred Percival Maudslay. Published 1974 by Milpatron Publishing Corp., Stamford, Conn. Further reproduction prohibited.

to the extent of using iconography, architecture, and inscriptions to reconstruct personalities and intentions of rulers (e.g., Jones 1977; Newsome 2001; Schele and Freidel 1990). Such an approach is grounded in Western art historical tendencies, exemplified especially by Ernst Gombrich's (1966: 35–57) attempts to glimpse the personalities of the Medicis through the works they commissioned. Despite this precedent, however, such an approach must proceed with caution, at least in the ancient Maya context (Fash 1998; Houston 1989). For example, it seems unlikely that we would be able to "reconstruct" the personality of a ruler, since the artifacts and the ruler are so tenuously associated. In particular, in ancient Maya art history we have very limited evidence concerning patterns of patronage and the specific relationship of the ruler to the artists.

The monuments of K'ak' Tiliw are particularly deceptive in this regard, as the main subject of both their texts and image is the king. The standard rhetoric of the inscriptions claims for the king sole responsibility for their dedication. Given this unitary "personal" focus, it seems only natural for the historian to look for the impetus for these works in the mind of the king himself. In addition, the themes of many of the images and texts are highly subjective, relating to dreams and trance experience. The small scale of the community and the centralization of art production only strengthen our suspicions that it was the king himself who planned the images. Nevertheless, while the king could have designed the monuments or have otherwise assumed some responsibility in their programming, it is essential to remember that we have no evidence to confirm or deny this supposition. It is also possible that the design could be attributed to a master scribe, another member of the royal family, a council of lineage heads, a shaman-priest, or some other religious specialist. In short, there is no documented connection between the king and the inception or execution of the work, making the attribution of intention to a particular person difficult.

On a more abstract level, the search for a basis of art in a single personality ignores the problems associated with the concept of artistic intentionality. While this study takes as given the proposition that humans are endowed with agency, it also recognizes that the attribution of artistic creativity to a reconstructed historical state of mind is problematic. In particular, the voluntary causes attributed to historical individuals may have been implicit in the cultural institutions in which the actors unreflectively took part. Other intentions may have become acquired through a history of behavior which had once been but was no longer consciously contemplated. In this view, artistic intentions are situated in the relationship between the context of artistic production and the object itself (Baxandall 1985: 42). Intentionality is thus one of the deceptions of art. While we assume that a specific group of people must have made the physical work of art, the integration of these people into a broader webs of social interaction inextricably links agency into systems of behavior that are not reducible to the sum of their parts. As stated by Alfred Gell (1999: 163), works of art seduce the viewer/interpreter into a "network of intentionalities whereby, although each individual pursues (what each takes to be) his or her own self-interest, they all contrive in the final analysis to serve necessities which cannot be comprehended at the level of the human being, but only at the level of collectivities and their dynamics." The indeterminacy of art lies in the magical ability of the artist to transcend the understanding of the spectator. Indeed, Gell (1999: 172) describes the artist as an "occult technician," whose work "mediates between creative agency and the power of the collectivity."

Such considerations suggest a different approach to studying the subjectivity and personalization of art at Quirigua, not based on personality as a fact or primal source, but rather with the goal of reconstructing the role of the "self" as defined historically by the society (see Mauss 1985: 3). A number of studies by Stephen Houston, David Stuart, and Carolyn Tate have proposed models for interpreting ancient Maya representations in terms of the "self" (Houston and Stuart 1996, 1998; Stuart 1996; Tate 1992: 11–25). Houston and Stuart in particular observed that Maya monuments were not conceived as false simulacra but rather as living entities that shared in the essence of the rulers. The term used to refer to such images, b'ahil, was derived from b'a(h), which meant not only "self" and "person" but also "head." As such, it identifies the head and face as a particularly significant locus of personality—a concept that goes far to explain the compositional focus on the king's face at Quirigua and other sites. Images of a ruler not only embodied the royal self in multiple permanent forms but were considered to function as active agents on the ruler's behalf. In this way, the Maya overtly acknowledged the general function of art and artifacts as secondary agents, capable of propagating causal sequences of events as extensions of the human agents who made them (see Gell 1998: 15–17).

Two examples of the attribution of agency to stone sculptures are illustrated in inscriptions from Quirigua. One is on Stela E east (Fig. I.27a), where the events of the period-ending are introduced with a glyph that assigns agency, followed by *ub'ahil* "his image." The next glyph block is of astronomical significance, preceding the name of K'ak' Tiliw.[29] This passage suggests that the ceremony was conducted under the authority of the royal image, depicted in an astronomical guise. A second reference to an active, living monument may appear in a partially eroded passage on the west face of Stela D (Fig. I.27b). Here the text records an event associated with the dedication date of the monument as *ajawaj*, or "it is made *ajaw*," a phrase related to expressions for royal accession.[30] Next may be the glyph for "his image" (*ub'ahil*), followed by a series of illegible signs. The final glyph of the clause is *tunil* "stone object." This passage, then, may suggest that for the period-ending ceremony a stone monument (presumably Stela D) was itself made *ajaw*.

The recognition that stelae function as surrogates for royal authority has further implications for the understanding of their imagery. In particular, it suggests that the monumental portraits may have served to propagate and perpetuate the gaze of the king. As discussed by Stephen Houston and Karl Taube (2000), ancient Maya conceptions of the sense of sight were not the same as the view developed by modern science, in which the eye is a passive receptor of light. In contrast, the ancient Maya eye was an "emanating eye" that actively changed the world by exerting the will of the viewer. Thus, a common title (or nominal component) of kings, *k'inich*, meaning literally "sun-faced" or "sun-eyed," expresses the searing heat and brilliant light that were believed to emanate from a ruler's face or eyes. Like the sun, the gaze of the ruler was probably credited with the capacity to engender life.

Part of the dedication of a monument was the witnessing of its sanctification by the ruler or some other noble, which may have animated the representation (Houston and Stuart 1998; Houston and Taube 2000). In particular, this event may have opened the eyes of the carved figure, investing them with the power of sight on the ruler's behalf. Indeed, the aloof gazes of ancient Maya stela portraits are strongly suggestive of the establishment of a wide visual field, with the implication of control of events within that field. For the contemporary Yukatek, an orientation above or movement upward is considered to be relatively powerful or beneficent (Hanks 2000: 26–28). The Classic Maya glyphic expression *yichnal* also expresses this notion of an encompassing visual field that was crucial in validating ritual (Houston and Taube 2000). Cognate with modern Yukatek *yiknal* "in front of," this expression is also inherently hierarchical, linking

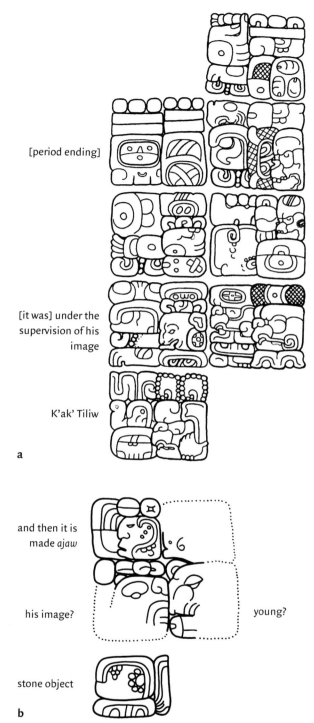

[period ending]

[it was] under the supervision of his image

K'ak' Tiliw

a

and then it is made *ajaw*

his image?   young?

stone object

b

I.27. References to agency of monuments at Quirigua: *a,* Stela E, D15–C19; *b,* Stela D, B22–A23a1. Drawings by author.

subordinate persons to a ruler or deity. In fact, certain texts from Quirigua use the *yichnal* in substitution for *ukab'jiy* "under his supervision" (Looper 1999: Fig. 15). Stelae such as those of Quirigua may have been conceived in part as instruments for extending and perpetuating the dominant gaze of the ruler, but also as a means for invigorating those in the visual field with the royal "heat."[31]

A group of portrait stelae such as those associated with K'ak' Tiliw, then, may be interpreted as a means of distributing royal agency throughout the landscape, embodied in a series of distinct visages. A study of ancient Maya personhood thus requires an examination of the meanings not of individuality but rather of the "dividuality" of the self—to borrow a term from Marilyn Strathern (1988)—which was achieved through representational art. In this view, there is no *a priori* category of the self separate from the collaborative practice of its figuration. Further, we must acknowledge that the self is not a static entity but one which changes and evolves over time.

In order to define the changes in self-presentation in Maya monuments and to interpret the social and historical forces that contributed to their making, a term employed in psychology and literary criticism is useful. The term "persona" is used in literature to distinguish between the author and the narrator (Fowler 1987: 176–177) and in psychoanalysis to refer to an "arbitrary segment of collective psyche" (Jung 1953: 105).[32] Both of these conventions make use of the metaphor of the mask or "second self"; and, in fact, the term "persona" originally denoted the masks worn by actors in Greek theater. Although the concept of persona is not often employed by art historians, this etymology suggests the applicability of the term to representational visual culture. In the present study, "persona" is used to define diverse "selves" as they are manifested in art, thereby implying the critical distinction between the identities of the subject of a portrait and the guises presented in a portrait image. Persona, unlike personality, is a culturally constructed mask or a conventional identity that may be changed in relation to dynamic social circumstances.

In ancient Maya culture, personae served as an important mode of mediation between the individual and society and are thus crucial in understanding the dynamics of agency. When manipulated by elites, personae expressed the nature of social hierarchy and inequality. This function of persona is grounded in the widespread Mesoamerican practice whereby rulers legitimated their authority through the display of powerful emblems, often tied to the body. Materials such as jade, shell, quetzal feathers, and bone were attached to the trunk, head, and limbs to infuse these various parts of the body with their power. Notably, many of these materials were derived from loci that were associated with supernatural forces. Bones were literally at the core of the living body, while other materials were acquired from distant, and therefore symbolically powerful, sources. Jade and quetzal feathers came from the mountains, suggesting a celestial identification, whereas shells came from the sea and were thereby associated with the aquatic underworld. Thus, ceremonial attire was cosmological and transformational, magically infusing the elite person with spiritual energy. These details are highly elaborated on Maya monuments, a testament to their iconic power. The principal emblem that served as a seat of spiritual power is a mask and/or headdress. During ceremonial performances, rulers could become one with the spirits that the mask or headdress embodied, thus effecting their physical and psychological transformation. Maya rulers also commonly signaled control over divine forces through the display of deity images in the hands. In this way, masks, headdresses, costume, and other regalia served as a means of forming and manipulating personae, defining the precise relationships between the ruler and diverse supernatural entities.

An examination of the supernatural personae of rulers entails a consideration of the nature of Maya supernatural identities themselves. Did Maya rulers identify with a generalized impersonal supernatural essence or with distinct divine personalities? The answer to this question, as can be imagined, is far from simple, mainly because the subject of the nature of Maya divinities is still debated (Houston and Stuart 1996; Marcus 1978; Proskouriakoff 1965: 470–471, 1978; Thompson 1970: 198; Vail 2000). The Maya spirit world was and remains complex, populated by entities of distinct types. One was known as *way*, the spiritual co-essence of a person, which usually took the form of a composite animal (Grube and Nahm 1994; Houston and Stuart 1989). In addition, the term *k'uh*, which was used to refer to an impersonal divine essence, could also reference a specific incarnation in a deity image (Houston and Stuart 1996). Such complexities suggest that to identify Maya supernaturals indiscriminately as "gods" is inappropriate. Among the most significant of the differences between Maya deities and the modern Western conception of gods is the Maya deities' nonexclusive association with fairly broad domains such as agriculture, war, and death. For example, in a statistical study of the Madrid Codex, Gabrielle Vail (2000) demonstrated that nominal glyphs and attributes are used to group diverse deities into three loosely defined, overlapping contexts. The fluidity of roles and attributes of ancient Maya deities helps to explain their tendency toward multiplicity and hybridity.

The spirits of lightning are a good example of an ancient Maya deity complex (Looper 1991a). Across the Maya area, derivatives of the proto-Maya term *kahoq are used to refer to the thunderstorm as either a physical or spiritual phenomenon (Kaufman and Norman 1984: 117; Spero 1987: 231). Thus, in Ch'ol the lightning spirit is called "Chaak" or "Chahk" (Attinasi 1973: 249; Aulie and Aulie 1978: 46), while in Yukatek "Chaak [cháak]" refers to rain or to the deities of thunder, lightning, and rain (Barrera Vásquez 1980: 77; Bricker, Po'ot Yah, and Dzul de Po'ot 1998: 61). In the Classic period, the term "Chaak" is attested as a designation for various supernatural beings, who share a core cluster of features (Fig. I.28). These include bivalve shell earflares, reptilian eyes, serpent markings on the body, a shell diadem, a knotted pectoral or belt ornament, and a snakelike snout. Many carry hafted axes and trefoil stones and are shown in a jumping movement.

Not only do these beings seem to preside over diverse domains (such as fishing, sacrifice, and caves), however, but most are named with qualifiers, such as Chaak Xib' Chaak, Ux B'olon Chaak, 'O/'Ohl Chaak, and Yax Ha'al Chaak. The distinctions seem to correlate to the ritual domains with which the deities are associated. For example, Yax Ha'al Chaak frequently appears in codex-style pottery scenes together with a particular "death god" and a jaguar deity who has been thrown upon a mountain (see Robicsek and Hales 1981: 39–43). Other lightning deities are similar in appearance to the Chaaks but are re-

ferred to in the inscriptions by the term "Yo'at/Yo'pat" and appear in scenes of the resurrection of maize (Fig. I.4). Despite these differences, the deities can be grouped into a single complex, based on their shared iconography and associations with thunderstorms and the portals between realms of the cosmos. Their particular manifestations depended on specific ritual requirements which, in turn, were grounded in local histories and traditions.

Likewise, the ethnographic record suggests that Maya divinities are not conceived as possessing timeless personalities or singular identities but rather undergo periodic and often seasonal transformation. As facets of a cosmic totality, Maya deities are born and die as they satisfy their roles in the universal biography. They may change names, appearances, attributes, specific domains of influence, age, and even gender. For example, one of the chief Ch'orti' deities is a solar being during the dry season but transforms into a maize spirit upon the arrival of the rainy season (Girard 1995: 350). In addition, Rafael Girard (1995: 278) observes the tendency for contemporary Maya deities to multiply geometrically into compound manifestations. The same phenomenon is well known from the Yucatan, where deities commonly have a quadripartite aspect, being associated with the four cardinal directions (Thompson 1970: 198–199). Such concepts provide a basis for the consideration of monumental images as aspects of royal personae, which change depending upon calendrical, historical, and ritual requirements. Multiple images required the intervention of diverse deities on behalf of the ruler.

While costume and other regalia represent an important dimension of royal personae, naming practices were also significant in communicating the divine attributes of a historical identity. In some instances, these identities converged, when headdresses were used to display deity heads and other elements that correspond to rulers' names (see Martin and Grube 2000: 77). Another approach to merging these identities was the performance of ceremonies appropriate to the domain of one's supernatural namesake. As we shall see, this particular strategy was highly elaborated during the reign of K'ak' Tiliw. Names, however, are not equivalent to personae but are a distinct mode of marking social identity. Distinctions are usually made between rulers and the deities after whom they were named. Personae seem to have more in common with royal titles, which often stress the performance of ceremonial duties or cosmological associations and which are not required to express the identity of the ruler as a historical entity.

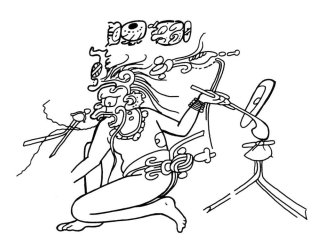

I.28. Yax Ha'al Chaak, from a Classic codex-style vessel (see Robicsek and Hales 1981: vessel 20). Drawing by author.

The potentially complex relationship of names to personae and other social identities is well illustrated by the example of seasonal ceremonial activity of the Kwakwaka'wakw people of the Northwest Coast (Jonaitis 1991). In the nineteenth century the Kwakwaka'wakw winter season was dominated by the *tseka* or Winter Dance. This was a season in which the spirit world spilled over into the human world, manifested in the performance of masquerades and the induction of men into initiation societies. During this season, people set aside their secular names and assumed sacred "winter names" and identities based on the nature of their participation in the ceremonies. Initiated persons were classified as Seals, who danced, and Sparrows, former dancers who now managed the performances. Participants were also organized according to secret societies, some of which involved masquerade performance as spiritually potent beings. Rights to these diverse identities were generally acquired through marriage.

How this system functioned in a person's biography is illustrated in a narrative called "The Acquisition of Names," recorded by Franz Boas (1925: 113–357). This story describes how a father prepared his son to succeed him by bestowing successive names upon him, accompanied by the distribution of gifts and observance of appropriate rituals. Manhood is marked by the presentation of a special name which gives the son the right to participate in feasts. Following this, the father, in conjunction with the son's father-in-law, sponsors a Winter Dance, in which the son appears as various characters, including Eater-of-the-Ground, a grizzly, and a fool dancer. After two winters, he retires as a Sparrow. This example shows that the purpose of Kwakwaka'wakw masquerade performance is not to illustrate a name but rather to support the change in social status signaled by the acquisition of the name. Both the name and masquerade participation are dictated by a complex genealogical system that is manipulated to enhance status.

Likewise, when considering ancient Maya identities, it is useful to consider them in the context of personal histories and political strategies. In contrast to the ethnographic case of the Kwakwaka'wakw, the only unambiguous evidence of ancient Maya elite ritual is provided by the ceremonial cities themselves, embellished with representational images and hieroglyphic texts. And while it would be inappropriate to treat Maya artworks as reflections of ritual akin to photographic documents, royal portraiture can be used to identify specific personae and to trace their development over time. Monumental personae may also be expected to vary among different sites.

Such comparisons suggest distinctive traditions of personae, which associate rulers with diverse sources of power. Usually, these traditions are grounded in local histories of representation; however, sometimes they can be shown to be borrowed from site to site and even to be manipulated competitively. The patterns of difference and correspondence among personae may be construed as evidence of political discourses, articulated through ritual. Ultimately, variation in personae reveals the manner in which power and authority were articulated and negotiated during the Classic period.

Methodologies

Having established the theoretical foundation of this study, it is useful to outline briefly the methodologies employed in the analysis. In particular, it is essential to discuss the value of each set of data in relation to the questions I have posed. One of the most illuminating of these data sources is the corpus of inscriptions that embellish the monuments of Quirigua. (Complete transcriptions and translations of the Quirigua texts appear in Appendix D.) These texts include declarations of dominance and subordination, warfare and alliance, and other political events that are frequently "disguised" in ritual terms. For example, a military victory is phrased as the throwing down of a war implement. The monumental texts thus provide a rich historical background for interpreting iconography and style. The basic approach to the decipherment of these texts is based on linguistic principles of syntax and phonetic substitution, as has been discussed elsewhere (Schele 1982; Schele and Grube 1994: 1–75; Stuart 1987b). Above the level of syntax, a discourse analysis of a text (or several related texts) allows for identification of major events and actors and of episodes in linked events (Josserand 1991). Such analyses expand the possibilities for reconstruction of political relationships, implicit in the actions of human actors and their supernatural patrons.

Epigraphers and archaeologists have occasionally expressed reservations about the relation of Maya inscriptions to history (e.g., Houston 1993: 9; Mathews 1985: 52–53). It has even been suggested that this is no "true history" but one so inextricably entwined with mythology as to render it useless as an interpretive category. Like any history, however, that inscribed on K'ak' Tiliw's monuments represents a carefully selected and integrated narrative mainly concerning human actors, the "truth" of which is dependent on the point of view of the compiler(s). Further, because any historical reconstruction is a dialogue with the past, but limited in that we must formulate the questions, an interpretation of ancient Maya texts is a political reconstruction. Thus, the goal of this project is to reconstruct the propositions made by the texts of Quirigua and contextualize them through local and regional comparisons.

In addition, it would be a mistake to assume that Maya hieroglyphic texts present a "confusion" between myth and history. On the contrary, ancient Maya texts reveal distinctive genres of history (stories about humans) and mythology (stories about the deified ancestors), identified through contrasting time frames, with mythic events taking place prior to and shortly after the renewal of the cosmos in 3114 B.C. (Marcus 1992: 8). In the inscriptions commissioned during the reign of K'ak' Tiliw, not only is this distinction rigorously observed through the temporal sequencing of narrative, but texts describing historical and mythical events are often relegated to different spatial zones on the monument. As at other Maya sites, mythic narratives provided the sacred charter for the actions of the king of Quirigua.[33] Thus, the distinction between history and myth was not one of truth versus invention as it is in the modern Western worldview. Indeed, mythic narratives were probably seen as inherently factual, being handed down through the generations and written in the movements of the stars and other natural cycles.

The Classic-period conceptualization of art and its production as strongly inspired by supernatural powers lent to artworks an *a priori* spiritual significance, a presence which demanded respect and awe. Such attraction was significantly reinforced by the emotional affectivity of form, whereby anthropomorphic or therianthropic images evoke sympathetic reactions in the viewer's body. In addition, Maya imagery is replete with symbols of spiritual and physical power, conveyed through an iconography of gesturing human figures in costume. As George Kubler (1969: 48) observed, the long duration of the Classic Maya style and iconography implies the existence of a generally agreed-upon system of symbolic values assigned to images. These values were surely stabilized to a considerable degree by the full integration of the writing system with iconography. Such considerations have supported the application of a structuralist approach to Maya iconography.[34] According to the structuralist paradigm, elements of dress, ritual objects, place of action, posture, and gesture all had conventional conceptual associations, which could be manipulated and configured with hieroglyphic texts into pointed rhetorical statements.

One area of structuralist research that has achieved particular prominence in recent years is the attempt to reconstruct a narrative of Maya cosmogenesis by combining Classic-period texts and imagery with passages from the *Popol Vuh*. This colonial-era K'iche' epic relates the story of Creation and the origins of the K'iche' people. The following summary of this narrative is based on the most recent reconstruction by Schele and Mathews (1998: 36–37). The basic plot of this narrative concerns the destruction of the previous, third Creation, which ended on 13.0.0.0.0 (August 13, 3114 B.C.), and the establishment of the present cosmos by a pair of Hero Twins named Junajpu and Xb'alanke' (in Classic times, Jun Ajaw and Yax B'alam) and their father and uncle, twin maize spirits. The story begins in primordial times, when the maize deities (called Jun Junajpu and Wuqub' Junajpu in the *Popol Vuh*) were playing the ballgame, a Mesoamerican sport in which two teams compete using a large hard rubber ball, scoring points by means of floor markers or rings installed in the court in which the game was played.

The vigorous actions of this game disturbed the lords of Xib'alb'a, the Maya underworld. The Xib'alb'ans, portrayed as spirits of disease and death, summoned the maize deities into their abode, subjected them to a series of tests, and then dismembered and decapitated them, burying their parts in a Xib'alb'an ballcourt. The skull of Jun Junajpu was hung in a tree adjacent to the ballcourt, where it remained until the daughter of a Xib'alb'an lord came up to the tree and spoke with the skull. When the woman held out her hand, the skull spat into her palm, whereupon she became pregnant. Fearing her father's wrath, the woman fled the underworld and eventually gave birth to a pair of boys, known as the Hero Twins. They are called heroes because one of their tasks was to destroy various monstrous beings which dominated the previous Creation, such as a false sun named Wuqub' Kaqix ("Seven Macaw").

These twins, like their father, were also avid ballplayers and were likewise called to stand trial before the lords of Xib'alb'a. Being more clever than their father, however, they survived all of the torments their hosts inflicted on them and eventually tricked the Xib'alb'ans themselves into being sacrificed. This being done, they attempted to resurrect their forebears in the ballcourt. The maize spirits, reborn as infants, grew quickly, like maize plants, into young adults and began to make preparations for the dawning of the new Creation. After being dressed by their sons and certain goddesses, they awakened a series of aged deities, including the Paddler gods and a patron of merchants known as God L, who helped cleanse the world through a great flood. The Paddlers ferried the maize deities to a place of Creation marked by a turtle, where they were resurrected through a cleft in the shell made the Yo'at/Yo'pat manifestation of lightning. On 13.0.0.0.0 the maize spirits directed the gods to set up three cosmic hearth stones. On the same day, celestial cords, probably identified with the umbilicus of the reborn maize deity, descended to earth bearing sustenance. On 13.0.1.9.2 (February 5, 3112 B.C.), 542 days later, the maize deities completed their work on this fourth Creation by establishing the three-dimensional space of the cosmos, conceived as a house. They marked the four corners, measured the sides, and in the center planted a great ceiba tree (*Ceiba pentandra*). As this took place in the dry season, the ceiba tree was in flower and thus was conceived as a tree of life. The final event in this cycle was the spinning of the tree as a world axis, setting the stars in motion.

This story as reconstructed above is not merely a model for the establishment of cosmic order but can be viewed as an allegory of ancestor veneration, a fundamental concept in Classic Maya religion. In addition, the narrative may be interpreted as a model for Classic Maya rulers as manifestations of the Hero Twins, keepers of cosmic order and caretakers of the ancestors. Further, Schele and Freidel suggested that this narrative was read in the movements of the Milky Way during the course of the year (Freidel, Schele, and Parker 1993; Schele 1992b). According to their model, certain canonical orientations of the Milky Way, such as the two extending from north to south and one from east to west, are symbolized by specific icons in Maya art, such as the crocodilian known as the Cosmic Monster and the centipede jaws that mark the entrance to the underworld. The linkage of the Creation narrative to regular celestial movements strongly implies not only its universality but also its coherence as a discrete sequence of events.

While there is much to be said for the idea of interpreting Maya iconography in terms of nocturnal celestial images, caution should be exercised in the application of the "master narrative" of cosmogenesis, as described above, to isolated examples of Maya art. In particular, it can be observed that the Creation story presented above is assembled through a process of bricolage, in which elements from diverse historical traditions and contexts are combined into a single historically disconnected narrative. The entire process is based on the assumption of the existence of an underlying collective and transhistorical Maya narrative that is expressed in fragmentary form in art and literature. In fact, such an approach is not

unique to Maya art history but has been attempted in diverse fields, such as the art of the Dogon (e.g., Laude 1973). In addition to the problem of historical confusion intrinsic to the pastiche, however, the very existence of elaborate collective myths is suspect. As noted previously in the discussion of the symbolism of stelae, it is highly unlikely that a cultural zone as large and diverse as that of the Classic Maya would be characterized by such uniformity in narrative traditions. In fact (as we shall see in subsequent chapters), not only were the monuments of Quirigua distinctive, but the stories of cosmic ordering inscribed on them preserve many unique motifs that are specifically tied to local historical circumstances. While structuralism is useful when developing theories about motifs, it cannot by itself explain why a motif appears in a given instance in history. A historically engaged interpretation of images must consider both structure and context.

The most basic level of contextual analysis is analysis of the program in which an image is located. In this book, the term "program" is used in its traditional art historical sense, as developed especially in the field of medieval and Renaissance art (Gombrich 1972; von Simson 1988: 228). It refers to a complex of images and texts and the conceptual scheme that underlies this complex. To be considered a program, a group of monuments must be located in a contiguous space, oriented in the same direction or along the same axes, and erected in the same general period. At Quirigua, as at many Maya sites, the webs of meaning established among written texts and images are not necessarily limited to single monuments but extend to multiple monuments arranged in groups. In this regard, Classic Maya art is highly sophisticated, comparable to medieval church portals or Buddhist architecture.

A focus on the programmatic aspects of art privileges the designer's point of view. This is an important point, because the Quirigua monuments were created within a multiethnic milieu, with a substantial non-Maya component. Presumably, different social groups at Quirigua would have participated in various ways in the execution and use of the sculptures, resulting in diverse interpretations of their meaning. Even within the Maya minority, distinctions in social status must have related to different points of view with regard to the monuments. A complete understanding of the social significance of the Quirigua program is beyond the scope of the present book, as it would necessitate a status-sensitive comparative analysis of both Maya and non-Maya monumental practices within the region (see Ashmore n.d.). In contrast, the explanatory perspective taken in the following chapters begins by reconstructing the often esoteric messages of the monuments themselves and then expanding their interpretations into ever widening social spheres by integrating archaeological data. The reader should remain aware of the limitations and biases of such an approach.

Because of the complexity of monumental sculpture programs, it is essential to characterize precisely the relationship of images to spatially linked written texts. As discussed by Janet Catherine Berlo (1983: 13), written texts that are physically linked to images may be either *conjoined* (juxtaposed) or *embedded* (integrated into an image). The standard monumental mode at Quirigua segregates pictorial images from written texts, placing them on distinct faces of the monument. In all cases, pictorial images are presented as primary information, placed on the broadest faces of the monuments or directed toward major performance areas or processional routes, while written texts are relegated to a secondary position, usually placed on the narrower sides of a monument or on the reverse. This hierarchy of image over written text is standard for Maya art and has implications for the interpretation of the meaning of monuments.

A useful model for understanding these relationships, presented by Flora Clancy (1986), draws on Roland Barthes's theories of relay and anchorage to suggest that written texts can either complement or supplement images in Maya art. Thus, texts may either constrain or *anchor* meaning, by describing the events depicted; or they may extend the significance of the image by providing additional information relating to it, through a process of *relay*. At Quirigua images and texts are related to each other through both of these processes. Because the texts often relate multiple events which take place at different times, the text is related to the image through relay. One or two of the clauses in a monument's text, however, will normally be referenced (anchored) in the image. Thus, there is often a clear resonance between the poetics of image and text that contributes to the aesthetic impact of the artwork. In addition, the reading order of the text may suggest a reading order of images, in the cases where there is more than one image. In the end, the decipherment of the patterns of relations of image, text, and space allows for the reconstruction of the particular message that the sculptures present to the audience.

Previous studies of Maya sculpture have noted a strong retrospective focus of iconography, wherein elements from earlier sculpture are frequently quoted in later works (Proskouriakoff 1950; Schele 1979). Such repeti-

tions through time contribute significantly to the local distinctiveness of art from the largest Maya centers. In addition, as Carolyn Tate (1992: xi) observed, the Maya "conceived the imagery of each monument in relation to nets of meanings woven by the symbols on previously existing monuments placed throughout the city." According to Tate, such webs of significance had a political interpretation, as they served to foster a sense of local identity among the inhabitants of the locales where the art was displayed. An implication of this observation is that deliberate copying of ritual iconography from site to site could be taken to indicate political relationships and positioning. Quirigua serves as an excellent test case for this theory, through the richness of its iconography and completeness of its sculptural record. It will become apparent that the sculptures of Quirigua are replete with iconographic quotations not only from the local past but from the ceremonial traditions of Copan. The specific iconographic and textual targeting of these works reveals the dynamism of local and regional ideologies of political ascendancy.

While an examination of iconography within a temporal and spatial matrix provides a means for evaluating the politico-religious history of art, stylistic continuities and disjunctions are also worthy of detailed analysis.[35] In the words of Willibald Sauerländer (1983: 254), "Style is the mirror which makes all the buildings, the statues, the images of the past accessible to aesthetic historicism, for its dreams and for its files." As will be demonstrated, clear patterns of stylistic development can be distinguished in Quirigua sculpture during the forty-year period of continuous sculptural commissions. The most obvious change is an increasing emphasis on the sculptural block and its rectangular cross-section. Further, relief becomes increasingly shallow, so that by the last decades of the eighth century carved designs are conceived and executed as little more than slightly "enriched" drawings, wrapped around the surfaces of a three-dimensional block. How can these changes be explained? Are they the result of an intentional move by the artist(s) to express some concept, or are they merely a sort of artistic "drift," the secondary result of other cultural processes? Moreover, can stylistic changes be related to political power—and, if so, how?

As noted by Whitney Davis (1990: 26), current conceptions of style are firmly rooted in traditions of Classical rhetoric, in which style involves rules for intended verbal effects, such as persuasion or elaboration. Accordingly, these discussions center on informational content of style and intentionality. Nevertheless, as defined traditionally in art history, style is not some inherent quality or occult entity residing in a work of art but an abstraction, based on comparison between artifacts. Further, patterns of similarity in artifact styles cannot necessarily be attributed to common historical causes; in other words, we cannot always successfully read "from style to history" (Davis 1990: 26).

This qualification is especially relevant to the case of ancient Maya sculpture, when we know relatively little about its context of production and use and even less about indigenous concepts of style. For example, the apparent conservatism in stelae from a certain site could be attributed to a number of factors, such as workshop histories, deliberate copying of models, or working practices. Judging from style alone and without independent data, it is not possible to determine which of these interpretations is correct. Conversely, neither can differences in sculptures, such as the changes in those at Quirigua, be taken as sole evidence of particular historical relationships. Instead, as argued by Davis (1990: 25), style is necessarily the index or symptom of the presence of a historical entity rather than the result of it. This being the case, considerable care must be taken in correlating sculptural style and politics. In this study, political relationships are constructed primarily by using inscriptional and iconographic data, with stylistic comparisons serving to enrich and extend these interpretations. In such a manner I hope to bridge the gap between style and social history, which has been a perennial problem in Precolumbian art history.

The strong historical focus of this book dictates its organization. It begins in Chapter 1 by tracing the origins of Quirigua as a Classic Maya center back to its very humble beginnings as a small trading colony. Despite its subordinate status, the artistic legacy of Early Classic Quirigua is of great importance for the development of more ambitious programs during the reign of K'ak' Tiliw. Chapter 2 documents the early years of this ruler's reign

(725–738), when Quirigua was directly subordinate to Copan and its sculptors worked closely in line with the practices of the larger center. This chapter theorizes that the concept of personae in sculpture, which was already present in the Early Classic period, was actively suppressed through the prohibition of portrait images during this period.

Chapter 3 discusses the political and religious significance of the sacrifice of Waxaklajun Ub'ah K'awil, which was celebrated in a series of portrait stelae erected soon after the event. These monuments, which become increasingly ambitious in scale and execution, reveal evidence of archaism, an apparent reference to the local dynasty and the ruler's legitimacy therein. In addition, the decapitation provided the basis for the development of a distinct association of K'ak' Tiliw with the lightning deity Chaak, which remained crucial to his legacy. Chapter 4 introduces the most complex program of K'ak' Tiliw's career, a group of stelae erected on Platform 1A-1 between A.D. 761 and 780. These sculptures imbued the site with a living presence and permanent ritual authority of the king through the inscription of multiple personae. Nevertheless, the entire program celebrates the cosmological significance of K'ak' Tiliw's dominant identity as a manifestation of Chaak. The climax of this program, discussed in Chapter 5, presents a local twist on the lore of Creation, demonstrating the cosmological implications of the dedication of thrones/platforms by the ruler.

Chapter 6 documents the transformation of the complex personae of K'ak' Tiliw after his death, by his successors. The change is dramatic, as his successors at first focused on K'ak' Tiliw as a great warrior then later shifted to a more ambiguous presentation under new political circumstances. Despite these transformations, the characterization of the deceased ruler as a source of divine power attests to the cumulative impact of K'ak' Tiliw's own monuments on historical consciousness at Quirigua.

1

LIFE AT THE CROSSROADS

Quirigua before K'ak' Tiliw

WHEN K'AK' TILIW assumed the throne as ruler of Quirigua in A.D. 725, the site over which he ruled bore little resemblance to the ruins we see today. Penetrations of the acropolis undertaken by the University of Pennsylvania Quirigua Project revealed that the complex was very small prior to the eighth century. In fact, before his accession, few architectural groups existed in the vicinity of the site core. Nevertheless, several monuments from the period before K'ak' Tiliw have been discovered, including two stelae dating to the late fifth century. Together with a circular mid-seventh-century monument, Altar L, the inscriptions, iconography, and styles of these monuments reveal that Quirigua was not politically or artistically isolated. These monuments provide insight into the political climate of this period but also constitute a historical legacy that was evoked in the sculpture programs of the Late Classic period. In addition, several retrospective accounts of the early history of Quirigua appear in the very late monuments of K'ak' Tiliw and his successors. These texts are the only sources relating to the founding events of the Quirigua dynasty and are crucial for understanding the rhetorical significance of K'ak' Tiliw's monuments.

The reconstruction of the origins of Quirigua is problematic due to its location on the lower reaches of the Motagua River. Situated at the point where the valley broadens into a huge plain, Quirigua has, over the centuries, been subjected to the periodic flooding of the river and the subsequent deposit of large quantities of silt. Not only do such floods tend to sweep away cultural remains, but the silt also buries early features, making their localization and identification difficult. Further, the frequent changes in the river's course may obliterate even the most

substantial structures. Nevertheless, there is evidence that the area may have been occupied as early as the Late Formative period (prior to A.D. 100; Ashmore 1987; Jones, Ashmore, and Sharer 1983). Although no structures in the vicinity of Quirigua have been securely identified as Formative in date, a small number of artifacts appear to be from this early period (Ashmore 1980a).[1] These include a group of sixty-three figurines and one chert blade, possibly from Loci 122 or 123, groups located on the floodplain south of the river (Fig. 1.1).[2] The layout of one of these compounds, the unexcavated Locus 122, suggests a similarity to certain architectural complexes of the Formative-period highlands, which are typified by a combination of pyramidal mound and elongated plaza, oriented northeast to southwest (Ashmore 1984: 372, 1987: 219; see also Borhegyi 1965: 12, 14).

On the north bank of the river, two sculptures, Monuments 29 and 30, hint at a parallel Late Formative–period occupation in this area (Ashmore 1984: 372, 1987: 219; Sharer 1990: Figs. 48, 49). These two sculptures were found together in a modern drainage ditch located to the north and northwest of the site core. Both are roughly columnar schist monuments, measuring just over 1 m in length. They are extremely eroded on all surfaces but appear to represent anthropomorphs or monkeys with their hands clasped to their chests, standing on pedestal supports. The form of these sculptures is related to traditions originating with the Olmec and flourishing during the Late Formative period in the Guatemalan highlands, Pacific slopes and coast, Honduras, and the Isthmus of Tehuantepec of Mexico (see Miles 1965: 248–250). The presence of the pedestal sculpture form at Quirigua suggests already at this early date the participation of the lower Motagua valley population in a cultural sphere that included many peoples in Honduras and highland Guatemala.[3] Such cultural similarities served as the foundation for more concrete political relationships between Quirigua and Honduran centers, which developed during the Early Classic period.

Quirigua in the Early Classic Period

Substantial archaeological evidence for a settlement at Quirigua appears after about A.D. 400. It was around this time that the first phase of the acropolis was built, in the form of a modest patio group oriented roughly to the cardinal directions (Jones, Ashmore, and Sharer 1983: 2–4).[4] Construction materials were crude, consisting mostly of silt fills with cobble and schist-slab faces for the mounds and cobble walls. The southern structure built during this phase of the acropolis, Structure 1B-1-2nd, consisted of a north-facing double-roomed building situated on a mound of about 1 m in height. On the east side of the court, Structure 1B-6-2nd was built on a terraced platform with a western stairway. The structure apparently served as a shrine for a burial which was located under the building. This tomb was intruded 1.3 m into sterile river silt lined with schist slabs and contained the remains of an elite person, probably male, with jade-inlaid teeth and a jade bead placed in the mouth (Jones, Ashmore, and Sharer 1983: 4). Ceramic offerings associated with this burial confirm its Early Classic date, although there is no firm evidence to prove that it belonged to the dynastic founder of Quirigua, as has been suggested (Sharer 1978, 1997). It is also possible that the burial may be that of a later ruler or even another elite person.

The Early Classic period also witnessed construction elsewhere in the region, including two Groups, 3C-7 and 3C-8, located on the floodplain north of the acropolis. In addition, several more distant settlements were established. These include Locus 002, founded on a lookout ridge west of the valley groups, Locus 011, located near the mouth of the Quirigua River, and Locus 057 on the Jubuco River, several kilometers southwest of the floodplain center (Fig. 1.1).[5] Typical of the construction of this period are low earthen platforms faced with small river cobbles or, for larger structures, rounded-faced rhyolite blocks, with clay mortar and crushed rhyolite floors. The source for this building material was a series of rhyolite outcrops located between four and eight kilometers up the Motagua River.

The arrangement of the earliest phase of the Quirigua acropolis is highly suggestive of the site's far-flung political associations during the Early Classic period. During the initial investigations of these structures, it was observed that the plaza arrangement with a square eastern burial shrine is similar to a pattern seen at Tikal (Becker 1972). This was taken to imply political or cultural ties between the two sites. The recent excavation of the Copan early acropolis, however, suggests a closer comparison of the Quirigua shrine with the fifth-century structure at Copan known as Hunal, which contains the burial of its founder and also faces west (Ashmore n.d.; Sharer 1997). While the structure was begun as a palace, the Copan founder's burial transformed it into a symbolic and spatial pivot for superimposed construction (Fash and Fash 2000; Sedat and López 1999; Sharer, Traxler, et al. 1999; Traxler 2001: 56, 58). Although the dates of construction of the early acropolis at Quirigua are uncertain, its broad similarity to the early Copan acropolis suggests its closer political ties to the Honduran center rather than to Tikal, where similar court structures do not appear until the Late Classic.

The intimate political relationship between Quirigua and Copan suggested by Early Classic architectural layouts is confirmed by historical data, recorded in both contemporary and retrospective inscriptions. The official history of the establishment of rulership at Quirigua is found in several cartouches on Zoomorph P, a monument dating to A.D. 795 (Fig. 1.2). The first of the events is the "coming" to what is known to Mayanists as a "founding house," a locus associated with the rituals through which dynastic founders connected their authority to the prestige of the central Mexican metropolis of Teotihuacan (Grube and Schele 1992; Grube, Schele, and Fahsen 1991; Schele 1992a; Schele and Grube 1992a; Stuart 2000). This event transpired on September 6, 426, but it did not necessarily take place at Quirigua. Three days later, on September 9, was the erection of a stone monument and the accession of Quirigua's first ruler, nicknamed Tok Casper, under the authority of the founder of Copan's Classic period dynasty, K'inich Yax K'uk' Mo' (Grube, Schele, and Fahsen 1991; Looper 1999; Schele 1992a; Stone 1986; Stuart 1992b; Stuart and Schele 1986b). A passage from the Copan Hieroglyphic Stairway may also refer to the accession of this Quirigua ruler (see Chapter 3). These events took place on precisely the same dates as founding events for the Copan dynasty, as recorded on CPN Altar Q in 775. On the first of these days, the Copan ruler is said to have received the God K scepter of kingship; and on the second, to have "come" to the "founding house."

These texts indicate that, at least from the perspective of Late Classic Quirigua, the foundation of the dynasty

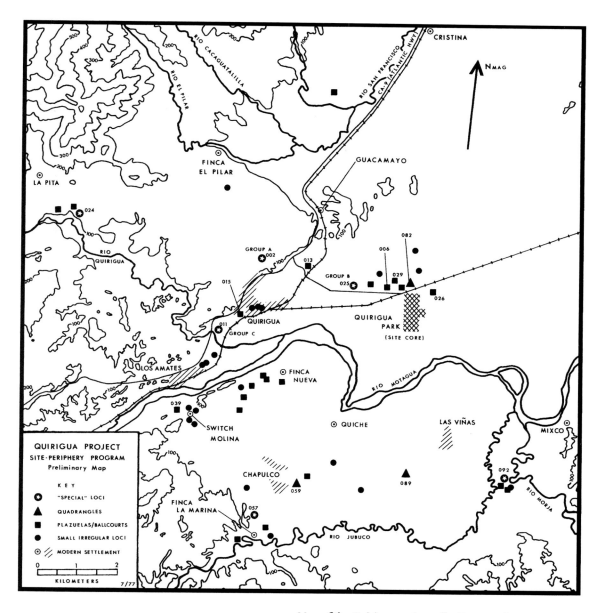

1.1. Map of the Quirigua region, after Jones, Ashmore, and Sharer 1983: Fig. 6.5. Courtesy University of Pennsylvania Museum of Archaeology and Anthropology.

occurred in conjunction with and overseen by the first king of Classic Copan. When considered in light of recent archaeological data from Copan,[6] however, the hand of Tikal can be detected in these affairs as well. This is suggested not only in the Tikal-style inset corners and apron moldings of the Yax platform commissioned by K'inich Yax K'uk' Mo' but also in later structures such as Yehnal, built by his successor, Popol Hol. The founder was also responsible for the introduction of art styles associated with Teotihuacan to Copan. For example, Hunal, the first structure in his building program and the

site of his eventual burial, was built in the talud-tablero style of Teotihuacan (Sharer, Traxler, et al. 1999). These innovations suggest the founder's origins from the central Peten, where Teotihuacan styles first appear in the Maya area. In fact, chemical tests of the remains of K'inich Yax K'uk' Mo' indicate that he was not a native of Copan (Buikstra 1997; Sharer, Traxler, et al. 1999). Further, a personage referred to as "K'uk' Mo' ajaw" appears in an early text from Tikal (Schele, Grube, and Fahsen 1993). Thus, although it is still not absolutely certain, there is considerable support for the thesis that Classic-period dynastic kingship at both Quirigua and Copan was instituted as part of a mission to establish Tikal's authority in the Southeast. This model explains the appearance of central Peten–derived features at both Early Classic Quirigua and Copan. It is to be expected as well that Quirigua would display numerous traits characteristic of Copan, the regional capital to which Quirigua was directly subordinate.

A second retrospective account of fifth-century rulers from Quirigua appears on Stela C, which dates to A.D. 775; but here there is no reference to external authority (Fig. 1.3). This inscription records the erection of a monument by a ruler named Tutum Yol K'inich in A.D. 455. While this ruler's name has sometimes been identified with that of the founder, Tok Casper, differences between the names of these persons suggest that they may have been successive rulers.[7] The Stela C text is crucial to K'ak' Tiliw's political rhetoric in that it establishes his links to a high king of Quirigua who was active less than thirty years after the founding of Copan's dynasty.

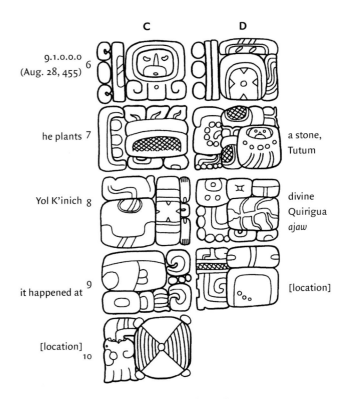

C   **D**

9.1.0.0.0 6
(Aug. 28, 455)

he plants 7

Yol K'inich 8

it happened at 9

[location] 10

a stone, Tutum

divine Quirigua *ajaw*

[location]

1.3. QRG Stela C, C6–C10. Drawing by author.

8.19.10.10.17
(Sept. 6, 426)

and then he comes

founding house

8.19.10.11.0
(Sept. 9, 426)

he plants

a stone,
he fastens the
headband

under his
supervision

K'uk' Mo'

divine
Copan *ajaw*

Tok Casper

[title]

K'inich *kalomte'*

1.2. QRG Zoomorph P, cartouches 7, 6, 5. Drawing by author.

Similar caching practices at the two sites add to the evidence for related elite traditions at Quirigua and Copan in the Early Classic period (Ashmore 1980b: 41; Ashmore, Schortman, and Sharer 1983: 59; Kidder, Jennings, and Shook 1946: 145; see also Schele 1990b). Not only are cache vessels of a type limited in range to Copan and Quirigua, but, in addition, the Maya of Copan and Quirigua (like those of the Guatemalan highlands) commonly burned cinnabar to yield mercury in caching rituals. Finally, jade "hunchback" figures found in monument caches are similar at Quirigua and Copan and related sites in central Honduras and the Guatemalan highlands. Such similarities parallel a general ceramic affinity between Copan and Quirigua documented in the Early Classic period. Some of Quirigua's Early Classic serving vessels and the majority of its storage vessels are similar to "southeastern" types, seen at Copan and Chalchuapa, in El Salvador (Ashmore 1984: 373; Willey et al. 1980). These relationships argue for Quirigua's participation on both elite and nonelite levels in the broad southeastern Maya cultural sphere centered on Copan, beginning in the Late Formative period. These cultural connections not only provide the basis for the political relationships documented between Quirigua and Copan during the Classic period but are also expressed in the sculptural traditions of the two sites during the Early Classic period.

Stela U

The earliest known inscribed monument from Quirigua, Stela U, provides a contemporary historical record that is consistent with the above official histories derived from very late sources. This monument is a schist stela, approximately 2.7 m in height, now broken in two pieces. Sylvanus G. Morley (1935: 49) found the monument lying on the lower terrace of Locus 002, the hilltop site west of the floodplain center which he named Group A. The monument had originally been set up on this lower terrace, in front of a stairway leading to the upper terrace and its south-facing, single-room building, Structure 1 (Sharer et al. 1983: 43). The stela foundation was of soil lined with stones; and its dedication cache, disinterred by vandals, consisted of ceramic vessels containing cinnabar, mercury, shale chips, and a bone fragment. Based on ceramic associations, the Stela U cache vessel type, and the round-faced masonry style of the first phase of Structure 1, it is certain that this was the original site of the stela (Ashmore 1980b: 36, 38, 42, 1981).

The figure on the obverse of Stela U is heavily eroded, but portions of the figure which continue onto the sides of the monument are well preserved (Fig. 1.4). This "wrap-around" compositional mode, seen here for the first time at the site, is typical of Quirigua sculpture (Clancy 1990). On both sides at the top are remains of the interlace and loop elements which are part of the figure's earflare assemblage, as preserved on the Early Classic Monument 26 (discussed below). The presence of interlace designs on the two sides of Stela U suggests that the front face of the stela represented a ruler in frontal view. Below the mat elements, open serpent maws disgorge profile faces adorned with earflares and wrapped headbands. The serpents are the termini of a double-headed serpent bar held by the figure on the obverse. The large tooth emerging from the mouth of the well-preserved head on the right side indicates that these heads represent supernatural beings, born out of the spirit world via the serpent. Glyphic elements which identify the deities appear above their foreheads.

A fairly well-preserved inscription with an initial series occupies the reverse of Stela U (Fig. 1.5). The date recorded is the *hotun* ending 9.2.5.0.0 10 Ajaw 8 Pop (April 18, 480), followed by a second date less than a year later (Looper 1999). Interestingly, the Long Count is truncated after the *tun*, and the calendar round is reversed, with the *hab'* coming before the *tzolk'in*. The reversal of *tzolk'in* and

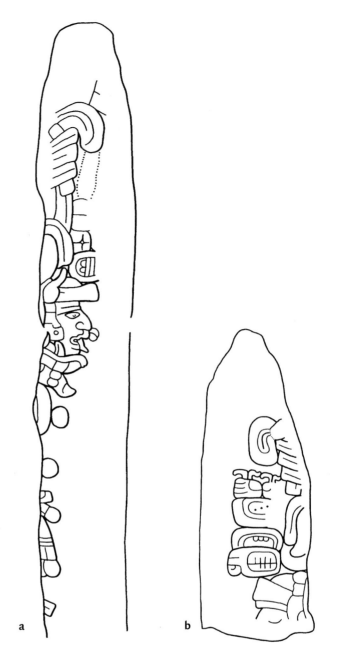

1.4. QRG Stela U: *a*, side 1; *b*, side 2. Drawings by author.

hab' is archaistic, recalling the text structure of the earliest lowland Maya stelae, such as the Hauberg Stela. It is also found on Copan Stela 16, which probably dates to 9.1.17.4.0 (A.D. 472; Schele 1990a; Schele and Miller 1986: 191). This suggests a connection between scribal traditions of the two sites at this early date. The personage mentioned on this monument is nicknamed "Turtle Shell," who completed his ritual under the supervision of a person bearing a west *kalomte'* title (Schele 1990b). This title, which is of considerable political significance, is

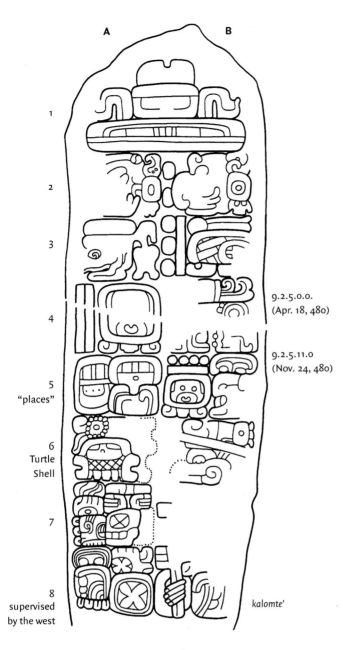

A   B

1

2

3

4

9.2.5.0.0.
(Apr. 18, 480)

5
"places"

9.2.5.11.0
(Nov. 24, 480)

6
Turtle
Shell

7

8
supervised
by the west

kalomte'

1.5. QRG Stela U, text. Drawing by author.

that Turtle Shell was acting under the auspices of an outsider, probably the ruler of Copan, who frequently assumed the title.[10] Although the personal name of the overlord is not given, he was probably Ruler 5 or 6. Whoever he was, his association with the west *kalomte'* title suggests political ties between Quirigua, Copan, and Tikal during this period.

Monument 26

Monument 26, a schist stela dedicated a few years after Stela U, confirms links between Quirigua and Copan in the Early Classic period but also implies connections with the larger sphere, including Tikal and Uaxactun (Figs. 1.6, 1.7). This shaft, which would originally have measured about 2 m in height, was found in 1979 by the University of Pennsylvania Quirigua Project. The monument was broken in antiquity, and only two large fragments are known: an upper fragment about 1 m in length and a lower piece about 0.6 m long. Both were found out of archaeological context in the vicinity of Group 3C-7 and were probably originally associated with a broad (more than 768 m²) earthen platform, 3C-1 (Fig. 1.8; Ashmore, Schortman, and Sharer 1983: 60).[11] The crushed rhyolite surface of Platform 3C-1 supported a flat, round schist altar, Monument 27, which was placed just south of the stairway that marked the north face of the platform. Atop the platform was constructed a single rectangular structure, 3C-14, made of earth and rhyolite rubble and faced with rounded-faced rhyolite masonry typical of the Early Classic period (Ashmore 1980b: 37).

Excavations near the eastern side of Structure 3C-14 encountered a well-built rhyolite chamber containing a collection (Cache 1) of three pairs of plain red everted-rim bowls, placed lip to lip and holding large amounts of cinnabar (partially burned to yield mercury), bits of pyrite, faunal remains, and six pieces of carved light green jadeite (Ashmore, Schortman, and Sharer 1983: 58). The jades included a pair of unfinished earflares, a pair of fists, and a pair of hunchback figures, which may represent shamans or shamanic assistants in trance (Schele 1990d). This cache probably served to dedicate Structure 3C-14, with the three vessels arranged in a triangle in reference to the three stones placed by the gods to organize space at Creation. Although the foundation for Monument 26 was not located with certainty, it is possible that a stone-lined pit located on an axis west of Structure 3C-14 served this purpose.

Like Stela U, Monument 26 bears a figure of the ruler on the obverse and sides (Fig. 1.6) and a text on the reverse (Fig. 1.7). The initial series of the text records a date

one of a set of compounds which couple a cardinal direction with *kalomte'*, a term of uncertain translation.[8] When combined with the direction "west," the title was restricted to the most powerful of Classic-period dynasties, especially that of Tikal, and seems to be closely associated with legitimation through reference to Teotihuacan. Accordingly, it is particularly associated with Tlaloc-Venus warfare, a martial complex of ritual and iconography adopted by the Maya from Teotihuacan.[9] As no known personage from Quirigua ever bore this title, it is likely corresponding to late 493, either October 28 (9.2.18.13.1) or November 6, 493 (9.2.18.13.10). While the initial series date has often been taken as the dedication date of the monument, there is good reason to think otherwise. A substantial portion of the text is, in fact, missing, which has destroyed critical details. On the lower fragment, however, a "scattering" ritual is followed by a "sky-god, earth-god" expression. In Maya inscriptions, this ritual formula is exclusively associated with period endings, implying that the broken area once included an explicit reference to the 9.3.0.0.0 k'atun ending that

shortly follows the initial series date. The dating of this stela to the period ending rather than the initial date is also consistent with other stelae from the site. Like Stela U, these are always associated with period endings, marking one of the four divisions of the k'atun. In addition, the date will have critical implications for the understanding of K'ak' Tiliw's later sculptural commissions, in particular, Stela H. The initial date of Monument 26 is nevertheless associated with several events, including the accession of a person named Mih Toh, who bears the title of "fourth in succession." A third successor is also mentioned, but in an uncertain context.[12]

While this text makes no explicit statement regarding relationships to Copan, it does suggest cultural connections to the larger center. In particular, the date of accession of the fourth successor is close to the date of maximum elongation of Venus as Morning Star on October 31. This astronomical association is in line with traditions of Copan, which favored this point in the Venus cycle for royal accession.[13] Although circumstantial, such a similarity in dynastic traditions between the two sites supports the inference that they were in close contact and even of common origin, as suggested by the text of Zoomorph P.

Conceived as a wrap-around composition, the Monument 26 figure bears strong stylistic as well as iconographic similarity to the slightly earlier Stela U. The portrait of the fourth successor is shown frontally, clutching a double-headed serpent bar to his chest (Fig. 1.6). The beads which surround the face probably symbolize petals and liken the ruler's face to a flower, a metaphor for life and fertility.[14] Below the nose are two additional beads (probably dangling from the pierced septum), also associated with flowers, which symbolize the sweet-smelling spirit essence embodied in the breath of the living king (see Houston and Taube 2000). The headdress of the lord consists of a single personification head, the forehead of which is wrapped with a band holding a T533 "Ajaw face" with side scrolls and a vertical blade. This feature is an Early Classic version of the personified royal headband or "Jester God" (see Fields 1989). Above the personification head is an oval cartouche containing what appears to be, on the left side, the mirror commonly included in Early Classic images of God K. Atop the cartouche is a large maize cob with the foliage peeled back to display the rows of kernels.

The king's earflare assemblages are very elaborate and stylistically typical of the Early Classic period. They feature interlaces at the sides of the face, loops emerging from the top of the interlaces, and pendant disks and

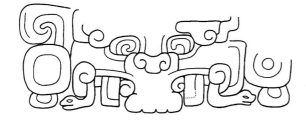

1.6. QRG Monument 26, figure. Drawing by author.

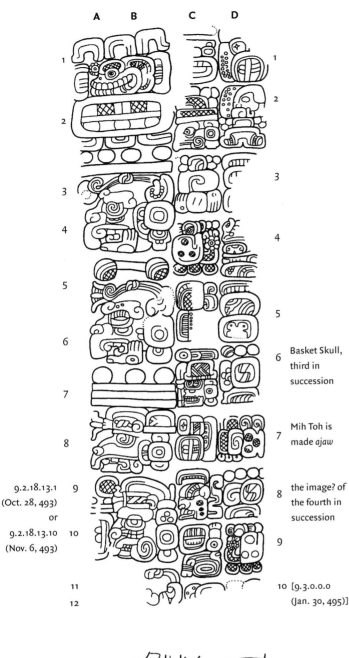

A B C D

1
2
3
4
5
6
7
8

9.2.18.13.1
(Oct. 28, 493)
or
9.2.18.13.10
(Nov. 6, 493)

9
10
11
12

1
2
3
4
5

6 Basket Skull,
third in
succession

7 Mih Toh is
made *ajaw*

8 the image? of
the fourth in
succession

9

10 [9.3.0.0.0
(Jan. 30, 495)]

Z1 scattering,
sky god

Z2 earth god

Z3

1.7. QRG Monument 26, text. Drawing by author.

bell-like ornaments below. The large earflare disks are displayed adjacent to the interlaces. Vertical struts emerge from the tops of the interlaces, pass through the mouth emanations of the personified headdress, and terminate in serpent heads. Sandwiched between the earflare disks and the personified headdress are braided elements with discoidal termini and, on the right side, a trilobed motif. These elements commonly appear as part of the ancient Maya earflare assembly (for example, on Tikal Stela 2 and Copan Stela P) and probably represent glyphs for *sak* "white." Together with the interlaces and serpent heads, these signs suggest a conceptualization of the earflares as a cosmological "white flower," an important Maya metaphor for breath and life force. In fact, earflares were often rendered as petaled flowers and sometimes had square-nosed serpent inserts that represented the stamen of the white flower of the ceiba tree (Freidel, Schele, and Parker 1993: 394; Looper and Kappelman 2001; Stuart 1992a). Part of the symbolism of the headdress of Monument 26, then, identifies the ruler with the ceiba tree, the principal biological metaphor for the cosmic axis that connects humans to the celestial spirit world.

Little else of the costume is visible on Monument 26, except the interlace-and-disk cuffs and matching belt and a beaded pectoral which includes a human head with closed eyes. To the figure's sides, just below the serpent heads, float two circular forms with hatched interiors, surrounded by curls. Below these medallions fall scrolls representing divine energy or *k'uh*. The position of the medallions, below the otherwise empty serpent jaws, suggests that they are to be read as the objects that emerge from the maws of the serpent bar. The falling scrolls support this contention, as they are shown emitted directly from a double-headed serpent bar on other monuments (for instance, K'ak' Tiliw's Stela H; see Chapter 3). Although the details of the medallions are unique to Monument 26, they are similar in design and location on the monument to the shields which appear on several Copan stelae, including I, 7, and 60 (Fig. 1.9). In the context of Quirigua Monument 26, shields are conjured from the spirit world through a vision rite, an image that underscores the king's control of the supernatural forces of war. This interpretation may be reinforced by the closed-eyed human head that the king wears as a pectoral, although usually such trophy heads are worn inverted.

Facing page

1.8. Map of QRG Group 3C-7. Drawing by Wendy Ashmore.

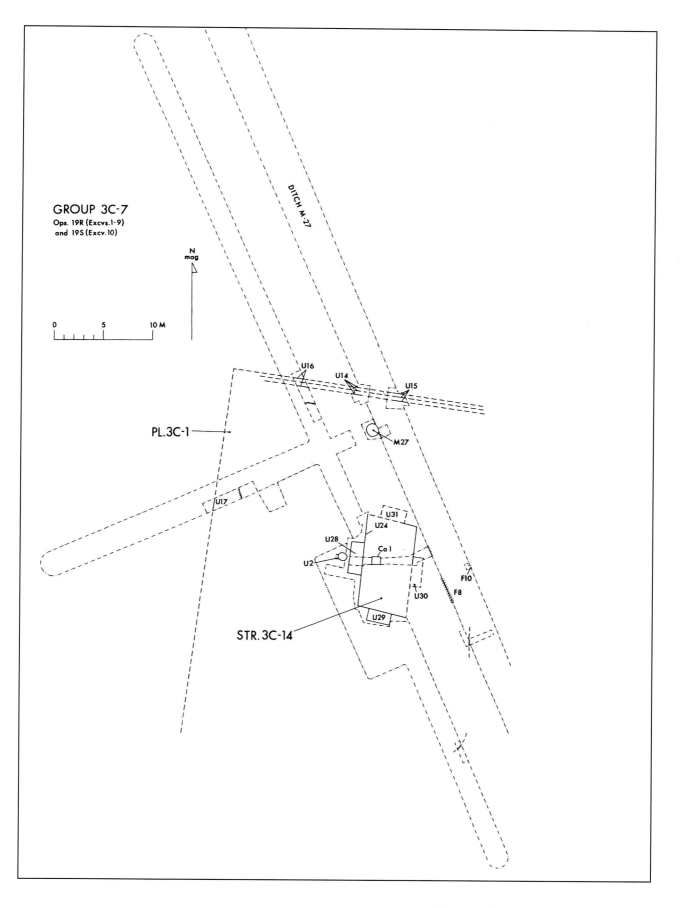

GROUP 3C-7
Ops. 19R (Excvs. 1-9)
and 19S (Excv. 10)

N mag

0   5   10 M

DITCH M-27

U16
U14
U15

PL.3C-1

M27

U17

U31
U24
U28
Ca 1
U2
F10
U30
F8
U29

STR. 3C-14

1.9. CPN Stela 60. Drawing by author after field drawing by Linda Schele, courtesy Instituto Hondureño de Antropología e Historia.

Although the feet of the figure are missing, the lower fragment of Monument 26 does preserve a basal register showing a personified mountain that is wrapped around to the sides of the monument (Fig. 1.6). The right side displays a stepped motif on the forehead, which corresponds to the cleft opening in the mythological mountain of Creation, which in the Classic period was called Yax Hal Witz "First True Mountain" (Schele and Freidel 1991). Analogous to the Broken Place, Bitter Water Place of the *Popol Vuh* where the seeds of all cultigens were kept and where humanity was created, the First True Mountain was a source of fertility and life for the ancient Maya, who believed that humans and maize contained the same divine essence. Further, the First True Mountain depicted on the Tablet of the Foliated Cross (Fig. 1.10a) is shown floating in the waters of the primordial sea, the place where souls go at death and out of which they emerge in resurrection.[15] The cleft at the top of the First True Mountain serves as the portal through which souls of ancestors, in the form of the spirit of maize, are resurrected

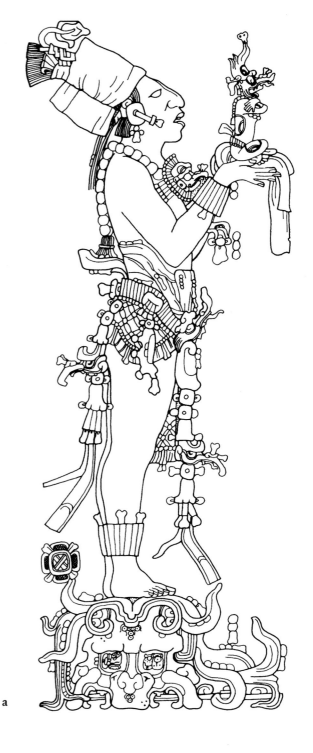

a

1.10. Sacred mountains with personifications of maize: *a*, Palenque Temple of the Foliated Cross, main panel, detail; *b*, Bonampak Stela 1, detail. Drawings by author and Linda Schele, © David Schele, courtesy Foundation for the Advancement of Mesoamerican Studies, Inc.

b

through the ritual acts of the descendant, as shown on Bonampak Stela 1 (Fig. 1.10b). In fact, standing atop the cleft in the mountain, the ruler on QRG Monument 26 is represented in the guise of the maize deity himself. This role is affirmed by the maize cob at the top of the head-dress. The figure on Copan Stela H wears a similar personification head and cob (Fig. 1.11). On this monument, the maize-deity costume is worn in the context of the carving of an ancestor's bones as part of the rituals leading to resurrection (Schele and Grube 1992b; Schele and Mathews 1998: 154–158). The same configuration appears on the Tablet of the Foliated Cross from Palenque, which shows K'inich Kan B'alam II dressed as the personification of maize standing atop the mountain where the plant first appeared (Fig. 1.10a).

Additional details of the basal register of Monument 26 suggest a second symbolic referent for the mountain upon which the ruler stands. The paired snakes that descend from the corners of the creature's mouth identify it as a version of Snake Mountain, a mythical place associated with the origins of warfare, civilization, and legitimate rulership. As such, this icon reinforces the symbolism of the shields that emerge from the double-headed serpent bar held by the ruler.

Although it appears widely throughout Mesoamerica, Snake Mountain is most familiar to modern scholars under its Nahuatl name, "Coatepec." As documented in central Mexican sources from the early colonial period, Coatepec was the birthplace of the Aztec patron deity Huitzilopochtli and the site where he defeated his enemies. Huitzilopochtli also initiated agricultural practices at this place, through the establishment of a well of water in the ballcourt at the base of the mountain. With its serpent balustrades, the Templo Mayor of Tenochtitlan itself represented this sacred location, combined with a manifestation of the mountain of sustenance or Tonacatepetl (Broda 1987: 77; Matos Moctezuma 1984, 1987; Townsend 1982).

The trope of Snake Mountain was not restricted to the Aztecs, however, nor to the Late Postclassic or colonial periods. It has been documented in architectural form at Teotihuacan and El Tajin as well as widely throughout the Maya area as early as the Late Formative period (Koontz 1994; Schele and Kappelman 2001; Schele and Mathews 1998). One of the most elaborate architectural versions of Snake Mountain among the Maya was Structure E-Sub-VII, built at Uaxactun in the Late Formative. Like the Templo Mayor, this structure included references to the Snake Mountain, through snake effigy masks on the lower tier of the façade, as well as to a

1.11. CPN Stela H, west face. Drawing by author.

mountain of sustenance (probably the First True Mountain), through the stucco masks installed on the middle tier (Ricketson and Ricketson 1937: Figs. 33, 37).

The combined references to warfare and sustenance on the Uaxactun building have a direct parallel in the iconography of Quirigua Monument 26. At Quirigua, however, the more complex stela format with its hieroglyphic text and royal portrait links these themes with concepts of ancestor veneration. Specifically, we may note the passage of the stela text that mentions rituals for the third successor. The maize iconography with which the fourth ruler is associated on Monument 26 may commemorate these rites of ancestor veneration. The same thematic convergence occurs on Copan Stela H (Fig. 1.11), where the ruler as a maize spirit wears "flapstaff" war banners in his headdress during the conduct of ancestral rites.

Sculptural Style in the Early Classic Period

The political relationship between Quirigua and Copan expressed by the inscription of QRG Stela U is mirrored by strong stylistic and iconographic similarities between QRG Monument 26 and the sculpture tradition of Early Classic Copan. The frontal representation of the king on Monument 26 is perhaps the most salient of these features, probably deriving in part from images such as Copan Stelae 60 (Fig. 1.9) and 53, dated to the last half of the fifth century A.D. (Schele 1990a).[16] Although only the waist sections of the figures on both monuments survive, the figure is clearly represented in frontal view. Stela 60 also shows the elbows of the figure as well as the lower parts of a serpent bar, which was evidently clutched to the chest in a manner similar to Monument 26. The pose and vision theme of Stelae 60 and 53, in addition to the shields visible on Stela 60, set a precedent followed by most of the later stelae of Copan. Their iconography was also followed closely at Quirigua. In particular, the Stela 60 and Monument 26 shields are placed in the same position relative to the figures (Linda Schele, personal communication, 1990).

Despite these similarities, the surface treatment and arrangement of forms are different at the two sites. The figure of Monument 26 is laid out in a rectilinear grid, divided into five horizontal registers on the front of the monument, visible in the upper fragment (Fig. 1.12). The divisions marking these registers are located at the belt, shoulder, forehead, and headband of the personification head. The lower fragment is composed of a single register. On the sides of Monument 26, like those of Stela U, individual elements of the front protrude into a blank

field but do not fill it completely (Figs. 1.13, 1.14, 1.15). Within the registers, forms are executed with slightly rounded outlines but retain vertical and horizontal lines, in harmony with the overall design. Of greatest importance in breaking the grid is the "crab-claw" posture of the ruler's arms, which form two strong diagonals pointing toward the face. A few asymmetrical details break the

1.12. QRG Monument 26, upper fragment, obverse. Photo by Thomas Tolles.

1.13. QRG Monument 26, upper fragment, side detail. Photo by Thomas Tolles.

1.14. QRG Stela U, detail, side. Photo by Thomas Tolles.

1.15. QRG Stela U, detail, side. Photo by Thomas Tolles.

rigid symmetry of the figure, such as the elements inscribed by the oval cartouche in the headdress and repeated diagonal details, such as the interlaced designs of the earflare assemblages and belt. The front of the stela displays very little ground, with individual forms distinguished by slight variation in relief depth.

Although incised lines accent some shapes, in general both Stela U and Monument 26 show an unusual simplicity and clarity of design. By contrast, the artist of Copan Stela 35 (Fig. 1.16), which dates to approximately the second quarter of the fifth century, enlivened the image with small dots, tickings, and double and triple contour lines.[17] Overlapping is frequent. The early Tikal stelae (1, 2, 28), which pack the visual field with minute zoomorphic heads, scrollwork, and beads, also differ from the simplicity seen at Quirigua (Fig. 1.17). At Tikal—and even more so at Copan—curved, diagonally placed forms create a sense of swirling motion around the king's body, while at Quirigua forms are locked within a static grid. Perhaps the most telling example of this is the rendering of the Quirigua vision serpent as a rigid bar, whereas at Copan the serpents have flexible bodies (Stelae 35, 60).

1.16. CPN Stela 35. Drawing by Barbara Fash, courtesy Instituto Hondureño de Antropología e Historia.

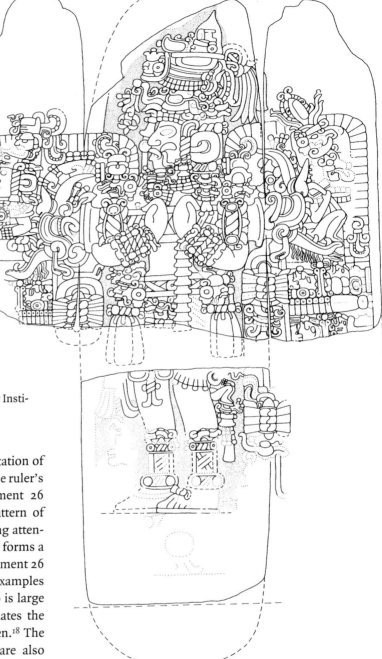

1.17. Tikal Stela 2. From Jones and Satterthwaite 1982: Fig. 2. Drawing by William R. Coe, courtesy of University of Pennsylvania Museum of Archaeology and Anthropology.

Also dramatically different from the representation of rulers elsewhere is the compositional focus on the ruler's face at Quirigua. This is achieved on Monument 26 through the frontal representation and the pattern of small beads that frames the ruler's visage, calling attention to it. The hand and arm posture of the ruler forms a pedestal for the face as well. Although the Monument 26 facial type can perhaps be traced ultimately to examples such as Tikal Stela 4, the face on Monument 26 is large compared to the monument width and dominates the composition more than examples from the Peten.[18] The faces portrayed in the Quirigua monuments are also more delicately modeled than the remainder of the compositions, thus lending them emphasis. This can be seen not only in the subtly curved eyebrow ridge and indentation of the eye socket on the lord's face on Monument 26 (Fig. 1.12) but also in the beautifully abstract cheekbone and nose of the deity emerging from the serpent on the side of Stela U (Fig. 1.18). The modeling of this figure's face contrasts with the flat serpent jaw and costume details below.

One additional prominent feature of Monument 26 and Stela U, the wrap-around composition, warrants further comment, as it is one of the major differences be-tween later Quirigua and Copan sculpture. Copan Stelae 60 and 53, which served as prototypes for later stelae at Copan, have a totally different compositional mode from the monuments of Quirigua, treating the front face of the slab as distinct from the sides. This approach to the stela figure, termed the "panel" compositional mode, contin-ued to be employed into the Late Classic period at Copan (Clancy 1990). Even the heavily undercut stelae seen dur-ing the reign of Waxaklajun Ub'ah K'awil represent the extreme of a series of experiments in high relief and un-dercutting, in which the figure, as if inflated, emerges from the flat slab to varying degrees.[19] The Quirigua ste-lae, in contrast, simply take a frontal design and wrap it around the monument, in the manner of Tikal Stelae 1, 2 and 28, which feature complex images of backracks on their side panels (Fig. 1.17). In fact, lacking more local precedents, these early- to mid-fifth-century Tikal monu-ments seem the most direct models for Stela U and Mon-ument 26 of Quirigua, which also adopt the personified basal register seen at early Tikal and at other more cen-trally located sites such as Caracol (Jones and Sharer 1980). Nevertheless, there are differences between the two compositions. The approach seen at Quirigua pre-serves the integrity of the stela as a four-sided monu-ment, without drawing attention to the interface of front and sides as do the Tikal stelae, which place backrack poles with knotted accents at the edges. The free play of continuous relief designs over both front and sides of the stela is a trait unique to Quirigua, developed to its fullest potential in the programs of K'ak' Tiliw, together with additional features of the Early Classic style.

While certain stylistic details suggest associations be-tween the Early Classic stelae of Quirigua and those of Tikal and Copan, one of the closest correspondences yet found is between Quirigua Monument 26 and Uaxactun Stela 20 (Fig. 1.19; Ashmore n.d.; Clancy 1999: 105; Jones

1.19. Uaxactun Stela 20. Drawing by author.

1.18. QRG Stela U, detail, side. Photo by Thomas Tolles.

and Sharer 1980; Rands 1968: 518). Although they differ markedly in execution, the two stelae share numerous iconographic and compositional features, including the frontal pose, crab-claw gesture, shields in association with the serpent-bar, and a zoomorphic headdress surmounted by a large cartouche.

The contexts of these two monuments are also closely comparable. Both were dedicated on 9.3.0.0.0 and in association with radial pyramids (pyramids with stairways on all four sides). Stela 20 at Uaxactun was set up in front of the eastern stairway of Structure E-VII. Although its precise dedication site is unknown, Monument 26 was found in the vicinity of Structure 3C-14, which also had four stairways. Furthermore, the iconographic references of Monument 26 to the mythic Snake Mountain and First True Mountain have a direct parallel in the Late Formative mask program of the Uaxactun pyramid, discussed above. Quirigua Monument 26 therefore represents a synthesis of the Uaxactun program, reflecting the iconography and composition of Stela 20 in its figural portion and commemorating the earlier E-Sub-VII mask program in its basal register.

Such correspondences among Early Classic monuments and buildings at Quirigua and Uaxactun were surely not accidental. They are probably related to the political reordering of the Maya area that began with the takeover of Uaxactun by Tikal in the late fourth century and continued with the establishment of new dynasties in the Southeast in the early fifth century. The similarities between Quirigua and Uaxactun monuments in the late fifth century imply that these ties remained vital, with a direct flow of artistic ideas among the various centers that composed the alliance network. Indeed, the early phase of Copan Structure 10L-4, located in the Great Plaza, is structurally comparable to the Quirigua radial pyramid (see Cheek and Milla Villeda 1983: 79). Both southeastern buildings apparently evoke prototypes from the central Peten. Like the Aztec Templo Mayor, these two Early Classic structures probably symbolized mountains of sustenance and warfare.

The Transition to the Late Classic Period

Shortly after the fairly active years of the late fifth century, Quirigua entered a period of misfortune. Not only are no monuments known at Quirigua between 495 and 653,[20] but building activities seem to have slowed or ceased during the period. In the absence of data, it is difficult to attribute the hiatus to a specific cause. One possibility is that Quirigua's malaise may have been related to the poor economic and political fortunes of Tikal in the Mid-

dle Classic, an interpretation supported by ceramic ties with the Peten through the seventh century (Jones and Sharer 1980).[21] In addition, Quirigua may have been the victim of an attack sometime in the sixth or seventh century. Evidence for this theory is seen in the condition of both Stela U and Monument 26. Both of these monuments were broken at the knees, and the left eye of Monument 26 was scratched away. These treatments are characteristic of stelae that have been subjected to intentional defacement, such as Tikal Stela 31, which may have been damaged by invading warriors from Calakmul and Caracol. In apparent conformity with a ritual proscription, royal portraits were selectively damaged in such raids, probably in order to limit the ability of the royal persona embodied in sculpture to exercise authority.[22] Also like Stela 31, Monument 26 shows very little weathering, suggesting that after its vandalism it was buried or otherwise protected from the elements.

While the agents responsible for the attack are unknown, there is some evidence that Quirigua maintained ties with Copan into the sixth century. Unlike Quirigua, Copan saw considerable expansion during the early sixth century, under the patronage of the seventh and eighth rulers in the line of K'inich Yax K'uk' Mo'. Ruler 8 oversaw a major expansion of the acropolis complex, including the structure called Ante, which bears a step dating to 542. The importance of Ruler 7 prompted his commemoration by the twelfth ruler of Copan, the great Smoke Imix, on CPN Stela E. A connection between Ruler 8 and Quirigua is found among the burial furniture of his tomb. Tests of ceramic vessels from this tomb suggest that several of the wares had been made in the vicinity of Quirigua (Reents-Budet et al. n.d.). Although they cannot be specifically linked to the rulers of Quirigua, these vessels indicate that there was a degree of contact between the sites around the mid-sixth century, with Quirigua possibly playing the role of a tributary to Copan. After this time, there is a silence in the archaeological record of about a century, when Quirigua seems to have lain virtually dormant. Archaeological evidence shows that the old floodplain center of Group 3C-7 experienced considerable damage wrought by heavy floods in the seventh century (Ashmore 1987: 219–221). This suggests that a natural disaster, such as a hurricane, may have contributed to Quirigua's woes.

Altar L

A revival of sorts at Quirigua may be documented with the dedication of Altar L, a large rhyolite disc about 1 m in diameter and 0.25 m thick, carved with a crude relief image of a ruler seated cross-legged on a pair of glyphs, facing right (Fig. 1.20).[23] Dating to A.D. 653, this monument was found out of primary context, reused as a "table altar" near the acropolis. The figure shown on Altar L wears a large mosaic collar with an overlying necklace and pendant, a large belt, wristlets, and anklets. His headdress is a personification head with serpent wings, surmounted by a Venus sign. A day-sign cartouche inscribes the figure, as well as accompanying texts, and the entire composition is framed by still more text on the right and left edges. A damaged double-bar coefficient appears atop the cartouche. The cartouche and coefficient identify Altar L as an example of a class of monument known as a "Giant Ajaw" altar. In this case, the day Ajaw is indicated by the portrait of the *ajaw* or king seated in the center of the cartouche. The date recorded by the large day sign is likely the same as the 12 Ajaw calendar round recorded on the lower right of the rim text, corresponding to the *k'atun* ending 9.11.0.0.0 (October

14, 652). The Venus sign in the headdress of the lord seated inside the cartouche commemorates the period ending, which coincided with the heliacal rising of Venus as Evening Star. Such commemorations are common at Copan. The monument itself was probably dedicated several months after the period ending, however, on the date inscribed to the left of the figure, 9 Chuwen 14 Sek, or 9.11.0.11.11 (June 2, 653). The event associated with this date is a "house censing," a ritual in which buildings were purified by incense,[24] followed by the expression *ak-'taj ti nep? nah* "dances with/at ?? building." The name of the current Quirigua ruler, K'awil Yo'at/Yo'pat, is written to the right of the figure. The ruler mentioned here is known only from this monument and is not given a succession number. In addition, because it was found out of primary context, the building commemorated by this altar is unknown.

Altar L implies connections with Copan not only through the commemoration of Venus events, which

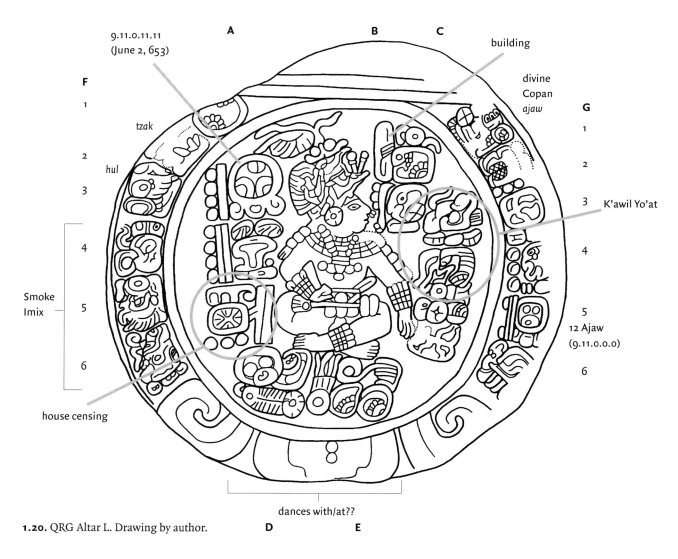

1.20. QRG Altar L. Drawing by author.

were so important to the rulers at Copan, but through the historical content of the text. The name of the twelfth ruler of Copan, Smoke Imix, appears in the rim inscription, beginning on the left side and ending with his emblem glyph title on the right. Although the event with which this king is associated includes the verb *hul* "arrive," it is preceded by a second verb, *tzak* "conjure," which makes it difficult to interpret.[25] During the same period ending, Smoke Imix dedicated a huge program of seven stelae at Copan, erected in the site core and periphery.[26] In addition, a stela was dedicated at the outlying site of Santa Rita. This program seems to have marked a critical point in a steady drive toward political expansion or consolidation that began during the reign of the previous ruler, B'utz' Chan (Fash 1983; Stuart 1992b: 175). By the 9.11.0.0.0 period ending, the kingdom of Copan already extended far beyond the valley pocket (Fash 1998: 248-249). Thus, the citation of Smoke Imix on Altar L may be interpreted as an attempt to bring Quirigua more

firmly into the political sphere of Copan. Until the precise meaning of the verbal expression that introduces the name of the Copan king is known, however, political interpretations of the Altar L text must remain tentative.

Adding to the mysteries of Altar L is its style, which is strikingly different from that of any known sculpture of Copan (Fig. 1.21). Not only are many of the glyphs executed in a peculiar style, with their lines left in high relief and the inner parts cut back to the ground, but crude incising completes their details. This carving style is unique to this monument, suggesting that Altar L was executed by local artists and not by members of a Copan workshop. Certain details of the glyphs, as well, point to the local inspiration of this altar, such as the form of T168 *ajaw* which appears in the two emblem glyphs (G1, C5). On Altar L the *po* elements of T168 feature a "+" shaped infix, recalling the Early Classic Quirigua convention that also appears on Stela U and Monument 26. This version of T168 was used at Copan through the reign of

1.21. QRG Altar L. Photo by Jesse L. Nusbaum, courtesy of Museum of New Mexico, neg. no. 60996.

B'utz' Chan (e.g., Stelae 7 and P) but was abandoned by the time of Smoke Imix.

The most striking divergence of Altar L from Copan tradition, however, is the format of the altar itself. Such "Giant Ajaw" altars are not known at Copan and seem to be most common at the site of Caracol.[27] At Caracol the "Giant Ajaw" format appears as early as A.D. 495 and usually depicts the Ajaw date of the dedication within a quatrefoil cartouche. Quirigua Altar L is a variant on the type, using the basic Caracol form but cleverly incorporating a historical figure into the composition to represent the day name. While the political significance of this form is unclear, it should be observed that there were long-standing political ties between Caracol and the Southeast. The most noteworthy of these connections was the mention of the Copan king Waterlily Jaguar on Caracol Stela 16, dated to 534 (Grube 1990b; Houston, in Stuart 1992b: 174). Unfortunately, the political interpretation of this reference to the Copan king is unclear.

Structure 1B-sub.4 and Altars Q and R

At about the same time that Altar L was dedicated, major modifications of the Quirigua acropolis were begun. Among the most significant of these was the first ballcourt constructed at the site, Structure 1B-sub.4.[28] This impressive structure was built of rhyolite blocks and closely approximated the Copan ballcourts in orientation and dimensions. Two small twin structures with north-facing doorways, 1B-sub.2-2nd and 1B-sub.3-2nd, were also built at this time at the northern end of the ballcourt. The axis between these two structures coincided with the alley axis of the ballcourt, suggesting that they may have been part of the same architectural complex. Although it has not been confirmed by excavation, two small rhyolite disks, Altars Q and R, probably originally functioned as alley markers for the court (Figs. 1.22, 1.23). With a third stone, they would have been installed along the major axis of the court, in typical Classic Maya fashion. In fact, Altars Q and R are almost identical to the markers of Copan Ballcourt IIa in size and shape, and their quatrefoil borders are similar to those of the markers pertaining to all known phases of the Copan court. The images and styles of the "altars" are also similar to each other, further supporting the idea that they were originally close in date, if not part of a single program. They are executed in a shallow relief style with the ground cut back from the figure and incising for most of the details, with relatively little modeling (Fig. 1.24).

Nevertheless, Altars Q and R are sufficiently different in style from Altar L to cast doubt on the notion that these

1.22. QRG Altar Q. Drawing by author.

1.23. QRG Altar R. Drawing by author.

monuments together formed a triad of ballcourt markers. Not only are Altars Q and R thicker and much narrower than Altar L, but the Q and R figures are executed with an elegance of line absent from the Altar L figure. Further, certain details of Altar Q, such as the *kawak* markings, give evidence of line control superior to Altar L. Unfortunately, because Altars Q and R were found out of their original context in the acropolis court in front of Structure 1B-6, these conclusions remain unproven; and the hypothetical third ballcourt marker is still missing.

1.24. QRG Altar Q. Photo by Thomas Tolles.

Both Altars Q and R show figures seated cross-legged on oval objects inscribed with plain borders. The figure on Altar Q faces to the viewer's right; that of Altar R, to the left. The figures have one hand placed on the hip, the other held out, palm up. Short texts once accompanied the figures, but these are now eroded beyond recognition. Because the Altar Q figure is in much better condition than its counterpart, the discussion of these monuments' iconography must focus on this image alone. The object on which the figure is seated can be identified as a stone, as it bears *kawak* markings: the "grape bunch" on its left half and a dotted semicircle on the right. Glyphs also appear on the stone; a *sak* "white" sign is visible next to the "grape bunch," while the other sign is not clear. The vertical strip which runs in front of the stone has double knots at its top, suggesting that the stone is tied with a band. This detail may relate to the Classic Maya practice of dedicating monuments by wrapping them with rope or cloth bands. The curved sign to the left of the figure is a moon symbol. The figure is dressed mostly in jewelry, including a huge mosaic collar with medallions at the chest and shoulders, each having pendant bead assemblages. The belt is also elaborate, featuring a large bivalve shell in front. The wrists and ankles are adorned with mosaic cuffs, while the head is wrapped in a cloth to which a bell-shaped element with projecting serpent head is added.

Several elements of the attire of the figure on Altar Q

identify him as a deity associated with maize and the moon, known elsewhere in Maya art (Fig. 1.25).[29] The large bivalve shell on the belt is typical of the maize deity, as are the abundant jewelry and headdress type. The hand posture may also reflect the typical dance pose of the maize deity. It is likely that a similar maize/moon deity is represented on Altar R. In the Classic period, the figure was connected to the ideology of ballcourts through a myth similar to that recorded in the *Popol Vuh*. A place of trial and death for the various heroic personages in the myth, ballcourts served Classic kings as a metaphor for warfare and a prime venue for captive sacrifice (Miller and Houston 1987; Schele and Freidel 1991; Schele and Miller 1986: 241–258). Ballcourts were a liminal space in the Maya architectural vocabulary, representing the entrance to the underworld. The cartouches of the Quirigua markers were "windows" through which the beings of the underworld could be witnessed, as through the mouth of a cave (Schele and Freidel 1990: 487–488). The skeletal centipede heads that appear at the notched corners of the cartouche symbolize the maw which leads to the underworld, thus stressing its identification as a spiritual portal.

A similar portal with an ancestor inside and also marked with skeletal heads appears on the center ballcourt marker from Yaxchilan Structure 14 (Fig. 1.26). Other portals are represented on stelae from Yaxchilan, usually in the upper registers and enclosing images of ancestors. Normally, the Yaxchilan stelae (1 and 10) have pairs of these cartouches, but Stela 4 (Fig. 1.27) shows a figure inside a moon sign instead of an ancestor cartouche. This lunar symbol recalls the final episode in the Hero Twins narrative of the *Popol Vuh*, in which Junajpu and Xb'alanke are apotheosized as the sun and moon. The context of this apotheosis is their attempt to reassemble the parts of their father and uncle, the equivalent of the maize deities, which had been buried in an underworld ballcourt. Thus, the appearance of the deity of maize on the altars is consistent with their proposed function as ballcourt markers, as these figures would have embodied the potential of the ballcourt for the resurrection of maize and ancestors, as well as death by sacrifice.

Stela T

The influence of Copan in the latter part of the seventh century seems to have motivated not only architectural projects at Quirigua but also a revitalization of the local stela tradition. This is marked by Stela T (Fig. 1.28), dedicated on the 9.13.0.0.0 period ending by an unknown ruler, possibly in conjunction with the modifications of Locus 002 (Group A; Morley 1937–1938, vol. 4: 86–89). A schist column of roughly the same size and format as Stela U, which was erected more than two hundred years before, Stela T exhibits a conservatism typical of early Late Classic Quirigua sculpture. Unfortunately, both text and image are so badly eroded as to preclude any extensive discussion of the monument's historical significance.

Quirigua as a Border Site

By the end of the seventh century, Quirigua was beginning to show signs of revival, having declined in the sixth century. Although the data indicate that Quirigua's closest political and cultural ties through this period were with Copan, several features also suggest an inter-

action with regions to the northwest. The material evidence first appears in the Early Classic period, when certain locally manufactured polychrome bowls found at Quirigua resemble late Tzakol wares from the Peten (Ashmore 1980b: 42; Ashmore, Schortman, and Sharer 1983: 60). Such influences parallel the introduction into Copan of forms of architecture, monumental modes, and iconography typical of Early Classic Tikal in the early fifth century. The Peten influences that begin to shape Quirigua in the early fifth century, then, seem likely to have resulted from a complex sequence of incursions into the Southeast by immigrants from Tikal, heading for Copan. Quirigua functioned as an outpost or "way station" in this relocation, established at a crucial transfer point for overland trade routes between the Peten and Honduras (Ashmore 1980a: 27; Jones and Sharer 1980). It also provided access to the sites in southern Belize, via water routes, and to the jade and obsidian sources of the highlands.

Thus, poised between major regions of the Maya world, Quirigua has all the hallmarks of a border site. Controlled directly through Copan, its art styles remained conservative and eclectic, exhibiting features typical of both Copan and the Peten. One of the best examples of this hybridity is in the monumental sculpture tradition, in which Stela U and Monument 26 have a wrap-around mode and basal register typical of early Tikal sculpture, a calendrical structure and ritual associations reminiscent of Copan, and a frontal composition and iconography related to monumental art at both Uaxactun and Copan. The Early Classic architecture of Quirigua also recalls both Copan and Peten prototypes.

The Sub.4 ballcourt may also have conformed to this pattern. Constructed during a period when Copan was exhibiting great political strength, the Quirigua ballcourt was designed in the same style as that of Copan and was of almost exactly the same dimensions and close to scale. The ballcourt was thus an overt sign of Copan's hegemony over Quirigua. But in addition the ballcourt may have had a symbolic dimension that marked Quirigua as a border site. Throughout the Maya area, ballcourts were closely associated with borders, on multiple symbolic levels. Not only did they represent a threshold between different cosmic realms, but they were often built in a transitional architectural space. For example, the Copan ballcourt is situated between the acropolis and Great Plaza, near the causeway entrance to the plaza. As Susan Gillespie (1991) has argued, the sacrificial ceremonies associated with the ballgame, particularly decapitation and dismemberment, ritually evoked the division of time

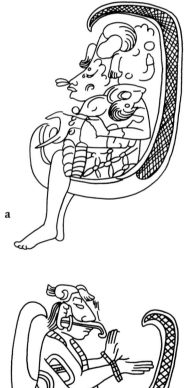

1.25. Maize/moon conflated deities: *a*, Classic incised vessel, detail; *b*, Pearlman conch, detail. Drawing by author.

1.26. Yaxchilan Structure 14 center ballcourt marker. From Tate 1992: Fig. 66. Drawing by Carolyn Tate.

1.27. Yaxchilan Stela 4, detail. From Tate 1992: Fig. 86. Drawing by Carolyn Tate.

into agricultural seasons, marked by the movements of celestial bodies. These ceremonies, and the architectural setting in which they occurred, constituted a mechanism for marking and maintaining social and political boundaries. Accordingly, Maya ballcourts were frequently associated with warfare and were sometimes built to commemorate conquest. This is documented in the Postclassic Guatemalan highlands at sites such as Cawinal, where ballcourts served to mediate between different lineages and even diverse ethnic groups (Fox 1991). A similar role may be suggested for the ballcourt of Quirigua, a site located in a border region with a population not ethnically related to the Maya elite (Scarborough 1991: 141). Here the ballcourt functioned as a venue for rituals that mediated not only between Peten and Copan Maya but between these and the local populations they dominated.

The subordinate political status of Quirigua may also be discerned from the titles borne by its rulers. Until the monuments of K'ak' Tiliw, no clear examples of the full emblem glyph are apparent. On Stelae U and T and Monument 26, erosion and breakage might be blamed for this deficiency; but even on Altar L the "Quirigua *ajaw*" title at C3 seems to lack the critical *k'uhul* "divine" prefix that identifies high kings. This is in marked contrast to retrospective accounts of the Early Quirigua rulers that were commissioned by K'ak' Tiliw and his successors. For example, K'ak' Tiliw's Stela C attributes a full Quirigua emblem glyph to Tutum Yol K'inich. The discrepancy between contemporary and retrospective histories is important in that it casts considerable doubt on the validity of dynastic continuity claimed by K'ak' Tiliw. There is no question that the texts exaggerate the autonomy of the Early Classic site. As will be seen in the following chapters, the veneration of the ancient rulers of Quirigua extended even to quoting many of the iconographic features of their stelae. In this way, the Late Classic rulers claimed a legitimate and ancient legacy of ancestral kingship.

2

A RESTIVE VASSAL

The Early Reign of K'ak' Tiliw

TODAY AN astonishing array of late-eighth- and early-ninth-century stone sculptures dominates the site of Quirigua. These were erected by rulers during an era in which economic conditions favored lavish patronage of the arts. The monuments of K'ak' Tiliw stand tallest in this group and were all carved after the approximate midpoint of his reign, several years after the site achieved independence in 738. The early years of this king's reign were also marked by significant art projects. And while they cannot equal the later monuments in scale or elaboration, they are nevertheless a testament to the political ambitions of the ruler and foreshadow the great works that were to come.

During the years between the accession of K'ak' Tiliw in 725 and the breach with Copan in 738, monumental artistic activity was focused on architectural programs in the acropolis. While remnants of these programs can be seen today, our extensive knowledge of them is largely due to the excavations carried out by the University of Pennsylvania in the 1970s. The structures, as well as the small sculptural monuments also commissioned during these years, enhanced the growing power of the ruler by evoking supernatural locations that were contacted during ritual performance, even while he was not yet represented in portraiture. Thus, they supported the later development of a series of supernatural personae for the king that were linked to the reordering of the cosmos in the remote past. In fact, the emphasis on developing supernatural identities for K'ak' Tiliw has somewhat hindered the understanding of this man as a "historical" figure. For example, it seems reasonably certain that K'ak' Tiliw was a local lord, as his emblem glyph title features the "gourd" sign that refers to the Quirigua polity.[1] Noth-

ing else is known about his ancestry, however, because parentage statements are entirely absent at Quirigua. This omission is noteworthy and stresses the distinctive quality of the persona at Quirigua as an identity that frequently shifts as it is presented in a series of composite supernatural guises.

The historical records relating to the first twenty years of K'ak' Tiliw's reign conjure a relatively tranquil image of Quirigua. We know of his accession only from monuments commissioned years after the event, which took place on 9.14.13.4.17 12 Kab'an 5 K'ayab' (January 2, 725) (Fig. 2.1). On Stelae E and F the accession is recorded as the receiving of a God K image, whereas Stela J commemorates the event as the fastening of the royal headband. Zoomorph G states that he was "seated in *ajaw*-ship." The age of the king upon accession was between twenty-eight and thirty-eight, as calculated from titles that appear on his late monuments.[2] One other piece of information included in the retrospective accounts of K'ak' Tiliw's accession is extremely important to the understanding of the political rhetoric of his monuments. Stela E states that the accession happened under the authority of Waxaklajun Ub'ah K'awil, the thirteenth ruler of the Copan dynasty (Fig. 2.1a; Stuart 1987a, 1992b). This pattern, in which Quirigua rulers were stated to be subordinate to those of Copan, is consistent with earlier inscriptions from Quirigua, such as Stela U. It is also in agreement with the interpretation of various mid- to late-seventh-century monuments, such as Altar L and the Sub.4 ballcourt, which suggest statements of subordination.

The retrospective texts of Quirigua also record events for two of the period endings during the early years of

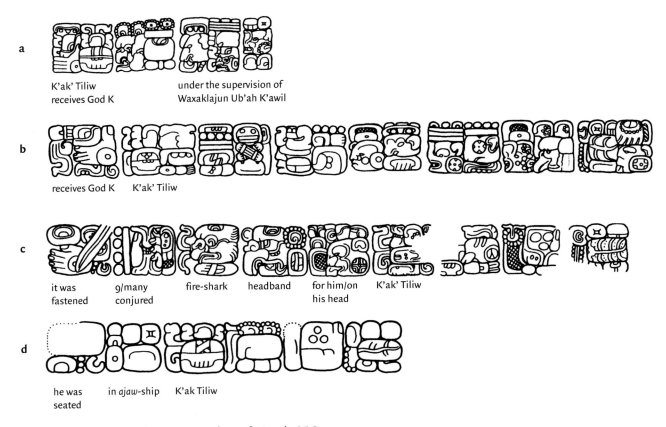

a
K'ak' Tiliw
receives God K

under the supervision of
Waxaklajun Ub'ah K'awil

b
receives God K   K'ak' Tiliw

c
it was   9/many   fire-shark   headband   for him/on   K'ak' Tiliw
fastened   conjured   his head

d
he was   in *ajaw*-ship   K'ak Tiliw
seated

2.1. Accession of K'ak' Tiliw: *a*, QRG Stela E, A8–B9a; *b*, QRG Stela F, B6–A10; *c*, QRG Stela J, F4–F8; *d*, QRG Zoomorph G, K'2a1–b1. Drawings by author.

K'ak' Tiliw's reign, although they are not well understood (Fig. 2.2). The earlier of the two happened in 731, on the first *k'atun* ending after his accession (9.15.0.0.0), and is recorded on Stela E and Zoomorph P. The account of Zoomorph P (Fig. 2.2a) is especially interesting as it records not only the dedication of a monument but also an event involving Sky Xul, the king who succeeded K'ak' Tiliw. Although this text is recorded on one of Sky Xul's own monuments and the actual monument to which the text refers has not been found, the passage suggests the possibility that this ruler was alive over fifty years prior to his accession and thus was possibly a son or younger relative of K'ak' Tiliw. Again, there is no genealogical statement at Quirigua to confirm their relationship. The second period-ending record relating to the early years of K'ak' Tiliw's reign is better understood. It appears on Stela I of Jade Sky and records the planting of a stela by K'ak' Tiliw (Fig. 3.7). The date is July 26, 736 (9.15.5.0.0), the last period ending before the capture of Waxaklajun Ub'ah K'awil (the following chapter discusses this period-ending record in greater detail).

Altar M (Dedicated September 15, 734)

Two small, stylistically similar rhyolite sculptures, Altars M (Fig. 2.3) and N (Fig. 2.4), can also be assigned to this period (A.D. 725–738). When Catherwood visited the site in 1840, these two monuments were found at the base of the east staircase of the Ballcourt Plaza, serving as supports for Altar L (Morley 1937–1938, vol. 4: 95; Stephens 1841, vol. 2: 122). Although this arrangement recalls the "table altar" forms of sites such as Piedras Negras, it could not have been their original configuration, because Altar L is earlier in date than M and N. It is likely that this rearrangement of the monuments can be attributed to the ninth-century occupants of the site. Unlike Altar N, Altar M can be dated with precision, as its inscription of four columns and five rows includes a dedication date of September 15, 734 (9.15.3.2.0; Fig. 2.5). In addition, the text names the monument with a compound that commonly refers to thrones and altars, perhaps reading *kuch tun*, literally "seat-stone" (MacLeod n.d.). Interestingly, the text seems to name the agent of this dedication as someone other than K'ak' Tiliw. This person is referenced only by a title, however, and therefore cannot be identified. The name and titles of the sponsor of the monument dedication, K'ak' Tiliw, complete this text.

The titles K'ak' Tiliw bears at this early date—"black Copan *ajaw*" and "south *kalomte'*"—have relevance to the political context of Quirigua at this time. The first of these titles has often been mistaken for the Copan emblem glyph and thought to imply a dominion over Copan following the capture of Waxaklajun Ub'ah K'awil (Fash 2001: 151; Fash and Stuart 1991: 167; Riese 1986: 95–96, 1988: 75). Not only is this title distinct from the emblem glyph (having a prefixed *ik'* "black" rather than *k'uhul* "divine"), however, but this example dates to the time prior to the conflict with Copan. Instead, the "black Copan *ajaw*" title is probably related to a number of locations mentioned in the Copan and Quirigua inscriptions that include the "black" sign (Schele 1989d; Schele and Grube 1990b). This title also appears on Nim Li Punit Stela 2, a monument erected in 731, only a few years before Quirigua Altar M, in the name of a companion of the agent of the stela erection (Schele and Grube 1994: 159). This occurrence suggests that it may be a title that indicates a lord's origin within one of the districts affiliated with the Copan polity. Thus, its use by K'ak' Tiliw is suitable for his role as a vassal of Waxaklajun Ub'ah K'awil.

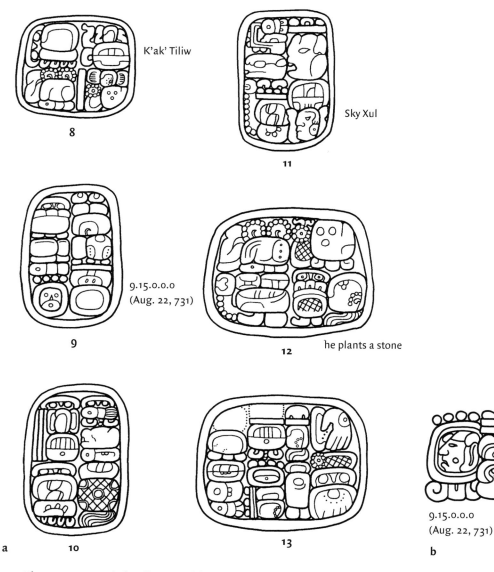

K'ak' Tiliw

8

Sky Xul

11

9.15.0.0.0
(Aug. 22, 731)

9

he plants a stone

12

a   10

13

9.15.0.0.0
(Aug. 22, 731)

b

2.2. The 9.15.0.0.0 period ending at Quirigua: *a,* QRG Zoomorph P, cartouches 8–13 (rearranged); *b,* QRG Stela E, B10–A11. Drawings by author.

2.3. QRG Altar M, side. Photo by Thomas Tolles.

2.4. QRG Altar N, side. Neg. no. 5126, McClure photo, courtesy San Diego Museum of Man.

Although it is unlikely that the "black Copan *ajaw*" mentioned on Nim Li Punit Stela 2 is K'ak' Tiliw, the passage indicates that at least one site in southern Belize was politically linked to Copan and Quirigua in the Late Classic period.

Various iconographic similarities in the art of Copan, Quirigua, and Nim Li Punit parallel the distribution of the "black Copan *ajaw*" title. Prominent at all three sites is the "turban" headdress, worn by rulers and high lords at Copan (e.g., Stela 6, Altar Q) and Nim Li Punit (Stela 15; Fig. I.19) and appearing on ceramic figurines at Quirigua (Altman and West 1992: Fig. 10).

The other title attributed to K'ak' Tiliw on Altar M has a less provincial significance. The "south *kalomte*" title, seen here for the first time at Quirigua, is used by rulers of Copan prior to the time of Altar M—for example, by Smoke Imix on Altar K. The title, therefore, is one borrowed by Quirigua from the Copan kings that bears no

connotation of political subordination or regional affiliation.

The final title appearing in the text of Altar M is partially eroded, but enough remains to identify it as a title that names K'ak' Tiliw as an *ajaw* of Quirigua. While this might be an example of the full emblem glyph, the first part is eroded, making this difficult to ascertain. A curved outline on the upper left implies the presence of a prefix, but this might be either a T228 '*a* complement or a T36 *k'uhul*. The first clear example of a full Quirigua emblem glyph (with *k'uhul*) is on Stela H. Epigraphers have noted that the name of the site incorporated into this title (or the full emblem glyph) is similar to that of Pusilha, suggesting a possible political relationship between the two sites (Marcus 1976: 45; Proskouriakoff 1993: 56). This correspondence is not exact, however, as the Quirigua gourd is usually represented on its side, whereas that of Pusilha is upright. Based on the known syllabic value of the gourd as *tzu*, Schele and Grube (1994: 118) suggested that the emblem glyph at both sites reads *tzuk* "partition, province," indicating the subordination of the two sites to Copan. A relationship between Pusilha and Copan also seems to be implied by the appearance of names similar to those of Copan rulers B'utz' Chan and Smoke Imix in the texts of Pusilha Stelae D and M, in association with the gourd emblem glyph. Along with the "black Copan *ajaw*" title which appears on Quirigua Altar M, such similarities may suggest inclusion of Quirigua in a large political sphere reaching from Copan into southern Belize.

Artistic traditions, however, draw finer lines between these diverse zones. The panel-style monumental format and marginally literate inscriptional style of most stelae from southern Belize clearly distinguish them from those of Quirigua and Copan, suggesting that artistic interchange between the Quirigua-Copan sphere and southern Belize was limited. Among the few artistic links between Quirigua and Pusilha are the zoomorphic sculptures of felines at Pusilha (Altars V, W, X), which may be related to the zoomorphic format of Quirigua (see Joyce et al. 1928: 339; Morley 1937–1938, vol. 5: Pl. 167). Not only is the iconography of the Pusilha sculptures different from that of the sculptures of Quirigua, but their date is uncertain. Further, at about 1 m in length, the Pusilha feline sculptures are somewhat smaller than Altar M (1.25 m) and Altar N (1.8 m) and certainly diminutive compared to the later massive zoomorphs of Quirigua.

In contrast, the artistic ties between Quirigua and Copan are strong and are clearly exemplified by Altar M. Although Morley (1935: 150) considered Altar M (Fig. 2.6) to represent a feline head, Stone (1983: 51) pointed out that the multiple curved fangs that emerge from the beast's mouth are characteristic of a reptile, either a crocodile or a snake. She suggested that the crosshatched *imix* (reading *ha'* "water") eyelid of the Altar M creature identifies it with a crocodilian shown on the "Vase of the Seven Gods," which bears an *imix* sign on its tail.[3] The creature may not be a specific animal at all, however, but rather a three-dimensional rendition of a rare toponymic glyph. This sign appears only twice in Maya texts, on Copan Stela B and on the Palenque Temple of Inscriptions, west panel (Fig. 2.7). In the Palenque example, the crosshatched glyph is placed in front of the head, instead of being infixed into the eyelid as in the Copan and Quirigua examples. In both glyphic contexts, the toponymic function is assured by the presence of T86 *nal* superfixes. In the example from Palenque at least, this location is on a supernatural plane.

In its original context as a monumental toponym, Altar M may have identified a structure or ritual area with this particular place name. In addition, when the king performed rituals in association with or even on top of the monument, it may have symbolically situated the lord in a supernatural domain. Unfortunately, because it was not found in primary context, we cannot be certain of its original function. The presence of the toponym on Copan Stela B (dated to A.D. 731) suggests that Copan was the specific inspiration for the iconography of the Quirigua sculpture, which was carved only about three years later. In fact, the inscription of Altar M uses a distance number to connect the dedication date of the monument specifically to the date on which Copan Stela B was dedicated. This strongly implies that Altar M was a direct response to the Copan stela.

Altar N (Dedicated ca. 734)

Altar N (Fig. 2.8) is sculpted in the form of a turtle shell, with an aged figure emerging from one end. At the other end is a skeletal head, turned sideways and with a mirror sign in the forehead (Fig. 2.9). Based on the turtle shell and head with aged features and net headdress, Stone (1983: 57) identified the sculpture as a representation of God N. Although this image is the unique example of a bicephalic God N in a turtle shell in Maya sculpture, there are several similar instances of God N on Classic vases. Usually, the rear head is not skeletal but rather takes the form of a waterlily-adorned aged god (see Robicsek and Hales 1981: vessels 57–59). The upper surface

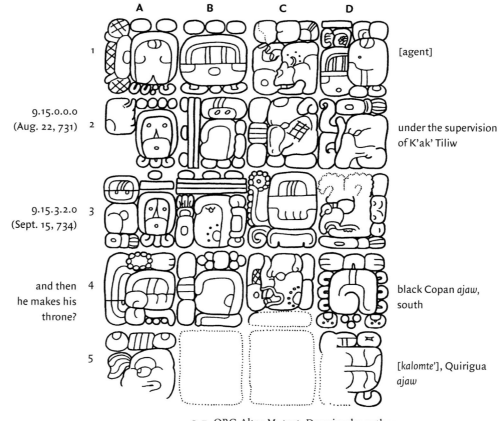

2.5. QRG Altar M, text. Drawing by author.

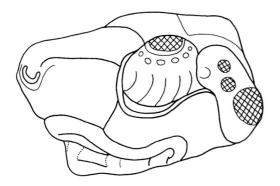

2.6. QRG Altar M, side. Drawing by author.

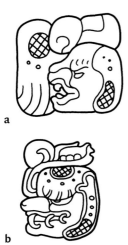

a

b

2.7. Toponyms: *a*, Palenque Temple of Inscriptions, west panel, J3; *b*, CPN Stela B, west face, E1. Drawings by author.

net headdress, the shells they often hold are one of their attributes, as is the star-shaped shell pendant worn by the emerging deity depicted in Figure 2.10. The deer ear sported by many of the trumpeting God N figures may symbolize his patronage of scribes.

Although the iconographic and thematic relationship of Altars M and N is unclear, the two monuments are stylistically similar (Stone 1983: 58). Both sculptures have characteristic bold, rounded forms, uncomplicated by small detail. The sculptures are also of comparable size and are made of rhyolite of very similar appearance. The stylistic qualities of Altars M and N yield other insights of political and historical significance. First, these two monuments represent the beginnings of the tradition of zoomorphs at Quirigua, a sculptural form that has a

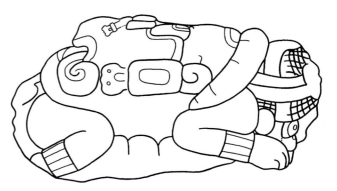

2.8. QRG Altar N, side. Drawing by author.

of the Altar N turtle shell is carved with an image of a squint-eyed, long nosed mask, identified as the Principal Bird Deity (Stone 1983: 58).

Called Pawatun, the deity that appears on Altar N was a prominent denizen of the underworld who had a number of roles in the Classic period, including patron of scribal arts, sky bearer, and, as a cognate of the highland god Mam, spirit of mountains, thunder, and the sacred calendar (Coe 1973: 14–15; Schele and Miller 1986: 54; Taube 1992: 92–99; Thompson 1970). A number of vase paintings depict vision serpents disgorging God N, either blowing shell trumpets or fondling women (Fig. 2.10). These vase scenes have been interpreted as representations of the conjuring of God N upon the birth of an infant, in order to determine the child's spirit companion (Taube 1994). As a lord of the earth, God N is charged with guarding these companions. Even though the God N variants in these scenes do not wear the usual

2.9. QRG Altar N, rear. Neg. no. 5123, courtesy San Diego Museum of Man.

2.10. God N emerging from serpent jaws. Classic polychrome vase (K1382), detail. Drawing by author.

number of historical antecedents elsewhere. Certainly, its use at Quirigua may be partly ascribed to a familiarity with the zoomorphic altars of Copan executed during the reign of Waxaklajun Ub'ah K'awil (Fig. 2.11). The rounded form of the Quirigua altars is surely a feature descended from the Copan experiments in plasticity that began during the reign of Smoke Imix and continued into the early eighth century with works such as CPN Stelae A, D, F, and 4 and Structure 10L-22 of Waxaklajun Ub'ah K'awil (Fash n.d.). The treatment of QRG Altars M and N is comparable to that of the Cosmic Monster sculpture that frames the inner doorway of CPN 10L-22 (Fash 2001: Fig. 77). Although there are no inscriptional records that confirm direct contact between the sculpture workshops of the two cities at this time, both stylistic similarities and the dramatically improved technique of the two sculptures compared to QRG Altar L seem to support the notion that the sculptors of Altars M and N were trained at Copan. It is reasonable to suggest that the stylistic similarities between these two altars and the monuments of Waxaklajun Ub'ah K'awil are symptomatic of a cultural interaction between Copan and Quirigua that paralleled the political relationship of the two kings who commissioned these sculptures.

The textual content of Altar M also clearly links this monument to those of Waxaklajun Ub'ah K'awil. As observed by Stuart (1992b: 170), Waxaklajun Ub'ah K'awil's monumental texts are distinctive in that they generally focus on rituals of dedication. With a few notable exceptions, such as Stela J, even fairly lengthy texts such as that

of Stela A convey little more than information concerning the dedication of the stone. Quirigua Altar M thus follows closely in the steps of the artistic developments of the larger center. This is not to say, of course, that the Quirigua monuments are wholly derivative of the traditions of Copan. On the contrary, not only is their subject matter distinctive, but the incorporation of a text into a zoomorphic altar was unprecedented, even at Copan. The zoomorphic altars at Copan have no inscriptions until the time of Yax Pasaj (Ruler 16). Nor is the graphic style of the glyphs on Altar M closely comparable to the texts of Copan.

In addition, the Quirigua zoomorphs, beginning with Altars M and N, are reminiscent of the very highly developed tradition of zoomorphic sculpture found in the Guatemalan highlands and Pacific coast during the Late Formative period (Stone 1983: 43–48). As discussed in Chapter 1, the pedestal sculpture tradition and caching practices at Late Formative and Early Classic Quirigua exhibit similarities to those of the highlands, suggesting the long duration of this influence and/or interaction. In addition, Stone (1983: 48) noted that QRG Altar V, a small sculpture representing a human head emerging from serpent jaws of probable Classic date, is very similar to serpent heads 1, 4, and 5 of Ballcourt 2 at Guaytan, a site located in the upper Motagua valley.[4] Indeed, of the major Classic lowland sites, Quirigua is one of the most closely connected geographically to the highland region, via the Motagua River. Quirigua's economic interests in the upriver jade and obsidian sources may have fostered

2.11. CPN Altar of Stela D. Photo by Thomas Tolles.

an artistic interaction with the sites a relatively short journey beyond.

Structure 1B-2 (Constructed ca. 720–740)

K'ak' Tiliw's accession not only heralded a revival of sculpture at Quirigua but also inaugurated major architectural renovations of the site core. The remodeling of the acropolis during this time copies quite closely the late architectural projects of Waxaklajun Ub'ah K'awil, reinforcing the sculptural statements embodied in Altars M and N and transforming Quirigua into a miniature replica of Copan. The origin of K'ak' Tiliw's architecture in that of Copan, however, could have had other interpretations than the expression of his political subordination. Like Altars M and N, the architectural projects of K'ak' Tiliw were double-edged, serving both as a statement of cultural and political connectedness and as a proclamation of the power of the Quirigua polity and the status of its ruler as king.

The acropolis construction associated with the period between the accession of K'ak' Tiliw and the sacrifice of Waxaklajun Ub'ah K'awil constitutes a distinct phase in which accessibility to the acropolis became significantly more restricted. The main structures include Structure 1B-2, an addition on 1B-1-2nd, and a wall connecting this addition to 1B-18-2nd, located on the east side of the court (Jones, Ashmore, and Sharer 1983: 4–5; Sharer et al. 1979; Sharer et al. 1983). The dating of this construc-

tion phase is based on stratigraphy and a comparison with the material used for the textually dated Altar M (Jones, Ashmore, and Sharer 1983: 7; Sharer 1978: 57). Like this monument, the construction facings are made predominantly of rhyolite, carefully cut into small, flat-faced blocks. As such, the style of masonry is a dramatic change from the cobble facings and silt fills used previously in the acropolis but also differs from the Early Classic round-faced masonry style.

The most ornate building of this period was Structure 1B-2 (Morley 1913, 1935; Sharer 1990: 86). Also termed Structure B, this edifice was first investigated by the archaeologist Earl H. Morris in 1912. The building was constructed on the southwest corner of the acropolis court upon a stepped platform and measures approximately 13.5 m long (E–W) by 8.2 m wide (N–S). Morley (1935: 135) estimated that it may originally have been about 5.2 m high. Subsequent acropolis building campaigns gradually but partially covered its supporting platform, front stairway, and south, east, and west sides. Nevertheless, the ritual and historical significance of this building was such that it remained accessible throughout the rest of the history of the acropolis.

The single centrally positioned doorway looks north upon the plaza and gives access to a transverse room with two doorways (Fig. 2.12). One doorway to the west leads to an L-shaped room fitted with a masonry bench. The other inner doorway is on an axis with the outer door and leads to three small rooms arranged in a series. In the last of these rooms, Morris found a polychrome vase in the form of a grotesque human head, now in the St. Louis Museum of Art (Morley 1935: 136–137). In addition, near the vase a set of hematite hexagonal disks about 1.6 mm thick and not more than 2.5 cm wide was recovered (Morley 1913: 358). One side was highly polished, and in some cases the edges were rounded. These objects probably had been attached to a backing and served as a mirror. Each of the three major doorways had two pairs of stone hooks for hanging curtains (one pair at floor level, the other about 1.2 m up the jamb). The stone bench in the western room measures about 2.3 x 1.1 m and is hollow, with an inner chamber measuring about 0.8 m wide and 0.8 m high running the entire length of the bench. Inside this bench, Morris found approximately twelve 3.6–4.5 kg smoke-blackened river cobbles.

The exterior of Structure 1B-2 was decorated on all sides with relief carvings, making it one of the most elaborately embellished structures of its time at Quirigua. Morley (1913: 357) reported that these sculptures included "grotesque head motives" on the four corners and in the middle of the south and west walls. His reference is to sculptural cornice decoration consisting of rows of incisors with curls at each side. These sculptural decorations are executed in a "mosaic" technique, in which large designs are built up of aggregated small, individually carved pieces, each attached to the façade with a tenon. Morley photographed the southern wall decoration, which has now been partially dismantled (Fig. 2.13). His photo shows that symmetrical stepped designs flanked the side curls, which were placed on a projecting panel just below the incisors. The Morley photograph also shows that a course of stones carved with a horizontal groove ran above the incisors. Other dotted curls occupied the register of the incisors, above the stepped elements. These are visible in the modern reconstruction of the building. At present, only one set of incisors is intact, located on the northwest corner (Fig. 2.14). Empty gum brackets flank the six teeth.

A second level of sculptural decoration on 1B-2 is located on the wall surface below the cornice with its incisors. Uncovered by the Pennsylvania Project, these mo-

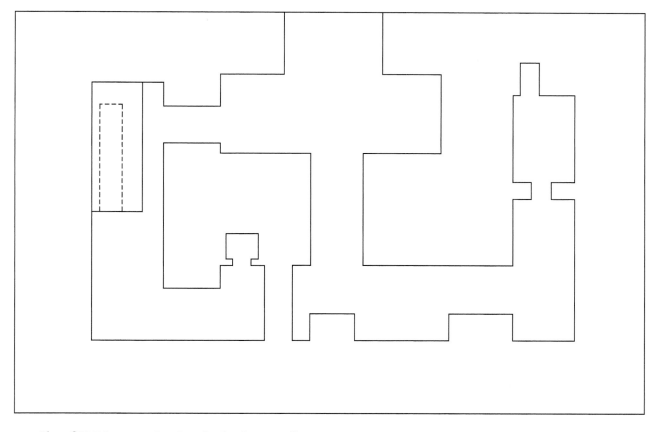

2.12. Plan of QRG Structure 1B-2. Drawing by Thomas Tolles.

2.13. QRG Structure 1B-2 south façade, ca. 1910. From Morley 1913: 359.

saic sculptures consist of rosettes with inset faces out of which emerge scrolls (Fig. 2.15). Today three of the upper termini of the scrolls may be seen, evenly spaced across the south façade of the structure, one directly below the location of the center maw. The west façade was found to have two rosette figures, one of which is partly visible. Morley (1937–1938, vol. 4: 82, 244) observed that a similar rosette and face embellished the north façade, just to the right of the doorway, partially buried by a later stairway. His illustration shows that this rosette had T533 Ajaw faces on either side (Fig. 2.16). These data indicate that the building originally had nine rosette mosaics: two on the north side, two each on the east and west, and three on the south. A schematic reconstruction of the south façade sculptural elements is shown in Figure 2.17.

Archaeologists traditionally interpret this building as functioning as a dwelling or palace (Morley 1913: 355; Sharer 1978: 66). An examination of the symbolism of its sculptural ornamentation, however, suggests that it had an additional sacred significance. The maws which adorn its cornice are found on many other Classic Maya buildings that seem to have served as temples. They are particularly prominent on temples that represent sacred mountains, such as Copan Structure 10L-22 (Fig. 2.18).

2.14. QRG Structure 1B-2, detail of northwest corner façade mosaic sculpture. Photo by Thomas Tolles.

The combination of sculpted elements on the cornice of 1B-2 recurs on the upper temple platform stucco masks from Tikal Structure 5D-33-2nd, which symbolize mountains (Fig. 2.19; Schele and Freidel 1990: 169). Based on the correspondence of elements between these two temple façades, the design of the 1B-2 cornice may be identified as a representation of a personified hill or mountain (Fig. 2.17). The symmetrical stepped elements correspond to the eyes of the mountain face; the incisors, to the mouth; and the upper dotted curls, to the forehead emanations, which probably represent maize foliage. Be-

2.15. QRG Structure 1B-2 south façade rosette mosaic sculpture. Drawing by author after Sharer 1990: Fig. 56.

2.16. QRG Structure 1B-2 north façade rosette mosaic sculpture. Drawing by author after Morley 1937–1938, vol. 4: Fig. 147.

cause the Quirigua design compresses the entire mountain face into a single cornice register, the eyes and mouth are placed on the same level. The eye icons closest to the corners of the building pertain to the mouths that occupy the corners. The rosette/face/foliage combinations that appear on the wall surfaces below the cornice also have an equivalent at another Classic site. For this design, the analogy is the mid-sixth-century temple at Copan known as Ani.[5] The Copan design, executed in stucco on the wall below the cornice, consists of squared niches framing aged faces (Fig. 2.20). One of these faces has star-shaped ear ornaments. Foliage emerges from the tops of the niches and cascades down the sides, and rosettes are located to the sides of the niches.

Assuming the equivalence of the decorations on the two temples, the designs may be interpreted. The aged faces and star-shaped shell earflares of the Ani niche figures identify them as God N or Pawatuns. The rosettes that appear on both temples are circular and inscribed with radiating arcs. Thus, they may be identified with a fairly common glyph, T538 (Fig. 2.21), which also functions iconographically as a flower in various contexts. One of the clearest examples is from an Early Classic tripod vessel, where the rosettes float among other floral glyphs that read *nikte' "Plumeria"* and are punctured by hummingbirds (Fig. 2.22). The Ajaw faces that flank the rosettes on the north façade of 1B-2 (Fig. 2.16) also reinforce their meaning as flowers, because the Ajaw face functions iconographically as a flower (Stuart 1992a). The foliage that sprouts from the niches of Ani is rather generalized, but that which emerges from the flowers on

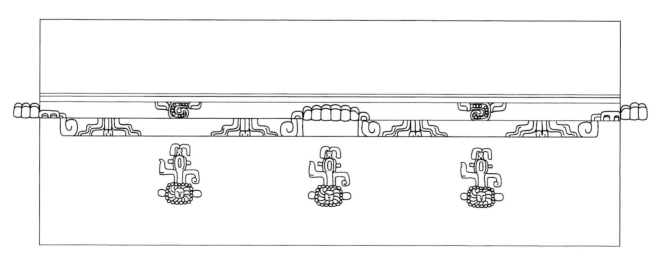

2.17. QRG Structure 1B-2, reconstruction sketch of south elevation (not based on precise measurements). Drawing by author and Thomas Tolles.

2.18. CPN Structure 10L-22, detail. Drawing by author.

2.19. Tikal Structure 5D-33-2nd stucco. Drawing by Linda Schele, © David Schele, courtesy Foundation for the Advancement of Mesoamerican Studies, Inc.

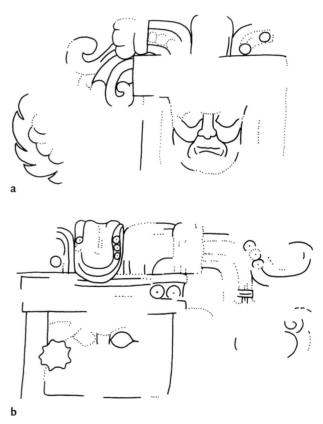

2.20. CPN Structure "Ani," details of façade stucco decoration. Drawings by author after field drawing by José Espinoza, courtesy Early Copan Acropolis Program, University of Pennsylvania Museum of Archaeology and Anthropology and Instituto Hondureño de Antropología e Historia.

1B-2 clearly is maize foliage. A cob-shaped form appears atop the stalk, and tassels issue from the floral sign just above it (Fig. 2.15).

The combination of Pawatun/flower/maize foliage on the temple façades recurs in a glyphic context as one of the toponyms on Copan Structure 10L-22A (Fig. 2.23a). Here the Pawatun head is employed to represent the numeral "five," and the maize foliage is *nal*, a toponymic identifier. The "Five-Flower" toponym refers to a specific supernatural location and is related to several similar flower-locations that appear widely in Maya art.[6] Although the glyphic elements that name these places do not precisely agree and therefore are probably not exactly the same as the 10L-22A toponym, it is apparent that floral places in general, and the Five-Flower place in particular, have strong associations with the realm of the dead as well as with the Creation of the world. The Five-Flower place also relates to the conception of a supernatural "Flower World" realm, documented among Uto-Aztecan speaking peoples of Mesoamerica and the Greater Southwest, at Teotihuacan, and among certain highland Maya groups (Hays-Gilpin and Hill 1999; Hill 1992;

2.21. T538. Drawing by author.

2.22. Hummingbird piercing flower, adjacent to rosette. Early Classic carved vessel, detail. Drawing by author.

Houston and Taube 2000; Taube 2000). In some ancient Maya inscriptional contexts, the Five-Flower place explicitly names a burial site of rulers. For example, on a panel from Cancuen, a "five-flower mountain" is referred to as a tomb (Fig. 2.23b). Similarly, on Piedras Negras Lintel 3, the burial of Ruler 4 also takes place in a "five-flower mountain" (Fig. 2.23c).[7] The identification of mountains as Five-Flower places in the Cancuen and Piedras Negras texts is also evident on a vessel from Tikal (Fig. 2.24), which couples an image of a mountain with the toponym. Flower icons also mark the mountain monsters in the basal registers of Caracol Stelae 4 and 11 (Beetz and Satterthwaite 1981: Figs. 5a, 12).

Other inscriptions suggest that the Five-Flower place is a mythological location where the rebirth of maize occurs. On the "Cosmic Plate" (Fig. 2.25), the toponym occurs in conjunction with references to a "Black Hole" place and a "Black Lake" location. This place clearly corresponds to the scene below, which shows Chaak partially submerged in the black water, framed by the jaws of the black hole. Below the Chaak is an image of the spirit of maize, rising from a skeletal head marked with per-

sonified waterlilies. Another example of the association of the Five-Flower place with the rebirth of maize appears in the text of Altar 1 of Piedras Negras (Fig. 2.26). This text begins with an account of Creation, including a reference to the manifestation of the First Three-Stone place where maize was reborn on August 13, 3114 B.C. Following additional information, the text states that a king of Piedras Negras (in this case, a divine ancestor) oversaw these events at the Five-Flower place. Thus, the Five-Flower place is a location where Creation and the primordial sprouting of maize took place.

The T538 dotted rosette of the Five-Flower toponym appears in iconographic contexts that feature themes of birth. A codex-style vase (Fig. 2.27) shows the spirit of maize being born out of a water register containing split *ajaw* signs as well as tiny rosettes. The glyphic caption

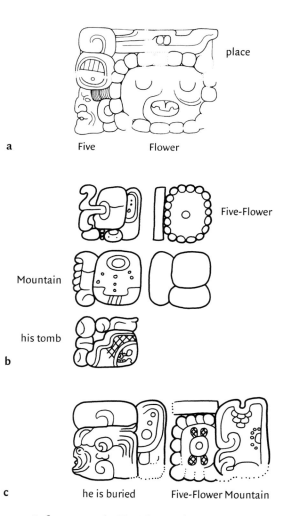

a   Five   Flower   place

    Five-Flower

Mountain

his tomb

b

c   he is buried   Five-Flower Mountain

2.23. References to the Five-Flower place: *a*, CPN Structure 10L-22A glyphic detail; *b*, Cancuen panel, O5–O7; *c*, Piedras Negras Lintel 3, V5–U6. Drawings by author and Barbara Fash, courtesy Instituto Hondureño de Antropología e Historia.

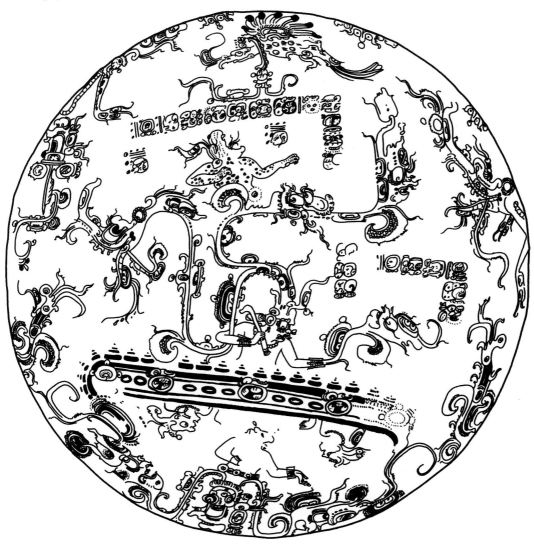

2.24. Five-Flower Mountain, details of a Classic-period vessel.
Drawing by author.

2.25. Classic codex-style vessel (the "Cosmic Plate," K1609).
Drawing by author.

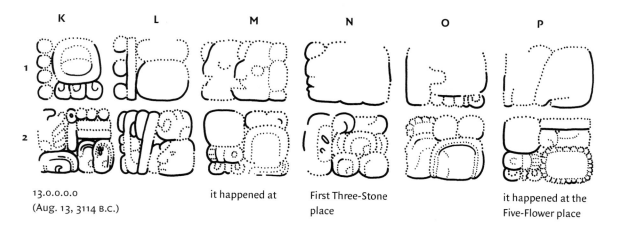

13.0.0.0.0
(Aug. 13, 3114 B.C.)

it happened at

First Three-Stone
place

it happened at the
Five-Flower place

2.26. Creation narrative. Piedras Negras Altar 1, K1–P2. Drawing by author.

which accompanies this figure in one scene may identify him as *aj siy ich* "he who is born from liquid" (Houston and Taube 2000: 281). Another vase (Fig. 2.28) shows a cacao tree bearing the head of a deity, which grows out of the same flower. This image—possibly related to the *Popol Vuh* tale in which the head of First Father, Jun Junajpu, is hung in a tree and comes to impregnate the daughter of one of the underworld lords (Taube 1985: 175)—underscores the association of this flower with reproduction. The flower occurs as well in a toponym which includes *ik'* "black" and *kab'* "earth," appearing on QRG Stela A (Fig. 2.29a) and Piedras Negras Stela 3 (Fig. 2.29b). At Piedras Negras the toponym adorns the legs of a throne upon which Lady K'atun Ajaw and her daughter are seated. The bench of this throne also bears the toponym as well as a scene in which a person holds a vision serpent. As these vision serpents are used in metaphorical scenes of birth on Yaxchilan Lintels 13 and 14, the Black Earth Flower place would seem to be a place of birth and ancestor communication, similar to the Five-Flower place.

The close associations between the Five-Flower place, a mountain, and a place of resurrection suggest that the Five-Flower place may be a variant of or qualifier for the Classic Maya Creation mountain, the Yax Hal Witz, out of which maize first emerged (Freidel, Schele, and Parker 1993: 138–139; Schele and Freidel 1991). The Classic-period practice of naming burial locations after the place of resurrection of maize reinforces the equation of the dead ancestor with the spirit of this plant. Although it is not known if Quirigua Structure 1B-2 marks a burial site, it seems likely that the mountain masks of its cornice together with the Five-Flower toponyms of its walls iden-

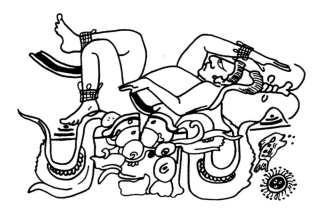

2.27. Deity born from a flower. Codex-style vessel (K2723), detail. Drawing by author.

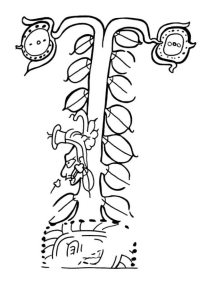

2.28. Cacao tree sprouting from flower. Polychrome vessel (K5615), Museo Popol Vuh, Universidad Francisco Marroquín, Guatemala, detail. Drawing by author.

black · place

earth · flower

a

Black Earth

Flower place →

b

2.29. Black Earth Flower place: *a*, QRG Stela A, D4; *b*, Piedras Negras Stela 3, detail. Drawings by author.

tify the building as an effigy of Quirigua's local maize-mountain. The symbolic significance of 1B-2 approximated that of Copan Structure 10L-22, although the Copan structure is also a local variant, perhaps identified with Mo' Witz or "Macaw Mountain" (Wagner n.d.).

This interpretation of 1B-2 is consistent with one of its peculiar interior features, the hollow bench of the west chamber in which Morris found a number of smoke-blackened river cobbles. Morley (1935) took these stones as evidence that the room may have been used as a sweat-bath for ritual purification. The stones, heated in fires outside the building, could have been introduced underneath the bench and, after dousing with water, could produce the steam needed for a sweat. In his analysis of

Maya sweatbaths, however, Linton Satterthwaite (1952: 25) expressed doubt about Morley's interpretation, pointing out mainly that 1B-2 does not have most of the architectural features commonly associated with Classic Maya sweatbaths. Most notably, it lacks the typical symmetrical layout and drains. Nevertheless, the boulders do suggest the possibility that the room was used as a sweatbath at least occasionally and was perhaps more symbolic than functional.

If the west room of 1B-2 was a sweatbath, even a symbolic one, then it would reinforce the meaning of the edifice as a whole. As discussed by Stephen Houston (1996), Mesoamerican sweatbaths have close symbolic associations with birth. One of the most common uses of the baths is as a treatment for the mother both before and after childbirth. In many Maya communities, parturition itself traditionally takes place in the sweatbath. In the Mam village of Santiago Chimaltenango, Guatemala, the structure is so closely associated with birth that the afterbirth is buried under its floor (Wagley 1957: 129). The design of one of the rooms of 1B-2 as a sweatbath could be seen as a means of providing a place where the ancestors could be reborn through the vision rite. This hypothesis might even be supported by the pyrite mirror pieces found in the structure, as such mirrors are associated with supernatural communication. Further, the placement of a sweatbath in a building that represents a mountain is consistent with the symbolism of sweatbaths as caves.

The construction of 1B-2 shortly after the accession of K'ak' Tiliw modified the meanings of adjacent structures, specifically the ballcourt, Structure 1B-sub.4. In the plans of the ceremonial centers throughout Mesoamerica, a ballcourt or sunken court was often located at the foot of or near the principal mound or pyramid (Freidel, Schele, and Parker 1993: 132–137, 146–155; Reilly 1989). In many cases, the principal mound can be interpreted as symbolizing the mountain of Creation for the city. This tradition is exemplified in the Middle Formative period by the Olmec site of La Venta, in which the conical mound of Complex C is axially aligned with the sunken court of Complex A. The twin embankments framing a plaza space between these two units may be an early ballcourt. The more complex architectural environments of the Classic-period Maya exhibit a number of variations on this pattern. For example, in the Copan acropolis the pyramid symbolizing the mountain of Creation, Structure 10L-22, is fronted by a "false ballcourt," a courtyard embellished with a triad of markers similar to those seen in masonry ballcourts. Both the sunken courts and ballcourts are often interpreted as places of sacrifice and entrances to the underworld. For the Maya, they are also manifestations of the cleft in the Creation mountain (Schele and Freidel 1991). Thus, Maya ballcourts functioned as the loci for sacrificial acts which magically induced the growth of maize and the rebirth of ancestors out of the watery underworld.

The Sub.4 ballcourt stressed the symbolism of the adjacent 1B-2 as the mountain of Creation of Quirigua because the ballcourt itself represented the cleft in this mountain. Both buildings were oriented on the same axis and opened onto the same ritual space, the acropolis court, thereby strengthening their mutual symbolic associations. The remodeling of the acropolis by K'ak' Tiliw in this particular manner, however, was by no means a simple expression of sacred geography. Taken in its historical context, the building program emerges as a profound statement of political authority and revitalization for the city. The construction of mound/pyramid plus plaza/ballcourt combinations in Maya sites often can be linked to the Mesoamerican concept of "centering," in which architectural groups replicate cosmic patterns in order to sacralize the constructed spaces (Freidel, Schele, and Parker 1993; see also Ashmore 1989). While such cosmological structures provided the basic spatial vocabulary for Maya architecture, it is also apparent that the Creation mountain is associated with the concept of city founding. The *Popol Vuh* defines historical cities in terms of mountains, thus associating them with the mythological mountain of origin, Pan Paxil, Pan Kayalaa, "Broken Place, Bitter Water Place." In addition, the mythological mountain is itself referred to as a *tinamit* "city, citadel" (Tedlock 1985: 163, 182). In the *Popol Vuh* the mythological mountain represents the supernatural prototype for urban settlement.

Using this analogy, the construction of Structure 1B-2 at Quirigua may be interpreted as a refounding or renewal of the city. Even though the structure added to an already existing architectural complex, its particular symbolism as a sacred mountain proclaimed Quirigua's self-identification as a polity. When seen in the context of the contemporary architecture of Copan, the early constructions of K'ak' Tiliw take on even more pointed significance. During the years preceding A.D. 740, Copan witnessed significant construction within the site center, overseen by the king Waxaklajun Ub'ah K'awil. Some of the most important of these projects centered on Structure 10L-26.

In the past, most archaeologists thought that the Hieroglyphic Stairway of Structure 10L-26 was built after the defeat of Waxaklajun Ub'ah K'awil (Marcus 1976; Riese 1980, 1986). It is now evident that Waxaklajun Ub'ah K'awil himself began this massive project, dedicating the lower section of steps in A.D. 710 (see Morley 1920: 272). According to a recent analysis of the style and discourse patterns of the stairway text by David Stuart (n.d.b), about half of the present height of the structure can be attributed to Waxaklajun Ub'ah K'awil. The upper sections of this text recorded accessions and death dates of the Copan rulers, possibly beginning with the founder, K'inich Yax K'uk' Mo'. The intact Steps 4, 5, and 6 feature a lengthy record of the death and burial of Smoke Imix, suggesting that the stairway bore a special dedication to this predecessor of Waxaklajun Ub'ah K'awil. The large and richly furnished Chorcha tomb found deep inside Structure 10L-26 (Burial XXXVII-4) was likely that of Smoke Imix himself (Fash 2001: 111). If this interpretation is correct, then the Hieroglyphic Stairway was conceived during Waxaklajun Ub'ah K'awil's reign as both a dynastic monument and a funerary memorial to Smoke Imix.

Structure 10L-26 was only one of many commissions sponsored by this ruler (Cheek 1986; Schele, Grube, and Stuart 1989; Stuart 1989a). In 715, a few years after the completion of the stairway, the Copan king completed the final version of Structure 10L-22. The ballcourt was remodeled during the following years, to be dedicated in 738. In addition, during this period considerable effort went into enlarging plaza areas and renovating structures on the east, west, and north edges of the site core. K'ak' Tiliw's 1B-2 can be seen as inspired by Waxaklajun Ub'ah K'awil's 10L-22, since both buildings represent the sacred mountains of their respective cities. Even its mosaic technique of sculptural adornment can be specifically linked to the Copan tradition (Riese 1986). The new form of the Quirigua acropolis featuring a symbolic Creation mountain deliberately emulated recent developments at Copan.

Conclusion

The imitation of diverse aspects of Waxaklajun Ub'ah K'awil's architectural and sculptural styles, formats, and imagery by Quirigua artists prompts reflection on the meanings of these influences. The stylistic and technical correspondences between Quirigua and Copan architecture are so close as to suggest that Copan artists actually worked at Quirigua or that Quirigua artists were apprenticed in workshops at Copan. Thus, stylistic similarities are a symptom of a political relationship of subordination and cultural exchange. A somewhat different read-

2.30. CPN Great Plaza. The stelae visible in this photograph were commissioned by Waxaklajun Ub'ah K'awil during the early eighth century. Photo by author.

ing is suggested by the iconography of these structures. As discussed above, the new temple built by K'ak' Tiliw represents a local sacred mountain. The construction of such a temple symbolized the refounding of the sacred center. The new constructions, then, suggest not only the connections between Copan and Quirigua but the growing political autonomy of Quirigua.

It is possible to discern in the early architectural projects of K'ak' Tiliw the germ of the idea to transform Quirigua into a new capital of the Maya Southeast, rivaling Copan. Beyond the symbolic meaning of these structures, the very mass of construction which was undertaken during this time—together with the commissioning of carved, inscribed monuments—speaks eloquently of the relative autonomy that Quirigua seems to have gained upon the accession of its new king. Indeed, the inscription of Altar M says nothing of the subordinate status of K'ak' Tiliw, a very bold omission for a lord supposedly subject to the Copan king's authority. In fact, this monument claims K'ak' Tiliw himself as the overlord of another unknown agent.

It should be noted, however, that in his early years as ruler K'ak' Tiliw commissioned no known portrait images. This is in dramatic contrast to Waxaklajun Ub'ah K'awil, who erected no fewer than five spectacular portrait stelae during this period. These monuments (CPN Stelae 4, H, A, B, and D) were placed in one of the most important public spaces at Copan, the Great Plaza (Fig. 2.30). In view of the importance of this genre at Copan, the total absence of monumental portraits at Quirigua seems significant. Furthermore, after Quirigua's independence, each monument commissioned by K'ak' Tiliw featured a royal portrait, and sometimes more than one. Given this radical change in art forms before and after the conflict with Copan, one could speculate that monumental portrait images may have been prohibited at Quirigua during the reign of Waxaklajun Ub'ah K'awil. Such images may have been seen as an overt public statement of political independence, inappropriate for a vassal lord. Instead, the monuments erected during K'ak' Tiliw's early reign suggest more general and depersonalized themes of city founding within a sacred landscape.

The possibility that portraiture was forbidden to K'ak' Tiliw while he was a vassal raises interesting prospects for the understanding of this genre of art. As discussed earlier, royal portraits served rulers as a principal mode of multiplying and memorializing personae. With each representation, the charismatic power of a ruler was dramatically enhanced as performance spaces were claimed and personalized. Without such images, rulers were severely restricted in their ability to generate a personal identification with a public ritual space and, by extension, with the polity. Portraiture, then, may have functioned as a means by which supreme rulers maintained their authority, literally embodying the cosmos and the polity. Subordinates such as K'ak' Tiliw had to be satisfied with building sacred landscapes and performing in them, their bodies only temporarily totalized though spirit possession. The tension between such fleeting experiences and a permanent cosmological identity fixed in portrait images may have contributed to the constant stress on the structures of political hierarchy during the Classic period.

When the early history of K'ak' Tiliw is considered as a whole, a picture emerges of a potentially volatile political situation, about which the overlord Waxaklajun Ub'ah K'awil would have had reason to worry. The sudden florescence of the former colony with new sculptural and architectural commissions speaks for a dramatically different political and economic climate in the lower Motagua valley. Even though the later monuments of K'ak' Tiliw imply that the decapitation of the Copan ruler in 738 formed the foundation of his authority, the archaeological and artistic evidence suggests that almost immediately after the accession of K'ak' Tiliw in 725 power was rapidly being consolidated around the ruler. Although it is tempting to ascribe this resurgence in part to charismatic performances of its ruler, supported by new art programs, the sudden and dramatic rebirth of Quirigua strongly hints at the presence of an outside hand in the affairs of the small site. Indeed (as will be seen in the next chapter), sometime between A.D. 725 and 738 K'ak' Tiliw ceased to be a loyal vassal of Waxaklajun Ub'ah K'awil and began conspiring with distant and powerful enemies of Copan. These developments soon unfolded into a series of events that would shape the history and art of the two cities for years to come.

3

REBELLION AND REVIVAL

The First Stelae of K'ak' Tiliw

THE INHABITANTS of Quirigua in the late 730s had reason to praise the ancestors. The population was expanding, and the surplus from agriculture and trade was being transformed into monumental architecture and sculpture in the site core. Presiding over this time of plenty was the ruler K'ak' Tiliw, whose monumental commissions simultaneously expressed the cultural bond with Copan and asserted the eminence of the local ruler. Monumental art and architecture during the first ten years of his reign boldly negotiated the line between subordination and independence. Finally, in 738, tensions between the two centers reached a critical point, resulting in the capture of the Copan ruler by Quirigua. Taking advantage of this unexpected maneuver, K'ak' Tiliw beheaded his former overlord in a ritual which would radically transform the ceremonial center of Quirigua. As later monuments clarify, this sacrifice was not merely a political act but one replete with supernatural significance. The ruler had demonstrated that he could wield the spiritual powers necessary to guarantee the safety, fertility, and prosperity of the polity.

Among the many events chronicled on Quirigua's monuments, only the sacrifice of the Copan ruler is given the same prominence as K'ak' Tiliw's accession. In fact, the same four monuments that record the accession also proclaim this victory. To judge from the monuments of K'ak' Tiliw and his successor, the two rituals set the course for the site's emergence as the new capital of the southeastern Maya area. At Quirigua these episodes are celebrated in two distinct programs of monumental sculpture for which an enormous ritual space north of the acropolis, the Great Plaza, was constructed. The earlier program, erected between 746 and 756, is the topic of the present chapter. This monument group occupied the southern part of the Great Plaza and consisted of two stelae, H and J, and possibly a third monument, Stela S. The later program, built upon a slightly raised platform to the north of Stelae H and J, is discussed in Chapters 4 and 5.

Although these two programs explicate the supernatural and political implications of the sacrifice of the Copan ruler, they also suggest that the event initiated an extended period of competition between Quirigua and Copan. This conflict apparently entailed the transformation of the Quirigua acropolis into a defensible citadel, fitted with high terraces and perimeter walls. Far from ignoring its aggressive neighbor, Copan was forced to deal with the political crisis, responding through a number of architectural and sculptural projects which alternately proclaimed the regional hegemony of the Copan polity and celebrated the heroism of its ruler. In sum, Copan rapidly rebounded from its defeat, led by two rulers whose art programs literally and symbolically built upon the works of their unfortunate predecessor.

The Defeat of the Copan Ruler

The defeat of Copan by its former colony is one of the most dramatic stories from ancient Maya history. The pivotal date in this episode, 9.15.6.14.6 6 Kimi 4 Sek (May 3, 738), corresponds to the date of sacrifice of the ruler of Copan, Waxaklajun Ub'ah K'awil.[1] The method used in this execution was decapitation, probably performed with a flint axe. In Maya art this technique is shown performed by supernaturals, as on the Altar de Sacrificios vase (Fig. 3.1). Chaak, the deity of lightning and thunder, also commonly wields the hafted axe used in this ceremony (Figs. I.28, 2.25, 3.13). The sacrifice was not a mere mortal act but was laden with supernatural overtones. Attesting to this significance, the event was mentioned on three of K'ak' Tiliw's stelae, J, F, and E, and posthumously on Zoomorph G (Fig. 3.2).

The death of the Waxaklajun Ub'ah K'awil is also recorded in a passage from the Hieroglyphic Stairway, the most important monument commissioned at Copan following the conflict with Quirigua (Fig. 3.3). The manner of presentation here is different from that at Quirigua, revealing distinct interpretations of the significance of the ruler's death at the two sites. The account of his death recorded on the Hieroglyphic Stairway uses a common metaphor which refers to the departure of the breath from the body and makes no reference to decapitation. This event is followed by the phrase *tutok' tupakal*, however, a couplet that literally reads "with his flint, with his shield." As this record is unusual, it is difficult to interpret. While it may allude to the death of the ruler by arms, it may also be read as a figurative reference to his death "in war." Whatever its precise translation, this inscription apparently presents Waxaklajun Ub'ah K'awil as a hero rather than a humiliated victim.

Apart from the accounts of the death of Waxaklajun Ub'ah K'awil, there is limited evidence for the context of the conflict. Certainly, there is no indication that lord was captured on 9.15.6.14.6, as implied by various au-

3.1. Self-decapitating deity. Altar de Sacrificios Vase, detail. Drawing by Linda Schele, © David Schele, courtesy Foundation for the Advancement of Mesoamerican Studies, Inc.

a he is decapitated   Waxaklajun Ub'ah K'awil

b he is decapitated   Waxaklajun Ub'ah K'awil   under his supervision   K'ak' Tiliw   it happened at   Black Hole place

c he is decapitated   Waxaklajun Ub'ah K'awil

d he is decapitated   Waxaklajun Ub'ah K'awil   under the supervision of K'ak' Tiliw

3.2. The death of Waxaklajun Ub'ah K'awil: *a*, QRG Stela J, H3–G5; *b*, QRG Stela F, A12b–B14a; *c*, QRG Stela E, B12b–A13a; *d*, QRG Zoomorph G, L'3b2–L'4. Drawings by author.

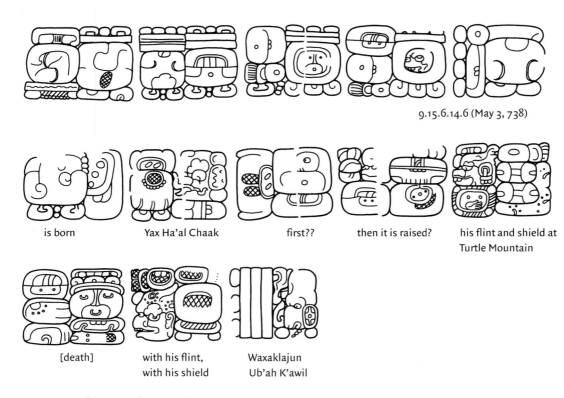

9.15.6.14.6 (May 3, 738)

is born Yax Ha'al Chaak first?? then it is raised? his flint and shield at Turtle Mountain

[death] with his flint, with his shield Waxaklajun Ub'ah K'awil

3.3. Events of May 3, 738, as recorded on the Copan Hieroglyphic Stairway. Drawing by the author based on Gordon (1902: plates 12 and 13).

thors (Riese 1986: 96; Sharer 1990; Stuart and Schele 1986a: 12). The last date associated with Waxaklajun Ub'ah K'awil at Copan prior to his execution was the dedication of Copan Ballcourt III on 9.15.6.8.13 (January 10, 738), only 113 days before his death (Grube et al. 1989). It has been suggested that Waxaklajun Ub'ah K'awil was captured when he went to war to secure captives to inaugurate this structure (Schele and Freidel 1990: 487). As there is no evidence that either Quirigua or Copan was attacked at this time, it is probable that Quirigua warriors ambushed the lord of Copan during an attempted attack on another site.

Although the details of the revolt remain elusive, a text on Stela I (a monument commissioned by the sixteenth ruler of Quirigua) suggests that the battle and sacrifice were separated by a few days (Fig. 3.4). The text begins with the date 9.15.6.14.0 (April 27, 738), which was six days prior to the decapitation of Waxaklajun Ub'ah K'awil, followed by two events.[2] The first is difficult to decipher but probably refers to the capture or piercing of wooden images, while the second refers to the kindling of a fire by drilling. The recipients of this action are named as ancestral deities of Copan or, in the words of this text, "Chante Ajaw, K'uy Nik? Ajaw, the gods of Wax-

aklajun Ub'ah K'awil." Although they are not otherwise mentioned at Quirigua, Chante Ajaw and K'uy Nik? Ajaw ("Four Lord" and "Ceiba Flower? Lord") are named frequently in the texts of Copan and are even depicted in sculptural form, on the bench from Temple 11 (Fig. 3.5). The Stela I passage may therefore be an account of the battle between Copan and Quirigua, phrased in ceremonial terms. Rather than describing the actual capture of the Copan king, the text records the capture and possibly the burning of wooden images of the ancestral deities of Copan.

This interpretation of the account on Stela I is supported by analogy with events in Classic Maya history and by comparison with ethnohistorical sources. In the Classic period, statues of patron deities or ancestors were frequently carried into battle on stepped palanquins or litters (Freidel, Schele, and Parker 1993: 310–317). Intact wooden statues are rare in the archaeological record. However, plaster casts were made from the remains of stuccoed wooden images found in Tikal Burial 195 (Harrison 1999: 102, Figs. 59, 60). In such a form, the gods could be captured, as, for instance, appears on the Naranjo palanquin taken by Tikal and shown on Temple 4 Lintel 2 (Fig. 3.6; Martin 1996). On this lintel the jaguar image is referred to as the god of the defeated Naranjo ruler, just as Chante Ajaw and K'uy Nik? Ajaw are called gods of Waxaklajun Ub'ah K'awil on QRG Stela I. Aztec ethnohistorical documents also refer to the capture and sometimes destruction of the god images of conquered cities (Hassig 1988; Sahagún 1950–1982, Bk. 2: 182).

The historical account of Stela I also contains crucial information for understanding actions taken by K'ak' Tiliw against Copan. Appearing above the details of capture or destruction of the Copan ancestor images is an account of the 9.15.5.0.0 period-ending rituals, including the erection of a stela by K'ak' Tiliw (Fig. 3.7). The following passage, beginning with a second unclear verb or relationship glyph, reveals that a second personage was involved in this period ending. This person is identified as Wamaw K'awil, the high king of Calakmul, located far to the northwest in Campeche, Mexico.[3] Consistent with the global politics of the Classic Maya realm, it is profitable to speculate about the reasons for the long journey of this ambassador. During the Classic period, Calakmul was the most powerful rival of Tikal (Martin and Grube 1995, 2000). Both sites focused much energy on forming alliances with smaller sites, which were sometimes quite distant from the "superpowers." For example, the ruler of Tikal, Shield Skull, visited Palenque

K'uy Nik?   Chante Ajaw

3.5. Ancestors from CPN Structure 10L-11 bench. Drawing by author.

in 659 and later clashed with Dos Pilas and Calakmul (Grube 1996: 8; Houston 1993: 102–110; Mathews 1979; Schele and Mathews 1993: 116). Copan as well had been closely connected with Tikal since the early fifth century.

Thus, a possible interpretation of the passage on Stela I is that Calakmul, intending to bring about the collapse of Tikal's allies, may have conspired with K'ak' Tiliw to turn against Copan. Even though it is not clear exactly how the Calakmul lord participated in the period-ending festival at Quirigua, the timing of this interaction is significant, occurring between the accession of K'ak' Tiliw as a vassal of Copan and his aggression against Copan. The text from Stela I, then, may be taken as evidence that the revolt was related to "superpower" politics of the northern Peten. Although the texts of Quirigua are silent with regard to exactly when the site became involved with Calakmul, there is reason to suspect that initial contacts were made soon after K'ak' Tiliw's accession. The rapid growth of Quirigua during this period suggests that the site received external political, and possibly military, support. In addition, the construction of such monuments as Altar M and Structure 1B-2—with their implications for political autonomy—strongly suggests that Quirigua had begun to break away from Copan early in his reign.

This interpretation of the text of Stela I brings into sharper focus the relationship of Quirigua to Copan in the early- to mid-eighth century. First, it provides an answer to the "David and Goliath" question, which asks how tiny Quirigua managed to defeat the ruler of much larger Copan. Furthermore, why did Copan not avenge the loss through a counterattack against Quirigua? In re-

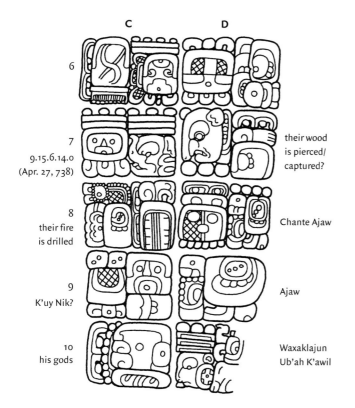

C   D

6

7
9.15.6.14.0
(Apr. 27, 738)

their wood is pierced/captured?

8
their fire is drilled

Chante Ajaw

9
K'uy Nik?

Ajaw

10
his gods

Waxaklajun Ub'ah K'awil

3.4. QRG Stela I, C6–D10. Drawing by author.

3.6. Tikal Temple 4 Lintel 2. From Jones and Satterthwaite 1982: Fig. 73. Courtesy of University of Pennsylvania Museum of Archaeology and Anthropology.

cent studies of the political machinations of Calakmul during the Late Classic period, it has been argued that an alliance with the great city often brought with it a promise of military support (Martin and Grube 1995, 2000). Although the evidence from Quirigua is circumstantial, it is highly unlikely that Copan would have failed to retaliate had there not been an implied threat of reprisals by Calakmul. It is probable that the involvement of Calakmul in Quirigua affairs after the accession of K'ak' Tiliw went far beyond the ritual act of stela dedication recorded retrospectively on Stela I. Calakmul may have encouraged K'ak' Tiliw to revolt against his overlord and provided troops to undertake the mission.

The identification of the role of Calakmul further suggests that Quirigua elites were close observers of political events elsewhere in the Maya world, probably through a network of diplomat-spies. As an example, it is difficult to conceive that they would have been unaware of events in the Petexbatun, where B'alaj Chan K'awil of Dos Pilas defeated the Tikal king Shield Skull in 679, under the auspices of Calakmul (Mathews 1979). While this history is not wholly analogous to Quirigua's revolt against an overlord, the benefits of an alliance with Calakmul would have been made clear from this episode.[4] Further, the dramatic expansion of Dos Pilas, with architectural and monumental art programs commissioned during the reign of Itzamnaj K'awil, would perhaps have convinced the leaders of Quirigua of the advantages of an alliance with Calakmul.

It is also interesting to observe that the account of K'ak' Tiliw's Calakmul connection on Stela I was not commissioned during K'ak' Tiliw's lifetime but long after his death. This treatment has parallels in Maya histories from other sites. At Caracol, for example, the ruler K'an II (r. 618–658) recorded the history of his father's move from the orbit of Tikal to that of Calakmul in the mid-sixth century on Altar 21 (Grube 1994). In contrast, the monuments of the father, Yajaw Te' K'inich II, lack references to external political powers. The same holds for the monuments of K'ak' Tiliw, which never acknowledge assistance in the revolt. During the reign of K'ak' Tiliw, it was probably not advantageous to admit dependency on a foreign power—and, at any rate, Quirigua was distant enough from Calakmul to have avoided true hegemonic control by the larger site.

The Great Plaza

While the text of Stela I contains information which enhances our understanding of the politics surrounding the revolt, the monumental programs of K'ak' Tiliw him-

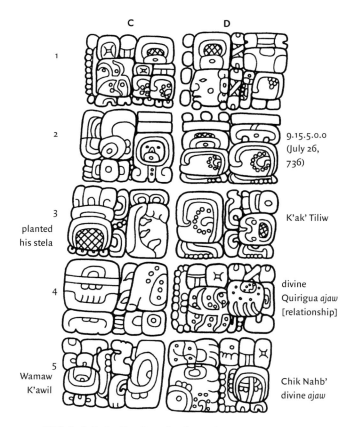

3.7. QRG Stela I, C1–D5. Drawing by author.

self emphasize those ritual actions that ensured independence, focusing on the contrast between his accession as a former vassal and the decapitation of Waxaklajun Ub'ah K'awil. One of the primary means of commemorating the decapitation is through the symbolism of the Great Plaza (Fig. 3.8), the huge public space that was built in the years after 738.[5] The original plaza consisted of two parts. The southern half, with a thin cobble and slab facing over naturally deposited silt, was chosen as the site for Stelae H and J. The northern part of the plaza, built to accommodate K'ak' Tiliw's later monuments (Stelae F, D, E, C, and A and Zoomorph B), was distinguished from the southern half of the plaza by being raised about 0.5 m above it (Platform 1A-1; Fig. 3.9). A series of seven low, narrow mounds formed the eastern boundary of the Great Plaza, at least two of which (Structures 1A-8 and 1A-10) were fitted with central, west-facing staircases. Excavations of the southernmost of these, Structure 1A-10, indicated that a small platform fronted the structure, and its summit platform also supported a superstructure made of adobe blocks. The western boundary of the plaza was formed by the channel of the Motagua River: flowing from the southwest past Loci 011 and 025, it made a sharp southward turn and, passing

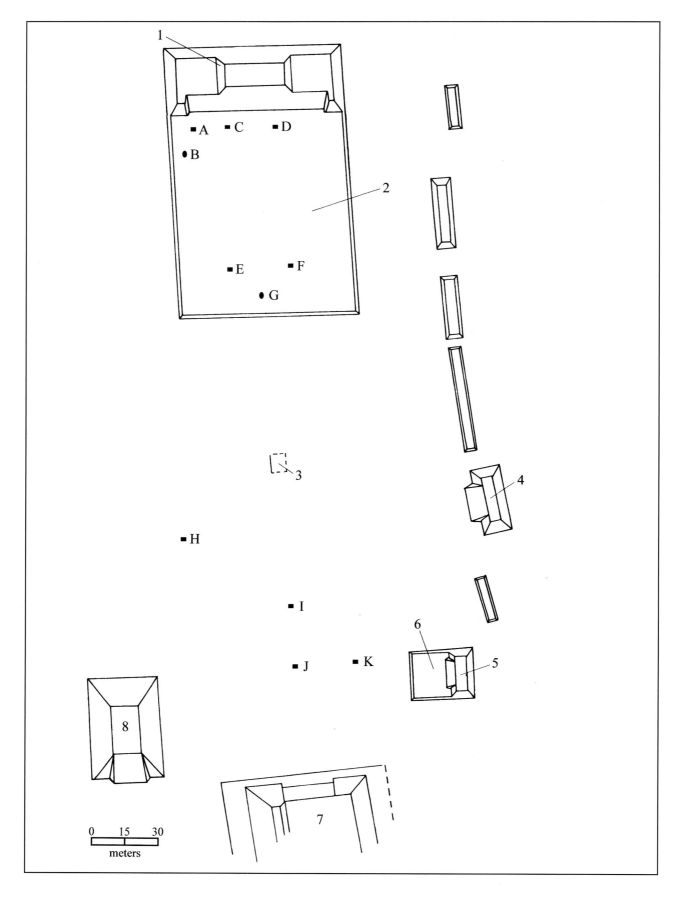

Facing page

3.8. QRG Great Plaza plan. Modified from Jones, Ashmore, and Sharer 1983: Fig. 6.3. Courtesy of University of Pennsylvania Museum of Archaeology and Anthropology. Key: 1. Str. 1A-3; 2. Platform 1A-1; 3. Platform 1A-3; 4. Str. 1A-8; 5. Str. 1A-10; 6. Platform 1A-2; 7. Acropolis; 8. Str. 1A-11; A. Stela A; B. Zoomorph B; C. Stela C; D. Stela D; E. Stela E; F. Stela F; G. Zoomorph G; H. Stela H; I. Stela I; J. Stela J; K. Stela K.

the acropolis, turned again toward the east. The plaza apparently served as a "gateway" to the ceremonial center, as it was fitted with a dock that extended from the plaza edge between Structures 1A-11 and 1B-21, west of the axis of Structure 1A-11 (Ashmore, Schortman, and Sharer 1983: 56, 61).

When visitors disembarked at Quirigua, they did not enter an ordinary public zone. On the contrary, the Great Plaza was symbolically identified with the place of sacrifice of Waxaklajun Ub'ah K'awil, thereby commemorating this pivotal event in Quirigua history. This meaning was inscribed in the texts and iconography of several monuments, including Stela F, which identifies the location where the decapitation occurred (Fig. 3.10a). This toponym consists of the glyph for "black" infixed into a grapheme representing skeletal jaws, used in Maya art as a marker for the cavelike entrance to the underworld. On other monuments K'ak' Tiliw is given a title that names him a lord of this "Black Hole" supernatural place. In several contexts, such as the "Cosmic Plate," this location is associated with a second toponym, "Black Lake place" (Fig. 3.10b; Stuart and Houston 1994: 77). In the accompanying image (Fig. 3.10c), the jaws that frame the composition symbolize the Black Hole place, while the Black Lake appears as the water band in which the central deity is shown partially submerged. The central deity of the Cosmic Plate is Chaak, the Maya patron of light-

ning and rain, who wields a type of hafted axe used in decapitation sacrifice. This image reinforces the association of the Black Lake and Black Hole with decapitation sacrifice. The Postclassic Maya Dresden Codex also shows a water-filled hole in the earth (a cenote) as the domain of Chaak (Fig. 3.10d).

Two monuments in the southern part of the Great Plaza at Quirigua refer to this supernatural location. One reference appears in the text of Stela H, naming the location where the monument was erected (the Great Plaza) as the Black Lake place (Fig. 3.11a). The "lake" grapheme from this toponym also appears on the northeast corner of the base of nearby Stela J (Fig. 3.11b; Grube, Schele, and Fahsen 1991). The toponymic references on these two stelae confirm that the Great Plaza was named after the Black Lake place. In addition, not only does the base of Stela J include the "lake" toponym, but the jaws which define the Black Hole serve as a basal register for the west-facing image of the ruler. These clues suggest that the Great Plaza represented the Black Hole, Black Lake place. The association of the plaza with an aquatic underworld is consistent with the symbolism of plazas in the Maya area (Schele and Grube 1990a). The passage of the Motagua River along the plaza's edge visually reinforced this symbolism at Quirigua.

In summary, the site of the decapitation of Waxaklajun Ub'ah K'awil was commemorated at the primary public space of Quirigua, identified with the entrance to the underworld, the "Black Hole." The "lord of the Black Hole place" title on monuments of K'ak' Tiliw serves as a memorial to the sacrifice in this location but also identifies the monuments as part of the extended metaphor of the plaza. The formulaic description of the sacrifice as a decapitation at Quirigua may be interpreted as a reference to the supernatural symbolism of the Great Plaza. This kind of sacrifice is the domain of the lightning deity Chaak, who presides over the same supernatural location, as seen on the Cosmic Plate (Fig. 3.10c) and in the

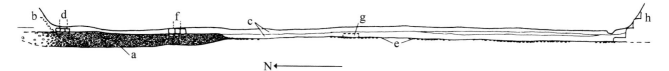

3.9. Schematic north–south section of the Quirigua Great Plaza, from Jones, Ashmore, and Sharer 1983: Fig. 6.4. Courtesy of University of Pennsylvania Museum of Archaeology and Anthropology. Key: a. Platform 1A-1; b. Str. 1A-3; c. silt strata overlying plaza; d. Stela D and its platform; e. discontinuous cobble stone surface; f. Stela F and its platform; g. Platform 1A-3; h. platform of Str. 1B-17 (acropolis).

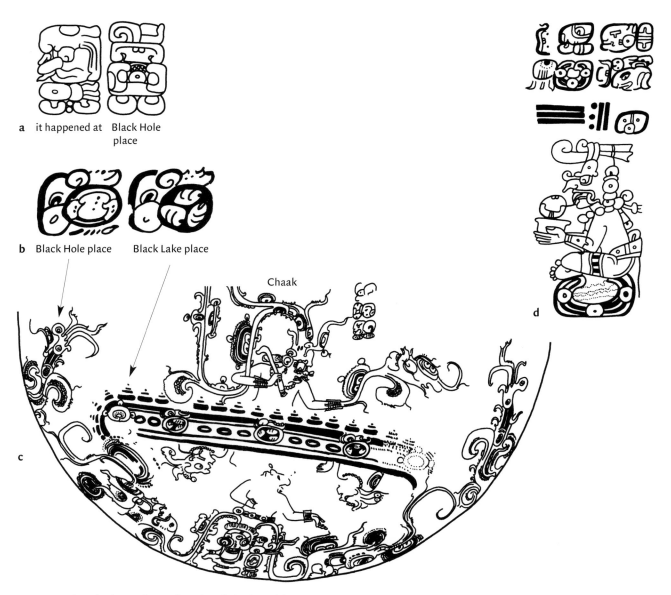

a it happened at Black Hole place

b Black Hole place Black Lake place

Chaak

c

d

3.10. Openings in the earth as a domain of Chaak and decapitation: *a*, QRG Stela F, A14b–B14a; *b*, "Cosmic Plate" (K1609) detail of text; *c*, "Cosmic Plate" (K1609) detail of image; *d*, Dresden Codex, p. 39c. Drawings by author.

Dresden Codex (Fig. 3.10d). As the agent who oversaw the decapitation, K'ak' Tiliw is presented as an incarnation of Chaak, akin to the supernatural beings illustrated in pottery images from other sites.

In assuming the ritual identity of a lightning god, K'ak' Tiliw drew upon deeply rooted associations of lightning with warfare. Indeed, one of the most common war titles in the Classic period was *kalomte'*, depicted as a Chaak holding the sacrificial axe.[6] Related beliefs survived the Spanish invasion. One of the most venerated Jakaltek culture heroes is El K'anil, the "man of lightning,"

who destroys enemies by transforming into lightning (Montejo 1984). Among the Ch'ol, the thunderbolt spirit Chahk protects towns from evil (Aulie and Aulie 1978: 46). The Tzotzil tell many tales about Chauk or Thunderbolt, who destroys enemy warriors with an electrical storm (Spero 1987: 92–93). War leaders of numerous Maya groups are reported to transform themselves into lightning in order to attack enemies. For example, a K'iche' captain named Izquín Ahpalotz Utzakibalhá, or Nehaib, assaulted the conquistador Pedro de Alvarado in this form (Recinos 1957: 88).

The reference to the place of sacrifice of Waxaklajun Ub'ah K'awil as the Black Hole may have yet another function: to commemorate the appearance of the sky on the night of the decapitation. According to Freidel, Schele, and Parker (1993: 87–88), the Black Hole was visualized in the sky when the Milky Way formed a partial ring around the horizon. On May 3, 738, the night of the sacrifice, the Milky Way reached this configuration after sunset. Thus, as the axe fell on the Copan ruler's neck on this evening, the Milky Way resembled a great portal or maw into which Waxaklajun Ub'ah K'awil's spirit fell upon death. A similar event is shown on the Palenque Sarcophagus Lid, in which the deceased ruler enters the road to the underworld through a skeletal maw (Schele and Miller 1986: Pl. 111). The construction and identification of the Great Plaza with the Black Hole, Black Lake place celebrated the sacrificial ritual which charged the plaza with sacred significance.

It is essential to remember that the Black Hole configuration is a seasonal orientation, visible at various times at night from mid-January to mid-June (Milbrath 1999: 288–291). Therefore, the Milky Way orientation alone can not explain why the sacrifice took place exactly on this date. In fact, May 3, 738, was likely chosen because it was the date on which the sun made its first zenith passage of the year at Quirigua.[7] That is, at noon on this date, the sun stood directly overhead. The Great Plaza's designation as the "Black Hole, Black Lake place" recalls the solar zenith passage because both the supernatural location and the zenith passage are closely tied to the beginning of the agricultural season. The image of the Cosmic Plate (Fig. 3.10c), in fact, shows that the Black Hole,

Black Lake place is the portal through which maize plants sprout, symbolized by the maize spirit shown directly below the Chaak.

The associations of zenith passage, decapitation, rain, and agriculture not only are expressed in K'ak' Tiliw's architecture and sculpture programs at Quirigua but also constitute essential elements of rites performed by the contemporary Ch'orti' Maya. As discussed by Rafael Girard (1966, 1995), the Ch'orti' officially inaugurate the rainy season on April 30–May 1, marked by the zenith passage of the sun. On this date, the Ch'orti' believe that the fertility god impregnates the earth when passing through the zenith at noon (Girard 1966: 36). This date is marked by astral phenomena, such as significant positions of Orion, the "Cross of May," and the Pleiades (Fought 1972: 59; Girard 1966: 63). In addition, a gnomon or the body may be used to verify that the "lord is moving straight" (Girard 1995: 183).

Even before this date, however, the Ch'orti' elders conduct crucial rain-making ceremonies both in the ceremonial house and at certain sacred locations in the landscape. The first is on April 22, when a cross is planted at the spring that is the source of the La Conquista River, symbolically identified with the underworld (Girard 1966: 66). This cross, made of the heartwood of the mother cacao (*Gliricidia sepium*) and covered with green conte leaves, is inscribed with the name of the elder who made it. It is set in front of the spring, added to the crosses planted during previous years. Stones are collected at the spring, later to be planted in the corners of the temple or in the lower corners of the saint's table. Shortly thereafter, at midnight on April 24 or 25, a cere-

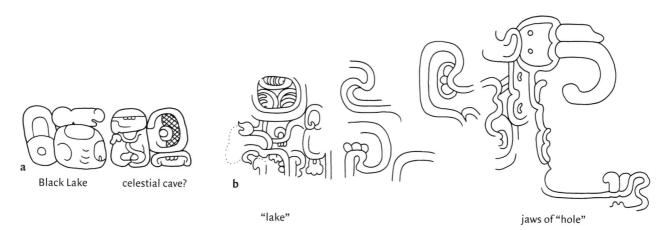

a   Black Lake   celestial cave?   b   "lake"   jaws of "hole"

3.11. Designations for the Great Plaza: *a*, QRG Stela H, N1–N2; *b*, QRG Stela J, rollout of basal register, north–northwest. Drawings by author.

mony is held at the La Conquista spring (Girard 1966: 68–79). Here two ritual structures are prepared: one between the cross and the spring which serves as an offering to the sky gods, and another near the fire, with a pit for offerings to the earth, termed *palangana, convento,* or *mesa* (Fought 1972: 525). Concerning this offering, Fought's (1972: 468) informant states: "They say that there it was put up, the basin of the spirit of the earth. They say that when everything is being set down, chilate, chickens, turkeys, incense, they say that it is as if on that table they had placed everything. And the spirit of the earth rises and takes everything which was placed in front of him."

The climax of the ceremony is the sacrifice of chilate and then two turkeys, which have been allowed to copulate:

> After the elder has poured the contents of the five containers of chilate into the sacred pit, to "feed" the Earth, he orders the number one slave to perform the sacrifice. The slave then holds the turkey in the air over the pit and with the help of the other slave, with a single slash of his sharp knife cuts off the head of the bird so it falls into the hole. The elder comes to verify that all the blood of the bird falls into the center of the pit, and personally lends his assistance by squeezing the turkey's neck. Then, the same slave opens the breast of the animal and with great dexterity takes out the heart and intestines, which he throws into the cavity; then he does the same with the legs. Next the slaves pluck the turkey completely and fill the pit with the feathers. The same operation is performed on the hen turkey. It is half past two in the morning. (Girard 1995: 113)

Regarding these opening rites of rainy season, Girard (1995: 199) states that "everywhere the blood sacrifice of birds is prevalent and indispensable" (see also Wisdom 1940: 437–440).

Back in the village, the elders induce the coming of rain using a variety of techniques. First, the foliage decorations of the saint's altar are renewed with green leaves gathered from the spring (Girard 1966: 89). Water, frogs, and fish collected from the spring are placed in the canoe, which symbolizes the underworld (Girard 1966: 77). In addition, the temple interior is moistened with sacred water (Girard 1966: 92). Next, two male and two female elders sit in chairs placed around the table located in front of the saint's altar and then stand simultaneously. This ritual, called "raising the sky," is conducted with close attention to synchronized action so as not to imbalance the cloud layer. Its function is to summon the Working Men to arise into the sky from their position at the corner posts (Girard 1966: 95). The gods are thereby summoned to come to the table to drink the chilate laid out for them. This complex ritual sequence is followed by the planting of the fields, accompanied by additional decapitations and blood sacrifices of turkeys in holes dug in the milpa (Wisdom 1940: 441–444). Girard (1966: 123, 126) states that the seed is consecrated on April 25 and that planting proceeds from this date until May 4, depending on the altitude. Similar ceremonies of rainmaking and offerings to the earth also occur later in the agricultural season in association with the second planting of the milpa, which occurs around August 12 or 13, marked by the second zenith passage. These ceremonies, however, are held on a smaller scale than those that are held around the first zenith passage (Girard 1966: 207).

The points of correspondence between the modern Ch'orti' rainmaking ritual and the ritual documented at Quirigua are remarkable. First is the decapitation of the Copan ruler on the date of first zenith passage at Quirigua, which recalls the annual turkey decapitation conducted by the Ch'orti' on the zenith passage, in order to cause rain to fall. In addition, both modern and ancient rituals took place at locations associated with the underworld. For the Ch'orti', the place of sacrifice is a sacred spring. At Quirigua the place of sacrifice is identified as a "Black Hole," recreated in the architectural form of the Great Plaza. The use of "black" in the name of this place may reflect the Ch'orti' association of rainy season rites with this color. As Girard (1966: 106) notes, the principal elder who conducts the rain ceremonies wears a dark (blue) headband.

In addition, at Quirigua, a ritual of fire-drilling occurred six days prior to the sacrifice of the Copan ruler (see Fig. 3.4). This is comparable to the ritual sequence of the Ch'orti' of Chiquimula, who perform a new fire ceremony prior to the rites of sacrifice at the beginning of the rainy season. This occurs at the end of a period of labor, in which the fields are cleared of vegetation, concluded by the time of the vernal equinox (March 20) or Holy Week. The peak of this sequence occurs on Saturday of Holy Week, when the officiating elder puts out the temple fire and starts a new fire, from which the domestic hearths are relit. Importantly, in Chiquimula, this ritual is conducted using the ancient technique of drilling, in which a stick that is placed in a socket on a board is spun between the hands until sparks appear. The same action is represented in the Dresden and Madrid Codices, conducted by deities (Fig. 3.12). This event signals that it is time to burn the fields. Although the modern ritual is timed according to the Christian calendar, it still precedes the solar zenith passage and is conducted specifically to produce the clouds from which the rain will eventually fall. Overall, then, both modern and ancient Maya ritual sequences include fire-drilling followed by decapitation events on the solar zenith passage, performed at an underworld location. It seems highly unlikely that this correspondence of multiple events is due to chance.

3.12. Deities drilling fire: *a*, Madrid Codex, p. 38b; *b*, Dresden Codex, p. 6b. Drawings by author.

Although scholars commonly associate Mesoamerican captive sacrifice with agricultural ceremony, the sacrifice of Waxaklajun Ub'ah K'awil represents the unique historically documented occurrence of this ritual sequence from Classic Maya history. An examination of the contexts of other fire-drilling and decapitation events yields no other examples which correlate with the inauguration of the rainy season. While it is likely that ceremonial cycles similar to the rainy season rites of the modern Ch'orti' were widely conducted during the Classic period, they were not generally raised to the level of high royal drama. This prompts a consideration of why the sacrifice of Waxaklajun Ub'ah K'awil was conducted in such a manner. Among the possible motivations may have been that such a ceremony was consistent with the ritual identity inherent in K'ak' Tiliw's name. As stated earlier, this name may be roughly translated as "fire-burning celestial lightning god," after a variant of the lightning and rain god that splits the carapace of the cosmic turtle to bring forth the sprouting of maize. The Great Plaza therefore can be interpreted as a ritual site that symbolically reinforced one of the most stable supernatural personae of K'ak' Tiliw, as an incarnation of the rain and lightning deity Chaak, who was closely associated with agricultural fertility.

Copan apparently acknowledged a variant of this persona in its own monumental programs. As part of the sequence which describes the conflict and the death of Waxaklajun Ub'ah K'awil, the Copan Hieroglyphic Stairway notes the birth of a supernatural entity called Yax Ha'al Chaak as well as an event involving martial emblems at a place called *kok witz* or "Turtle Mountain" (Fig. 3.3). This particular manifestation is also shown on painted pottery in a dance performance accompanied by a Waterlily Jaguar and a death god (Fig. 3.13). According to David Stuart (personal communication, 2002), this passage explains the supernatural context for the sacrificial event, in which the Quirigua ruler took on the guise of a "First Rain Chaak." This text is significant not only because it confirms the interpretation of the sacrifice of the Copan ruler as a meteorological ceremony but also because it affirms the authenticity of Maya supernatural personae even between competing historical traditions that emphasize distinct aspects of the event. At Quirigua the identity is conveyed through the creation of a symbolically charged ritual setting associated with performances of the victorious ruler. In contrast, at Copan a concise and explicit text names only the supernatural cause of the Copan king's downfall.

3.13. Yax Ha'al Chaak in a scene of sacrifice, from a codex-style vase (K1152). Drawing by author.

Stela S (Dedicated June 4, 746)

The supernatural events set in motion by the conflict between Copan and Quirigua are recorded only long after the event; in fact, more than seven years elapsed before the historical record resumed at Quirigua. Although the retrospective account of Stela I mentions the planting of a stela for the 9.15.5.0.0 period ending, this monument has not been located; nor has the stela associated with the next period ending, 9.15.10.0.0, also mentioned in a later account. This second celebration is cited on Stela F and includes an enigmatic statement reading merely *la-kamtun xukpi* "huge stone [stela] Copan" (see Fig. 4.6). The lack of actual monuments from this early period following the conflict with Copan suggests that this was a time of economic consolidation and restructuring, during which new (sandstone) quarries were opened at a site approximately 3.5 kilometers north of Quirigua. We may assume that technological infrastructure was being developed at this time to support the transportation of multi-ton stones to the site core.

For the next *hotun*, however, an actual stela has survived: Stela S. It was found in Group 7A-1 (Morley's Group B; Fig. 1.1), the westernmost floodplain group located on the north bank of the ancient Motagua River (see Morley 1923, 1935, 1937–1938). Its excavators remarked that the Stela S foundation in Group 7A-1 is characteristic of the late Stela I and unlike the foundations of the other early K'ak' Tiliw stelae, H and J (Jones, Ashmore, and Sharer 1983: 19–20). Thus, the monument must have been translated to this site from another location, possibly in the Great Plaza. Even though the original location of Stela S has not been securely identified, a likely candidate is the small Platform 1A-3 located about 80 m south of the edge of the north monument platform (1A-1; Fig. 3.8). Although of unknown size, Platform 1A-3 was identified by a single course of masonry aligned north–south and faced on the west side. If this platform did indeed serve as the foundation for Stela S, its placement would put the monument close to the alignment of Stela J with the north–south axis of the Great Plaza.

Stela S is badly eroded on all sides, possibly in part as a result of having been dragged from place to place in antiquity (Fig. 3.14). The monument was carved of sandstone, the preferred material for architecture and sculpture during the later part of K'ak' Tiliw's reign, and features a figure representing the ruler on the obverse. Texts occupy the reverse and sides. The text begins on the reverse, with a record of the dedication of the monument (Fig. 3.15a). Unfortunately, most of the reverse text is difficult to read, and the side to the right of the figure is totally illegible. A few glyphs on the left side, however, are readable, including the name of the ruler K'ak' Tiliw, spelled syllabically, in typical early fashion (E1–E2; Fig. 3.15b). The figural side of Stela S (Fig. 3.16) preserves little more than the general outlines of the royal image, evidently in frontal pose. A few details of the headdress are in slightly better condition, including fanlike projections of feathers, over the left side of which is superimposed a vertical device that includes zigzag struts. This element may represent a staff, similar to those held by rulers of Tikal, as on Stela 30 (Jones and Satterthwaite 1982: Fig. 50). Zigzag staffs also appear on Copan Stela A (Fig. 3.40), and this would appear to be the most direct source for the image on Stela S.

Although very little can be said about Stela S due to its poor preservation, aspects of its style and compositional mode may be placed within a historical context. Most secure is the frontal representation, which clearly derives from the earlier stelae of Quirigua, such as Stela U and Monument 26. The dedication date of the monument on a *hotun* may also be compared to earlier practices at Quir-

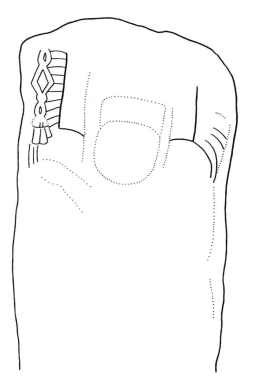

3.14. QRG Stela S, reverse. Neg. no. 5120, courtesy San Diego Museum of Man.

3.16. QRG Stela S, figure. Drawing by author.

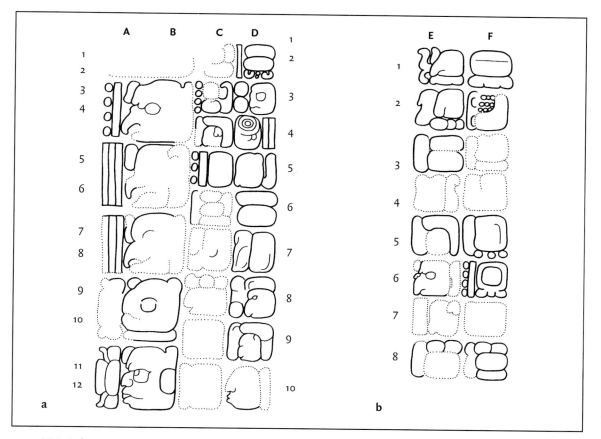

3.15. QRG Stela S, text: *a*, reverse; *b*, left side. Drawings by author.

igua. For example, Stela U has an initial series date of 9.2.5.0.0, and the other three early Quirigua monuments (Monument 26, Altar L, and Stela T) celebrate *k'atun* endings. Judging from the retrospective account of Stela I, the practice of regular *hotun* monument dedications began on 9.15.5.0.0, two *hotuns* before the dedication of Stela S.

Stela S is also the earliest known example of the dramatic increase in monument size, one of the artistic innovations that took place at Quirigua during the reign of K'ak' Tiliw. The height of the carved part of the shaft is about 2.8 m, whereas the basal dimensions are approximately 1.6 x 1.2 m. Thus, even though Stela S is small compared to the colossal monoliths that followed, it is much more massive than the slender Early Classic stelae of Quirigua. In this respect, the stela seems to manifest a general trend in Late Classic monuments toward increased size (Proskouriakoff 1950). The confinement of the figure to the obverse of the stela and the lack of a basal register also diverge from local tradition and perhaps betray Quirigua's lengthy domination by Copan. The general format of the monument, with a figure on the obverse and texts on the other three faces, may derive from formulae established at Copan. No earlier monument at Quirigua displays this format, and the mode is very common at Copan, appearing in the stelae of the seventh, tenth, eleventh, twelfth, and thirteenth rulers. In the end, very little can be said about Stela S because of its badly eroded state of preservation. Nonetheless, the sculptural composition suggests continuities with the traditions of both Quirigua and Copan.

Stela H (Dedicated May 9, 751)

To celebrate the second *k'atun* ending of his reign, K'ak' Tiliw commissioned Stela H, a monument which makes a pointed political statement during the period following the sacrifice of Waxaklajun Ub'ah K'awil. The stela was erected adjacent to Structure 1A-11 and to the west of the plaza axis, roughly opposite Structure 1A-8, one of the markers for the plaza's eastern edge (see Fig. 3.8). The figural side of Stela H faced the river, oriented toward the river traffic (Fig. 3.17). Its foundation consisted of a deep pit, dug through the plaza pavement and filled with rock and clay. A 25-cm-long flint blade, interred below the stela butt, served as the dedication cache for the monument (Strömsvik 1941: 81–82). The foundation of Stela H was built up to form a roughly square platform about 0.5 m high and 8.5 m on a side, framed by large blocks and filled with rubble. In effect, this platform created a separation between the viewer and the monument, enhanc-

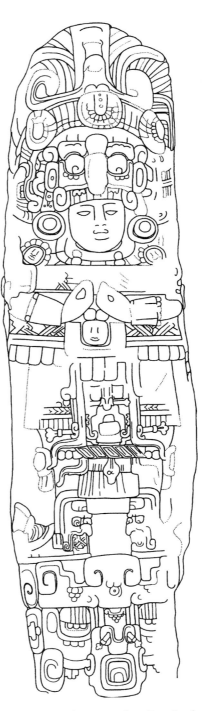

3.17. QRG Stela H, west face. Drawing by author.

ing both the rectangular cross-section of the sculpture and its inaccessibility. The visitor to the plaza could not casually brush against the monument but had to make the conscious decision to mount a rather substantial step and enter into a new and more intimate space. In the public context of the Great Plaza, this arrangement seems meaningful and may be viewed as an attempt to enhance the sacrosanct qualities of the stela. The subtle spatial barrier could have been understood as a metaphor for social hierarchy and in particular for the esoteric knowledge and power possessed by the ruler, whose image dominates the composition.

In contrast to Stela S, the format of Stela H is remarkably similar to the Early Classic Quirigua Stela U and Monument 26. The figure on the obverse (west) is portrayed frontally, standing on a zoomorphic basal register, with portions of the figure wrapped around the north and south sides. This model, with the reverse (east) devoted to the text, is also found on the early stelae. In addition, the imagery of Stela H is nearly identical to that of Monument 26. The heavy eyelids, mirror nose marking, *kawak* markings, and stepped forehead of the agnathous zoomorph on which the ruler stands identify the basal register as a personification of a hill or mountain, following the iconography of Monument 26.[8] On the relatively well-preserved north face of Stela H (Fig. 3.18a) the wraparound design of the mountain can be seen as a full-figure personification of maize, identified by his jewelry, high hairline, and the maize plant that emerges from his head. Here the deity is shown clinging to the foliage that sprouts from the earflare scroll on the mountain personification. Although absent on the much smaller Monument 26, the Stela H maize spirit appears in the same structural position as the maize deities that emerge from the mountain earflare curls on other Classic monuments, such as Bonampak Stela 1 (Fig. 1.10b).

The figure standing on top of the mountain basal register is shown holding the rigid double-headed serpent bar, as on Monument 26. Also similar to Monument 26 is the use of scrolls of sacred energy and the implements of war which emerge from the bar on the north and south sides of Stela H (Fig. 3.18). On the more elaborate Stela H, however, spears are shown together with shields. God K figures, identified by the smoking torches embedded in their mirrored foreheads, manipulate these war emblems. In some texts, God K is called *k'awil*, a term which has been interpreted as a statue into which a supernatural being is called in ritual as well as the spirit itself (Freidel, Schele, and Parker 1993: 199).[9] The combination of God K and weapons portrayed on Stela H may thus be interpreted as an image that expresses the supernatural basis of warfare. The scrolls that surround the God K figures as they emerge from the serpent-headed bar signify the sacred energy that the king manipulates through the emblems of war. The spears held by the deities may also relate to the dedication cache for Stela H, which consisted of a flint blade.

An astronomical interpretation of God K adds another dimension to our understanding of this iconography. In a survey of Classic Maya monuments, Susan Milbrath (1999: 233–240) found a correlation between appearances of God K imagery and certain positions of the planet Jupiter, especially with periods of retrograde motion. Significantly, the dedication date of Stela H, May 9, 751, approximated the first stationary point of Jupiter. A monument dedicated on the same day, Tikal Stela 20,

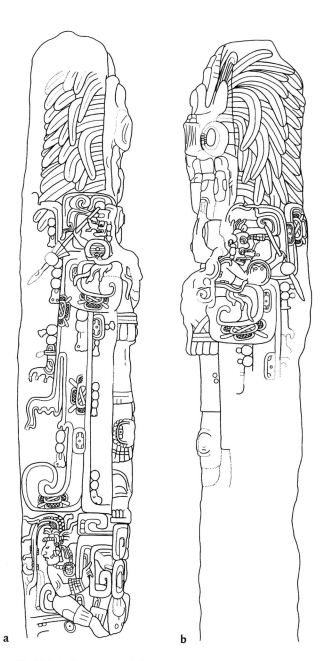

3.18. QRG Stela H: *a*, north face; *b*, south face. Drawings by author.

also commemorates this event through a prominent God K image, positioned at the apex of the ruler's headdress (Milbrath 1999: 237, Pl. 17). Such events may have been interpreted as astrologically auspicious for conducting certain ceremonies because they offered access to sacred energies. The imagery of monuments such as Stela H suggested that the rulers were able to direct these energies, through their manipulation of instruments such as the double-headed serpent bar. The regular association of iconography with celestial events implies the ruler's ability to predict such auspicious moments when access to celestial power is possible. Thus, the power of the ruler derived from his or her knowledge of celestial cycles and the rituals necessary to direct these energies toward earth.

The costume of the Stela H figure (Fig. 3.17), like that of Monument 26, is largely standard for Classic-period royal portraiture, although the later monument is better preserved. The lord is shown with typical high-backed sandals, here given personification heads and elaborate conical instep tassels. The better-preserved examples of these sandals at Quirigua (Stelae F, D, and E) demonstrate that these heads and adornments represent waterlilies and thus mark the cosmic zone at the lord's feet as the aquatic realm of the underworld. Representations of the ruler's jade or shell jewelry include large earspools, a mosaic necklace bearing medallions with inset faces on the shoulders, and mosaic cuffs. Knee ornaments take the form of medallions with pendant beads. The ruler wears a heavy belt with repeating interlace adornment and pendant *Oliva* shell tinklers, worn over a jaguar-skin skirt bordered with chevrons and probably a feather fringe. Because of the association of such heavy belts with the ballgame, a metaphor for war and agriculture, it is possible that the belt symbolizes the earthly realm of the cosmos. The celts that dangle from the front belt head may also imply this, given their general association with maize. In the context of the stela composition, the belt marks the midpoint between the underworld zone of the feet and the celestial zone identified with the head. The headdress itself features a large personification head with "serpent" wings surmounted by a canopy-like version of the headdress of the creator deity and archetypal magician, Itzamnah. One unusual costume element appearing on this stela is the scroll device at the headdress apex. This may correspond to the maize foliage that occurs in the equivalent position on Monument 26. Both monuments show the ruler as the resurrected maize deity, standing on the mountain of Creation.

The king's loincloth on Stela H further emphasizes the symbolism of the vertical axis of the royal body. In the form of a standard "God-C" apron, it is rendered as a frontal face bordered on the sides by two serpent heads and below by a woven pattern with leaves. These elements serve to identify the ruler's body with the sacred ceiba tree, demonstrating his ritual role as a cosmic pillar and pathway for supernatural forces (Schele and Miller 1986: 77). In addition, the interlace, leaves, and other elements that spill from the apron deity's mouth refer to a complex of floral imagery that embodies the ruler's reproductive capacity (Looper and Kappelman 2001). As a whole, the king's costume on Stela H develops a cosmological persona for the ruler, in which his standing body becomes an axis of communication between sky, earth, and underworld.

The correspondence between the iconography and format of Stela H and Monument 26 is striking and suggests that Stela H may represent a conscious decision to appropriate or quote the older monument. In fact, the spatial contexts of the two monuments were similar in that both Monument 26 and Stela H were erected adjacent to radial pyramids. Just as Monument 26 was set up near Structure 3C-14, Stela H was planted next to Structure 1A-11. Stela H and Structure 1A-11 thus serve to recreate the original Group 3C-7 program, presumably paying homage to the ancient rulers of Quirigua.

Confirming the parallels between the two monument groups is the dedication date of Stela H, which is recorded on the east face (Fig. 3.19). The Long Count and Calendar Round date of 9.16.0.0.0 2 Ajaw 13 Sek (A1–E2) is followed by additional calendrical information and the dedication sequence, which identifies the place of stela erection as the Black Lake, a name for the Great Plaza (Fig. 3.11a; Grube, Schele, and Fahsen 1991). Remarkably, the *k'atun* ending recorded on Stela H fell exactly thirteen *k'atuns* after the period ending celebrated on Monument 26, 9.3.0.0.0. Owing to the structure of the calendrical systems, both dates also occurred on 2 Ajaw. The symmetry of these two dates as 2 Ajaw *k'atun* endings provided a basis for comparing K'ak' Tiliw to the Early Classic rulers of Quirigua, reinforced through the iconography and format of Stela H. There is no doubt, however, that the ruler who commissioned Stela H was willing not only to appropriate the power of his ancestors but also to proclaim his control over maize and war. The martial iconography of Stela H, which was commissioned on the first *k'atun* ending after the decapitation of Waxaklajun Ub'ah K'awil, reinforces the ritual identity of the ruler as an embodiment of the lightning deity that decapitates enemies and splits the shell of the cosmic turtle to yield sustenance for the people. It may likewise be interpreted as a warning to Copan and its allies that the Quirigua ruler could wield the supernatural and physical forces of war.

This pattern of quoting an earlier iconography within the context of a calendrical cycle is not unique to Quirigua. At Tikal, several years before the dedication of Quirigua Stela H, the ruler Jasaw Chan K'awil installed a series of lintels in the superstructure of his future burial pyramid, Temple I. On the third lintel of this structure, a hieroglyphic text records a series of events conducted to celebrate the defeat of the lord of Calakmul. These events took place on the date 9.13.3.9.18 12 Etz'nab' 11 Sak, which fell exactly thirteen *k'atuns* after another important date in Tikal history, 9.0.3.9.18 12 Etz'nab' 11 Sip, the last date recorded on the Early Classic Stela 31. This was the date of death of Spearthrower Owl, a lord possibly from Teotihuacan whose son began a new lineage of rulers at Tikal. The origins of this figure are reflected in the iconography of the sides of Stela 31, which show warriors dressed in Teotihuacan garb. Apparently in commemoration of these historical figures, the central Lintel 2 of Temple I depicts Jasaw Chan K'awil ("Ruler A") as a Teotihuacan warrior, seated on a palanquin that is also adorned with Teotihuacan imagery. As observed by Schele and Freidel (1990: 210–211), the jaguar imagery assumed by the ruler on the obverse of Stela 31 recurs on Temple I Lintel 3 in the form of a large Waterlily Jaguar protector figure. Thus, even though the references are much more complicated at Tikal, the specific quotation of imagery in conjunction with the completion of large cycles of time is similar to the case of Quirigua Stela H. Further, such parallels could serve to reinforce the identification or even to suggest the reincarnation of ancestors through their descendants. Stela H draws on the authority of the earlier stela, suggesting the antiquity of the local dynasty and the continuity of rulership.

With the recognition of this citation of earlier iconography, different modes of archaism may be identified in Maya art. The distinction between revival and survival provides a useful model for understanding such citations (Greenhalgh 1987: 20–24). A revival results from the direct copying of an "original" ancient object and may be understood as an intentional reference to some aspect of the past. In contrast, a survival derives from a continuous series of replications of a form, with no necessary knowledge of its source.[10] Instances of survivals of ancient forms are numerous in Maya art, such as the use of double-headed serpent bars at Late Classic Copan, which are part of a chain of representations extending back to the

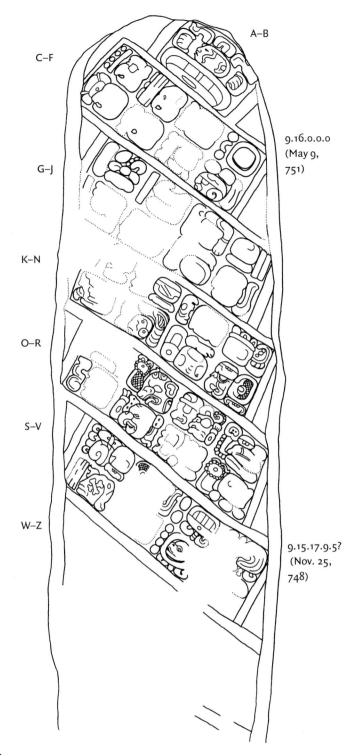

C–F

A–B

G–J

9.16.0.0.0
(May 9,
751)

K–N

O–R

S–V

W–Z

9.15.17.9.5?
(Nov. 25,
748)

3.19. QRG Stela H, east face. Drawing by author.

Early Classic period. Because the tradition of erecting stelae at Quirigua was interrupted for a period of nearly two centuries, between the dedications of Monument 26 in 495 and Stela T possibly in 692, Stela H can assuredly be classified as a revival. Because it was found out of precise context, it is not known if Late Classic sculptors had access to Monument 26 itself. Even if the stela had been lost, however, the imagery of the monument could have been preserved in manuscripts.

But not all features of Stela H derive from Monument 26. Many novel elements are stylistic or relate to format, such as the interlace pattern used as a frame for the inscription (Fig. 3.20). Although various scholars have posited Cancuen Stela 3 as the inspiration for the Stela H interlace, the Cancuen stela very likely postdates QRG Stela H and is probably not its model.[11] Rather, the text format of QRG Stela H is likely a greatly simplified variation on the text frame of the east face of Waxaklajun Ub'ah K'awil's Stela J at Copan (Fig. 3.21; Fash and Stuart 1991; Morley 1937–1938, vol. 4: 111; Proskouriakoff 1993: 131; Riese 1986).[12] Not only do the relative dates of the two

monuments support this contention, but Stela H at Quirigua occupies an analogous position to Stela J at Copan. Just as Stela H addresses those who enter the Quirigua Great Plaza near its main point of entry, so was Stela J erected at the entrance to the Middle Plaza at Copan. At Copan the stela was located at the terminus of the causeway from the urban zone of Sepulturas (Fig. 3.22). Likewise, Structure 1A-11, the radial pyramid built adjacent to QRG Stela H, may have been partly inspired by Structure 10L-4, the radial pyramid located at the boundary of the Copan Great Plaza and Middle Plaza. Such similarities argue that the Quirigua artists were looking to Copan for some concepts of format, planning, and programming.

Further, the analogous position of Quirigua Stela H and Copan Stela J supports the interpretation that the Quirigua Great Plaza was itself a variation on the Copan Plaza (Ashmore 1987; Maudslay 1889–1902, vol. 5: 6; Morley 1920: 428). At Quirigua, however, the programmatic idiom of Copan is used to express a distinctly aggressive message through the militaristic imagery of Stela H and the symbolism of the Great Plaza as a monu-

3.20. QRG Stela H, east face. Photo by Jesse L. Nusbaum, courtesy of Museum of New Mexico, neg. no. 60956.

3.21. CPN Stela J, east face. Drawing by author and Linda Schele.

ment to the sacrifice of the Copan ruler. Indeed, the patronage of the Copan Great Plaza and its sculptures by Waxaklajun Ub'ah K'awil adds an ironic twist to their reinterpretation by K'ak' Tiliw. Beginning with Stela H, the Quirigua monuments significantly surpass the stelae of Copan in height, as his Great Plaza also eventually outstripped that of Copan in scale. K'ak' Tiliw's new monuments suggest both the military superiority of Quirigua over Copan and the autonomy of the Quirigua polity achieved through revolt.

Because it is the first well-preserved stela of K'ak' Tiliw, Stela H merits a detailed stylistic analysis. Like its great size, the stylistic features of the stela are surprising, representing a mélange of features with diverse origins. One stylistic feature seen on Stela H that later becomes standard for Quirigua sculpture is the conformation of lines to a rectilinear grid. This can be seen clearly in the scroll designs on the sides of the monument, as well as in the basal register (Fig. 3.23). While diverse origins have been posited for this style, including sculpture of Veracruz or Yaxchilan or San Agustín Acasaguastlan pottery, a local source seems more likely (see Miller 1983: 133; Proskouriakoff 1950: 144). As discussed in Chapter 1, a strong sense of rectilinear composition is typical of Early Classic Quirigua sculpture. In addition, it can be found in architectural sculpture from the early part of K'ak' Tiliw's reign. For example, many of the leaf forms from Structure 1B-2 have squared outlines, a tendency that probably derives from the Copan architectural sculpture tradition. At Quirigua this aesthetic preference became thoroughly incorporated into freestanding sculpture. It is useful to compare, for example, the basal register mountain from Stela H to the mountain masks from the corners of Copan Structure 10L-22 (Fig. 2.18). Both examples show a similar squaring of earflares and scrolls, especially evident above the earflares. In addition, certain details of the Quirigua mask, such as the heavy striated eyelids and *kawak* markings on the forehead rendered as disks with inscribed circles, seem closely linked to the Copan precedent. While the squaring of forms at Copan could be explained by the necessity to fit forms onto rectangular stone blocks, at Quirigua the preference is purely an artistic choice that mimics the forms of an architectural façade.

Stela H also incorporates specific stylistic elements typical of the sculpture of Waxaklajun Ub'ah K'awil. These include the rounding of the face and headdress elements as well as the frontal representation of the earflares (Fig. 3.24). Like the early Monument 26, the face of the Stela H figure receives emphasis. On the later monu-

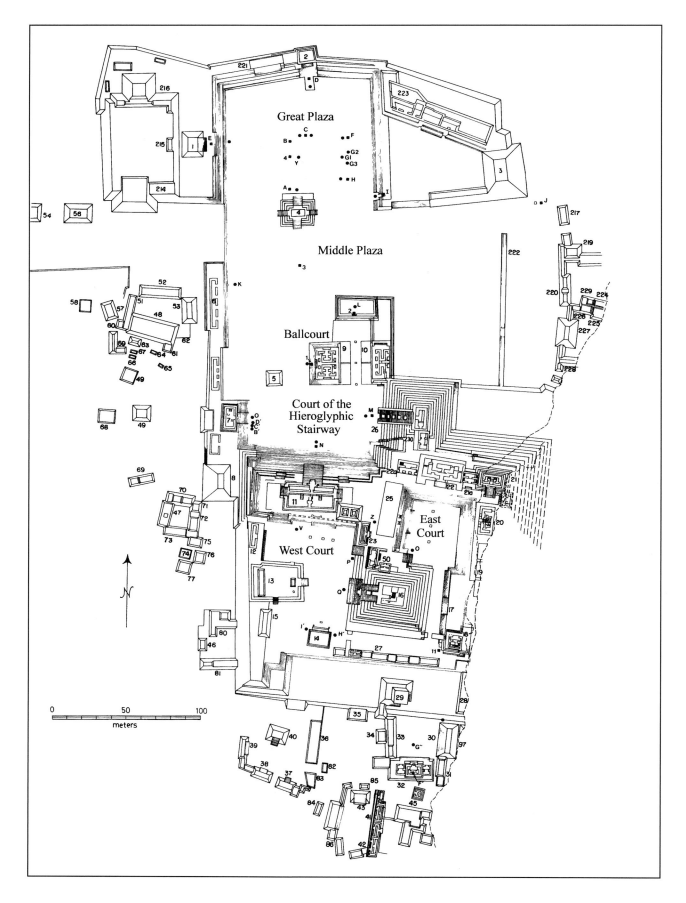

Great Plaza

Middle Plaza

Ballcourt

Court of the
Hieroglyphic
Stairway

West Court

East
Court

N

0   50   100

meters

3.22. Plan of CPN main group. Drawing by Barbara Fash, after Hohmann and Vogrin 1982. Courtesy Instituto Hondureño de Antropología e Historia.

Other stylistic features of Stela H suggest even closer ties to Copan sculpture, and especially to the stela tradition. Adjacent to the God K figures (Figs. 3.25, 3.26), the ground is deeply cut away, leaving dark pools of shadow out of which the gods appear to leap. The treatment of hairlike, trailing features, such as the serpent beard on the north face, approaches that of equivalent elements

3.23. QRG Stela H, west face, detail of basal register. Photo by Thomas Tolles.

ment, however, it is achieved in a different manner. On Stela H the dark cavity produced by the headdress emphasizes the face which emerges into the light below, a technique clearly derived from the Copan sculptors' interest in dramatic shadow effects. In fact, the use of contrasting shadows is a dominant design concept seen on the obverse of this stela. The arms and belt are surrounded by deep cuts, producing dark shadows. The entire leg zone is cut deeply from the ground, but with little rounding. This aspect of Stela H recalls earlier stelae at Copan. So too does the relaxed hand position of the figure on Stela H, which is different from that of the Monument 26 ruler and much closer to Copan Stela 4, for example.

3.24. QRG Stela H, west face. From Morley 1937–1938, vol. 5: Plate 178d, courtesy Carnegie Institution of Washington.

on certain Waxaklajun Ub'ah K'awil stelae. On Copan Stelae H and D, for instance, these elements flicker across the dark holes in a dramatic staccato effect. Both the diagonals formed by the curvilinear elements of the snake head and beard and the deity's posture and spear angle recall the sculpture of Waxaklajun Ub'ah K'awil, as does the appearance of the God K itself. Copan stelae, in general, are noted for the abundant small spirit beings that float about the main figure, but the animated expression and very large oval eye of the God K on Stela H seem particularly close to the figures conjured by Waxaklajun Ub'ah K'awil (Fig. 3.27).

Despite these similarities, the overall approach of the sculptors of Stela H was to emphasize four flat faces of the stone block. For example, above the God K figures appear broad, flat expanses of simplified, tonguelike feathers. Further, below the deities, the scrolls of sacred energy unroll along the empty ground, strongly emphasizing the block of the stela. An emphasis on flatness is

3.26. QRG Stela H, south face, detail showing God K with war implements. Photo by Thomas Tolles.

3.25. QRG Stela H, north face, detail showing God K with war implements. Photo by Thomas Tolles.

especially evident on the basal register of the north face (Fig. 3.28). Here the maize deity is rendered in a single plane, with little more than incised details. In this respect, the maize deity passage closely follows the style of certain earlier Quirigua sculptures, in particular, Altars Q and R and even Altar L. This emphasis on planarity and blockiness of the stela represents a marked difference from previous figural stelae at Copan, in which flattening is seen only in text areas. On most Copan stelae, especially those of Waxaklajun Ub'ah K'awil, the figures are surrounded by small superimposed, obliquely placed, dynamic masses that fill all available space. In addition, the human figure at Copan often projects out into space, rather than being confined within the "bounding planes of the prism," as at Quirigua (Kubler 1984: 253).

Stylistic inconsistencies are also clearly apparent on the obverse of Stela H, in which the rounded modeling of the figure's head and headdress strongly contrasts with the extremely flat rendering of the figure from the ser-

3.27. CPN Stela D, detail showing God K. Photo by author.

pent bar downward (Fig. 3.24). In this lower area of the obverse, and in the squared scrolls of sacred energy on the north and south sides as well, is plainly evident the preference at Quirigua for the integrity of the squared stone block, documented as early as Monument 26. Also divergent from Copan sculpture is the level of the horizontal compositional break on Stela H. While compositions at Copan usually break at the waist, QRG Stela H is divided at shoulder level, above the serpent bar. As such, it strongly recalls the prototype of Monument 26. This interpretation of the local derivation of flattened planes typical of Late Classic Quirigua sculpture differs from that of Arthur Miller (1983: 133), who attributed this feature to influence from Yaxchilan. It seems much more likely that the preference for flattening is a deliberate archaism deriving from local Early Classic monuments.

An additional interpretation of the emphasis on the low-relief sculptural style at Quirigua deserves comment. This is the notion that the style of carving at Quirigua is limited by the potential of the material out of which the monuments are carved. For example, Mary Ellen Miller

(1999: 82; see also Proskouriakoff 1993: 132) stated that the sandstone of Quirigua is "a particularly hard and resistant red rock that defied attempts to transpose the three-dimensionality of Copan, try as Quirigua sculptors might to achieve it." This view contradicts that of Morley (1935: 28), who observed: "The Quirigua sandstone, for the most part, is close grained and of even texture. When first quarried it is somewhat soft but hardens with exposure to air. The close even grain of this stone made for uniform results under the chisels, since it provided an evenness of resistance upon which the ancient sculptor could rely, thereby permitting him to carve as and how he would; while its softness, when first quarried, made for ease in carving with his tools of flint, diorite and basalt."[13] In fact, sandstones vary greatly in compactness

3.28. QRG Stela H, north face, detail of basal register, showing maize deity. Photo by Thomas Tolles.

and durability, their hardness depending upon the relative porosity and type of material that binds the sand grains that compose the stone. The cementing substance of the hardest sandstones is nearly pure quartz, whereas other agents such as iron oxide, clay, and calcite can produce far softer stone. A surface examination of the Quirigua sandstone reveals fairly large pores, suggesting relative ease of carving; however, this appearance may be the result of weathering. Without scientific testing of stone taken directly from the ancient quarries, the degree of hardness of the Quirigua sandstone will remain unknown.

Regardless of the properties of the medium, we can see that hardness does not seem to have been particularly limiting to the development of Quirigua sculpture. This is readily apparent in the areas adjacent to the face of many stelae (including H), in which large quantities of stone were removed to create three-dimensional modeling. In general, hardness or softness does not dictate sculpture style; it only determines the length of time required for carving. Other stone qualities such as tensile strength or friability may limit the sculpture process, although only in extreme cases. The potential of sandstone to allow highly plastic effects is readily seen outside of the Maya sculpture tradition, in Jain sculpture of India, for instance. In this tradition, sculptors pushed the medium to its limits, producing works with lacelike perforation and extreme undercutting. As noted by Arthur Miller (1983: 130), Maya art styles were not so much driven by medium but depended upon workshop traditions, with little encouragement of deviation from established norms. This type of process, called "formed habit style" by Miller, is structured according to cultural institutions or technologies and supported by a visual tradition.[14]

One iconographic feature of Stela H that is also different from Copan representations is the sandal style with a conical instep tassel. While many Copan portraits are shown with elaborate sandals, they often feature inverted personification heads as ankle-guards (as on Stela C) and elaborate knotting but without conical decoration. The decoration of the sandals on QRG Stela H more strongly recalls designs seen frequently in the Peten, as on the contemporary Tikal Stela 20, but also on Piedras Negras Stela 32 (Jones and Satterthwaite 1982: Fig. 29; Proskouriakoff 1950: Fig. 30). While there is no known precedent for this type of decoration at Quirigua, this should not immediately be taken as evidence of external "influence," as none of the known earlier Quirigua monuments preserve the foot area of the figure. This area is missing in both Monument 26 and Stela U, and Stelae S and T are hopelessly eroded. Therefore, it is impossible to determine whether there was a local precedent for this iconography.

In sum, Stela H is an example of both stylistic revival and survival. Many elements, especially the flattening of the figure and the emphasis on the rectangular block of the monolith through a wrap-around composition, seem to have been deliberately copied from the local Early Classic tradition. Some stylistic qualities, such as squared forms, seem related to eighth-century architectural sculpture, which in turn is highly derivative of the Copan tradition. Other stylistic features, including dramatic shadow effects, appear to be more directly comparable to Waxaklajun Ub'ah K'awil's stelae, resulting in a peculiar tension in the monument's overall effect. The most direct explanation for this divergence in style would be a relative lack of centralization in the sculpture workshop responsible for the execution of the stela. In contrast to later Quirigua sculptures, which were clearly dominated by a master who ensured a relative stylistic unity, Stela H shows a mixture of styles that are not resolved or integrated. What is particularly interesting about the trajectory of Quirigua sculpture following the conflict with Copan is that it reveals no evidence of influence from Calakmul, which is supposed to have assisted Quirigua in its rebellion. This observation supports the theory that the interaction between Quirigua and its ally was of limited extent and duration, perhaps involving only military and ritual assistance. There is no significant impact of the sculpture, architecture, or literary traditions of Calakmul on the art of Quirigua. In contrast, the art of Copan continued to exert a powerful influence over Quirigua, as can be seen in subsequent monument commissions.

Stela J (Dedicated April 12, 756)

Although it was erected only one *hotun* after Stela H, Stela J not only manifests a different aesthetic conceptualization but also demonstrates the quality expected from a well-coordinated workshop. At about 5 m in height, Stela J approximates its predecessor in scale and was erected as the central pivot of the southern part of the Great Plaza (Fig. 3.8). It was placed close to the major axis of the Great Plaza but farther south than Stela H. Strömsvik (1941: 82–83) describes the Stela J foundation as a rectangular platform 6.5 m to a side and 0.5 m high built on the cobble plaza surface and bordered by large stones. The stela butt rested on a large stone and was braced by stone wedges and a clay, pebble, and rubble fill. The cache was a house-shaped clay box, the contents of which were not preserved. The association of Stela J and Stela H as a single program is suggested not only by their similar size but by the orientation of both monuments with the figure facing west toward the river. Both monuments also share the conception of a stela as a four-sided monument with a figural obverse and reverse inscription. Stela J does, however, diverge from Stela H in its use of the side panels to display additional texts.

The inscription on Stela H is badly damaged, but it is likely that it was a straightforward dedication text with little narrative complexity. The text of Stela J, in contrast, is both beautifully carved and elegant in its rhetorical structure, pointing the way toward the elaborate narratives seen in the later monuments of K'ak' Tiliw, starting with Stela F. The text begins on the east side (Fig. 3.29), with an enormous ISIG occupying the entire width of the rectangular panel of the inscription. The following Long Count date of 9.16.5.0.0 (A6–B10), written using only head variants, represents a technical advance over the previous two monuments of K'ak' Tiliw. Additional chronological and dedicatory records follow, including an account of penitential bloodletting rites and the resulting materialization of a vision serpent. K'ak' Tiliw's name and titles appear next and include "south kalomte'," "black Copan ajaw," "fourteenth in succession," and "Black Hole" titles.[15] The east text of Stela J thus constitutes a very elaborate description of the period-ending ritual, in which K'ak' Tiliw erected the monument, made offerings, and manifested a vision serpent through trance.

Although most of these titles have been discussed previously, the "fourteenth in succession" title appears for the first time on Stela J and has been valuable for the political interpretation of K'ak' Tiliw's reign. This title includes a T573 "hel" sign, identified by Riese (1984) as a count of rulers from a founder. Here it is combined with a coefficient of fourteen, therefore identifying K'ak' Tiliw as the fourteenth successor of the "founding house." The next glyph, ch'ahom(a) "incense-offerer," is probably used here as a reference to the founder. Noting that the lord sacrificed by K'ak' Tiliw was the thirteenth successor of the Copan dynasty, Riese (1986) proposed that K'ak' Tiliw's use of the "fourteenth in succession" title was an attempt to usurp the Copan succession, through a reference to Copan's dynastic house. Jones and Sharer (1980) suggested instead that the succession referred to in the Stela J text is the local Quirigua line, given the references to an Early Classic fourth successor on Monument 26 and a probable founder of Quirigua on Zoomorph P.

These two interpretations may be resolved through the acknowledgment of the common origins of the two dynasties with K'inich Yax K'uk' Mo', according to the official histories of the Late Classic period (Grube, Schele, and Fahsen 1991; Looper 1999; Looper and Schele 1994). As discussed in Chapter 1, Zoomorph P, a Late Classic monument, records the founding of the Quirigua dynasty under the authority of the Copan founder on the same dates as the establishment of rulership at Copan. The ambiguity of the reference to the succession may be interpreted as an attempt to imply the position of K'ak' Tiliw as the inheritor of the succession of K'inich Yax K'uk' Mo' and thereby cast Quirigua as the preeminent capital of the Southeast. It seems likely, as Riese (1986) proposed, that the use of the "fourteenth in succession" title was indeed a statement of rivalry between K'ak' Tiliw and the fourteenth ruler of Copan, K'ak' Joplaj Chan K'awil ("Smoke Monkey").

The texts that occupy the north and south sides of Stela J (Fig. 3.30) seem to convey the same message, for they cleverly compare K'ak' Tiliw's accession and the decapitation of Waxaklajun Ub'ah K'awil, suggesting the necessary link between the two events. Both texts have the same basic structure and begin with distance numbers that count from the period ending recorded on the east face. As the north text returns to an earlier date than the south, it is probably meant to be read first. The event featured on the north text is the accession of K'ak' Tiliw on 9.14.13.4.17 12 Kab'an 5 K'ayab', recorded as the fastening of the headdress. The south text, in contrast, records the decapitation of Waxaklajun Ub'ah K'awil on 9.15.6.14.6 6 Kimi 4 Sek. Following this phrase is a record of the ruler's receiving of the God K scepter, a phrase usually associated with accession to the throne. Because the verb recording this event is not otherwise marked, it can be assumed that the time frame has shifted to the period ending when the monument was dedicated.

Not only do these texts compare the events of accession and decapitation through their placement on opposite north and south sides of the stela, but they are also both tied to the 9.16.5.0.0 period ending through distance numbers. As such, the events of accession and decapitation are given as background information for the period ending, thus presenting them as dual supports for the ruler's power. A similar rhetorical strategy is utilized on Caracol Altar 21, albeit in a much more complicated manner. On Altar 21 both the accession of Yajaw Te' K'inich II under the authority of Tikal and an attack by Tikal against Caracol appear as background information supporting subsequent aggression against Tikal (Grube

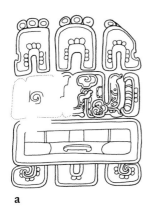

a

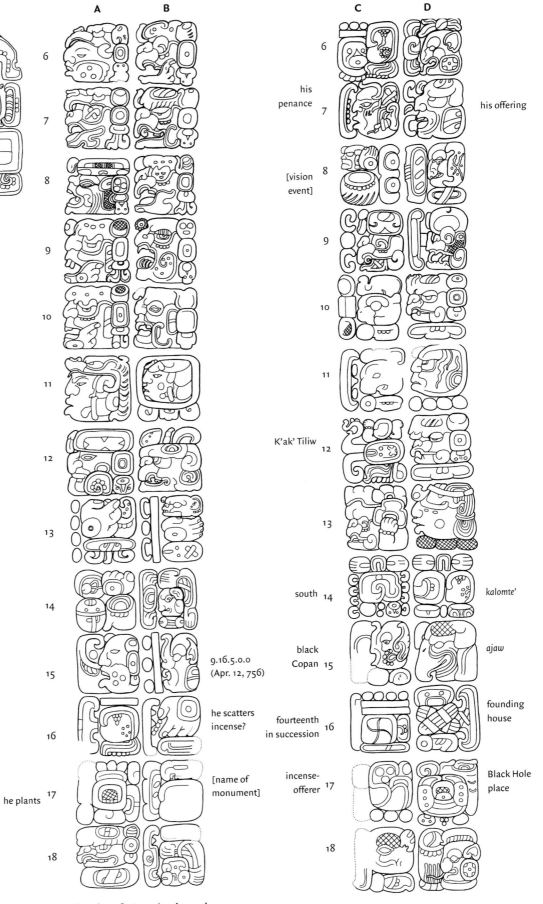

A **B**

6

7 — his penance

8 — [vision event]

9

10

11

12 — K'ak' Tiliw

13

14 — south

15 — 9.16.5.0.0 (Apr. 12, 756) — black Copan

16 — he scatters incense? — fourteenth in succession

17 — he plants — [name of monument] — incense-offerer

18

C **D**

6

7 — his offering

8

9

10

11

12

13

14 — kalomte'

15 — ajaw

16 — founding house

17 — Black Hole place

18

b

3.29. QRG Stela J, east text: *a*, ISIG; *b*, A6–D18. Drawing by author.

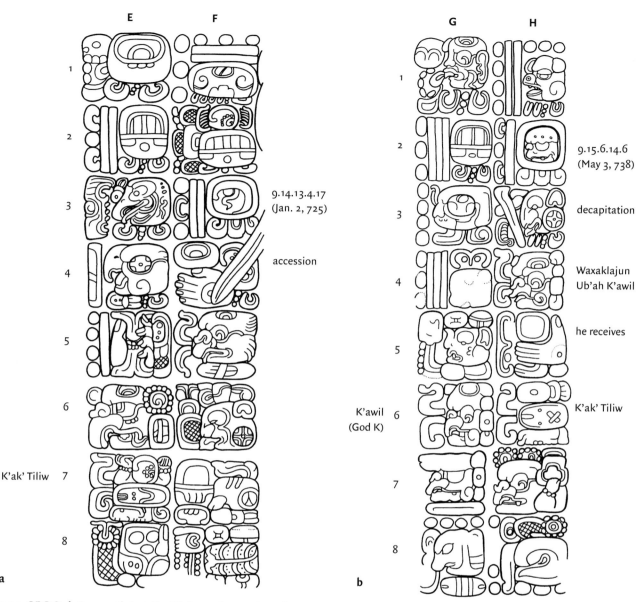

E   F   G   H

9.14.13.4.17
(Jan. 2, 725)

accession

9.15.6.14.6
(May 3, 738)

decapitation

Waxaklajun
Ub'ah K'awil

he receives

K'awil
(God K)

K'ak' Tiliw

K'ak' Tiliw

a   b

3.30. QRG Stela J: *a*, north text, E1–F8; *b*, south text, G1–H8.
Drawing by author.

1990a; Schele and Grube 1994). The pattern at Quirigua is closely analogous, presenting K'ak' Tiliw's accession under external authority as the justification for his action against the overlord. While one view might characterize this "retaliatory" rhetoric as pure propaganda, this might miss the mark. It may be possible to consider these accounts of victimization as an exhortation of the ancestors to protect their dependents. Certainly, such accounts contradict the notion that ancient Mesoamerican texts selectively omitted defeats from official histories (Marcus 1992: 360). In contrast, defeats as well as statements of subordination were crucial to native accounts, often serving the purpose of highlighting more momentous events in which the victory was achieved.

The imagery of the obverse (west face) of Stela J amplifies selected themes from the monument's text (Fig. 3.31). The figure is shown in the frontal mode typical of Quirigua stelae. This portrait deviates from local tradition, however, in that the ruler holds a God K scepter in the right hand (now almost totally eroded). The grasping of the God K scepter probably illustrates the text at H5–G6, which records the taking of a God K image or *k'awil* on the period ending. It is thus a somewhat different configuration than that seen in the earlier Stela H, in which God K figures emerge from the double-headed serpent bar.

The diverse contexts of this deity suggest that it had complex meanings in ancient Maya art. As a scepter, God

K seems to have particularly close associations with royal blood and bloodlines (Schele 1976; Tate 1992: 55). This symbolism is conveyed through several aspects of the deity, primarily through the transformation of its leg into a serpent. Images from ceramics suggest that the serpent-leg of God K is in actuality a vision serpent induced by bloodletting, through which the will of supernaturals and ancestors is made apparent to the living. Further, God K has a close association with mirrors, one of the most ancient Mesoamerican symbols of the portal to the spirit realm, out of which gods and ancestors are reborn. Finally, as a scepter (actually a personified axe) the being represents the power of lightning, wielded by the king (Baudez 1992; Coggins 1988a). It is this last symbolic value that seems most relevant to the interpretation of Stela J, as it complements the meanings conveyed through the monument's textual reference to the decapitation of Waxaklajun Ub'ah K'awil and its location in the Great Plaza. Together, these elements develop a persona for the ruler as lightning deity.

On Stela J the meanings of the God K scepter are expanded through its display with other emblems. One of these key elements, a shield emblazoned with an image of the Jaguar War God, is held in the left hand, opposite the scepter. Although badly eroded, diagnostics of this deity—the "cruller" under the eyes and shell beard—are still visible. The significance of the shield as a war implement is clear, as is the jaguar emblem, which evokes the powers of a great nocturnal hunting animal.[16] Further, as a possible symbol of the moon during the dry season (Milbrath 1999: 124–126), this deity may reflect the season when men typically went to war.[17] The round shape of the shield also may suggest this astronomical identification.

In addition to these two hand-held emblems, however, the king also wears a distinctive pectoral, consisting of a central medallion with infixed deity head, flanked by arcing panels from which emerge a tab and volutes. The form of the pectoral is related to the glyph reading *sak* "white," suggesting a designation of this emblem as the "*sak*-pectoral" (Fig. 3.32).[18] All elements are rendered as mosaic, with individually cut pieces (possibly shell or stone) attached to a backing. This type of object may be worn either as a belt or as a pectoral by the rain and lightning deity Chaak, as depicted on pottery and monumental art such as Quirigua Altar O′ (Fig. 3.32b). Rulers wearing regalia of Chaak also may wear the pectoral, as on La Pasadita Lintel 2, Yaxchilan Stela 11, the Dumbarton Oaks panel from Palenque (Fig. 3.32c), and several stelae from Naranjo (6, 7, 12, 13, 20, 28).

3.31. QRG Stela J, west face. Drawing by author.

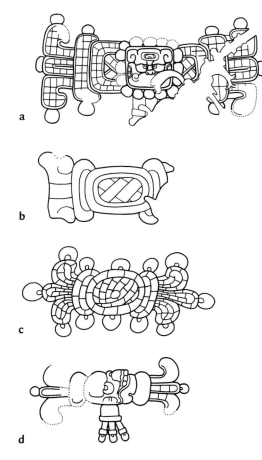

3.32. *Sak*-pectorals: *a*, QRG Stela F north, detail; *b*, QRG Altar O′, detail; *c*, Dumbarton Oaks panel, detail; *d*, Naranjo Stela 7, detail. Drawings by author.

One example of the *sak*-pectoral from Naranjo is particularly interesting, as it features a skull in place of the central disk, oriented sideways (Fig. 3.32d). This detail suggests an iconographic merging of the *sak*-pectoral with another common type of pectoral, which I refer to as the "bar pectoral."[19] This type of pectoral usually has bell-shaped ends, out of which emerge three bell-and-bead elements. On some monuments, the bar and *sak*-pectorals are worn together, as on Dos Pilas Stela 15 and Tikal Stela 16. A survey of Maya iconography suggests that, when accompanied by the Jaguar War God shield and God K scepter, the *sak*-pectoral or bar pectoral is closely associated with period-ending ceremonies.[20]

But what can be concluded about its specific symbolic reference? In Maya iconography, both *sak* glyphs and bell-and-bead elements such as those attached to the bar pectoral are part of a complex of floral imagery (Stuart 1992a). Positioned horizontally at the chest level of the ruler, the *sak*-pectoral suggests an identification with the

flowering branches of a cosmic tree. While this association is vaguely suggestive of fertility, it is not very conclusive. A better clue comes from the identities of the medallion infixes. In some examples from Quirigua, the infixed emblem is the Jester God, a deity that not only personifies the royal headband of kingship but also has aquatic traits (Fig. 3.32a).[21] For example, several examples of Jester Gods have features typical of the "Xok," a supernatural shark, such as barbels or fins on the cheek and triangular shark teeth (Fig. 3.33). A principal role of this creature in Maya mythology was as the vehicle for the rebirth of maize; in fact, the maize deity commonly wears a Xok headdress or belt to commemorate the event (Fig. 3.34).

The aquatic characteristics of the Jester God seem to justify the association of the pectoral with the rain deity Chaak. But in addition these iconographic elements underscore the association of the pectoral with the rebirth of maize. The floral qualities of the pectoral also suggest this attribution, as the resurrecting maize spirit is shown bedecked with floral regalia. Further, some variants of the pectoral have infixes of small human faces with stepped haircuts that may represent the personification of maize. The skull which sometimes appears on these pectorals may likewise refer to the resurrection of maize. In Maya thought, corn kernels are conceptualized as tiny skulls which, even though dry and hard, contain the powers of life. The same concept is realized in the ceremony of accession, in which the Jester God headband is presented to the king. As discussed by Karl Taube (1994), this ceremony involved the ritual death of the ruler through a surrogate human sacrifice, followed by

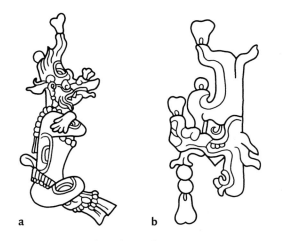

3.33. Jester Gods with Xok features: *a*, Palenque Temple of the Foliated Cross, main panel, detail; *b*, Palenque Tablet of the Slaves, detail. Drawings by author.

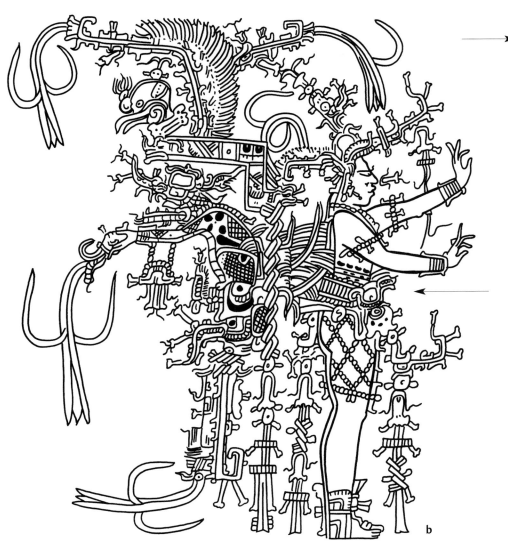

3.34. Maize deities with Xok attributes: *a*, QRG Stela J, A11; *b*, Classic Holmul-style vessel (MS1416), detail. Drawings by author.

his mystical rebirth, likened to the resurrection of the maize plant. The *sak*-pectoral is a key symbol of this new status, embodying the powers needed to enter the bloody, watery realm of the underworld and emerge triumphant, a manifestation of life and sustenance.

As noted above, the triad of shield, scepter, and pectoral is closely associated with period-ending ceremonies of the Classic period. Further, they were likely displayed in remembrance of the three stones of Creation which established the basis for the ceremony. Supporting this conclusion is the close correspondence between the identities of the three stones and the domains signified by the triad of regalia. The first stone of Creation, a jaguar platform/throne stone, corresponds to the Jaguar War God shield, while the second (snake) platform/

throne matches the snake-footed God K scepter. The identity of the third stone as a "water platform/throne" is consistent with the aquatic associations of the storm deity Chaak and with the theme of the rebirth of maize from the underworld. The triad of emblems also commemorates three principal ritual domains of the ruler—warfare, communication with ancestors through bloodletting, and mystical death/rebirth—symbolized by the three stones of Maya Creation mythology. The God K/Jaguar War God shield/pectoral complex of imagery appears on QRG Stela J in order to forge an analogy between the period ending and cosmic renewal.

Many of the other costume elements worn by the ruler on Stela J refer to cosmological concepts commonly attributed to Late Classic rulers. The elements that identify him with a cosmic tree include the "God-C" apron, ear-flares, and a tall headdress consisting of three stacked personification heads topped by the Principal Bird Deity. This sacred bird is frequently shown perched atop trees in supernatural contexts. The heavy belt with shell tinklers may symbolize the earthly realm pierced by the cosmic axis. The ruler's large jade or shell mosaic collar with frontal and shoulder medallions, knee bands with medallions, skirt, and headdress flanges with interlaces and serpent heads are all familiar from Stela H and are found frequently in Late Classic royal costume.

At the top and bottom of the royal image, however, appear icons which are not common on Maya stelae and which refer to victory over Copan through a supernatural metaphor. The basal register upon which the figure stands consists of a head, probably that of a personified waterlily, held between open profile centipede jaws (Fig. 3.31). These jaws are skeletal and have the long "snaggle teeth" that identify them with the portal to the underworld, elsewhere known as the "Black Hole."[22] The jaws wrap around to the north and south sides of the stela and are connected by scrolls to heads which have glyphic elements for "lake" in the forehead (Fig. 3.35). On the east side of Stela J (Fig. 3.36), this basal register continues as a panel that represents the surface of the underworld using a structure formed by parallel horizontal dotted layers separated by dotted diagonal bars. Inside the frame formed by these bars is a large *le* glyph, which is also commonly found in images of the surface of the underworld and which stresses the powers of fertility inherent in these waters. In Yukatek, *lel* is a word for "semen" (Barrera Vásquez 1980: 445). As discussed previously, the combination of elements appearing on the basal register of Stela J identifies the plaza where the stela stands as a replica of the "Black Hole, Black Lake" supernatural location where the sacrifice of Waxaklajun Ub'ah K'awil took place.

The headdress also contains prominent martial imagery, displayed on the north and south faces (Figs. 3.37, 3.38). Emerging from behind the serpent wings of the Principal Bird Deity and a stepped skyband device portrayed on the west face are huge skeletal centipede maws out of which issue serrated flint blades. On the north side are preserved three knots at the base of the centipede head, indicating that these blades are the termini of staffs. The same type of staff is shown in varied configurations in Maya art (Fig. 3.39). On Copan Stela A they emerge from the serpent bar and descend adjacent to Waxaklajun Ub'ah K'awil's legs (Fig. 3.40). They also appear in headdresses on several monuments, including

3.35. QRG Stela J, north, detail of basal register. Photo by Thomas Tolles.

3.36. QRG Stela J, east basal register. Drawing by author.

Tonina Monument 3 and Naranjo Stela 8. A variant of the skeletal centipede/flint combination appears as a frontal badge of the headdress worn as part of the Tlaloc-Venus war costume, for example, on Piedras Negras Stela 35 (Stone 1989). On the Naranjo example a stepped skyband similar to that on Quirigua Stela J appears in the headdress, suggesting that the skyband and centipede/flint staff may form an iconographic unit. The emergence of the flint from the portal to the spirit world represented by the centipede implies the supernatural origins of war, a theme strongly underscored by the shields and trapezoidal banners that dangle from the centipede chins. On Stela J the shields have three dots, a pattern also seen on the shields at Copan and on those held by warrior figures on painted ceramic vessels (Fig. 3.41). The trapezoidal

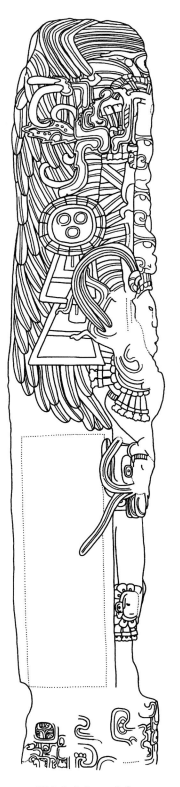

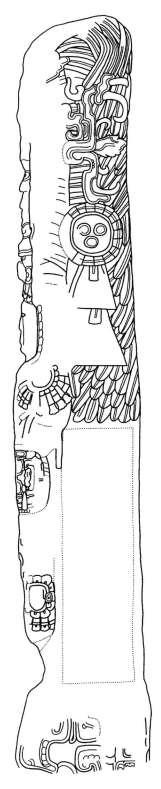

3.37. QRG Stela J, north face, text removed. Drawing by author.

3.38. QRG Stela J, south face, text removed. Drawing by author.

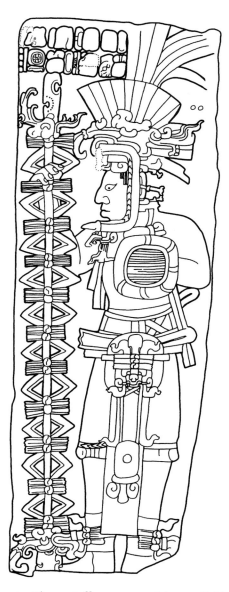

3.39. Zigzag staff as a ceremonial spear, Reitberg Stela. Drawing by author.

3.40. Zigzag staff with shield adjacent to ruler's leg, CPN Stela A, detail. Drawing by author and Linda Schele.

3.41. Warrior with dotted shield. Classic codex-style vessel (K1248), detail. Drawing by author.

banners are a part of Tlaloc-Venus warrior attire, for example, dangling from the kneebands of the Naranjo Stela 2 figure and the warriors from Copan Structure 10L-26 (Fash 2001: Fig. 91). Thus, while the basal register of Stela J commemorates a specific victory of K'ak' Tiliw, the ruler's headdress voices a challenge to the current enemies of Quirigua. The persona conveyed on Stela J, like that of Stela H, is pointedly martial.

The design of the text and image of Stela J in order to promote K'ak' Tiliw's status and announce the independence of Quirigua is echoed by transformations in the monument's style of carving. When compared to Stela H, it is clear that the execution of Stela J is more consistently focused on interpreting features characteristic of the Early Classic stelae of Quirigua. The sophisticated low-relief carving of Monument 26 (Figs. 1.12, 1.13), which raises individual forms away from the block almost entirely in parallel planes, frequently employing double outlines to emphasize individual shapes and linear continuity, is recalled throughout Stela J (Fig. 3.42). The relatively blocky qualities evident in Monument 26 are also apparent and indeed exaggerated in Stela J, in which the rounding of edges and slightly curving lines of Monument 26 give way to a stricter adherence to precise verticals and horizontals, even more than in Stela H. Compare, for example, the earflares of the early and late monuments, which in Monument 26 (Fig. 1.13) are relatively rounded, gently slipping from the grid and on Stela J (Fig. 3.42) are far more rectilinear, with only slight rounding of the corner lobes. The format of the rear text with its large ISIG may also have been inspired by the Early Classic local corpus. The ISIG of Stela U, for instance, is double sized, extending across both columns of text.

As on Monument 26 and Stela H as well, the face is a major compositional concern on Stela J; but in this case the emphasis is achieved through the breadth and simplicity of execution of the face relative to the surrounding ornament. In this respect, Stela J is closer in style to Monument 26 than to Stela H. Whereas the Stela H face protrudes abruptly toward the viewer, that of Stela J floats gently from the shadows. And yet Stela J does not totally escape the legacy of Copan. The frontally placed earflares and the graceful sweep of the feathers on the stela sides toward the front derive ultimately from Copan sculptures (Fig. 3.43; Proskouriakoff 1950: 131). The legs of the QRG Stela J figure also stand out from the ground and are even slightly undercut, recalling Copan models. Significantly, however, all of these features are apparent on QRG Stela H, suggesting again that they were residual, having been reinterpreted through their execution in local modes to become typical of the Late Classic monuments of Quirigua.

Further contributing to the distinctiveness of this sculptural style is the rendering of the hieroglyphs of Stela J. In harmony with the geometric qualities of the frontal figure, the glyphs conform to a strict grid and are broadened, thus straightening the edges of the individual signs (Fig. 3.44). Moreover, the simplicity and the flatness of the glyphs draw attention to the flat plane of the block, as do the parallel relief planes of the figure. Such treatment of glyphs is distinct from Copan glyphic styles, which are notable for the complexity of linear de-

3.42. QRG Stela J, west face. From Morley 1937–1938, vol. 5: Plate 178d, courtesy Carnegie Institution of Washington.

tail, curvilinear execution, and, during the reign of Waxaklajun Ub'ah K'awil, conception of glyphic blocks as plastic masses (Fig. 3.45). The tradition of broad, flat treatment of glyphs at Quirigua seems to have been begun on Stelae S and H but is only seen clearly for the first time on Stela J. As will be seen, this stylistic tendency becomes increasingly exaggerated during the reign of K'ak' Tiliw, culminating in the squared, platelike glyphs of Stelae E, C, and A. The only feature of the Stela J text that seems clearly to evoke Copan is the full-figure form of the *hab'* patron in the ISIG, which may have been inspired by the remarkable CPN Stela D of Waxaklajun Ub'ah K'awil. Full-figure glyphs also appear on earlier Copan monuments, such as Stela 19, and contemporary sculptures at Copan (as discussed below). The animated expressions and widely opened mouths of many of the glyphs on the Quirigua monument may also be related to

the appearance of the CPN Stela D glyphs. Nevertheless, when rendered according to local aesthetic rules of drawing and modeling, these features are transmuted into a distinctive new style.

Perhaps most salient of the non-Copanec features on Quirigua Stela J is an emphasis on the squared shape of the stone block. Prior to the reign of Waxaklajun Ub'ah K'awil, stela figures at Copan protruded little from the block. Beginning with CPN Stela C, however, they began to be increasingly undercut, suggesting a projecting figure and an irregular silhouette when viewed from the side. Carvings such as CPN Stela D are so plastically conceived as to seem akin to clay figures, fused to almost invisibly thin rectangular slabs (Fig. 3.46). Quirigua Stela H, despite its exaggerated wrap-around composition, retains something of this quality in the deep modeling of the head area. In contrast, the figure of QRG Stela J clings tightly to the massive block of the stela, with most of the forms arranged in a single plane (Fig. 3.47). The only deep carving occurs in the area around the face and headdress personification heads and adjacent to the legs, and yet the facial treatment is much shallower than that seen on QRG Stela H. Overall, the monument is treated as a squared shaft sheathed in delicate, overlapping shallow-relief forms. The plumes that wrap sharply around the sides of the stela, superimposed upon other continuous elements, only exaggerate the blockiness of the stone mass and the flatness of its faces (Fig. 3.48). As on Stela H, areas of ground are plainly visible, especially adjacent to the legs and on the monument sides. The emphases of both of these monuments on empty ground, four distinct faces, and flattened forms recall the Early Classic tradition and may have been interpreted as a means of forming an identity distinct from Copan, based on patently local models. The implementation of the basal register in Stela J also continues the Quirigua tradition established in the Early Classic period. Because it is absent at Copan, this compositional element points to the antiquity of the Quirigua tradition and continuity with the nearby QRG Stela H.

The attempt to redefine local Quirigua sculpture may have extended to the iconography of Stela J, as well. As Kubler (1969:14) noted, the God K scepter which appears on Stela J is seen nowhere at Copan (see also Stone 1983). Although it is possible that this iconographic complex was derived from Petexbatun sites such as Dos Pilas, we might be advised to use caution in interpreting the source of the imagery on Stela J. Given the precise copying of the iconography of the Early Classic Monument 26 in Stela H, it is possible that Stela J quotes some other

3.43. QRG Stela J, north face, detail of headdress. Photo by Thomas Tolles.

3.44. QRG Stela J, east text detail. Photo by Thomas Tolles.

as yet unknown antique local sculpture. Nevertheless, its presence on Stela J and repetition on K'ak' Tiliw's next three stelae argue for its interpretation as an iconographic complex that was identifiably non-Copanec and that could be used to develop a local identity.

To recapitulate, Stela J represents the first unified and confident expression of a local Late Classic sculptural style at Quirigua. Apparently, between 751 and 756, the workshop responsible for stela carving was radically overhauled, replaced by highly skilled artists who were overseen by a strong master sculptor. But where did this master originate? Although work on the acropolis at the time involved some sculpture, there are no known buildings that approach the refined control exhibited on Stela J. At present, archaeological evidence does not support the identification of this master with another site. The style is utterly foreign to contemporary Copan; nor does southern Belize offer a likely candidate. Whoever the art-

3.45. CPN Stela A, detail of text. Photo by Thomas Tolles.

ists of Stela J were, their attention to detail and control of technique represent a refocusing of energy in monumental art at the site. From this point on, each stela is conceived as a challenge, as if the power of high-quality sculpture was suddenly recognized and as much energy as possible was invested in each new project.

These changes in sculpture at Quirigua may be interpreted in several ways. On the one hand, exquisite sculptures may have awed the people who visited the Great Plaza, suggesting the power and sophistication of its ruling elite. The reinterpretation and exaggeration of local Early Classic stylistic features on a colossal scale may also bespeak the role of this and subsequent stelae as memorials to the antiquity and independence of Quirigua. The texts of Stela J complement these stylistic suggestions through accounts of the period-ending rituals of K'ak' Tiliw that demonstrated his possession of the supernatural powers of a sovereign ruler. The texts also tout the crucial violent action of K'ak' Tiliw that formed the foundation of his power. Reinforcement for this message comes through the placement of the stela itself in the plaza, which was a memorial to the sacrifice of Waxaklajun Ub'ah K'awil, and through prominent symbols of warfare displayed in the figure's headdress. But in addition to these political considerations, it is important to

3.46. CPN Stela D, west face. Photo by author.

3.47. QRG Stela J, view of north and west faces. Photo by Jesse L. Nusbaum, courtesy of Museum of New Mexico, neg. no. 60958.

3.48. QRG Stela J, north face, detail of glyph panel. Photo by Thomas Tolles.

recognize that the sweat and toil of hauling, erecting, and carving these great sculptures surely was conceived as a pious offering to the gods and ancestors and a plea to obtain their blessing. For those responsible for their creation, as well as their patron, such actions were a form of both social currency and magical propitiation.

Copan's Response to the Quirigua Conflict: Structures 10L-22A and 10L-26

Even though there is no evidence that Copan suffered any ill economic effects from the capture of their ruler by Quirigua, the art programs of the two rulers to succeed Waxaklajun Ub'ah K'awil express profound concern with the ideological implications of the sacrifice of the local ruler and the fragmentation of the Copan hegemony (Fash 1983, 1986). Promptly after K'ak' Tiliw dispatched the thirteenth successor of the Copan dynasty, a new ruler assumed the throne at Copan on 9.15.6.16.5 (June 11, 738; Stuart and Schele 1986a). The approach to monumental art during the reign of this rival of K'ak' Tiliw,

K'ak' Joplaj Chan K'awil, was markedly different from that of his predecessor. Instead of amplifying the persona of the ruler as mythic hero, stress was placed on the political unity of the various lords subordinate to the high lord of Copan. A forum for this strategy was the building of Structure 10L-22A, which was probably dedicated on 9.15.15.0.0, the same date as Quirigua Stela S (Fig. 3.49a).[23] This structure has been identified as a Popol Nah or Sak Nikte'il Nah, a council house in which the various lords of the polity would meet for festivals and learn sacred dances. The adjacent Structure 10L-25 probably served as the platform on which the lords' dances were performed (Fash 1992).

Eight sculpted toponymic glyphs adorned the cornice of Structure 10L-22A, above which were seated figures that may depict lineage heads from the locations named by the glyphs. Although it is clear that some of these toponyms correspond to supernatural locations, we have already seen that such names could be used to refer to the built environment, especially ceremonial centers. Further, one of the place name glyphs on Structure 10L-22A corresponds to glyphs found on three different buildings in Group 10L-2, a palace compound south of the Copan acropolis (Andrews n.d.; Andrews and Fash 1992). The roof comb of Structure 10L-22A featured a large figure seated on a jaguar-headed throne, presumably an image of K'ak' Joplaj. Thus, the sculptural program of the temple stresses the subordination of minor lords to the divine lord but at the same time recognizes the increasing importance of these lesser elites in the political structure of the polity, especially through their associations with sacred locations.

At first glance, Structure 10L-22A seems to ignore the recent conflict with Quirigua. The building of the temple itself may have been compelled by the capture and sacrifice of the previous ruler, however, as a means to garner support from the nobles at a time when confidence in the ruling lineage may have been shaken. Certainly, the program is a dramatic departure from the emphasis on royal portraiture in the monuments of Waxaklajun Ub'ah K'awil. But in addition Structure 10L-22A may even include a reference to Quirigua among the cornice toponyms. On the northeast corner of the building was found the "Black Lake" place (Fig. 3.49b), the location so prominently cited at Quirigua. The toponym appears on the base of Quirigua Stela J and the inscription of Stela H and is also featured in a large round cartouche associated with one of the temples from the Quirigua acropolis, now located in the sculpture stacks near the site warehouse. The prominence of the location at Quirigua sug-

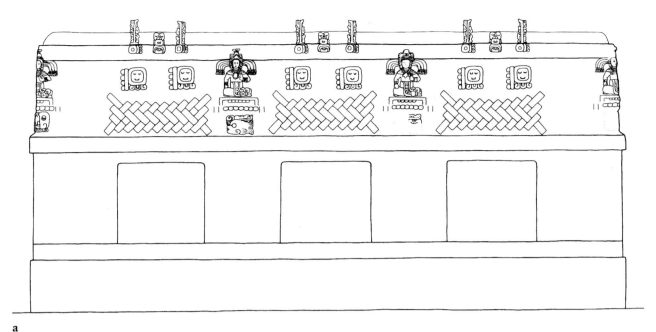

a

3.49. CPN Structure 10L-22A: *a*, elevation; *b*, "Black Lake place" toponym. Drawings by Barbara Fash, courtesy Instituto Hondureño de Antropología e Historia.

b

gests that the toponym may have been included on Structure 10L-22A as an oblique reference to the continued inclusion of Quirigua as a part of the Copan polity. If Quirigua is indeed the referent of the Structure 10L-22A glyph, it would have been a very subtle and clever political statement, one which denied the defeat of Waxaklajun Ub'ah K'awil as justification for Quirigua's independence.

Although K'ak' Joplaj's Structure 10L-22A may have partially inspired the subsequent pronouncements of political autonomy in Quirigua Stela H and J, it seems much more likely that K'ak' Tiliw's early stelae were more directly engaged in an aggressive dialogue with the art of the next Copan ruler, K'ak' Yipyaj Chan K'awil ("Smoke Shell"), who acceded on 9.15.17.13.10 (February 18, 749). While he may have commissioned several buildings, including Structures 10L-20 and 21, K'ak' Yipyaj's first major project was the completion of the final phase of Structure 10L-26, which included the upper section of the immense Hieroglyphic Stairway and its crowning temple (Fig. 3.50). The stair was dedicated on 9.16.4.1.0 (May 8, 755), about a year before K'ak' Tiliw set up Stela J. The temple was completed on the *hotun* ending 9.16.5.0.0 (April 12, 756; Stuart and Schele 1986a). As discussed in the previous chapter, this project had been initiated by Waxaklajun Ub'ah K'awil, who completed the lower por-

tion of the stairway in 710 (Stuart n.d.b). Rather than destroy or cover over this monument, it was decided to resume construction using the same iconography, adding the upper section of the stair and supplementing its remarkable display of images deriving from the art of Teotihuacan.[24]

At Copan the significance of Teotihuacan imagery is extremely complex and rich. Like most other Maya sites, its principal reference is the ceremonial complex of Tlaloc-Venus warfare. Indeed, the center axis of the Hieroglyphic Stairway is marked with seated warriors, presumably representing the former rulers of Copan, shown reborn from the spirit world out of snake maws. In addition, however, the proliferation of Teotihuacan iconography on Structure 10L-26 was closely associated with the founder of the dynasty, K'inich Yax K'uk' Mo', as demonstrated by the imagery of Structure 10L-16, Altar Q, and a ceramic figurine found in the Chorcha tomb within 10L-26 itself (see Fash 1992; Freidel, Schele, and Parker 1993: 309). In the context of 10L-26, Teotihuacan imagery commemorated the warlike prowess of the dynasty that originated from the founder's control of powerful

3.50. CPN Structure 10L-26 and Hieroglyphic Stairway, reconstruction. From Proskouriakoff 1946: 37, courtesy Carnegie Institution of Washington.

spirit beings from the venerable distant metropolis (Stuart 2000, n.d.b).

The temple superstructure, also dedicated by K'ak' Yipyaj, was richly adorned with mosaic sculptures representing the goggle-eyed butterfly derived ultimately from Teotihuacan warrior imagery (see Berlo 1984). The roof comb featured six seated warrior images in addition to other motifs related to the iconography of Tlaloc-Venus warfare (see Fash 1992: Figs. 15, 16; Schele and Miller 1986). Inside the temple, perhaps along the back wall, were three panels of text as well as a long horizontal glyphic band that decorated the vault spring (Fig. 3.51). In some ways, this "Temple Inscription" is even more remarkable than the text of the stairway, as its full-figure glyphs are composed in two parallel "fonts," one conventional Maya and the other with Teotihuacan iconography (Stuart 2000, n.d.b). The context of these inscriptions, located in a chamber at the apex of the most important dynastic shrine at Copan, suggests that the mortal audience for these texts was highly restricted. Rather, the text (and probably the entire Structure 10L-26 art program) was designed to be read by spirits, including the very ancestors it commemorated, who by virtue of their diverse origins were pleased to read inscriptions in both Maya and Teotihuacan styles. It is essential to recognize that the Structure 10L-26 program did not ignore the impact of Waxaklajun Ub'ah K'awil on the site's history. On the contrary, not only did the stairway feature a prominent portrait of the thirteenth ruler dressed as a warrior, but K'ak' Yipyaj's additions include extensive historical accounts of his reign as well as the record of his death in war, attributed to supernatural causes. Thus, in its final form, 10L-26 may be interpreted as a memorial to a hero. There is certainly no indication that the defeat was seen as "humiliating" to Copan, as has often been suggested. From the point of view presented by Structure 10L-26, Waxaklajun Ub'ah K'awil died gloriously, defending his people, and thus merited a place in the local ancestral pantheon.

Seen in the context of the Copan Hieroglyphic Stairway, the imagery of Quirigua Stela J—in particular the prominent display of the banners on the north and south sides of the monument—gains new meaning. As these banners are part of the same iconographic complex of warfare that appears on CPN Structure 10L-26, their display on the Quirigua monument dedicated shortly after K'ak' Yipyaj's Hieroglyphic Stairway suggests a specific response to the Copan ruler's program. The banners may have been interpreted as a reference to the derivation of the Quirigua dynasty from the same figure as that of Copan, the paramount Tlaloc-warrior of the Southeast, K'inich Yax K'uk' Mo'.

An additional aspect of Stela J suggests that the Quirigua design was a direct response to the Hieroglyphic Stairway. The decidedly elaborate and historical nature of the inscription is of particular interest, as such an account is totally unprecedented in earlier monuments of K'ak' Tiliw. This was probably inspired by the Structure 10L-26 program at Copan, which, for the first time, features personalized historical accounts of an almost encyclopedic scope. The stairway was, in fact, dedicated prior to QRG Stela J, suggesting that the Quirigua designers had ample time to ponder the latest art produced at Copan. The impact of the Hieroglyphic Stairway may have affected the text even to the level of content, as the reference to the decapitation of Waxaklajun Ub'ah K'awil on Stela J is the first of its kind at Quirigua. As we have seen, the death of the thirteenth ruler was a featured event on

3.51. Temple inscription from CPN Structure 10L-26. Photo by author.

the stairway. Indeed, one wonders whether the notion of developing the rain deity as a persona of K'ak' Tiliw at Quirigua was a direct reaction to the inclusion of the passage relating to the birth of Yax Ha'al Chaak in the stairway text (Fig. 3.3).

Additional passages from the Hieroglyphic Stairway may also have been intended for a Quirigua audience. On Step 62 is recorded the taking of God K by a lord bearing the Quirigua emblem glyph (Fig. 3.52). Unfortunately, the name of this lord does not correspond precisely to any other known ruler; nor is the context of this phrase known. The name of this person is similar to that of the first ruler of Quirigua, Tok Casper, as inscribed on Zoomorph P. Although some details of these names/titles differ, the appearance of this text on the Hieroglyphic Stairway may have been a way of reaffirming the integrity of Copan's political sphere or, at least, of glorifying its past unity. Without the context of this passage, its full political significance remains elusive.

If Structure 10L-26 celebrates the Copan dynasty as a whole, K'ak' Yipyaj's Stela M seems to point to one ruler in particular (Baudez 1994: Fig. 30). The stela and its small altar, dedicated on the same date as the temple of Structure 10L-26 and Quirigua Stela J, were set up at the base of the Hieroglyphic Stairway by K'ak' Yipyaj, as a finishing touch to the great war monument (Fig. 3.50; Baudez and Riese 1990, vol. 2: 134; Morley 1920: 279). Like Quirigua Stela J, the monument had a single figure on the obverse and an inscribed reverse, but its style is utterly different from that of its Quirigua counterpart. In its heavy undercutting, vision rite theme, and scale, Copan Stela M is strongly reminiscent of the sculptures of Waxaklajun Ub'ah K'awil, such as Stelae 4 and F. Even its glyphic style recalls the sculpture of the thirteenth successor. For instance, the Ajaw face in the day-sign cartouche at B2b has the same U-shaped eyes and mouth that appear on several of Waxaklajun Ub'ah K'awil's later monuments, such as CPN Stela 4, Stela H, and Altar S.

Stela M also replicated the glyphic format of its antecedent by one k'atun, Stela D, which opened with an ISIG that occupied a single glyph block. Indeed, because Stela D was dedicated only twenty years before Stela M, it is possible that the same master who oversaw the design of Waxaklajun Ub'ah K'awil's last stela was still alive to direct the execution of Stela M. The altar of Stela M, which took the form of a Cosmic Monster, also recalls the sculpture of Waxaklajun Ub'ah K'awil in its rounded, expanding masses. The retrospective qualities evident in these two monuments of K'ak' Yipyaj yet again suggest an emphasis on the continuity of the dynastic tradition of Copan and of the sculptural styles that developed in association with one of the greatest art patrons in the city's history, Waxaklajun Ub'ah K'awil.

Although it is badly damaged, enough of the iconography of CPN Stela M is visible to discern its general themes. Like many of Waxaklajun Ub'ah K'awil's stelae, the main figure holds a double-headed serpent bar, which emits God K figures wrapping onto the sides of the shaft. Seven miniature figures, representing the spirits conjured through the vision rite, originally appeared atop and to the sides of the headdress and adjacent to the legs. The frame for the inscription on the reverse (east) probably represents a backrack, of which only beaded feathers are visible, as seen earlier on CPN Stela 4. The feathers also are visible wrapped onto the monument sides. The headdress of the ruler is especially interesting from the standpoint of Quirigua iconography. It represents a zoomorphic head with long spotted ears, similar to QRG Altar M. Although this being has been taken for a crocodile, the split upper lip and nonspiral eyes are more reminiscent of feline representations (Baudez 1994: 74). From behind bivalve shells located to the sides of this head, spears emerge; the struts of one are just visible on the right-hand side. These images are wrapped onto the monument's sides, where they terminate in open centipede maws emitting personified flints. This

receives God K?   Tok Casper?   divine Quirigua *ajaw*

3.52. CPN Hieroglyphic Stairway, Step 62, detail. Drawing by author based on Maudslay 1889–1902, vol. 1: 32.

imagery is identical to that appearing on contemporary Quirigua Stela J. This parallelism suggests that both monuments promote a martial agenda through the use of exactly the same ceremonial complex. In the case of Stela M, the headdress spears also connect the monument thematically to the Hieroglyphic Stairway, in front of which it stands.

Yet another direct iconographic parallel exists between CPN Stela M and QRG Stela J. Appearing on the sides of the Copan monument, behind the ruler's legs, are large skeletal jaws, a visual metaphor for the portal into the world of the spirits and the dead. As we have seen, the same icon appears in the basal register of Quirigua Stela J; but in this case the jaws are composed in a basal register, visible on the west face beneath K'ak' Tiliw's feet (Fig. 3.11b). This image may be interpreted in more than one way. Like the Quirigua jaws, the image may commemorate the appearance of the night sky on the monument's dedication date, in which the Milky Way took the form interpreted as the "Black Hole." In addition, the jaws probably unite Stela M with the adjacent Hieroglyphic Stairway and its overall theme of ancestor communication. Indeed, the entire stairway is conceived as a vision image, in which the altar at the base takes the form of an inverted vision serpent head, out of which the ancestral images located at intervals on the stairway are conjured (see Freidel, Schele, and Parker 1993: 369–372). The stairway balustrades define the edges of the serpent's mouth, with large curls representing its fangs. The appearance of the maw on Stela M, then, may be read as a reference to the position of the ruler in the spirit world.

In conclusion, the 9.16.5.0.0 period ending prompted commemorative art programs that were remarkably similar in theme at both Quirigua and Copan. Both sites focused on militarism and attempted to capitalize on the defeat of Waxaklajun Ub'ah K'awil. Copan Stela M and Quirigua Stela J even feature some identical iconography. Nevertheless, the particular uses of imagery were different. At Quirigua martial personae functioned in concert with texts and siting to recall the decapitation of Waxaklajun Ub'ah K'awil and the advantages this event was considered to have brought to Quirigua. At Copan militarism is presented in the context of ancestor veneration, in which control of powerful war gods is traced genealogically to the founder of the local Classic dynasty. In this account the audience, including the deceased Waxaklajun Ub'ah K'awil, is asked to witness the heroism of the divine lords of Copan and approve of the current ruler, who sought to honor them in such a manner. We

shall see that the contrasting role of ancestors in the histories authorized by rulers of Copan and Quirigua is a difference between the two sites that persisted until the end of K'ak' Tiliw's reign.

The Late Architecture of K'ak' Tiliw

The architectural embellishments of the Quirigua acropolis undertaken following the defeat of Waxaklajun Ub'ah K'awil echo the martial themes of Stela H and J, in that they focused on enhancing the defensibility of the complex. The predominant masonry style of this period consisted of well-carved flat-faced blocks, predominantly sandstone, the same material employed by K'ak' Tiliw for his stelae. Even though the material differs from the rhyolite preferred during the early reign of K'ak' Tiliw, the flat-faced carving style continued earlier traditions. Following the sacrifice of the Copan ruler, work at the Quirigua acropolis focused on restricting access to the western side of the court, through the construction of the massive, steep-sided Western Platform, which buried the Sub.4 ballcourt. A new ballcourt (Structure 1B-7), now visible in the ruins of Quirigua, replaced the buried structure (Sharer 1990: 78; see also Strömsvik 1952: 203–204).

Atop the Western Platform was a freestanding wall, Structure 1B-Sub.1 or the "K'inich Ahau Wall," which measured over 23 m long and 1.5 m thick and was centered over the stairway which led to the acropolis court (Coe and Sharer 1979: 18; Sharer et al. 1979: 50–51). The western face of this wall, which overlooked the river, bore a series of five mixed sandstone and rhyolite mosaic masks, which alternated between serpents with human arms and solar deities. A frieze consisting of two concentric ovals flanked by large profile serpent heads supported these masks. Although it is extremely difficult to date this sculpture precisely, given that it represents the unique known example of figural architectural sculpture in stone from this period, stratigraphy suggests that it may be have been completed around A.D. 750. This is consistent with certain stylistic details of the wall, such as the rendering of the feathers with a simple incised midrib, which is similar to Stela H (dated to A.D. 751). Beginning in 756 with Stela J, feathers at Quirigua are carved with parallel incisions to represent the hollow shaft. Interpreting the symbolic and programmatic significance of the wall is also difficult given its uniqueness, although it may have served as a symbolic marker for the ritual area in front of the platform or for the platform itself. The image of solar deities emerging from watermarked bands may relate to the meteorological themes promoted by the monuments.[25]

Additional development of the western side of the acropolis followed the construction of 1B-Sub.1, with the construction of Structure 1B-4 on its northern end. This project coincided with the enlargement of the northern platform of the acropolis, beginning with Structure 1B-5-2nd. Just to the west of this structure, 1B-Sub.2-2nd and Sub.3-2nd were buried and replaced by Structures 1B-Sub.2 and 1B-Sub.3, which had north-facing doorways as did their predecessors. Although situated on a slightly lower level than 1B-5-2nd, Structure 1B-Sub.3 was connected by a wall to the earlier edifice, further restricting access to the acropolis from this side.

At the same time that access to the Quirigua acropolis was becoming increasingly restricted, sites at crucial entrance points to the Motagua valley adjacent to Quirigua were elaborated. During the eighth century, construction was carried out at Loci 002, 011, 089, and 092 and probably also at 023/024, 057, and 059 (Fig. 1.1; Ashmore 1984: 380; Schortman 1993: 214–215). At greater distances from the site core, numerous sites in the lower Motagua valley saw major construction at this time. Nearly all of these valley centers date between 740 and 850 and were probably not politically subordinate to Quirigua. Their growth attests to a regional prosperity during much of the eighth and early ninth centuries. Usually, construction at the site-periphery loci employed the flat-faced sandstone facing typical of acropolis construction. Several of these sites seem to have functioned as "traffic control stations," including Loci 011 and 057, which were located at the points at which the Quirigua River and the Jubuco River entered the Motagua valley, and Locus 002, which was situated on a promontory overlooking the entire upper valley. Locus 092 might also be placed in this category, as it was situated at a point where the Jubuco and Morjá Rivers bent toward each other, near their confluences with the Motagua.

Intriguingly, Locus 057 was located on one of the most probable routes to Copan, suggesting that the site at this time may have been a lookout station for enemy troops coming from Copan or its allied towns, presumably in Honduras. Such an interpretation is consistent with the consideration of contemporary acropolis construction as defensive in nature and with the celebration of Quirigua's military power through the Great Plaza and Stelae H and J. In addition, these outlying sites may have been way stations designed to mediate diplomatic relationships between Quirigua and small Honduran centers. As we will see in the next chapter, K'ak' Tiliw succeeded in 762 in allying himself with one of the former enemies of Copan that may have been located in this region.

Conclusion

During the twenty years following the defeat of Waxaklajun Ub'ah K'awil, not only was the military prowess of Quirigua celebrated, but the site core of Quirigua and outlying centers were readied for additional military action. By 756, the year in which Stela J was dedicated, Quirigua was being transformed from a scattering of small settlements into an independent polity with controlled access points at its periphery and a defensible citadel at the center. At the focal point of this activity was a newly planted group of stelae that celebrated both the history of the center and the power of its vigorous ruler. These increasingly tall and sophisticated monuments (Stelae S, H, and J) were set up in a huge new plaza space that symbolically recreated a sacred location associated with the rain deity where K'ak' Tiliw claimed to have sacrificed his former overlord. As such, the portrait images became vehicles for promoting the persona of the ruler as an aspect of this divine entity, which was also conveyed by his royal name. The texts and imagery of the monuments served to affirm this victory as well as to promise the continuing protection of Quirigua and the fertility of the land through the patronage of the ruler possessed by the power of lightning and rain. As colossal sculpted monuments, these stones were also evidence of Quirigua's newfound wealth. The message was not ambiguous: sacred warfare promises prosperity and fertility.

Each monument in the series is distinctive, not only representing changes within the sculpture workshops but also suggesting an intense dialogue with Copan through iconography, form, and siting. Quirigua Stela H in particular seems to reinterpret specific features of previous Copan monuments, such as the interlaced glyphic frame of CPN Stela J and its location at an equivalent position in the overall site plan. Quirigua Stela J seems to address more contemporary developments and can be seen as a response particularly to CPN Stela M and the Hieroglyphic Stairway. As such, the early stelae of K'ak' Tiliw are symptomatic of the rapidly evolving political stance at Quirigua. The precise manner in which imagery is adapted from one monument into another is also highly suggestive of the notion that Maya monumental images functioned as active surrogates for royal authority, which exercised considerable sway over political events. From this perspective, the recurrence of formal features among several monuments could be interpreted as a map of the political landscape, embodied in human form.

Deeply ingrained in this aesthetic discourse, however, is an attempt to ground the revival of Quirigua in local traditions. Stela H in particular suggests a revitalization of the polity through compositional and iconographic references to Monument 26, dedicated more than two and one-half centuries previously by the fourth Quirigua ruler. Additionally, this monument was set up next to Structure 1A-11, a replica of the ancient Structure 3C-14, which served as the original context of Monument 26. In fact, the plaza associated with Structure 3C-14 was used as a place of ritual after its destruction (Ashmore n.d.). This activity was apparently condoned by the court, so that the site was left unmodified, to serve as a place of public gathering for commemorative ceremonies. Because the Early Classic may have been seen as a time in which Quirigua was a growing and possibly even an independent center, as implied by the inscription of Stela C, the comparison between these two monumental groups may have suggested the dawning of a new age of prosperity and sovereignty during the reign of K'ak' Tiliw. While making no known reference to a specific antique monument, Stela J further enhanced K'ak' Tiliw's prestige through its meticulous execution and emphasis on a blocklike sculptural mass, legitimated by the great works of the past. In these features, it distinctly foreshadows the sculptural developments that were to follow in the newest performance space at Quirigua—Platform 1A-1.

4

DREAMS OF POWER

Stelae F, D, and E

OF CENTRAL IMPORTANCE in the promulgation of the divine personae of K'ak' Tiliw during the last twenty years of his sixty-year reign was a program of six colossal stone sculptures, including five stelae and one zoomorphic throne. Continuing the tradition of monument dedications every *hotun*, these monuments were arranged in a rectangular pattern, marking off twenty-five *tuns* of history and defining a grand ritual space. Conceived as a unified program, this group of monuments represents an elaborate manipulation of the central concepts of Classic Maya elite lore and serves as both a memorial and a political statement. Part of the significance of this statement derives from the adaptation of numerous iconographic and rhetorical concepts from earlier sculpture programs at Copan, particularly from those of Waxaklajun Ub'ah K'awil. Taken in the context of recent events, these similarities suggest an attempt to appropriate the traditions of Copan, thereby legitimating K'ak' Tiliw's political ascendancy. Because of the complexity of the program, however, only the first three stelae of Platform 1A-1 are discussed in this chapter.

As a setting for this program, the Great Plaza was enlarged northward through the construction of Platform 1A-1 (Fig. 4.1). This enormous platform (about 100 x 85 m) was built in two phases, the first supporting Stelae F and D with a later westward expansion to support Stelae E, C, and A and Zoomorph B. The platform was made primarily of river cobbles, filling in a natural depression and rising about 0.5 m above the level of the southern portion of the plaza, which displayed Stelae H and J.[1] Like the southern portion of the Great Plaza, the surface of Platform 1A-1 was paved with stone slabs and joined to the southern portions by a simple sloping cobble wall.

Like Stelae H and J, the northern stelae were surrounded by raised platforms with large rectangular stone perimeters (Fig. 4.2a). Instead of the simple intruded pit of Stela H, however, the northern monuments were set in their foundations upon stone slabs and braced with other large stones set against the shaft (Fig. 4.2b). Gaps in the north sides of these foundations suggest that the stelae were first placed with the upper shaft pointing to the south and then raised up toward the north, with the butt slipping into the socket.[2] In their original appearance, the elevated platforms of the stelae planted atop Platform 1A-1 enhanced the height of the monuments and created a perimeter that separated the viewer from the shaft by 4 to 6 m.

Platform 1A-1 also supported a large mound, Structure 1A-3, built on its northern edge in two phases, corresponding to each of the phases of the adjacent platform. The first phase of the structure measured 82.5 m from east to west, 20 m from south to north, and 7 m in height. An inset stairway extended along most (63 m) of the south face of Structure 1A-3. A later addition to 1A-3 was undertaken mostly on the northern side of the structure and was never finished. Formally, this structure served as the backdrop for the program of monuments placed in front of it, indicating that the program's "front" face was directed toward the south. Further, the raised mound suggested a new symbolic dimension for the Great Plaza, with designated celestial and underworld zones. The raising of Structure 1A-3 and Platform 1A-1 seems to have identified the northern reaches of the plaza with the sky, which complemented the aquatic, underworld associations of the southern part of the Great Plaza. The arrangement of these two spatial zones along

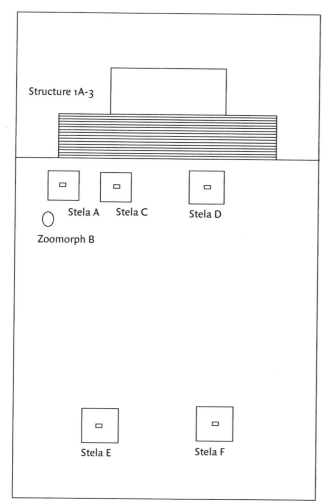

4.1. Platform 1A-1 plan. Drawing by author.

a north–south axis evokes a widespread Mesoamerican template for the creation of sacred landscape, in which a vertical axis connecting earth with sky and underworld is reoriented horizontally as a north–south axis (Ashmore 1989; Reilly 1994). While continuing the tradition of monument dedications in a plaza as seen at Copan, the Platform 1A-1 program represents a distinctive symbolic elaboration that connected Quirigua's performance areas into some of the most ancient concepts of architecture in Mesoamerica.

Stela F (Dedicated March 17, 761)

The first monument erected on Platform 1A-1 was Stela F, an immense (7.3 m) sandstone monolith carved with images of the king on the south and north sides and texts on the east and west faces (Figs. 4.3, I.5). A model for iconography, composition, programming, and textual formats that would follow, Stela F is of fundamental im-

portance to the 1A-1 program. Indeed, the monument is one of the great masterpieces of Quirigua, leading Morley (1937–1938, vol. 4: 130) to opine that "Quirigua had reached its sculptural apogee by the time this monument was erected, 9.16.10.0.0. The glyphs on the sides of Stela F [Fig. 4.4] are among the most beautiful in the Old Empire, indeed the writer feels that the *glyphs* on Stelae F and D at Quirigua are the finest in the Corpus Inscriptionum Mayarum." A slender shaft, tapering gently toward the top, Stela F dwarfs its predecessor, Stela J, and grandly proclaims the beginning of a new program of monuments. In fact, at the time it was dedicated, Stela F was the tallest monument yet erected by the Maya and was only surpassed ten years later by QRG Stela E.

Although both the east and west texts of Stela F begin with initial series statements, the two texts are not independent but rather represent a single continuous narrative (Figs. 4.5, 4.6). Like all of the monuments erected on

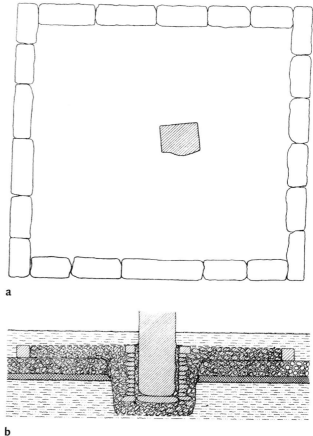

4.2. QRG stela foundations: *a,* Stela F platform, plan. From Strömsvik 1941: Fig. 8d; *b,* Stela E foundation, section. From Strömsvik 1941: Fig. 9f, courtesy Carnegie Institution of Washington.

4.3. QRG Stela F, south face. From Maudslay 1889–1902, *Archaeology*, vol. 2, Plate 34 (reversal corrected). From the facsimile edition of *Biologia Centrali-Americana* by Alfred Percival Maudslay. Published 1974 by Milpatron Publishing Corp., Stamford, Conn. Further reproduction prohibited.

4.4. QRG Stela F, east text detail. Photo by Thomas Tolles.

Platform 1A-1, the Stela F texts read from the east to the west, following the movement of the sun.³ This reading order is suggested by comparison of its texts with each other and with the predecessor, Stela J. In particular, the east text of Stela F begins with a statement of the current period ending, while the west text ends in the same time frame. This suggests that these points represent the beginning and end of the overall narrative, as otherwise they would be separated by a redundant initial series. In addition, as discussed in the preceding chapter, the Stela J text begins on the east face (reverse) with a description of the period-ending ritual then shifts time frame to the recent past on the sides and continues back to the present. If read from east to west, the text of Stela F follows a similar narrative pattern, beginning with the current period ending then shifting time frame to the past and continuing through historical time back to the present.

The east text begins with a Long Count date of 9.16.10. 0.0, 1 Ajaw 3 Sip (March 17, 761) followed by a full lunar series (Fig. 4.5). The dedication rites are the scattering of incense and the planting or erection of the stela by K'ak' Tiliw.[4] The clauses that follow are presented in a different time frame, however, associated with dates in the distant past that constitute a supernatural precedent for the current period ending. The shift backward in time frame is indicated by the affixation on the "completion" verb at

C14.[5] The scale of the shift, however, is truly astonishing, recorded as the passage of 0 alawtuns [20^6 tuns], completion of 19 x 20^7 tuns, ending on a Calendar Round of 1 Ajaw 13 Mol. Placing this date in the Long Count proves problematic, in that there is not enough information to firmly associate it with a particular period ending in the

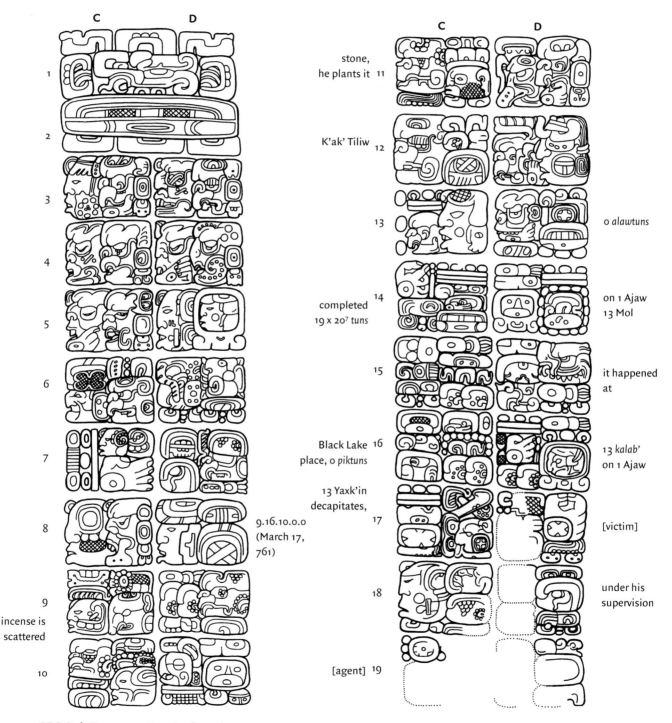

4.5. QRG Stela F, east text. Drawing by author.

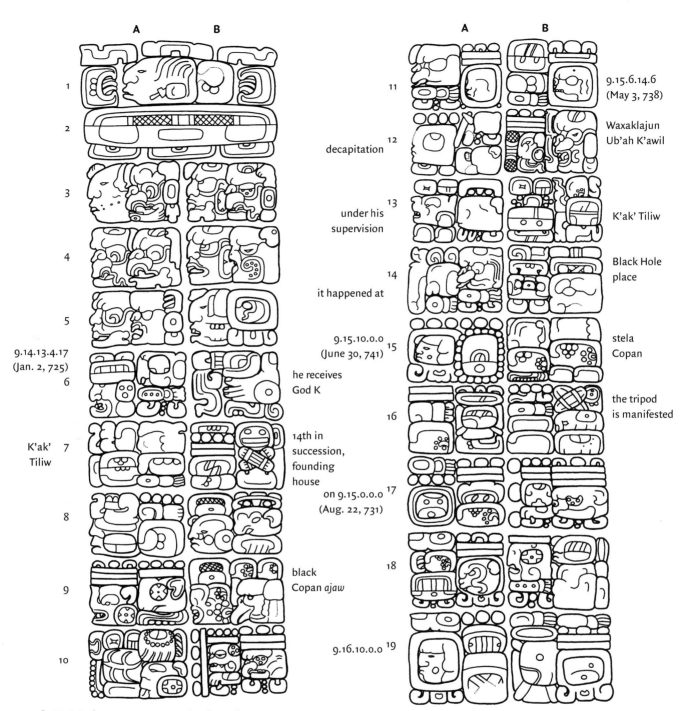

A B   A B

1   11   9.15.6.14.6
                                      (May 3, 738)

2   12
              decapitation   Waxaklajun
                                     Ub'ah K'awil
3   13
              under his
4   supervision   K'ak' Tiliw
                             14
                                    Black Hole
5   it happened at   place
                             15
9.14.13.4.17 9.15.10.0.0   stela
(Jan. 2, 725) (June 30, 741)   Copan
6   he receives   16
              God K   the tripod
                                    is manifested
K'ak' 7   14th in
Tiliw   succession,
              founding   17
8   house
              on 9.15.0.0.0
              (Aug. 22, 731)
              black   18
9   Copan ajaw

10   19   9.16.10.0.0

4.6. QRG Stela F, west text. Drawing by author.

past.[6] The completion of 19 x 20[7] *tuns* on 1 Ajaw 13 Mol occurs about every 24 trillion years. In essence, this unimaginably large cycle of time suggests that the event happened "ages ago," prior to the present Creation. The justification for the inclusion of this date is that it provides a mythological precedent for the period ending celebrated by K'ak' Tiliw on 9.16.10.0.0. The following passage further compares the period endings, giving one of the locations where the ancient period ending took place as the Black Lake place. This toponym is identical to the location where Stela F was planted, the Great Plaza, so named on Stelae H and J. The homology of toponyms casts the dedication of Stela F in a supernatural context.

The passage which terminates the east-face text of

Stela F gives a second mythic prototype for the 9.16.10.0.0 period ending. It begins with 0 piktuns (20³ tuns), 13 kalab'tuns? (20⁴ tuns?), followed by a Calendar Round date of 1 Ajaw 13 Yaxk'in. Like the previous supernatural period-ending records, it is not possible to place this Calendar Round in the Long Count, according to standard arithmetical rules. Nonetheless, the placement of this date on 1 Ajaw represents a manipulation of the calendar in order to compare the period ending and mythological dates. The event on this date is a decapitation, followed by what must be the name and titles of the unknown supernatural victim, followed by the agent.[7]

The text then continues on the west side of the stela, moving into a historical temporal frame (Fig. 4.6). In addition to being a summary of historical events, however, the west text of Stela F is composed in a narrative sequence that specifically enhances the ritual identity of K'ak' Tiliw as an incarnation of the lightning god, Chaak. The initial series is written in abbreviated form, without a lunar series: 9.14.13.4.17 12 Kab'an 5 K'ayab'. The event is the accession of K'ak' Tiliw, described as the receiving of a God K image, followed by K'ak' Tiliw's names and titles.[8] As on Stela J, the "fourteenth in succession of the founding house" title appears in this sequence, stressing the antiquity of the Quirigua dynasty and its ultimate origins at Copan. Further, K'ak' Tiliw is referred to as a "black Copan ajaw," thereby expressing his relationship to a greater polity. Like the text of Stela J, the text of Stela F proceeds to compare the accession to the decapitation of Waxaklajun Ub'ah K'awil. This, then, is the historical event for which the supernatural analogy was provided on the east face. An agency expression names K'ak' Tiliw as the supervisor of this ritual. As discussed in the previous chapter, the Black Hole location of decapitation follows. Next is a record of the 9.15.10.0.0 period ending, noted with only the nonverbal glyphs la-kamtun xukpi "huge stone [stela] Copan." Oddly enough, no stelae are known to have been erected at Quirigua or Copan for this period ending. Hence the complete significance of this passage is unclear.

The next event in the Stela F text is of key significance. The text records the previous period ending as a half-period of the k'atun noted at A17, 9.15.0.0.0 4 Ajaw 13 Yax. The event recorded for this k'atun ending is the "era event," a verbal phrase otherwise associated with the beginning of the current era, 13.0.0.0.0 4 Ajaw 8 Kumk'u (see Introduction and Fig. I.11). While its appearance on Stela F in a historical context is anomalous, it is worth noting that the date upon which the 9.15.0.0.0 period ending fell was August 22, 731, only nine days after the

solar day corresponding to 13.0.0.0.0 (August 13). The Stela F "era event" thus likens the k'atun ending to the primordial reordering of the cosmos. Moreover, the citation of this expression in the context of the 9.15.0.0.0 period ending highlights the identity of its tzolk'in position with that of 13.0.0.0.0 4 Ajaw 8 Kumk'u. This phrase also incorporates a term spelled k'o-b'a, which has been interpreted as k'oob' "hearth stones," based on a Yukatek word (Freidel and MacLeod 2000: 3). In Ch'orti', however, the cognate of this term, ch'uhp' or ch'uhb'(en), refers not only to the three stones of a hearth but also to the groupings of stones laid at either end of the house as a base for the ridge pole (Fought 1972: 336; see also Wisdom 1950: 708). Thus, the "era event" may refer to the foundation of the cosmic house in terms of various supporting tripods, not only the hearth. The stone tripod was likely seen by the Maya in the constellation of Orion, partially overlapping with the turtle seen in the belt stars (Fig. 4.7; Freidel, Schele, and Parker 1993: 79–83). In fact, Orion was visible near zenith before dawn on 9.15.0.0.0 (August 22, 731).

Taken in the context of the other events recorded on the west text of Stela F, the "era event" may also be interpreted as an important element of rituals of rainmaking (Looper 2003). This interpretation follows from a comparison of the Stela F narrative with contemporary Ch'orti' meteorological practices. As described by Girard (1966: 8–32) for Quetzaltepeque, the ceremonies commence on February 8, a date corresponding to cosmic Creation. The initial act is a pilgrimage to a sacred pool called El Orégano, located to the west of town. This pool is considered to be a portal to the underworld as well as a

4.7. Celestial turtle bearing a stone tripod, Madrid Codex, p. 71a. Drawing by author.

cosmic basin that feeds the clouds. At the pool a cloth is spread on the ground, and upon it are placed five gourds of chilate, a ceremonial drink made of maize and cacao. Arranged in a quincunx, these offerings constitute a "payment" to the gods (Fought 1972: 416), an enticement to the directional deities that are asked to withhold the wind and rain until the proper time. Upon return to Quetzaltepeque, the elders perform a ritual in the confraternity house in which malevolent winds are captured and sealed in jugs. Otherwise, these winds might escape from the underworld, causing disease and crop failure (see Fought 1972: 266–267). The jugs are placed under the altar, a table upon which the image of the local saint stands, together with containers of virgin water from Esquipulas and a "canoe" or wooden trough (see Wisdom 1940: 147). These objects are arranged in a quincunx, with the canoe in the center, the two vessels of water to the east, and the two jugs of "wind" to the west. A second quincunx, this time of river stones gathered previously at the El Orégano pool, is erected on top of the table, underneath the saint's seat. Finally, a feast is served on an adjacent table.

The purposes of the rites of early February are therefore to gather the sacred materials needed for subsequent rituals and to arrange them in the agricultural temple in preparation for the inaugural ceremonies for the rainy season, which include the planting of an inscribed cross at the sacred spring on April 22 and the turkey sacrifice on the zenith passage (discussed in the previous chapter). The correspondence between the Ch'orti' ritual sequence and that described on Quirigua Stela F is shown in Table 4.1. It is, of course, true that the events at Quirigua unfolded over a period of several years and that their sequence in the solar calendar is the reverse of that of the Ch'orti'. Nevertheless, the similarity in content of the ancient and modern narratives suggests that the ceremonies at Quirigua were based on meteorological models, like those of the Ch'orti', but performed as royal drama. The prominent place of meteorological rituals on the monuments of the Great Plaza, and particularly on Stela F, suggests the importance of the supernatural persona of Chaak to K'ak' Tiliw's political agendas in the years following the decapitation of Waxaklajun Ub'ah K'awil.

The final passage of the text of Stela F brings the narrative back to the current period ending. A distance number of 1.16.13.3 counts from the accession, 12 Kab'an 5 K'ayab', to 9.16.10.0.0 1 Ajaw 3 Sip. A half-period expression anchors this period ending to the next k'atun ending, 9.17.0.0.0, foreshadowing the pairing of the

monument with Stela E, which would be dedicated on 9.17.0.0.0 in the southwestern corner of the platform. To summarize the entire inscription, the east text of Stela F records the dedication of the monument, provides an ancient, supernatural background for the period ending, and gives an account of a mythical decapitation. The west text cites the accession of the king, connects it through a distance number to the decapitation of the Copan ruler, and then proceeds through historical period endings to the current celebration. The west text of Stela F presents the history of Quirigua as if it were a grand meteorological ceremony. This theme is prefigured by the content of the east-face inscription, which highlights a supernatural decapitation, a ritual action used by the Ch'orti' to control rain. While their specific content varies, we shall see that the narrative structure of Stela F serves as the basic pattern for the subsequent two stelae of K'ak' Tiliw, D and E, the figural images of which are also similar to Stela F.

Like all the other monuments of Platform 1A-1, Stela F features royal images that explicitly relate to and expand upon specific passages of its inscription. The texts and images of the six monuments are thus woven into patterns, binding them together into a unified program. In the case of Stela F, the passage elaborated is the Creation event cited in the context of the 9.15.0.0.0 period ending at B16b. As viewed from the dock-entrance to the plaza and the acropolis, the 1A-1 program has a clear front side, which faces south. Beginning the analysis on this side, the obverse of Stela F bears the image of the king in a standardized frontal pose, standing upon a basal register (Fig. 4.8). Reinforcing the main theme of the inscriptions, this register is carved in the image of Chaak, the deity of lightning and rain (Fig. 4.9). Diagnostic fea-

Table 4.1. Comparison of Ch'orti' Rainmaking Sequence and Events Recorded on Quirigua Stela F, West Text

Ch'orti'	Quirigua
"Creation"; setting stones in shrine (February 8)	"era event" (establishment of a stone tripod?) (August 22, 731) (Stela F, B16)
erection of inscribed cross (April 22)	"stela Copan" (June 30, 741) (Stela F, B15)
decapitation of turkey at underworld location (April 30–May 1)	decapitation of ruler at underworld location (May 3, 738) (Stela F, A12–B14)

4.8. QRG Stela F, south face figure, rolled out. Drawing by author.

4.9. QRG Stela F, south face basal register, rolled out. Drawing by author.

tures of this god are the shell earflares and its long, protruding nose. Emerging from the top of this zoomorphic head is a human (possibly an ancestor) wearing the attributes of royalty, including a mosaic collar, earflares, and a personified headdress. The hands of this figure emerge from above the shell earflares of Chaak.

The main portrait of K'ak' Tiliw shows him in the ritual role as an axis linking earth, sky, and underworld. His personified-waterlily sandals mark the aquatic underworld in which he stands, while the huge feathered headdress with personification heads places his head in the celestial realm. The heavy belt assemblage, associated with the ballgame and agriculture, suggests a symbolic earthly pivot between the realms. The main heads of the headdress are the same as those of Stela J, possibly personifications of the royal crown or "Jester Gods." Abundant jewelry in the form of knee ornaments, armbands, cuffs, collar and shoulder medallions, and earflares represents the flowers of the ceiba tree, as do the square-nosed serpent heads that border the loincloth and flank the T1017 ("God C-variant") head at the apex of the headdress. This T1017 head is also characteristic of the cosmic ceiba tree and appears repeatedly in the royal costume of Stela F south, on the shoulder medallions and loincloth. The loincloth is particularly significant, as its large size draws attention to the genital area of the ruler. The open mouth of the deity emits a complex of interlace designs, leaves, beads, earflares, and glyphs reading *sak* "white" and the T533 "Ajaw face." These elements are a metaphor for breath or life force, implying that life forces originate in the loins of the king. This symbol, which appears prominently in the stelae of Quirigua, identifies the ruler as a source of life through manifestation of male sexual potency. Similar combinations of interlaces, flowers, and serpent heads are common in headdresses at Quirigua (as on Stela F south), probably symbolizing the cosmic umbilicus drawn from the sky by the ruler.

Additional references to the ritual manifestation of vital forces by the king appear in the upper area of Stela F south. Here an image of a celestial bird or Principal Bird Deity perches at the top of the headdress, out of which descend bell-like forms linked in vertical strands. These bell-shaped elements are profile representations of the central element of earflare assemblages, which symbolize ceiba flowers in Maya iconography.[9] The king's hands grasp these strands of effigy flowers, which descend past his chest, to the bottom of his belt, where they terminate in snake heads, splayed outward. The lower jaw of each serpent is replaced by an assemblage composed of an irregular shape with two spots, from which are suspended a mat, two beads, and an earflare (out of which emerge three additional earflares), followed by textile strips. The same combination of elements emerging from double-headed serpent jaws appears in the central icon of the main panel of the Palenque Temple of the Cross (Fig. I.9b). This image has been interpreted as a representation of the Milky Way in its configuration as the "world tree," in which the snake represents the ecliptic running from east to west (Freidel, Schele, and Parker 1993: 78–79). Somewhat closer to home, the same combination is held in twin serpent mouths that flank the ruler's feet on the base of CPN Stela I (Fig. 4.10). The direct substitution of snake, bird, and king/cross in the Palenque

panel and QRG Stela F argues for the interpretation of the Quirigua snake as the ecliptic. Indeed, like the ecliptic, it is arranged on the stela stretched from east to west. The double-headed serpent ecliptic on the Palenque sarcophagus is composed of bell-shaped elements akin to those of QRG Stela F south.

The Principal Bird Deity appears in many ancient Maya images, marking a celestial zone and grasping a snake-like twisted cord in its beak, as on Caracol Stela 5 or Piedras Negras Stela 14 (Fig. 4.11; Taube 1994: 659–660). Such images are metaphorical representations of the conjuration or birth of supernaturals, in which the Principal Bird Deity focuses supernatural powers which are then transmitted into the world through the serpent. In this interpretation, the double-headed snake is the analog of both the birth rope which hangs from the center of the ceiling of a house (onto which a woman holds when giving birth) and the Yukatek *utáab'al 'e ka'an* "drawstring of the sky," a vine that is manipulated in rain ceremonies to guide prayers skyward magically.[10] Both ropes are symbolic umbilici, capable of channeling divine energies or blessings. The Yukatek cosmic rope is connected to a portal in the center of the sky, where the sun sits at zenith.

In Classic Maya images, the manifestation of cosmic umbilici is associated with the northern sky, as on a polychrome vessel from Motul de San José (Fig. 4.12).[11] In this image gods are seated among twisted, snake-headed cords, while the text records a divine birth at *nah ho' chan witz xaman* "first five sky, northern mountain." The importance of the northern location for the manifestation of the cosmic umbilicus is tied to the arrival of the rainy season. In the Maya area the onset of the rainy season coincides with the movement of the sun northward, from its southern, dry-season path, toward its zenith. Thus, as the ecliptic travels northward over the course of the year, it appears to "pull" the sun toward zenith. As noted in the previous chapter, the date of the first zenith passage was celebrated at Quirigua on May 3, 738, by the decapitation of the Copan king Waxaklajun Ub'ah K'awil. In addition to being a political event, this ritual magically induced rainfall through the flow of blood onto the earth. It was thus in part an agricultural ceremony, assuring that, while the sun was in the north, the rainfall needed to nourish growing maize seedlings would come.

Several scenes from the Postclassic Madrid Codex reiterate these concepts. On page 10, twisted cords fall from heaven, bearing a deity enclosed in a shower of rain (Fig. 4.13a). This scene is elaborated on page 5, where the twisted cords are rendered as entwined snakes that

4.10. Serpent with spotted element in place of lower jaw. CPN Stela I, west face detail. Drawing by author.

4.11. Principal Bird Deity holding cosmic umbilicus in its beak. Piedras Negras Stela 14, detail. Drawing by author.

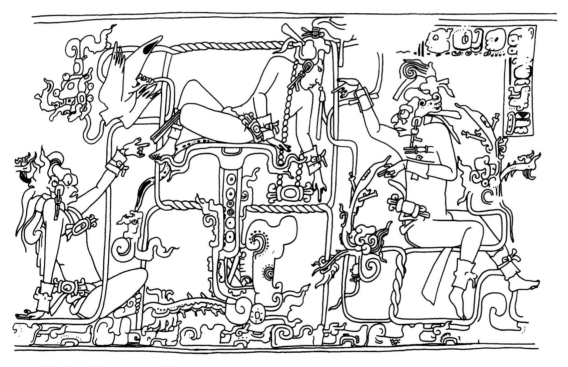

4.12. Classic polychrome vessel from Motul de San José. Drawing by author.

descend from the sky and support Chaak, who expels moisture on a prone deity below (Fig. 4.13b). Such images prefigure contemporary Maya beliefs in supernatural snakes that bring rain (such as the Chikchans of the Ch'orti') and represent a continuation of Classic-period notions of the cords as sources of life and vitality (Spero 1987). Another image that connects the twisted celestial umbilicus to the rainy season appears on page 19 of the Madrid Codex (Fig. 4.14). This image shows deities performing blood sacrifice using a rope threaded through their penises. The rope used in this ritual is marked with a "sun" glyph, identifying it as the ecliptic (Pope 1999).

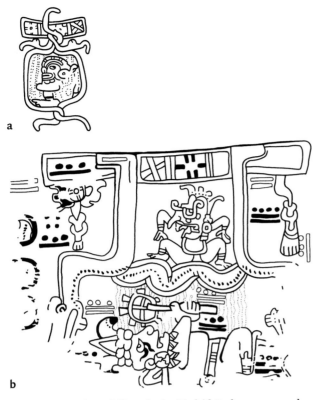

a

b

4.13. The cosmic umbilicus in the Madrid Codex: *a*, p. 10*c*, detail; *b*, p. 5, detail. Drawings by author.

This image represents yet another way in which the coming of rain (symbolized by the sacrificial blood of celestial deities) is closely related to the manifestation of the cosmic umbilicus-ecliptic.

The Principal Bird Deity from which versions of the celestial umbilicus emerge, as on Quirigua Stela F, probably identifies the Classic Maya celestial portal. It is likely that the bird symbolizes a constellation located near the north celestial pole, such as the Big Dipper. This being may have been seen as the agent that actually pulled the ecliptic northward. When it reached this point, the cords fell to earth, bringing rain. Indeed, the name of this bird incorporates the root *itz*, meaning "sap, dew, nectar" or other types of seeping liquid (Freidel, Schele, and Parker 1993: 410–412). The same root is used to form the Yukatek term *yíitzil ka'an*, which refers to a cosmological fluid conduit that connects sky and earth (Sosa 1985: 435–436). The Principal Bird Deity's flower diadem with flowing nectar also refers to this aspect. The name of the bird connotes its associations with earthly fructification—in particular, the flowering of the earth that follows the rains.

The south image of Stela F, then, represents the king manifesting the floral path of the sun, the ecliptic, which emerges from the region of the north celestial pole

marked by the Principal Bird Deity. This could be interpreted as a ritual action meant to induce rainfall. The king's action recalls specifically the posture of the young goddess shown on side I of a Classic-period vessel (Fig. 4.15), who is represented giving birth with the supernatural midwife, Goddess O, in attendance (Taube 1994). The image not only implies that the king gives birth (to gods) but—because his birth rope is the ecliptic—casts him as a creator god, pulling from the sky the umbilicus of Creation.[12] Such an act relates closely to the passage in the west text of the stela, which mentions the appearance of the cosmic stone tripod (B16). In Maya myth these stones were carried on the back of the turtle out of which maize was reborn through the agency of the lightning deity, Chaak. The appearance of this deity's face on the basal register of Stela F seemingly relates to this mythic sequence. The imagery of Stela F south may thus be characterized as embodying a dual ceremony, in which rainmaking is combined with world-creation. The image is a prime example of the linkage between these two domains in Classic Maya royal ritual, in which the period-

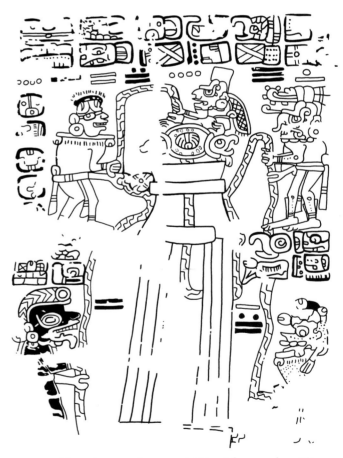

4.14. Deities using cosmic rope to let blood from penises. Madrid Codex, p. 19. Drawing by author.

4.15. Classic polychrome vessel (the "Birth Vase"; K5113), side I, detail. Drawing by author.

lily signs, indicate the surface of the underworld elsewhere in Maya art, as on Copan Structures 10L-22 and 11. The skeletal heads upon which the waterlily personifications of the headdress perch also signal the surface of the underworld. Atop their heads appear dotted leaves, bearing doubled diagonal marks. Similar diagonal marks appear on the waterlily personification heads which adorn the ruler's sandal backs.

A second major difference between the two faces of Stela F is that on the north side the king wears a large trilobed mosaic pectoral emblazoned with the Jester God and holds in his right hand a God K scepter and in his left a shield bearing the image of the Jaguar War God. One of the most remarkable compositional aspects of this image is the manner in which the scepter is held, fully visible in the right hand and bisecting the entire composition in a bold diagonal. This dramatic break in the rigid bilateral symmetry which otherwise dominates the entire composition serves to emphasize this emblem and, secondarily, the shield. This triad of emblems repeats iconography seen on Stela J, erected five tuns earlier. Its significance is to identify the ruler with the powers of Creation inherent in growing plants. The shield and scepter symbolize warfare and ancestral connections, respectively, while the pectoral is associated with transformation and rebirth through ascension to rulership. In addition, as a lightning axe, the scepter relates to the king's role as a rainmaker (Chaak).

The imagery of the south and north sides of Stela F thus amplifies the reference to Creation appearing in the west text, through a dramatic display of the king dressed as a cosmic tree, surrounded by the paired forces of birth. The south face depicts celestial forces, embodied in the cosmic umbilicus, while the north features the fecund waters of the underworld, identified with afterbirth. As the monument's text relates the appearance of the image of the turtle in the sky, the imagery shows the forces of birth that were contained within this turtle, brought forth and successfully organized and controlled by the king during the period-ending celebration which reenacted Creation. These images of birth constitute the foundation for the interpretation of the king's accession as a mystical rebirth. The accession is implied by the *sak*-pectoral/God K/shield combination of attributes appearing on the north side and reinforced by the highlighted textual account of this event. On Stela F the placement of accession text and image within the context of Creation stresses the congruency of these two events with each other and with the period ending, celebrated through the dedication of the monument itself.[13]

ending ceremony allowed kings to claim powers over both (pro)creation and production. More specifically, it elaborates the cosmic domains appropriate to K'ak' Tiliw as a manifestation of the rain deity and the source of sustenance.

The north (reverse) face of Stela F (Fig. 4.16) shows the ruler wearing a nearly identical costume to that on the south side, but there are a few salient differences. First, while a celestial cord descends from the headdress on the south, here a water band springs out of skeletal heads, flanked by full-figure waterlily personifications. The basal register of Stela F north also differs from that of the south, representing a skull marked with curls surrounded by rings of dots inscribed within half-quatrefoils (Fig. 4.17). These markings on the basal skull identify it with the aquatic domain of the underworld (Stone 1983). Similar skulls, often marked with water or water-

4.16. QRG Stela F, north-face figure, rolled out. Drawing by author.

4.17. QRG Stela F, north-face basal register, rolled out. Drawing by author.

While the monument celebrates the ruler's control over the feminine powers of birth, his masculinity is emphasized. This quality is apparent in his nudity, the phallic upright quality of the monument, and the stiff apron that covers (and thus emphasizes) the genital area. It is also seen in the short beard that the ruler wears on both obverse and reverse. In fact, this beard recurs on all royal portraits of the 1A-1 program but is absent on Stelae H and J, suggesting that it has an iconographic function related to the symbolism of the program as a whole (as discussed below). In the context of Stela F, the beard contributes to the mixed sexual persona portrayed by the ruler, in which the costume signals control of male reproductive powers, while the posture grasping the celestial cords is associated with feminine powers of birth.

Relations with K'ak' Yipyaj of Copan

The statement of the origins of royal power that derive from the birth of the cosmos conveyed through the carefully coordinated text and image of Stela F is much more elaborate than that of Stela J, its predecessor by a *hotun*. Notably absent from Stela F is the martial imagery seen on Stela J. Such an iconographic shift, however, does not imply that relations with Copan had cooled. On the contrary, just as the victory over Waxaklajun Ub'ah K'awil is recorded on the west side of Stela F, so K'ak' Tiliw was engaged in courting former enemies of Copan. The records of these events appear several years after the fact on Stela E and on Altars O' and P', commissioned by his successor, Sky Xul. The date was November 28, 762, and the event was the taking of a palanquin or litter of the type that the Maya employed to transport deity images (Fig.

4.18a). The agent is named with a glyph that includes a sun sign placed above a compound of a jaguar head with upraised arms. This entity, nicknamed K'in B'alam, is termed an *ajaw* of a site provisionally read as "Xkuy."[14] Elsewhere in the text of Stela E the same title appears, together with a toponym composed of a numeral six, a "shell-in-hand" sign, and *nal* (Fig. 4.18b). The "Xkuy *ajaw*" is mentioned here as an observer of the period ending. The passage recording the receiving of the palanquin concludes with an agency expression, indicating that K'ak' Tiliw supported the military actions of this lord.

Although the Xkuy/"Six Shell-in-Hand" place cannot at this time be identified with an actual site, it is also mentioned on an inscribed cylindrical stone fragment from Copan. This text names both Xkuy and the Six Shell-in-Hand place as a site that was burned by the king Waxaklajun Ub'ah K'awil on February 20, 718 (Fig. 4.19).[15] The use of the bat head to name this site also suggests that it was in the Copan hegemony, as the Copan emblem glyph includes a bat main sign (T756ab). The name of Copan may have been Xukpi or Xukup, after the motmot, a type of flycatcher (*Momotus momota*). Additional toponyms at Copan derive from the names of

birds, such as Mo' Witz ("Macaw Mountain").[16] Whatever its location, the texts suggest that many years after the defeat of Waxaklajun Ub'ah K'awil, K'ak' Tiliw was still engaged in military actions in the former sphere of Copan. In this case, he provided aid to a small site that previously had been a victim of Copan aggression. The citation of this lord on Quirigua monuments implies that the Xkuy lord's assistance was important in maintaining Quirigua's sovereignty. In fact, we might speculate that this site provided support during the war of 738. Such disgruntled enemies of Copan would have made ideal allies for K'ak' Tiliw. Unfortunately, there are no texts to confirm this.

The reference to Xkuy so many years after the sacrifice of the Copan king also gives substance to the interpretation that warlike iconographic programs at Copan and Quirigua were directed specifically at each other. Moreover, it shows that the interaction between the two sites falls within well-known patterns of Classic Maya warfare. Military campaigns often not only were conducted over long periods and in series of battles but were carried out against smaller sites allied to the enemy. Xkuy lords were present at the death of K'ak' Tiliw and were involved in another war in concert with Quirigua in 786 (see Chapter 6). Further, K'ak' Tiliw's relationship with Xkuy in 762 provides circumstantial support for the involvement of Calakmul in Quirigua's affairs after 736, as this would have discouraged Copan from suppressing alliances between Quirigua and Copan's enemies, such as Xkuy. With the protection of Calakmul, K'ak' Tiliw and his successor Sky Xul could conduct wars with impunity, not only gaining trophies, tribute, and prestige for Quirigua but also serving Calakmul's relentless campaign to destabilize Tikal and its allies.

The continuing antagonism between Quirigua and Copan in the 760s is paralleled by contrasting political programs expressed through monumental art. Dedicated by the ruler K'ak' Yipyaj on the same date as QRG Stela F, CPN Stela N (Fig. 4.20) draws on the most ancient iconographic traditions of Copan, depicting the conjuration of supernatural beings through a vision rite. Intriguingly, like Stela F, K'ak' Yipyaj's monument presents figures on opposite faces, oriented to the north and south. At Copan this choice may be understood as a revival of local modes of the past, since Waxaklajun Ub'ah K'awil and his predecessor, Smoke Imix, both commissioned double-figured monuments. The earliest of these was CPN Stela 3, erected by Smoke Imix in 652. Next was Waxaklajun Ub'ah K'awil's Stela C in 711 (Fig. 4.21). Both the north and south sides of CPN Stela N feature

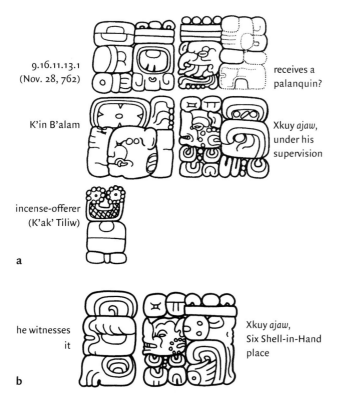

9.16.11.13.1 (Nov. 28, 762)

receives a palanquin?

K'in B'alam

Xkuy *ajaw*, under his supervision

incense-offerer (K'ak' Tiliw)

a

he witnesses it

Xkuy *ajaw*, Six Shell-in-Hand place

b

4.18. References to the Xkuy ajaw on QRG Stela E: *a*, A14–A16a; *b*, A20a–B20. Drawings by author.

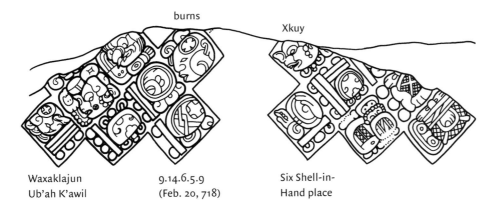

burns   Xkuy

Waxaklajun   9.14.6.5.9   Six Shell-in-
Ub'ah K'awil   (Feb. 20, 718)   Hand place

4.19. Inscribed cylindrical monument, Copan museum. Drawing by author.

similar imagery, with aquatic iconography dominant. The headdresses consist of zoomorphic heads topped with large waterlily pads and blossoms. Small ancestor figures are seated at the top of the headdress. On the north face (front), water bands—marked with *le* glyphs similarly to QRG Stela J—descend from the headdress and are terminated by reptile heads, which wrap around the sides of the stela. These heads are capped with "smoking *ajaw*" faces that symbolize the vital force of breath and have a jaguar ear, a "cruller" wrapped about the eye, and a long "shell beard." These elements identify the creature as an aspect of the Jaguar War God, which may symbolize the dry season moon (Milbrath 1999: 124–126). The date of dedication of CPN Stela N corresponded to the date of new moon during the height of the dry season. Glyph C of the monument's lunar series records this event as the first day of the Jaguar War God lunation. The God K figures conjured from the double-headed serpent bar by the ruler may refer to the appearance of Jupiter at two weeks past its stationary point.

Among the most remarkable features of this stela, however, are the twisted snakes, terminating in square snouts, that writhe along the edges of the figure on both sides. These snakes, clearly examples of the cosmic umbilicus, emerge from the earth out of supernatural maws that open behind the ruler's legs. Shooting upward, the bodies twist about one another, as on the Motul de San José vase (Fig. 4.12). Also, like the vase, they bear images

4.20. CPN Stela N, south face. From Maudslay 1889–1902, *Archaeology*, vol. 1, Plate 81. From the facsimile edition of *Biologia Centrali-Americana* by Alfred Percival Maudslay. Published 1974 by Milpatron Publishing Corp., Stamford, Conn. Further reproduction prohibited.

4.21. CPN Stela C, west face. Photo by author.

of deities and ancestors seated along their length. Some of these spirit beings have turban headdresses, as if representing ancestral rulers of Copan. The name of the monument appears to reference this iconography: *yax pasaj ha' ?? tunil* "first dawn, water ?? stone object" (A17–18). The "dawn" is represented as the earth opening its maws to the east and west, so that spirit beings may be reborn.[17] The emphasis on twisted celestial cords seen in CPN Stela N recalls a similar iconographic theme on the south face of QRG Stela F, although the Quirigua monument shows the cords descending from the sky and rendered as strings of earflare assemblages. The fundamental difference between the two stelae is that the Co-

pan monument attempts to materialize a supernatural entity, whereas the Quirigua monument depicts a costume element that perhaps actually descended from a headdress worn by K'ak' Tiliw.[18] Certainly this iconographic over-lap cannot be attributed to chance, any more than the emphasis on aquatic imagery on both monuments. Like the monuments commissioned a *hotun* earlier, Stela F and Stela N employ similar iconography to express a common ritual base for competing period-ending ceremonies.

A different form of competition between the two sites is uniquely expressed in certain features that K'ak' Tiliw's stela clearly adapts from various Copan sources.

Outstanding is the inclusion of references to supernatural period endings in the east-face text, which was unprecedented at Quirigua but which is also employed on CPN Stela N on the west face. Here the text shifts temporal frames, moving backward by a distance number of 14.17.19.10.0.0 to a 1 Ajaw 8 Ch'en period ending. In what was doubtless a response to this rhetorical strategy, the Quirigua text includes not one but two equivalent period endings, both calculated on a scale that dwarfs that of Copan. Coupled with the huge scale of Stela F, the attempt to surpass Copan on many levels—economic, intellectual, artistic—is readily apparent. But it was not merely an attempt to better the art of K'ak' Yipyaj, whose stela recalls the precedent of format and textual rhetoric established by earlier stelae at Copan. The inclusion of supernatural prototypes for period endings had been initiated decades earlier on CPN Stela C, which includes at least four ancient period-ending records, one on the south side and three surviving dates on the north. On Stela C the distance between the dedication date of the monument and the first ancient period ending is 4,617 years, while the second date on the north side corresponds to the end of 13 kalab'tuns (2,050,146.46 years) prior to Creation.

Through appropriation and adaptation, CPN Stela N draws on the prestige of Waxaklajun Ub'ah K'awil's great stela and, in turn, on the models of that monument. Therefore, the double-faced format, iconography, and textual rhetoric of Stela F erected by K'ak' Tiliw may be interpreted as an attempt to appropriate the sculpture tradition of Copan and in particular the royal ceremonial heritage that reached back from K'ak' Yipyaj to Waxaklajun Ub'ah K'awil and beyond. The reference to CPN Stela C is especially strong, as this monument shows the Copan ruler in contrasting guises. On the east side, Waxaklajun Ub'ah K'awil wears a caiman apron that probably identifies him with the appearance of the Milky Way at sunset on the night of the monument dedication in 711 (Schele and Mathews 1998: 142–144). Further, CPN Stela C features twisted cords adjacent to the headdress, symbolically analogous to the earflare strings manipulated by K'ak' Tiliw on Stela F south. The west face of CPN Stela C shows the king, this time bearded, standing before an altar in the form of a turtle (Fig. 4.21). While it is not certain, this image may represent the ruler participating in one of the supernatural period endings mentioned in the north text, in which a turtle is said to be dedicated at a place called ik' hun ?? nal (B5–B6). If this interpretation is correct, it sets the precedent not only for QRG Stela F but also for QRG Stelae D and E.

While the iconography and texts of QRG Stela F and CPN Stela N are similar, the styles of the two stelae are strikingly different. Even compared to its antecedent QRG Stela J, Stela F is far more columnar in conception and tapers gradually toward its apex, enhancing the impression of its height. To retain legibility of the king's face at such a height, the sculptors realized the facial form and the personification heads of the headdress as rounded masses cut deeply from the ground. Such execution allows the face of the king to be visible from a great distance, even in the blazing sunlight of the Great Plaza, which tends to flatten surfaces. The remainder of the figure is executed consistently in an accomplished low-relief style, which distinguishes elements of anatomy and costume in layered, parallel planes, following the technique of Stela J. Recalling its predecessor as well are frequent double outlines and the gentle rounding of selected shapes, such as serpent heads and medallions. Glyphic renderings are similar to Stela J, but the blocks are more rectangular (Fig. 4.22). Stela F also evokes the style of the Early Classic Monument 26, especially in its rectangular cross-section with clearly defined edges and the wrapping of the figure continuously onto the sides. Whereas Stela J emphasized the wrapping of the headdress only onto the sides of the monument, myriad costume elements of the Stela F figures intrude onto the east and west panels (Fig. 4.23), including the faces of personified waterlilies, which provide visual interest adjacent to the fields of feathers that occupy the upper half of the east and west sides. The king's elbows, collar, medallions, and belt heads, in addition to feathers, stress the wrap-around compositional mode in a much more consistent manner than on Stela J, the lower section of which is conceived relatively three-dimensionally, akin to Stela H. The emphasis on a wrap-around composition strongly evokes the sculptural tradition of Early Classic Quirigua.

In dramatic contrast to these tendencies at Quirigua, Copan Stela N is executed with exaggerated undercutting over the entire monument that nearly surpasses the most flamboyant of Waxaklajun Ub'ah K'awil's stelae (Fig. 4.20). The twisted celestial cords that the figure manifests during the vision rite writhe along the length of the monument's edges, breaking up the silhouette of the shaft. The glyphs, too, retain the rounded puffiness of Waxaklajun Ub'ah K'awil's Stelae A, B, F, and H (Fig. 3.45). Such adherence to the sculptural aesthetics of the reign of his predecessor stresses dynastic continuity at Copan. A similar message may be discerned from the text on the rectangular slab base of Stela N, inscribed on

4.22. QRG Stela F, east text, detail. Photo by Thomas Tolles.

representations of cloth bindings. Two of these strips record the accession of K'ak' Yipyaj's predecessor, K'ak' Joplaj, while the other two record the ruler's own accession, naming him the son of the former ruler. Thus, the accessions of the two rulers inscribed on these bindings provide a symbolic support for the current period ending. The style of the monument seems to echo this emphasis on dynastic continuity. Whether or not these correspondences were intentional, the contrasts between Copan Stela N and Quirigua Stela F are indexes of local developments, referencing the sophistication and distinctiveness of native sculptural traditions.

Stela D (Dedicated February 19, 766)

Marking the second corner of the 1A-1 platform is Stela D, placed at the foot of Structure 1A-3 about 63 m north of Stela F (Fig. 4.24). At about 6 m in height, the shaft is somewhat shorter than Stela F but still follows its predecessor in basic format. Inscriptions occupy almost the entire east and west faces, with the first seven glyphs on

4.23. QRG Stela F, east face, detail. Photo by Thomas Tolles.

each side realized in spectacular full-figure form (Fig. 4.25). The text begins on the east side with the date of the monument erection, 9.16.15.0.0 7 Ajaw 18 Pop (February 19, 766) and, like Stela F, with a lunar series (Fig. 4.26). The dedication rites include both erection of the stone and a scattering ritual by K'ak' Tiliw. The name of the monument, *k'an te' nah chan yo'at/yo'pat* "yellow tree building/first, celestial Yo'at/Yo'pat," is crucial to the interpretation of its ritual significance. This name is clearly a celestial reference, as Yo'at/Yo'pat is the name of the lightning deity responsible for splitting the turtle shell out of which maize is reborn. The first part of this name relates closely to this myth as well: it is the same as that of the Foliated Cross motif at Palenque—a deified maize plant. The monument, then, is named through a specific reference to astronomical phenomena that symbolized the critical moment in Creation lore when maize was resurrected through the actions of a lightning deity. This designation explicitly identifies the stela, adorned with colossal portraits of the king, as the vehicle for K'ak' Tiliw's persona as Yo'at/Yo'pat.

Subsequent events serve to develop this theme. Following the pattern established by Stela F, the Stela D east text next records the completion of a period ending in the far distant past, of 13 *k'inchiltuns* followed by the Calendar Round 7 Ajaw 3 Pop. Once again, the precise placement of this date in the Long Count remains problematic. The event recorded for this date is *yilijiy ahkul k'an nun?* "he witnessed the turtle yellow ??"—probably a reference to the vision of the turtle constellation in Orion's belt. The agent, K'ak' Tiliw, is indicated only by a title that he also carries on Stela F. This passage suggests that K'ak' Tiliw saw the turtle through a vision or dream in which he traveled into the past. Further, in view of ancient Maya notions of the vitalizing force of royal sight, it is likely that this passage implies that through his altered state of consciousness K'ak' Tiliw was able to enact the events of Creation. The place of the vision is indicated also, with a toponym composed of a *yax* sign, a dotted skull with T-shaped pupil, and *nal*, the toponymic marker. This "dream sequence" is echoed by the final passage of the east side, which records the witnessing of the current period ending by K'ak' Tiliw. The parallel *tzolk'in* positions and verbs of ancient and contemporary period endings recorded in this text suggest that K'ak' Tiliw also witnessed the turtle constellation at 9.16.15.0.0. In fact, on the evening of monument dedication (February 19, 766), the turtle constellation in Orion would have been visible to all at Quirigua, appearing high in the sky at sunset (Fig. 4.27).

4.24. QRG Stela D, north. From Maudslay 1889–1902, *Archaeology*, vol. 2, Plate 22. From the facsimile edition of *Biologia Centrali-Americana* by Alfred Percival Maudslay. Published 1974 by Milpatron Publishing Corp., Stamford, Conn. Further reproduction prohibited.

The time frame of the west text of Stela D again shifts back to the past, beginning with a record of the date 9.16.13.4.17 8 Kab'an 5 Yaxk'in (June 6, 764), once more followed by the lunar series (Fig. 4.28). The event is the completion of two k'atuns of reign by K'ak' Tiliw, including the location where the anniversary was celebrated. Next is an event involving a deity named Jun Pih K'uh, followed by a reference to vision rites similar to that recorded on Stela J. The time frame then returns to the current period ending, on which the stela is invested with the status of *ajaw* and K'ak' Tiliw performs a scattering ritual.[19]

Following the pattern established by Stela F, the figures of Stela D amplify an astronomical event mentioned in the text: the appearance of the turtle constellation cited in the east inscription. The figure on the south side (Figs. 4.29, 4.30) stands on a basal register in the form of the skeletal waterlily personification head, a variant of which also appears on the Stela F north basal register. In this case, however, the skull has a *yax* in the forehead, dots on the cheeks, and T-shaped pupils. It is thus identical to the place mentioned in the east text where the ancient 7 Ajaw 3 Pop period ending was observed. This basal register gives the context for the image of the ruler above as a supernatural location, to which the king has

literally time-traveled through a vision or dream. The king's attire on Stela D south as well as north includes most of the botanical symbols seen previously on Stela F (e.g., the waterlily sandals, God C-variant loincloth, heavy belt, ornaments, and earflares). The headdress flanges on both faces feature floral rosettes to which are attached serpent heads and, on the north face, interlaces and earflares. These motifs symbolize the celestial umbilicus and probably relate to the naming of the monument after the *k'an te' nah* place of the maize deity's rebirth. Following Stela F north, the portraits of Stela D show the king holding the God K scepter and shield and wearing a medallion ornament, a triad of emblems that underscores his association with the regrowth of maize and other plants. Although almost completely eroded, remaining outlines of the scepter indicate that it was held diagonally, while the shield is frontal. In the uppermost register of the south-face headdress appears an image of the Principal Bird Deity. This image, of astronomical significance, also reinforces the supernatural nature of the imagery, as this being is associated with the era before the cosmos was put in order in 3114 B.C.[20]

The north-face figure (Fig. 4.31) is similar to that of the south face, although far better preserved. Again the king wields the emblems of power, although oddly the

4.25. QRG Stela D, east text, detail. Photo by Thomas Tolles.

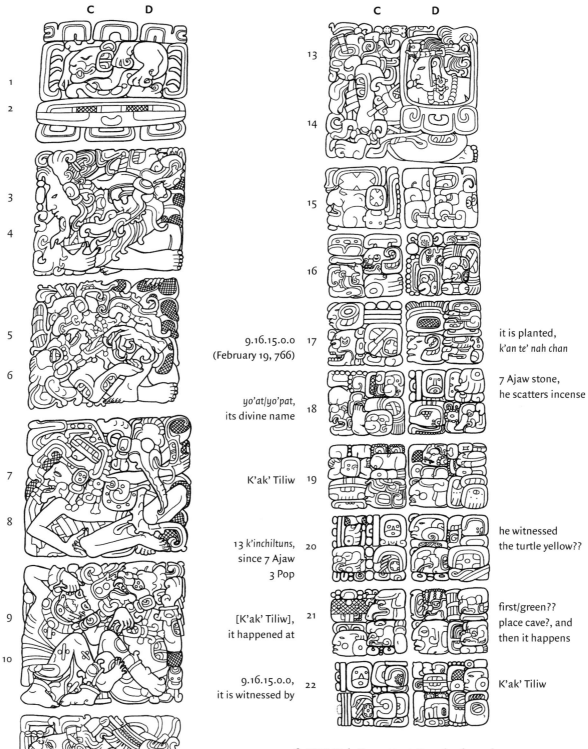

C D

C D

1

2

3

4

5

6

7

8

9

10

11

12

13

14

15

16

9.16.15.0.0
(February 19, 766)   17   it is planted,
                              k'an te' nah chan

yo'at/yo'pat,
its divine name   18   7 Ajaw stone,
                           he scatters incense

K'ak' Tiliw   19

13 *k'inchiltuns,*
since 7 Ajaw   20   he witnessed
3 Pop   the turtle yellow??

[K'ak' Tiliw],   21   first/green??
it happened at   place cave?, and
                          then it happens

9.16.15.0.0,   22   K'ak' Tiliw
it is witnessed by

4.26. QRG Stela D, east text. Drawing by author.

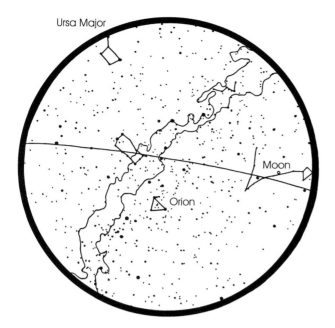

4.27. Sky map, February 19, 766, sunset. Drawing by author..

God K scepter is held in the left hand. This is unique in the Quirigua corpus. Further, the scepter is held horizontally, at waist level, and the shield is represented in profile. The headdress is also different from the south face, featuring a skull with moon signs replacing the lower jaw, placed atop double avian *chan* "sky" personification heads. While Kelley (1977a: 61) took this image to be a reference to a lunar eclipse, it is more likely that it symbolizes the moon on the dedication date of Stela D, which corresponded to the first day of the skull lunation as noted in the east-face lunar series (C16b). An alternative interpretation is that the headdress skull is a reference to Venus, which was in conjunction with the moon on this date (Milbrath 1999: 137).

A second reference to the moon may also appear in the basal register of Stela D north, which depicts the Jaguar War God combined with a glyph having the phonetic value *sa*. This deity is probably a reference to the dry-season moon, while its positioning in the basal register may suggest invisibility or a horizon phenomenon. Although the precise combination of Jaguar War God plus *sa* is unique in Maya art, the *sa* sign may relate to the record of the new moon on the Palenque Palace Tablet, which is composed of *sa* and the head of a Death God, which represents "completion" or "zero" in texts. In Ch'ol, *sahten* means "gone (moon, new moon)" (Attinasi 1973: 313). Although technically the moon was 1.3 days old on the night of dedication, it was recorded as dark in the lunar series of the east text.[21] The loss of the moon in the glare

of the sun is probably also implied by the design of the king's earflares, which, in contrast with those of the south face, are rendered as *k'in* "sun" glyphs. Yet another astronomical reference may be embodied in the odd gesture of the ruler with the God K scepter. As the date of dedication of Stela D was close to the second stationary point of Jupiter, the holding of the figure downward may symbolize the stasis of the planet.

The imagery of Stela D thus shows the king in contrasting celestial personae. The south face depicts the ruler in a dream or trance state, journeying into the remote past to witness (and thereby set in motion) an ancient period ending. The south basal register gives the name of the place where the turtle constellation was witnessed in the remote past, while the Principal Bird Deity in the headdress reinforces the pre-Creation context of this event. The north face, in contrast, shows the king performing the period ending in 766, with current astronomical (principally lunar) events symbolized by the basal register and headdress. Thus, while Stela F shows the ruler in the diverse cosmic realms of sky and underworld, Stela D emphasizes contrasting temporal frames. Even so, it continues the precedent for double-faced portraits established by Stela F and, by extension, Copan Stelae N, C, and 3.

Stela D is also closely related to Stela F stylistically, with its carving retaining most of the principles of modeling, overlapping, and design of its predecessor (Fig. 4.32). The most significant innovation of Stela D is the modification of the upper portion of the stela into a box-like frame in which projecting columns of feathers bracket the flat panels to the sides of the face and headdress. On the north side (Fig. 4.33), this frame is only partial, beginning at the level of the first personification head of the headdress and increasing toward the chin of the king's face. On the south, twin columns of feathers extend over the entire length of the headdress, creating dark recessed areas on either side of the royal visage, thus enhancing the illumination of the face (Fig. 4.30). First articulated on Stela D, this effect appears consistently in the subsequent stelae of K'ak' Tiliw, both increasing the dramatic focus on the face and headdress and emphasizing the four sides of the monument. Additional sculptural passages call attention to the rectangular cross-section of the monument, such as a sharper wrapping of the design around the edges relative to Stela F. The projection of the edge is even used to give convexity to the maize deity head still intact on the southeast corner (Fig. 4.34). This emphasis on the wrap-around composition recalls Monument 26 as well as earlier stelae of K'ak' Tiliw.

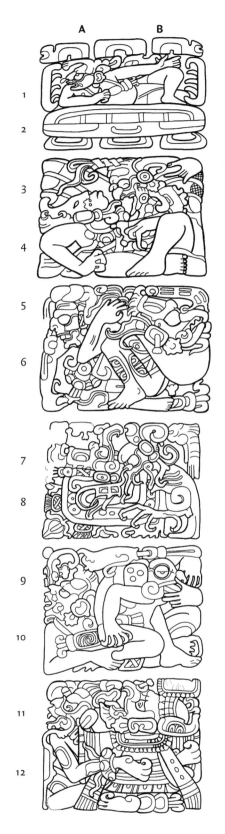

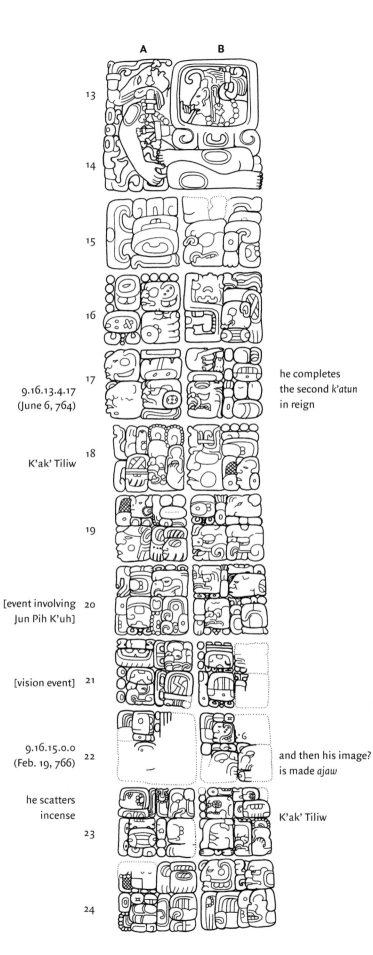

A   B

13

14

15

16

17   9.16.13.4.17
      (June 6, 764)

18   K'ak' Tiliw

      he completes
      the second *k'atun*
      in reign

19

20   [event involving
      Jun Pih K'uh]

21   [vision event]

22   9.16.15.0.0
      (Feb. 19, 766)

      and then his image?
      is made *ajaw*

23   he scatters
      incense   K'ak' Tiliw

24

4.28. QRG Stela D, west text. Drawing by author.

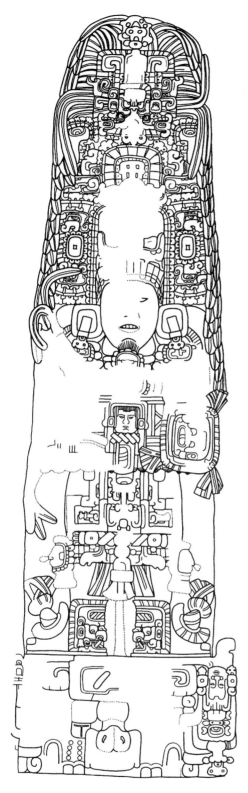

4.29. QRG Stela D, south face, rolled out. Drawing by author.

4.30. QRG Stela D, south. Neg. no. 346, photo by Dr. Gafford, courtesy San Diego Museum of Man.

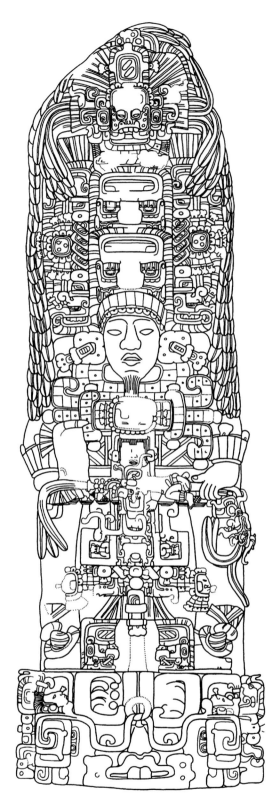

4.31. QRG Stela D, north face, rolled out. Drawing by author.

4.32. QRG Stela D, north face, detail. Photo by Thomas Tolles.

4.33. QRG Stela D, north face, detail. Photo by Thomas Tolles.

4.34. QRG Stela D, east face, detail. Photo by Thomas Tolles.

Stela E (Dedicated January 24, 771)

In his book *Incidents of Travel in Central America, Chiapas, and Yucatan,* John Lloyd Stephens (1841, vol. 2: 121–122) published vivid impressions of Quirigua that made the site and its monuments world-famous, including Stela E (Fig. 4.35). He described the monument as

> an obelisk or carved stone, twenty-six feet out of the ground, and probably six or eight feet under. . . . It is leaning twelve feet two inches out of the perpendicular, and seems ready to fall, which is probably prevented only by a tree that has grown up against it and the large stones around the base. The side toward the ground represents the figure of a man, very perfect and finely sculptured. The upper side seemed the same, but was so hidden by vegetation as to make it somewhat uncertain. The other two contain hieroglyphics in low relief. In size and sculpture this is the finest of the whole.

Over the years, the monument gradually tilted farther and farther from the vertical, inspiring much speculation as to the length of the butt needed to sustain the massive strain. By 1917 heavy rains had finally softened the monument's foundation so much that Stela E fell over completely yet remained unbroken. The stela's butt thus revealed was found to be less than 3 m long, with the total length of the monument being 10.6 m. Weighing in at around sixty-five tons, the stela is the largest stone ever quarried by the ancient Maya. In 1934 the archaeologist Gustav Strömsvik attempted to raise the monument using a winch and steel cables. Sadly, just short of success, the cable broke, sending the monument plummeting to the ground and breaking it cleanly in two pieces. The concrete used to reconnect the fragments is today clearly visible near the figures' necks. The nose on the north side also has a complicated history, having twice been cemented to the shaft, only to fall off each time. All that remains of it now is an iron reinforcing rod installed in the last futile repair attempt.

Stela E begins the elaboration of the west side of Platform 1A-1, located on its southwest corner. Like Stelae F and D, the figures on the north and south faces show the ruler holding the God K scepter and Jaguar War God shield and wearing the *sak*-pectoral (Figs. 4.36, 4.37). As on earlier stelae, these emblems are emphasized by the fact that they break the compositional symmetry. Also following the two previous stelae, Stela E features a text read from east to west, in two initial series inscriptions. The east text records the raising of the monument by K'ak' Tiliw, following an initial series date of 9.17.0.0.0 and a Lunar Series (Fig. 4.38).[22] The proper name of the monument derives from the two supernatural beings that occupy the headdress on the north and south faces. The first glyph (C10), *yax chit?* (Fig. 4.39a), corresponds to the north-face image of a supernatural with "squinting" eyes, a T580 forehead infix (Fig. 4.39b). The *yax* sign is located to the left of this head, atop a God-C variant head. The second glyph (D10; Fig. 4.40a) consists of a "shell-in-hand" sign, which signifies "zero" or "completion," followed by a compound that refers to the life-force residing in breath: *sak nik ik'*. The first part of this glyph refers to the being in the south-face headdress, which has hands replacing the lower mandible and "percentage sign" markings on its cheeks (Fig. 4.40b). This being substitutes for the "shell-in-hand" sign in the inscriptions. The second part of the glyph at D10 is probably referenced by the flower and serpent imagery in the headdress flanges, which refers to the celestial umbilicus.[23]

Facing page

4.35. QRG Stela E, south face. From Maudslay 1889–1902, *Ar-chaeology*, vol. 2, Plate 27. From the facsimile edition of *Biologia Centrali-Americana* by Alfred Percival Maudslay. Published 1974 by Milpatron Publishing Corp., Stamford, Conn. Further reproduction prohibited.

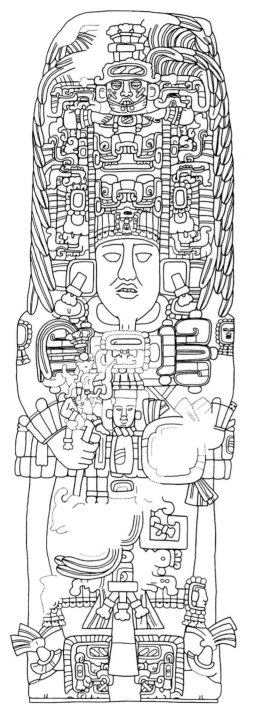

4.36. QRG Stela E, south face, figure, rolled out. Drawing by author.

4.37. QRG Stela E, north face, figure, rolled out. Drawing by author.

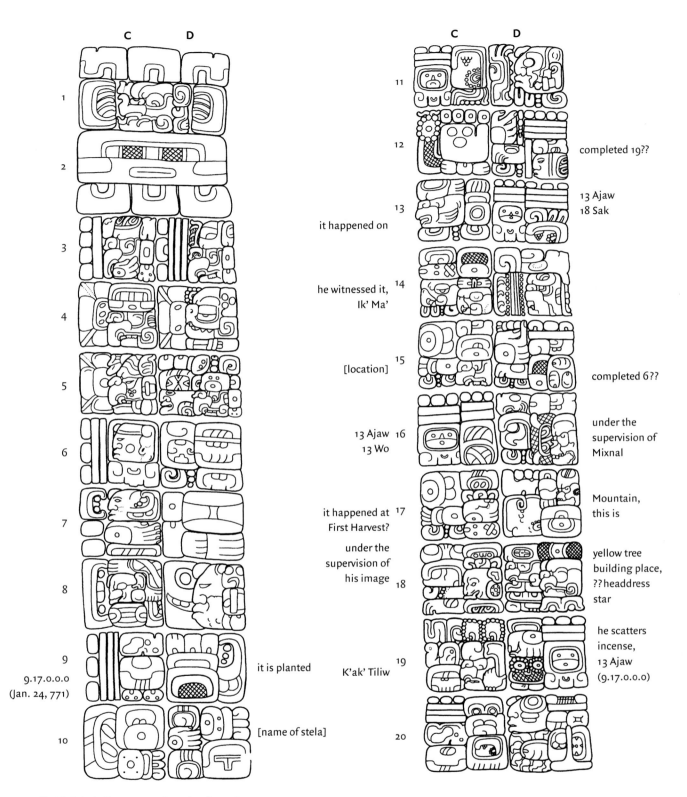

C   D

1

2

3

4

5

6

7

8

9
9.17.0.0.0
(Jan. 24, 771)

10

it is planted

[name of stela]

C   D

11

12   completed 19??

13   13 Ajaw
                                      18 Sak

it happened on

he witnessed it,   14
Ik' Ma'

[location]   15   completed 6??

13 Ajaw   16   under the
13 Wo   supervision of
                                     Mixnal

it happened at   17   Mountain,
First Harvest?   this is

under the   yellow tree
supervision of   building place,
his image   18   ?? headdress
                                     star

K'ak' Tiliw   19   he scatters
                                     incense,
                                     13 Ajaw
                                     (9.17.0.0.0)

                20

4.38. QRG Stela E, east text. Drawing by author.

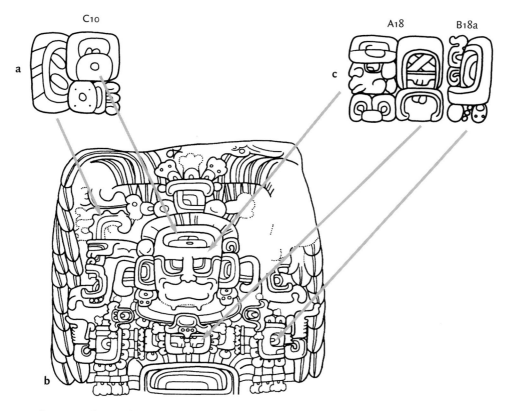

4.39. Correspondence of text and image, QRG Stela E: *a*, C10; *b*, north face; and *c*, A18–B18a. Drawings by author.

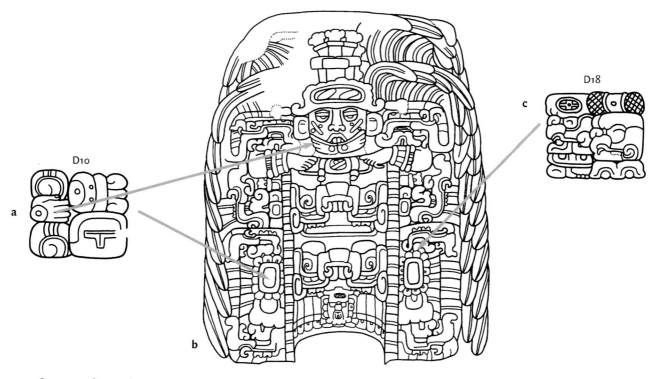

4.40. Correspondence of text and image, QRG Stela E: *a*, D10; *b*, south face; and *c*, D18. Drawings by author.

Following the model of Stela F, the text shifts the time frame back to record two period endings in the remote past, overseen by supernatural beings. The first follows the completion of nineteen units of an unknown period, with the Calendar Round written as 13 Ajaw 18 Sak. It is witnessed by a being also mentioned on a carved bone in the Dallas Art Museum, at an unknown location (see Schele 1992b: 166). The second period ending is associated with the completion of six units of unknown magnitude on 13 Ajaw 13 Wo, at a place possibly translated as "First Harvest Mountain."[24] Interestingly, the temporal unit noted here is the same as the name of the Great Plaza as recorded on Stela H (M2). It is also mentioned as the location of a supernatural event on Stela F (C16). Many of the high temporal cycles have names that are similar or identical to known supernatural locations, suggesting that visits to supernatural locations by Maya kings were understood as being synonymous with time-travel. One being who oversaw this second period ending, Mixnal, is also mentioned at Yaxchilan in a title for the ruler Bird Jaguar (Werner Nahm and Nikolai Grube, cited by Schele 1991a: 47).

In addition, a second supervisor is said to have overseen this ritual, who is not K'ak' Tiliw himself but the *b'ahil* or "image" of the ruler. This strongly suggests that portraits of rulers were capable of acting as agents on behalf of the rulers themselves. As long as monuments endured, so the kings' power was continuously deployed. Further, just as monuments perpetuated the royal body into the future, they may have been seen as allowing the king to visit remote places and times through the integration of his spirit with the primordial material of stone. Again, the precise Long Count placement of the ancient period endings mentioned in the Stela E text is not possible. The reader is clearly meant to interpret these events as supernatural prototypes for K'ak' Tiliw's current period ending, for they are immediately followed by an account of the dedication ritual for Stela E, in which drops of incense were scattered.

The west text of Stela E follows exactly the narrative structure of Stela F, beginning with an initial series record of the accession of K'ak' Tiliw but here followed by a lunar series (Fig. 4.41). The accession is written as the receiving of God K, under the authority of Waxaklajun Ub'ah K'awil, Copan *ajaw*. The next date recorded is the 9.15.0.0.0 period ending (A.D. 731), on which an unknown event occurred, followed by records of the decapitation of Waxaklajun Ub'ah K'awil in 738 and the taking of war trophies by K'in B'alam of Xkuy, the ally of K'ak' Tiliw, in 762. Finally, the text returns to the current pe-

riod ending, with the event recorded as a scattering of incense. The final clause of the text refers to the witnessing of these events by the *ajaw* of Xkuy. This passage underscores the importance of this ally to K'ak' Tiliw, who was present at Quirigua to witness and, by implication, to supervise the dedication of this great monument.

In addition to providing a selective political history of Quirigua and the supernatural prototypes for the period ending, the text of Stela E helps in the decoding of the figural portions of the monument. The description of the current period-ending ritual in the west text is particularly informative, as preceding the name of K'ak' Tiliw is a series of glyphs consisting of a "squint-eyed," long-lipped head suffixed by what is probably the syllabic sign *wo*, followed by *chan* "sky" and *k'awil* (Fig. 4.39c). These glyphs correspond to the iconography of the north-face portrait, which features the same "squinting" deity with a necklace composed of a "sky" glyph and the flanking smoking mirrors of God K (*k'awil*) (Fig. 4.39b). Thus, the north-face portrait is that of K'ak' Tiliw performing during the 9.17.0.0.0 period ending. Logically, we would expect that the corresponding passage on the east text would correspond to the headdress on the south face; however, a conclusive comparison is not possible. The compound naming the headdress at D18 reads *k'an te' nah nal? ?? hun ek'* or "yellow tree building/first place? ?? headdress star" (Fig. 4.40c). The first part of this compound, *k'an te' nah*, may refer to the iconography of the south-face headdress flanges, which feature rosettes with snake heads (Fig. 4.40b), identical to those of Stela D south. In the Stela D text the same *k'an te' nah* combination names the monument. In conclusion, the two faces of Stela E may represent a program exactly analogous to Stela D, with the south side depicting the ruler conducting the mythic 13 Ajaw 13 Wo period ending and the north showing the ruler in the historical present (A.D. 771).

The interpretation of the south-face image as the ruler conducting a supernaturally ancient period-ending celebration is supported by the iconography of the basal register of this side (Fig. 4.42). This image depicts a personified hill or mountain holding the Principal Bird Deity in its mouth (Stone 1983). The wings of this bird are wrapped around on the east and west faces of the monument. Above the wings appear personification heads that emerge from the mountain. At the termini of these heads are flower signs with emerging fragrance scrolls. These flowers probably underscore the symbolism of mountains as sources of fertility. As noted in the context of Stela D, the Principal Bird Deity probably has

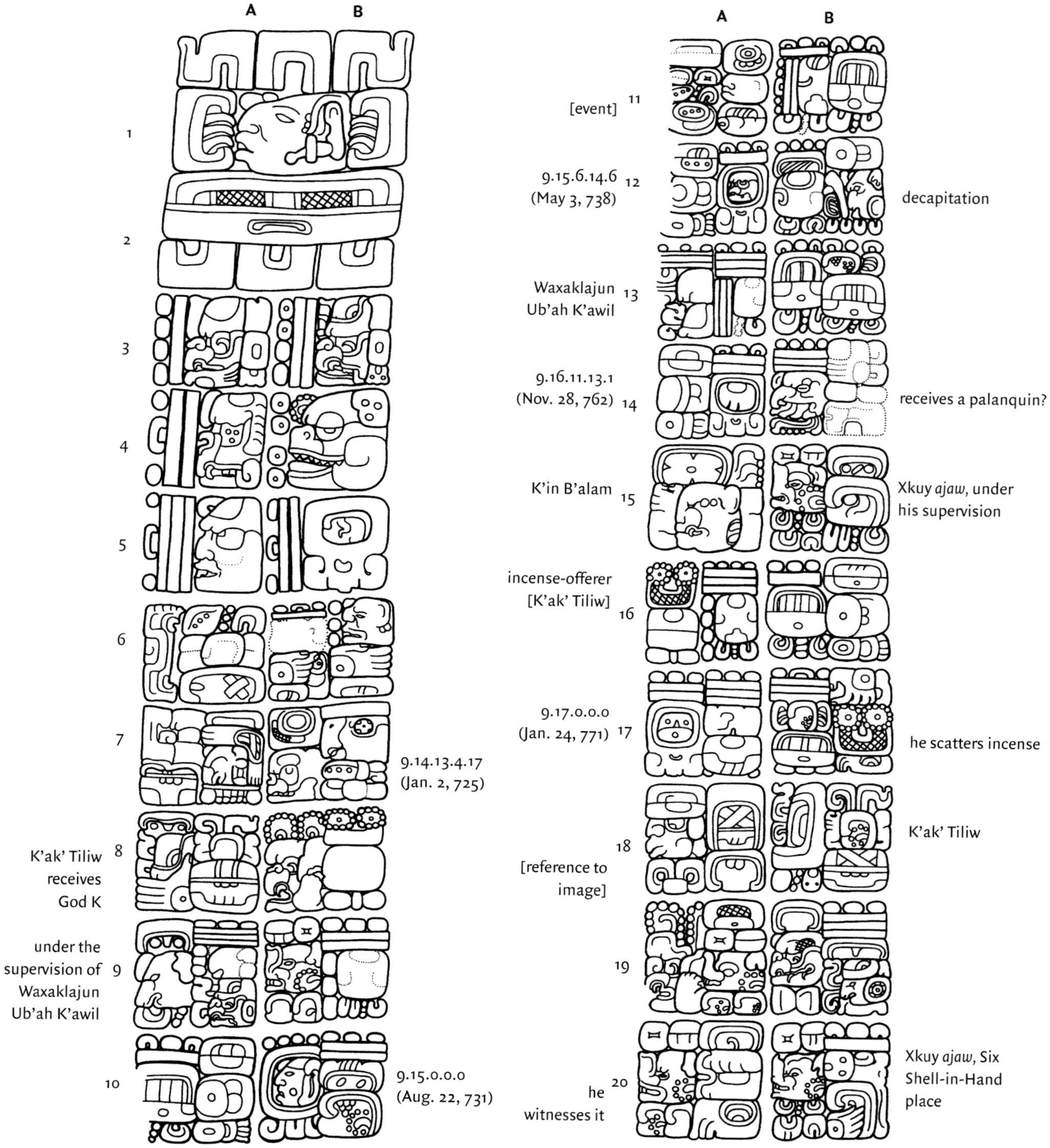
A
B
1
2
3
4
5
6
7
9.14.13.4.17
(Jan. 2, 725)
K'ak' Tiliw
receives
God K
8
under the
supervision of
9
Waxaklajun
Ub'ah K'awil
10
9.15.0.0.0
(Aug. 22, 731)
A
B
[event]
11
9.15.6.14.6
(May 3, 738)
12
decapitation
Waxaklajun
Ub'ah K'awil
13
9.16.11.13.1
(Nov. 28, 762)
14
receives a palanquin?
K'in B'alam
15
Xkuy *ajaw*, under
his supervision
incense-offerer
[K'ak' Tiliw]
16
9.17.0.0.0
(Jan. 24, 771)
17
he scatters incense
18
[reference to
image]
K'ak' Tiliw
19
he
witnesses it
20
Xkuy *ajaw*, Six
Shell-in-Hand
place

4.41. QRG Stela E, west text. Drawing by author.

astronomical symbolism but also is utilized as a marker for a pre-Creation context. This meaning may apply to the case of Stela E, suggesting that the above image takes place on an extremely ancient period ending at a supernatural location, possibly the First Harvest? Mountain mentioned in the east text at C17–D17.

The equivalent basal register on the north face has three linked personification heads that emerge from the mountain (Fig. 4.43). These heads wrap around the side of the monument and run the entire vertical length of the basal register. Emerging directly from the mountain mouth on the north face is the youthful visage of a deity

4.42. QRG Stela E, south basal register, rolled out. Drawing by author.

with a jaguar pelt on his cheeks, jaguar ears, a beard, and a headdress with three leaflike projections. The combination of these traits identifies the being as the personification of the number nine, who in other contexts is the Hero Twin named Yax B'alam.[25] Clenched between the teeth of this god is a phytomorphic element which branches to the right and left then bends upward. Attached to this element on both sides, hanging upside down, are heads with Roman noses, pointed incisors, "squinting" eyes, jaguar paws above the ear, and scrolls with leaves emerging from the agnathous mouth. These heads belong to the god who is the patron of the month Pax, known to have a phonetic value of *te* in the inscriptions. Thus, the combination of elements in the basal register may be read as a glyphic compound *b'olonte witz* "nine mountains," an expression known from the inscriptions of Copan, appearing on Stela I (Fig. 4.44). In the Copan text "nine mountains" occurs in a sequence that appears to name patron deities of Copan. The reason for citing this location on Quirigua Stela E is unclear but may have been meant to imply K'ak' Tiliw's dominion over a location sacred to Copan. This reference to a Copan location on Stela E reinforces the political statement made through the prominent references to a former enemy of Copan, the lord of Xkuy, as an ally of K'ak' Tiliw in the west text. The mountain imagery may also relate to the citation of an event on 9.15.0.0.0 in the west text. The monument dedicated on this date at Copan was Stela B, which features the ruler standing at the entrance of a cave in Macaw Mountain (Fig. 4.45). The mountain imagery of QRG Stela E may paraphrase the iconography of the Copan stela.

In its sculptural style, Stela E maintains the tradition of excellence begun with Stela J but also continues the trend toward flattening and wrapping of images seen in Stelae F and D. Stela E has clearly defined corners for the length of the shaft, increased squaring of scrollwork and costume elements relative to Stelae D and F (Fig. 4.46), and substantially more squared glyphs, which press against each other in a strict rectilinear grid. The glyphs eschew excessive detail, stressing the integrity of the flat vertical surface of the stone. Like Stela D, Stela E employs sunken areas on either side of the king's face in order to emphasize the royal visage (Fig. 4.47). The gradual development of this feature from Stela F to D to E shows that the final extreme contrast between the high-relief face and low-relief figure is a formal development internal to Quirigua. It cannot be convincingly attributed to an "influence" from other sites such as Piedras Negras, as suggested by Arthur Miller (1983).[26] In addition, Proskouriakoff (1950: 144) suggested that

> there is a particular quality of some of the Quirigua scroll designs which vaguely recalls the decoration of yokes found in the Totonac region, and the panels of the ball courts at Tajin. . . . This type of design is characterized by abrupt changes of direction in the outline of forms, by the use of interlaced elements, and by features of internal decoration of scrolls not typical of pure Maya forms. A striking example of this style of decoration is the lower panels of Stela E, which uses superimposed heads, with the headdress of one serving as the mouth of the next, and in which the motifs are almost entirely obscured by the decorative pattern [see Fig. 4.48].

But even in this case the search for precedents for such features outside Quirigua is not necessary. The "abrupt

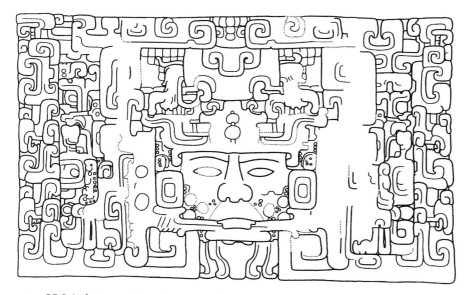

4.43. QRG Stela E, north basal register, rolled out. Drawing by author.

4.44. "Nine mountains" toponym, from CPN Stela I, C3a. Drawing by author.

changes of direction in the outline of forms" have been noted previously in the squared scrolls of such monuments as Structure 1B-2 and Stela H. The style of personification heads seen on Stela E basal register is entirely comparable to squared glyph styles of both Stelae D and E. Furthermore, the scrolls on the base of Stela E are not interlaced or "decorative" but represent distinctive iconographic elements, such as the forehead, tooth, nose, nostril, and mouth scroll of the personification heads. Nor are there scrolls with inner decoration. In short, the stylistic features of Stela E have a clear local lineage and may even have been emphasized in order to draw attention to that heritage.

4.45. CPN Stela B. Photo by Thomas Tolles.

Left

4.46. QRG Stela E, north face, cast. From Maudslay 1889–1902, *Archaeology*, vol. 2, Plate 28a. From the facsimile edition of *Biologia Centrali-Americana* by Alfred Percival Maudslay. Published 1974 by Milpatron Publishing Corp., Stamford, Conn. Further reproduction prohibited.

4.47. QRG Stela E, north face, detail of face. Photo by Thomas Tolles.

Conclusion

The complex of texts and images of Stela E develops webs of meaning in the Platform 1A-1 program through iconographic similarities with Stelae F and D. Aside from their headdresses and basal registers, the royal portraits of all three stelae are virtually identical, depicting the king in association with triadic emblems. These identify him with domains of warfare, supernatural communication, and rebirth through the universal metaphor of maize. The God K scepter held by the ruler on all three monuments further suggests his control of the power of

4.48. QRG Stela E, east face, detail. Photo by Thomas Tolles.

umental practices at Copan. While Stela F continues the trend established by Stela J, quoting iconography directly from contemporary monuments at Copan, the later Stelae D and E make reference only to earlier sculptures at Copan and their patrons, such as the reference to the decapitation of Waxaklajun Ub'ah K'awil on Stela E. This shift coincides with the accession of a new ruler at Copan and suggests that the political relationship between the two sites became less antagonistic after the death of K'ak' Yipyaj. As the next chapter shows, the culminating monuments of the Platform 1A-1 program continue this trend through an almost total disengagement from the sculptural rhetoric of Copan. Instead, they focus on continuity of rule within Quirigua and promote the role of the king as a universal architect.

lightning. Despite subtle differences among the monuments, these are the dominant personae conveyed through the iconography and texts.

The first three stelae of Platform 1A-1 are also unified in other ways. The thematic correspondence of Stelae E and D is close: both depict the king celebrating an ancient period ending on the south face and the historical period ending on the north. The narrative structures of the hieroglyphic texts of Stelae E and F are similar, proceeding from a historical period ending through two paradigmatic supernatural period endings on the east side. The contrasting west-facing texts summarize the history of the king's reign from accession, through the decapitation of Waxaklajun Ub'ah K'awil, to the present period ending. Stela E thus generates links to Stela F through its text and to Stela D through its iconography. Formally, too, Stela E is related to both monuments but is especially connected to Stela F by its extreme height. Exceeding Stela F only slightly in height (8 m as opposed to 7.3 m for Stela F), Stela E functions with Stela F as a huge gateway into the north monument group of K'ak' Tiliw.

At the same time, a distinct shift can be noted in the way that the Quirigua sculptures make reference to mon-

5

FOUNDATION OF THE COSMIC HOUSE

Stelae C and A and Zoomorph B

THE THREE monuments erected for the last two *hotun* celebrations of K'ak' Tiliw's reign constitute the climax of the Platform 1A-1 program. They also stand as one of the most remarkable statements of the divinity of a Maya ruler known from the Classic period. Although Stelae C and A were dedicated as a pair on 9.17.5.0.0 and Zoomorph B five tuns later, these three sculptures constitute a single symbolic unit, a program within a program, which I refer to as the "A-B-C program." In addition, the monuments were clearly designed to be "read" in a sequence, beginning with the easternmost monument, Stela C, then Stela A, and finally Zoomorph B. Likewise, within each monument, texts are read from east to west and images from south (obverse) to north (reverse). In order to convey a clear understanding of the meaning of these monuments, this chapter begins with a discussion of the group as a whole, before analyzing each monument in succession.

The A-B-C program is inaugurated by the east text of Stela C with an account of the creation of the cosmos (Fig. 5.1; see Freidel, Schele, and Parker 1993; Looper 1995b; MacLeod 1991; Schele 1992b). The two crucial events noted here are the appearance and bundling of the cosmic stone tripod. The wording used in reference to the appearance of the tripod is identical to that of Stela F, dedicated fifteen tuns earlier. The text goes on to describe the establishment or dedication of each of these stones, noting the agents of dedication, the identity of the stone, and its location. The first stone is a "jaguar platform," set up by the Paddler deities at a place called "First Five Sky." The second stone, a "snake platform," is planted by an unknown deity at "Large Town(?)." The third stone is a "water platform," erected by the god Itzamnah at "??-

Sky, First Three-Stone place." Their dedication is overseen by an entity called "Six Sky *ajaw*," which Freidel, Schele, and Parker (1993: 73–74) identify with the "Maize God." In my view, there is insufficient evidence to support this identification.

This text is of great importance not only because it is the unique record in the Maya inscriptional corpus of the identities and agents of the three cosmic platforms or thrones but also because it introduces the entire A-B-C program by identifying the mythological reference for the three monuments as the three stones of Creation. The sequence in which the supernatural thrones are presented establishes the pattern for the dedications of the three Quirigua monuments from east to west, with Stela C located farthest to the east and Zoomorph B placed just to the south and west of Stela A (Fig. 5.2). In addition, the first two platforms are depicted prominently on the obverse faces of Stelae C and A. Stela C shows an image of K'ak' Tiliw holding in his arms a platform made of jaguar pelt and crossed bones, with jaguar heads adorning the two sides (Fig. 5.3). Great floods of divine energy spew forth from the ends of the object, emphasizing its supernatural nature and its identity with the first platform of Creation. The second platform is pictured on Stela A, cradled in the arms of K'ak' Tiliw and matching the first object in all respects, save the snake head termini which mark it as the second platform (Fig. 5.4). This object is differentiated from a double-headed serpent bar (such as shown on Stela H west) by its bone and jaguar pelt construction and by the lack of spirit beings emerging from the ends.

Finally, the third platform or throne is recreated in effigy at Quirigua, embodied in Zoomorph B (Fig. 5.5).

This monument, identified as a platform by analogy with the other zoomorphs at Quirigua, is carved in the form of a crocodilian, known to Mayanists as the Cosmic Monster (Stone 1983, 1985).[1] Not only does the aquatic realm of the crocodilian correspond to the third Creation stone's symbolism as a "water platform," but the patron of the third platform, Itzamnah, is closely associated with the Cosmic Monster. For example, polychrome ceramics depict the deity seated on thrones or benches that take the form of a skyband, a device which often represents the body of the Cosmic Monster (Fig. 5.6; Carlson and Landis 1985; see also Taube 1992: 36–40). The glyph which names Zoomorph B also includes a water-lily-adorned creature (Fig. 5.7).

In the previous chapter it was suggested that the root metaphor of the three cosmic platforms was a tripod of stones used as an architectural support. And indeed, the three Quirigua monuments are set up in a triangle rather than a line, thus evoking this metaphor. Yet the three monuments are not equivalent. Although the two stelae are set up as a pair and share size (ca. 4 m in height), shape, composition, and dedication date, both artistic form and dedication date distinguish the stelae from the zoomorphic throne (Figs. 5.8, 5.9). Such patterns of

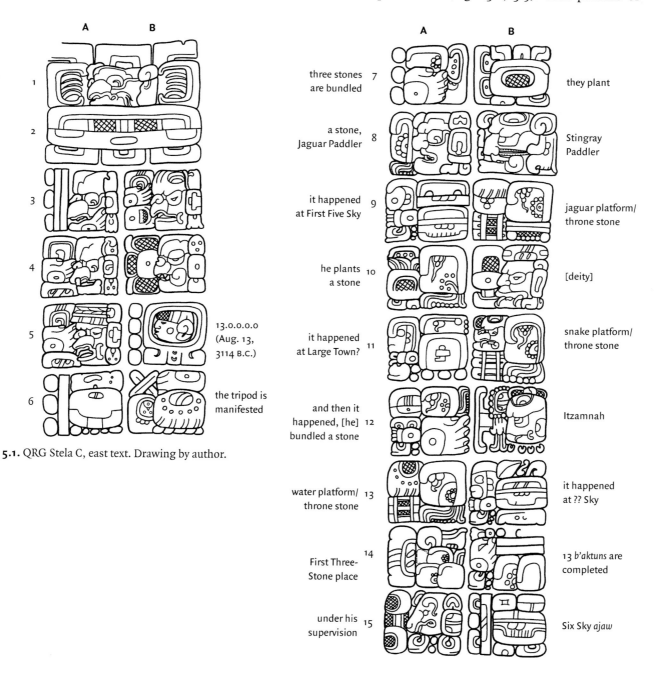

5.1. QRG Stela C, east text. Drawing by author.

(Left column, figure labels A / B, rows 1–6)

1

2

3

4

5 — 13.0.0.0.0 (Aug. 13, 3114 B.C.)

6 — the tripod is manifested

(Right column, figure labels A / B, rows 7–15)

three stones are bundled — 7 — they plant

a stone, Jaguar Paddler — 8 — Stingray Paddler

it happened at First Five Sky — 9 — jaguar platform/ throne stone

he plants a stone — 10 — [deity]

it happened at Large Town? — 11 — snake platform/ throne stone

and then it happened, [he] bundled a stone — 12 — Itzamnah

water platform/ throne stone — 13 — it happened at ?? Sky

First Three-Stone place — 14 — 13 b'aktuns are completed

under his supervision — 15 — Six Sky ajaw

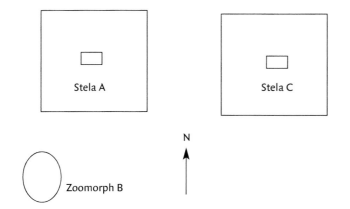

Stela A   Stela C

N

Zoomorph B

5.2. QRG Platform 1A-1, plan showing arrangement of Stelae A and C and Zoomorph B. Drawing by author.

5.3. QRG Stela C, south face, detail. Photo by Thomas Tolles.

5.4. QRG Stela A, south face, detail. Photo by Thomas Tolles.

complementation and hierarchy apparent in the monument program suggest that the three stones of Creation are not equivalent entities.

This conclusion is supported by a close reading of the syntactic structure of the Stela C east text (Fig. 5.1). The first two throne-settings are described in a parallel construction or couplet, which emphasizes their complementary relationship. Both clauses begin with an identical verb (*utz'apaw* "he plants it"), followed by the agent, location, and name of the stone. Hierarchy between the first pair of thrones and the third is conveyed both by the highlighting of the dedication passage of the third throne by the conjunction *i-* "and then" and by the use of a different verb (*k'alaj* "it is bundled") from that employed in reference to the first two dedications. The syntax following the dedication verb of the third stone also differs from the first two phrases, reversing the sequence of location and stone name. The syntactic and verbal variance of the first two passages from the third characterizes the third throne as distinct, defining its dedication as a climactic event. In this sense, the narrative structure of the Stela C text is comparable to the triadic parallel poetic form common in spoken Maya verse. In this style, a variation in the third line of a parallel sequence of three lines signals the end of the verse (Tedlock 1983: 220).

The patterns of complementation and hierarchy established by the narrative of Creation of Stela C are replicated in numerous images and art programs in the Maya area. The Palenque Palace Tablet, for example, depicts the very thrones described in the text of Stela C in order to support the cosmological connotations of the accession ceremony depicted (Fig. 5.10). The ruler, seated in central position atop a throne marked with aquatic (Xok) heads, is flanked by his parents, who are shown atop jaguar- and snake-headed thrones (MacLeod 1991; Schele 1979: 58; see also Hellmuth 1987: 111–129). These heads identify the thrones with the three platforms of Creation. In this image the positioning of the jaguar and snake thrones to the left and right of the king, as well as their association with the ruler's father and mother, suggests their complementary relationship. In contrast, the third throne is placed in the center of the composition and has two heads instead of one, implying its hierarchical distinction from the others. The Xok-headed water throne is also the seat of the living king, thereby distinguishing it from the others by age and generation. This association of youth with the water throne is consistent with the Quirigua Stela C text, which cites this throne as the newest of the triad.

The three thrones represented on the Palace Tablet

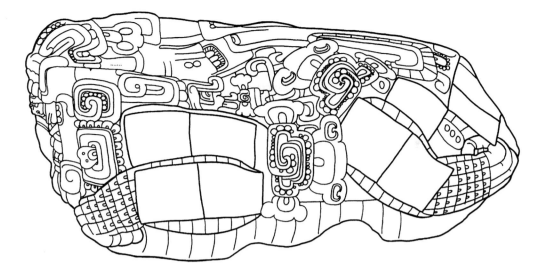

5.5. QRG Zoomorph B, east face, text removed. Drawing by author.

5.6. Itzamnah and moon goddess enthroned. Classic polychrome vessel (K504), detail. Drawing by author.

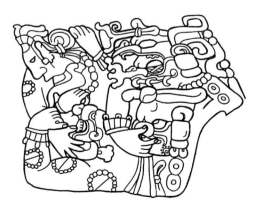

5.7. QRG Zoomorph B, glyph 13. Drawing by author.

also correspond to the identities of three supernatural patrons of Palenque: GI, GII, and GIII (God One, God Two, and God Three) (Berlin 1963; Schele 1979: 61). The jaguar throne corresponds to the jaguar features of GIII; the snake throne matches GII, a snake-footed deity related to God K; and the piscine head of the central throne refers to the aquatic features of GI. At Palenque the major monument associated with these three deities is the Cross Group, a triad of pyramids located in the site core (Fig. 5.11). Arranged around three sides of a rectangular plaza, each pyramid supports a shrine dedicated to one of these gods. On the west and east sides of the plaza, the Temple of the Sun and Temple of the Foliated Cross are associated with GIII and GII. Framed by these two pyramids and dominating them in height and axial position is the Temple of the Cross, dedicated to GI. The triadic structure of pyramids in the Cross Group thus replicates in architectural form the complementary relationship of the jaguar and snake thrones seen at Quirigua and on the Palace Tablet. The hierarchical dominance of the Temple of the Cross corresponds to that of the third throne, the water throne. The identities of the supernatural patrons of the Palenque Cross Group suggest that the triadic structure of Maya architecture could codify the same domains of royal power as the three stones of Creation.[2]

Yet another example that links this poetic patterning to Creation is found in the period-ending emblems discussed in the context of QRG Stela J (see Chapter 3). These insignia include a shield and scepter held in the two hands and a pectoral worn on the chest. The shield, emblazoned with a Jaguar War God image, stands for the first throne, while the serpent-footed God K scepter corresponds to the second throne. Held in the hands, these two elements form a complementary pair and are distin-

5.8. QRG Stela C, south face. Photo by Jesse L. Nusbaum, courtesy of Museum of New Mexico, neg. no. 60884.

5.9. QRG Stela A, south face. Photo by Jesse L. Nusbaum, courtesy of Museum of New Mexico, neg. no. 61305.

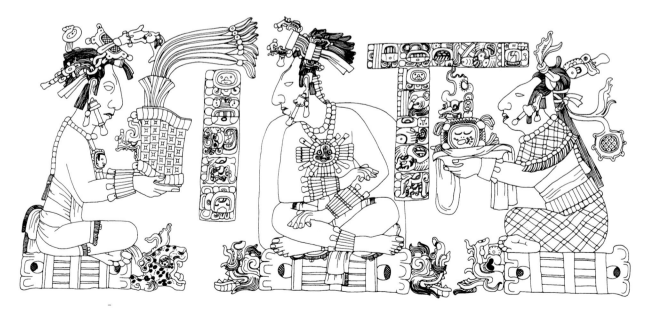

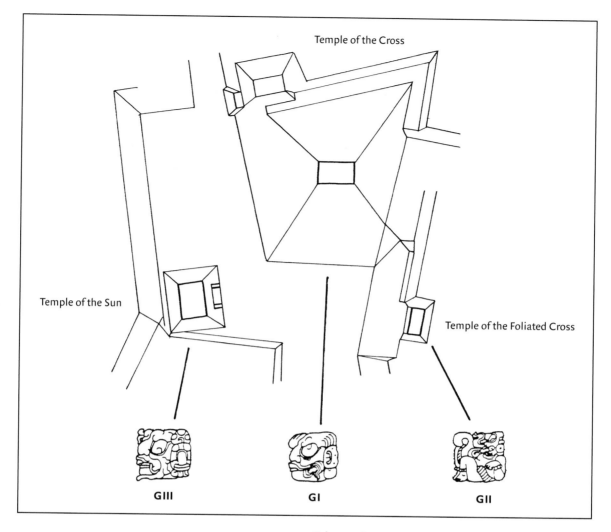

Temple of the Cross

Temple of the Sun

Temple of the Foliated Cross

GIII   GI   GII

5.11. Palenque Cross Group, with corresponding supernatural patrons. Drawing by author.

inguished hierarchically from the third element, whose aquatic symbolism indicates the third throne. Triadic emblems thus cast the king as a creator deity, endowed with the powers to set up space and time through the period-ending celebration. The body is conceived as an expressive medium through which symbolically significant poetic structures can be manipulated.

The three stones of Creation are distinguished not only through formal and compositional relationships in texts and images but also by gender associations. For example, the Palace Tablet image assigns the king's father

Facing page, bottom

5.10. Palenque Palace Tablet, detail. drawing by Linda Schele, © David Schele, courtesy Foundation for the Advancement of Mesoamerican Studies, Inc.

to the jaguar throne, while the mother sits upon the snake throne (Fig. 5.10). While the jaguar throne represents the canonical masculine domain of warfare, the association of the mother with the snake throne recalls the close association of the female gender with rituals of bloodletting and ancestor communication.[3] Based on the biological potential of a woman as mother, this association is supported by texts and iconography. A number of monuments principally from Yaxchilan show royal women bearing the instruments of bloodletting or communicating with ancestors through vision serpents.[4] In addition, some women were named after vision serpents, such as Lady Yax Rabbit of Yaxchilan, shown on Bonampak Stela 2 (Mathews 1980: Fig. 3). Yaxchilan Lintel 14 even names a vision serpent as the spirit companion of one of these women (Houston and Stuart 1989: Fig. 4). A mythical prototype for the ritual role is recorded in the text of the Temple of the Foliated Cross at Palenque, where the primordial conjuring of gods through bloodletting is performed by a maternal goddess, Lady Beastie (Schele and Freidel 1990: 254–255). The supernatural patron of the Temple of the Foliated Cross (GII, God K) is itself the embodiment of the portal of ancestral rebirth, matching closely the stereotypical female role as mother.

In contrast to the first two thrones, the third is associated with mixed gender identity, embodied in the spirit of maize (Looper 2002a). The special association of the third throne with maize is also seen in the elaborate symbolism of the Temple of the Cross at Palenque. Although the primary deity to whom the temple is dedicated was GI, the main panel text of the temple also features an account of the birth and actions of the father of GI, identified as a personification of maize.[5] In fact, the text suppresses the name of GI in order to focus attention on the father. At Palenque the GI portrait head is used in both the names of the father and the son, highlighting the conceptual overlap between the two deities, who are likely aspects of each other. In sum, in the Cross Group two flanking temples embody masculine and feminine gender statuses, while the third axial and dominant structure represents the domain of the androgynous ancestral spirit of maize. The dominant metaphor of Creation conveyed in the Cross Group texts and architectural layout legitimated the claims of its patron to supernatural ancestry.

Stelae C and A (Dedicated December 29, 775)

Having outlined the key symbolisms of the primordial platforms or thrones of Creation, it is possible to interpret additional aspects of the iconography and texts of QRG Stelae C and A in relation to these domains. On the obverse of Stela C the king's costume includes several elements associated with warfare, including the trapezoidal banners and triple knotted zigzag staffs that appear in the headdress flanges (Fig. 5.12). In the headdress shown on QRG Stela J, trapezoidal banners hang below the circular shields attached to spears. Elsewhere in Maya art the knotted zigzag staffs are terminated with flint blades and associated with war costume (Fig. 3.39). Also related to military imagery are the anklets worn by K'ak' Tiliw on Stela C. Although somewhat unclear, they appear to represent the head of the war serpent, which also occurs as anklets on Naranjo Stela 2 as part of a complete martial costume. These militaristic symbols reinforce the meaning of the first Creation throne that the ruler holds in his hands.

5.12. QRG Stela C, south face, rolled out. Drawing by author.

In contrast, the corresponding face of Stela A depicts the king with symbols of bloodletting (Fig. 5.13). His headdress consists of an exploded version of the "Quadripartite Badge," a Classic Maya icon interpreted as the deified plate of sacrificial offering (see Freidel, Schele, and Parker 1993: 216–217). Although the sacrificial plate itself is not present, the sun signs adjacent to the king's own earflares take the place of the sun-marked plate. Atop the headdress personification head are several elements, including a crown of crossed bands surmounted by a trilobed element. This combination of motifs stands for the crossed-bands pectoral element that usually appears in the Quadripartite Badge. The other two elements of the Quadripartite Badge—a shell (embodying powers of fertility) and stingray spine (used in bloodletting)—also appear in this array. Flanking the upper register of the headdress are profile heads of an anthropomorphic deity associated particularly with cache offerings, identified by the youthful face, the T-shaped sign on the cheek, and the smoking element replacing the lower jaw (Freidel, Schele, and Parker 1993: 420–421). The deified plate of sacrifice represented by the aggregation of elements of the royal headdress on Stela A constitutes a compact symbol of the ritual of autosacrifice and ancestor communication, a domain which was codified by the second stone of Creation held by the ruler.

The remaining texts of Stelae C and A also contain elements that reinforce the ritual domains codified by the first two Creation platforms. The west text of Stela C, in particular, features a monument dedication by Tutum Yol K'inich, an early king of Quirigua in A.D. 455, more than three centuries before the carving of Stela C (Fig. 5.14).[6] The date of this event, 9.1.0.0.0 6 Ajaw 13 Yaxk'in, shares its *tzolk'in* position with the dedication date of Stelae C and A. This text underscores the association of the first Creation stone, depicted on Stela C itself, with a male ancestor. In addition, the location for the monument erection is noted with a combination of undeciphered signs followed by *tz'unun* "hummingbird." The martial and ancestral associations of this highly aggressive bird were well developed in Aztec culture, in which a major patron of warfare and great male ancestral god was Huitzilopochtli, whose name translates as "Hummingbird-on-the-Left." Among the Maya there is some evidence for similar associations; for example, the glyph for a war palanquin at Tikal includes a hummingbird superfix.[7]

The east text of Stela A (Fig. 5.15) features a restatement of the current period ending, 9.17.5.0.0 6 Ajaw 13 K'ayab', and monument erection. As with the previous stelae, F, D, and E, the text then moves to the far distant past and, on the west face, records the completion of nineteen cycles of an unknown period on 6 Ajaw 13 Yax (Fig. 5.16). A god named Ik' Hun ("Black Headband") is said to have supervised this period ending at a supernatural location called "Black Earth Flower place." The text closes with a restatement of the scattering event by K'ak' Tiliw on the current period ending. The relationship be-

5.13. QRG Stela A, south face, rolled out. Drawing by author.

tween this text and the domain of the second Creation stone is embodied in the toponym at D4, where the supernatural period ending took place. An identical version of this toponym appears on the legs and front panel of a bench upon which the wife and daughter of the Piedras Negras ruler K'inich Yo'nal Ahk II are shown seated on Piedras Negras Stela 3 (Fig. 2.29b). Not only does the as-

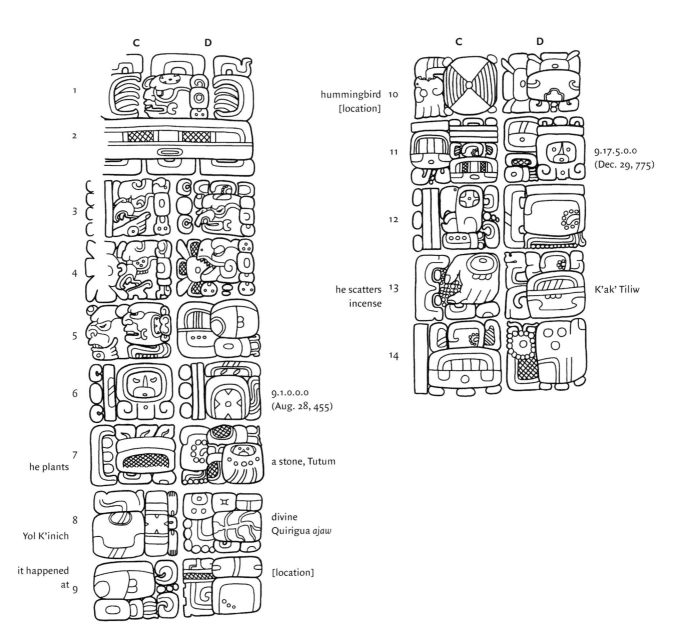

5.14. QRG Stela C, west text. Drawing by author.

sociation of this toponym with women recall the feminine connotations of the second throne of Creation, but the bench panel shows a vision rite taking place in association with the toponym. The mention of this location in the text of Stela A at Quirigua, then, highlights the symbolism of the throne that the monument commemorates.

Like the two south (obverse) faces of Stelae C and A, the imagery of the north (reverse) faces of the monuments also features themes related to cosmic renewal (Figs. 5.17, 5.18). In addition, like the south-face scenes, the north faces of the two stelae have similar composi-

tions, suggesting their interpretation as a pair. The text which serves as a basal register for both the south and north scenes of Stela C defines the relationship between the two faces. On the south face (Fig. 5.19a), the text records the Calendar Round date 1 Eb' 5 Yax (9.17.4.10.12) followed by an unknown verb and then "6 Ajaw stone." Since the main logograph of the verb consists of a stela-like sign with *kawak* (stone) markings and "6 Ajaw stone" is the monument name given on Stela A, it seems likely that the passage is a record of a prededication event involving Stela C or A or both monuments, possibly their quarrying. The text and image, therefore, record historical events, although it should be noted that the text does not precisely illustrate the scene that appears above. Rather, it contains supplemental information which expands on the significance of the scene.

The north text of Stela C (Fig. 5.19b) includes a distance number of eight days, which, taken from the Calendar Round on the south face, leads to 9.17.4.11.0 9 Ajaw 13 Yax, recorded as 9 Ajaw. The verb is not presently decipherable, but the topic is named as Jun Ajaw and Yax B'alam, the Hero Twins of Classic Maya lore. Even though the precise relationship of these texts to the images above them is uncertain, two points can be made. First, given that both text and image on the south face seem to record a historical event, it stands to reason that the north-face figure represents a supernatural or mythological event, following the sense of the text. Second, the

two texts are continuous (read from south to north), implying that the scenes are to be interpreted as related and sequential (read from south to north), like the iconographic sequence of previous monuments of the 1A-1 platform.[8]

The figure on Stela C north (Fig. 5.17) is anthropomorphic, with aged features and a crossed-banded leaflike element emerging from his mouth and wearing a circular nose ornament decorated with three flowers. These features identify this being as the patron of the *hab'* period Pax, which functions in inscriptions as phonetic *te'* "tree/plant" and, in iconography, as a personified tree. His counterpart on Stela A (Fig. 5.18) is an aged, bearded god with jaguar feet and a jaguar ear. The eye of this deity has the remains of a curled pupil and is framed by a "cruller."[9] This deity probably corresponds to Ik' Hun,

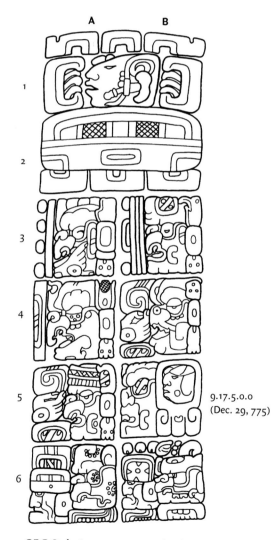

9.17.5.0.0
(Dec. 29, 775)

it is
planted

6 Ajaw

stone 11

5.15. QRG Stela A, east text. Drawing by author.

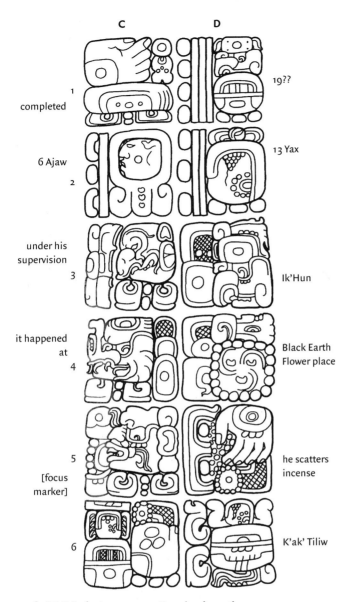

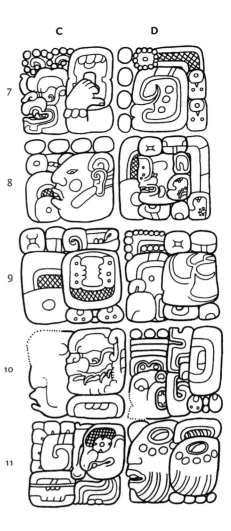

	C	D	
1	completed		19??
2	6 Ajaw		13 Yax
3	under his supervision		Ik'Hun
4	it happened at		Black Earth Flower place
5	[focus marker]		he scatters incense
6			K'ak' Tiliw

5.16. QRG Stela A, west text. Drawing by author.

who is mentioned as the patron of a supernatural period ending on the west face text of Stela A (D3). The deities on the reverse of both Stelae C and A wear *sak*-pectorals with crossed-band infixes. They dance with one heel raised, under canopies formed of skyband elements. The avian creatures perched atop the canopies may be identified as the Principal Bird Deity, based on remains of pectoral elements on Stela A. The skyband canopy and the snake head with a glyphic "sky" cartouche at its tip imply that these are astronomical representations.

Emerging from the register of the bird are thin cords, which descend along the east and west sides of the scenes, twisting about each other as they are manipu-

lated by the gods. Their descent from the realm of the Principal Bird Deity and the east–west orientation suggest that these cords are analogous to the strung ear-flares that the king manipulates on Stela F south (Fig. 4.8). Both represent the cosmic umbilicus as ecliptic. This identification is confirmed by the flower signs that label the Stelae C and A north cords as well as by the heads that terminate the cords (Fig. 5.20a), dangling inverted at the sides of the figures. These heads are similar to those which terminate the breath scrolls that emanate from the mouth of the figure on Quirigua Altar P', which are glyphically marked as "white flower? breath/spirit" (Fig. 5.20b; Stone 1983). These cords embody the es-

5.17. QRG Stela C, north face. Drawing by author.

5.18. QRG Stela A, north face. Drawing by author.

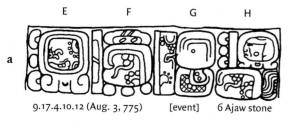

E	F	G	H
9.17.4.10.12 (Aug. 3, 775)		[event]	6 Ajaw stone

5.19. QRG Stela C basal texts: *a*, south; *b*, north. Drawing by
author.

I	J	K	L
9.17.4.11.0 (Aug. 11, 775)		[event]	Jun Ajaw, Yax B'alam

sence of life that animates the cosmos, manifested by the actions of the gods during Creation.

While the scenes of dancing deities manifesting celestial umbilici as depicted on Stelae C and A are unique in Maya sculpture, they may be compared with depictions from other media. In particular, they bear close correspondence to the scene from the Motul de San José vase discussed in the context of Stela F (Fig. 4.12). The correspondences between the vase scene and Quirigua Stelae C and A (Figs. 5.21, 5.22) include not only the cords but also the identity of one of the supernaturals. The Pax patron shown on Stela C seems to correspond to the god at the

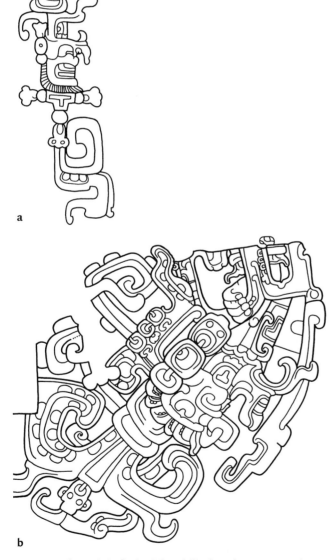

5.20. Head termini of celestial umbilical cords: *a*, QRG Stela C, north, detail; *b*, QRG Altar P′, detail. Drawings by author.

right in the vase scene, located beneath the L-shaped text. The jaguar paw behind the ear of this figure is an attribute of two Maya gods, the youthful god of the number nine and the aged Pax patron. Judging from the aged features of the god on the pot, his identification as the Pax patron is likely. Another feature shared by the monuments and vase is the location of the action as a mountain.

In the context of the Quirigua stelae, this location is indicated in the basal register of Stela A north, which shows a mountain personification head with a fragrant flower infixed into the forehead (Fig. 5.23a). This flower-marked mountain may refer to a sacred mountain of Quirigua, possibly the Five-Flower Mountain that K'ak' Tiliw created in effigy early in his reign, in the form of Structure 1B-2. This toponym contrasts with that shown on the south face of Stela A, which represents a personified waterlily (Fig. 5.23b). The basal registers of Stela A, then, place the king's platform dedications in the plaza, the Black Lake (or waterlily) place, and situate the supernatural result of this action in the context of the Creation mountain of Quirigua. The orientation of the supernatural scenes of the stelae to the north is consistent not only with the northern associations of the Principal Bird Deity but also with the northern mountain where the cosmic umbilicus is manifested on the vase. The birth theme suggested by the vase image also fits well with this interpretation, since the Classic Creation mountain floated upon the primordial sea and contained the seed of future generations as well as the bones of the dead.

The squared pattern woven by the umbilici on the vase and on the stela is also highly symbolic. It recalls the Maya use of ropes for measuring spaces, including architectural sites. It also evokes crucial events mentioned in the *Popol Vuh*, where the gods laid out the horizontal space of the cosmos by stretching cords in a squared pattern (Tedlock 1985: 72). This cosmic diagram is based on the perceived annual movement of the sun in the tropics from its southern rising point in December, through the zenith position, to the northern solstice point in June, and back again southward. Girard (1966: 33–34) explicitly related this text to Ch'orti' notions of perpetual cosmic Creation through the measuring of space by solar movement from east to west and north to south and back again. On the two days of zenith passage, the sun at midday passes directly overhead, precisely in the center of the cosmogram. The zenith passage had special associations with Creation for the ancient Maya as well and may have been used for establishing the base date of the Long Count calendar, which fell on August 13, 3114 B.C. (Lounsbury, in Freidel, Schele, and Parker 1993: 423).

5.21. QRG Stela C, north face. From Maudslay 1889–1902, *Archaeology*, vol. 2, Plate 20. From the facsimile edition of *Biologia Centrali-Americana* by Alfred Percival Maudslay. Published 1974 by Milpatron Publishing Corp., Stamford, Conn. Further reproduction prohibited.

5.22. QRG Stela A, north face, detail of cast. From Maudslay 1889–1902, *Archaeology*, vol. 2, Plate 8. From the facsimile edition of *Biologia Centrali-Americana* by Alfred Percival Maudslay. Published 1974 by Milpatron Publishing Corp., Stamford, Conn. Further reproduction prohibited.

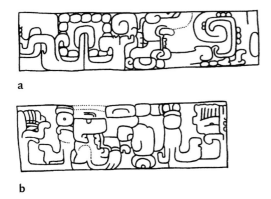

a

b

5.23. QRG Stela A basal registers: *a*, north; *b*, south. Drawing by author.

Stela C confirms the association of the twisted cords with the zenith passage, as the text below the image of the dancing god who pulls cords from the sky bears a date corresponding to August 11, 775—the date of second zenith passage at Quirigua.

A final clue to the significance of these images for the program is the abundance of triple-knot motifs that the gods wear on both stela scenes. The triple-knot motif is a pervasive symbol of ritual bloodletting, adorning both bloodletting instruments and penitents (Joralemon 1974).[10] A sacrificial motif also appears on the Motul vase, in the form of the plate in which the young god is shown seated atop a crocodilian (Fig. 4.12). In fact, as Karl Taube (1994) has pointed out, the central deity on this vase combines features of the "Maize God" and the Baby Jaguar, deities which are commonly shown as sacrificial victims. He suggests that the scene on the vase is an image of a *k'ex* "substitute/replacement" sacrifice, in which a god is killed in order for the succession or birth of another being to occur. In the scenes of Quirigua Stelae C and A north, the sacrificial iconography is worn by the supernatural beings, suggesting that it is their personal sacrifice that allows for the succession of the *k'atun*. The two gods are also shown in the conventional Maya dance position, with a heel raised, imparting to the period ending the transformational, liminal quality inherent in Maya dance.[11] As the king's blood sacrifice was believed to give birth to the gods, so the sacrificial dance of these patrons of the period ending caused the cosmic umbilicus to fall from heaven.

In sum, the reverse scenes of Stelae C and A show the supernatural events of the period ending which replicate the events of Creation. They are the divine counterpart for the obverse faces, which depict K'ak' Tiliw setting platforms to renew the cosmos. The imagery of the south

and north faces of Stelae C and A sacralizes the period ending, linking royal ritual acts and supernatural events through the symbolism of cosmogenesis. Implicit in each of these images is an architectural metaphor, involving the placement of a stone tripod by the ruler and the measurement of the sacred house symbolized by Platform 1A-1 and its monuments.

Zoomorph B (Dedicated December 2, 780)

In contrast to the complex evocation of the ritual domains symbolized by the first two Creation stones in QRG Stelae C and A, Zoomorph B is remarkably simple, at least in its programming of text and image (Fig. 5.5). The approximately 4-m-long monument was originally raised above the platform surface by three huge stone slabs, with its head facing the front of the program, toward the south (Strömsvik 1941: Fig. 8c).[12] Although the creature represented in this sculpture has been identified variously as a tiger, dragon, turtle, and toad, it is actually a supernatural crocodilian, sometimes termed the Cosmic Monster (Stone 1983). The clawed forelegs and hind legs of the creature are represented folded on the east and west sides of the monument, the joints marked with huge water scrolls accented with flower signs. Such symbols allude to the animal's identification with the underworld or primordial sea that supports and surrounds the earth. The earth itself is represented on the back of the creature, as if floating on it, as an enormous *witz* "mountain, hill" mask that runs the entire length of the monument (Fig. 5.24). The front head of the Cosmic Monster has eyes represented with crossed-bands, in typical fashion, and the mouth open wide (Fig. 5.25). Out of this maw emerges a figure with headdress and abundant jade jewelry (Fig. 5.26). The beard on this figure's chin leaves little doubt that it represents K'ak' Tiliw himself, who is shown on all other Platform 1A-1 monuments with the same facial feature. Footprints are carved at the bottom of the front jaw, oriented with the toes pointed toward the open maw, as if to mark the royal path.

Like other Cosmic Monsters, that of Zoomorph B bears on its posterior (the north side; Fig. 5.27) a huge mask of the Quadripartite Badge. Here it lies on its side, with the stingray spine pointing toward the west. Emerging from the tip of the spine is a crossed-bands symbol and flower, probably an allusion to the cosmic umbilicus manifested through bloodletting (Fig. 5.28). Behind the flower and spine, also wrapping around the monument's west side, is the tail of the crocodilian, marked with dotted ovals. At the end of the tail is a head identified as that of the Principal Bird Deity. In its elaboration of ex-

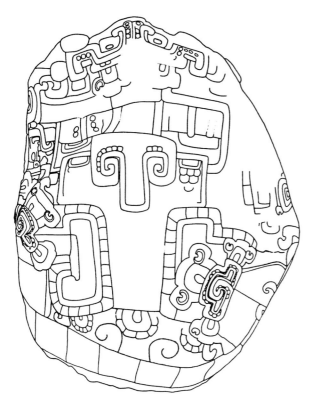

5.24. QRG Zoomorph B, upper. Drawing by Andrea Stone.

5.26. QRG Zoomorph B, south, detail. Photo by Thomas Tolles.

5.25. QRG Zoomorph B, south face. Drawing by author.

ecution, the text of Zoomorph B (Fig. 5.29), carved along the Cosmic Monster's limbs, parallels the iconography of the monument. It includes a Long Count date and lunar series, followed by a dedication phrase, all rendered in full-figure form.

In spite of its conventional image and text, the association of Zoomorph B with Stelae C and A permits a richer interpretation of its meaning in the context of Platform 1A-1. As previously noted, the Stela C text gives the mythological counterpart of Zoomorph B as a "water platform/throne stone," that is, a platform associated with the aquatic underworld. Zoomorph B itself was set in place on the western edge of Platform 1A-1, just as the primordial sea surrounds the earth. But the monumental image also has an astronomical dimension. In the sky the Cosmic Monster form of the Milky Way is the only conformation that stretches east to west, with the rift in its western extremity interpreted as the mouth of the creature (Freidel, Schele, and Parker 1993: 85–87; Milbrath 1999: 291). After sundown on the evening of the dedication of Zoomorph B (December 2, 780), the Milky Way was visible in this conformation. The monument,

5.27. QRG Zoomorph B, north face. Neg. no. 5102, courtesy San Diego Museum of Man.

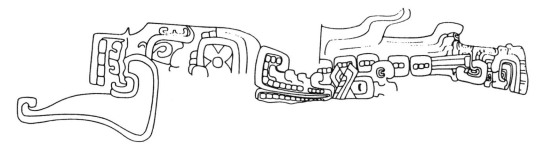

5.28. QRG Zoomorph B, rollout of north–west details. Drawing by Andrea Stone.

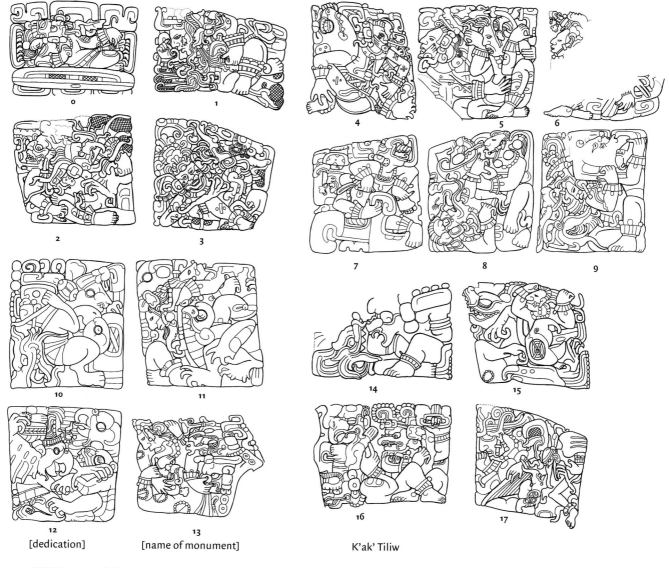

0

1

2

3

4

5

6

7

8

9

10

11

12
[dedication]

13
[name of monument]

14

15

16

17

K'ak' Tiliw

5.29. QRG Zoomorph B, text. Drawing by author.

therefore, represents the sky as it was seen on the evening of its dedication: a gigantic crocodile bearing the sun on its tail, floating in the waters of the underworld.

The crocodilian embodied by Zoomorph B relates the ruler to powers of transformation, death, and rebirth, expressed by the emergence of the ruler from the animal's maw. As a manifestation of the sea or ocean that surrounds the earth, Zoomorph B embodies a great portal that connects the world of the living to that of the dead. The patron of the corresponding cosmic platform mentioned in the Stela C Creation account is Itzamnah, who also functions as the canonical shaman or magician of the ancient Maya (Freidel, Schele, and Parker 1993: 211; Taube 1992: 31–41). The association of this divine figure

with Zoomorph B, through the mediation of the Stela C text, draws attention to the monument as a site of the ruler's transformation. Symbolizing this same process is the *sak*-pectoral worn by kings in the period-ending ceremony, which commemorates the third platform. The pectoral identifies the wearer as having been reborn into the status of ruler.

Likewise, the aquatic symbolism of Zoomorph B firmly identifies it with royal accession, by analogy with the fish-headed throne on which the Palenque king accedes on the Palace Tablet. Zoomorph B bears even closer comparison with the scaffold thrones upon which Piedras Negras rulers become kings (Fig. 5.30; Stuart 1984). On these stelae the skyband bodies of Cosmic Monsters surround the ruler. The bloody footprints on the cloth that leads to the scaffold on the Piedras Negras stelae also appear on Zoomorph B, just below the creature's maw, pointing toward the figure of the king. The monument, therefore, is both an image of enthronement and a platform or throne effigy. The footprints indicate the sacrifice of a captive that preceded royal accession. In the Piedras Negras monuments this sacrifice sometimes takes the form of a body, probably a child, placed in a bowl and laid at the foot of the scaffold throne. The function of this offering is to compensate the spirit world for the ritual rebirth of the king upon accession. The symbolism of the Cosmic Monster correlates precisely with the union of death and birth in the platform of accession, as it symbolizes the aquatic underworld surface out of which life springs and into which the souls of the dead fall.

The personified mountain which dominates the upper surface of Zoomorph B also emphasizes the intersection of death and rebirth represented by the Cosmic Monster platform of accession. This image identifies the monument with the Maya mountain of origin, a place where birth cords are manifested, as depicted on Stela A north. On Zoomorph B the ruler emerges from the mouth of the crocodilian just as the maize deity is reborn from the cleft shell of the cosmic turtle. Supporting this interpretation are multiple examples in which the Creation mountains are associated with Cosmic Monsters. Several architectural versions of the Maya mountain of Creation are fitted with Cosmic Monster iconography, such as Copan Structure 10L-22 and Tikal Structure 5D-33-2nd (Freidel, Schele, and Parker 1993: 149–152; Schele and Freidel 1990: 169–170). In addition, the other two Quirigua Zoomorphs (O and P) that represent Cosmic Monsters portray personified mountains on their upper surfaces. The altars associated with these monuments show Chaaks bounding out of cave mouths (Taube 1986: 57). The combined imagery of these programs represents rebirth from the Creation mountain (Fig. 5.31).[13]

As a symbolic equivalent of the Piedras Negras platforms, Zoomorph B represents the culmination of the sacrifice/rebirth cycle begun with Stelae C and A north. The south faces of Stelae C and A show the king's ritual actions that demonstrate his possession of ancestral powers of Creation. The north images of Stelae C and A show sacrifice and rebirth on the supernatural plane, which serve as a basis for the k'ex sacrifice and royal rebirth which take place in the context of Zoomorph B. The three monuments contrast the two major symbols of rebirth: C and A show the cosmic umbilicus, while B itself

5.30. Piedras Negras Stela 6. Drawing by author.

represents the aquatic surface of the underworld out of which rebirth occurs. These two elements are analogous to the umbilical cord and afterbirth of a natural birth. The A-B-C program suggests that these elements proceed in a sequence, with umbilicus preceding aquatic imagery. In this regard, the program matches the pattern established by Stela F, with the south face (cords) preceding the north (aquatic imagery). Following the same model, the A-B-C program conflates accession iconography with symbols of the underworld surface. It offers an expanded narrative of rebirth and accession, incorporating the elements of sacrifice as well as explicitly identifying the three monuments as the three stones of Creation.

Also like Stela F, the A-B-C program was erected to celebrate period endings, implying yet again the symmetry of Creation, period ending, and royal accession. The conflation of accession and period-ending costume shown on Stelae F, D, and E supports this conclusion, as does the patterning of texts of these stelae, which consistently contrasts period ending and accession (or accession anniversaries) on opposite faces of the monuments. Because the period ending is an anniversary of the creation of the cosmos, it provided an occasion through which K'ak' Tiliw's accession could be compared to the Creation. The imagery of Stela F conveys this relationship in one way, fusing accession iconography and symbols of the rebirth of maize. The A-B-C program implies it in another, representing the ruler's accession throne as a primordial platform of Creation and backing this throne with images of the ruler setting the other two Creation thrones.

Like a period ending, in which the king's bloodletting gave birth to the gods, the accession of K'ak' Tiliw constituted a new beginning. It represented a renewal of the basic patterns of space and time first established on 4 Ajaw 8 Kumk'u, when the gods set three stones. Further, when a stone image of the king was ritually bound in the period-ending ceremony, it became an *ajaw*, a new extension of the king's persona. Like a newborn child, it was swaddled in white cloth to indicate its recent arrival from the supernatural realm. K'ak' Tiliw's program of two stelae and zoomorph constitutes a remarkably comprehensive statement of the supernatural origins of the king's power, weaving accounts of ancestral history, extremely ancient supernatural events, and an elaborate story of Creation into a fabric that supports the king's own crucial rituals of warfare, bloodletting, accession, and period-ending celebration.

Although many other Maya rulers employed elements of Creation mythology to sacralize dynastic history, nowhere is the rhetoric so focused upon the amplification of the cult of the autonomous king as at Quirigua. For instance, while Creation thrones on the Palenque Palace Tablet create a cosmic setting for the king's accession, exclusive agency over the thrones is not claimed. Also, the ruler is shown together with his father and mother.

This parallels the genealogical structure of the narrative of Creation at Palenque. In contrast, K'ak' Tiliw is himself portrayed on Stelae C and A in the guise of an architect of Creation, setting up sacred platforms or thrones. His actions and costuming shown on these monuments manifest his personal appropriation of twin ritual domains of warfare and autosacrifice/ancestral communication. In the Creation narrative of Stela C, these domains are personified by a series of gods who act under

5.31. Arrangement of monuments at Quirigua: *a*, Altar P'; *b*, Zoomorph P, upper. Drawing by author.

the authority of a higher entity, the "Six Sky *ajaw*," and who are completely different from the divinities mentioned at Palenque. Stelae C and A are themselves presented as a backdrop for the ruler's own accession and ritual rebirth, embodied by Zoomorph B. As such, the program expresses very much the same political statement noted in the text of Stela J, in which the king's personal actions are put forward as the foundation of rulership. Thus, the A-B-C program may be interpreted as the climax not only of the program of Platform 1A-1 but also of a lifelong artistic agenda that sought to proclaim sovereignty for Quirigua and to assert K'ak' Tiliw's personal and divinely sanctioned role in effecting this independence.

The Platform 1A-1 Program

While it has been argued that Stelae C and A and Zoomorph B constitute a distinct program, the meaning of the group must be contextualized in terms of the larger program associated with Platform 1A-1. Although it was constructed in two phases and took roughly two decades to complete, the significance of the Platform 1A-1 program develops through the complex referencing of inscriptions and images among monuments that are spatially integrated. The major organizing feature (barely visible today) would have been the platform itself, which frames the monuments and sets them apart from the other stelae. Structure 1A-3 serves as a backdrop to this platform, unifying the stelae through their visual and spatial association with an imposing solitary structure. The six monuments also share relegation of dedication texts to east and west faces and images of the king to the south.

These royal images are unified, in that all are bearded and conform to a similar youthful facial ideal with wide-open eyes and parted lips. In fact, the beards may have a specific iconographic function. As a sign of great age and wisdom, they may have symbolized the king's ability to travel into the remote (supernatural) past, as described on several of the monuments. A likely model for such use of the beard is Copan Stela C, the west face of which may show the bearded ruler in a supernatural context (Fig. 4.21). In their usage at Quirigua, the beards may also constitute a visual pun in that the Maya word for "beard," *tzuk*, also means "partition." Therefore, the monuments mark cosmic partitions along east–west and south–north axes.[14] The same symbolism is implied by their axial placements and the rendering of the stelae with four distinct faces. The reading orders of the texts of the monuments call attention to these axes, leading on all monuments from east to west and on Stela C from south to north. The complementary imagery of the monuments on the platform also draws attention to the axes defined by southern and northern images.

Other correspondences and repetitions among the texts and images bind them together organically. On Stelae F, D, and E, the textual narratives proceed from the monument dedication to a mythical precedent, to the king's accession or anniversary, and then recapitulate the period ending. The climactic A-B-C program differs from the other three stelae, supporting the monument dedications with accounts of Creation mythology, a fundamental historical monument dedication, and a mythological period ending. The variance of the final monumental triad from the norm of Stelae F, D, and E recalls the standard narrative pattern of most lengthy Maya texts, in which the climactic event is marked by "disturbed syntax" (Josserand 1991). Thus, the texts of the monuments of Platform 1A-1 may be considered a coherent, continuous narrative.

Although the narrative formula and compositional structure of Stelae F, D, and E contrast with those of the northwestern triad, the personae embodied by the portraits in the final group are related to those of Stela F in particular. In the A-B-C program, K'ak' Tiliw is associated with the sacred energies of growing maize through his rituals of cosmic renewal. On the obverse of Stelae C and A, he performs with cosmic thrones, akin to images of maize deities on polychrome ceramics who dance with the same thrones in their backracks (see Freidel, Schele, and Parker 1993: 276–277). Zoomorph B shows the ruler within the mountain of Creation, out of which the maize is reborn. Stela F cultivates similar personae, depicting the king with paired symbols of the rebirth of maize.[15] The remaining two monuments of Platform 1A-1, Stelae D and E, convey similar personae, depicting the king in contrasting supernatural and historical time/space-frames. Such thematic patterning creates correspondences between opposite corners, binding the monument group together crosswise (Fig. 5.32). Appearing in the context of monumental themes of cosmogenesis, the cross-point of these thematic lines, the center point of Platform 1A-1, becomes analogous to the center of the universe. The establishment of a cosmic center and the erection of a tree at the heart of the world is a major theme of Maya Creation, just as the rising of the constellation of three stones in Orion on 4 Ajaw 8 Kumk'u placed the nexus of Creation near the center of the sky at dawn.

The monumental art program of Platform 1A-1, however, does not float freely in two dimensions but has a fixed front, established by Stelae F and E. These two ste-

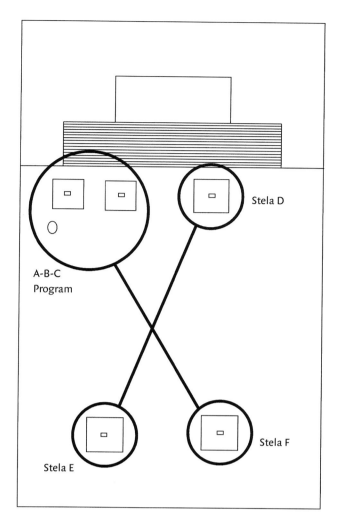

5.32. Diagram of programmatic correspondences of QRG Platform 1A-1 monuments. Drawing by author.

lae are similar in height and proportion, forming what amounts to a gateway into the platform space. Their texts are also alike, both incorporating accounts of the decapitation of the Copan king. The resulting emphasis on the southern edge of the platform as the program front ties the program of monuments firmly to the greater Classic-period stela tradition which places stelae in front of architecture. Although K'ak' Tiliw's program comes close to liberating the stela from architecture, it does not quite break the symbolic bond between the structures, established centuries earlier by the Olmec.

The strong directional patterning of the program, with east and south dominant, suggests analogies to modern Maya beliefs concerning world directions and their associations. Nearly universal among the Maya is the association of east and west with birth and death, modeled on the movement of the sun during the day and of stars,

planets, and the moon at night (see Thompson 1950: 249–252). The concept of east as dominant is expressed in the Ch'olti' term for east: *tzatzib quin* [*tzatzib' k'in*], literally "strong sun" (Moran 1935: 48). In Ch'olti' south is *nool* [*nohol*] (the "great" or "right-hand" side of the sun), and in Ch'orti' *tz'ik ik'ar* (literally "left-hand wind") refers to the north wind (Moran 1935: 60; Wisdom 1950: 739). This ranking corresponds exactly to the iconographic sequence identified at Quirigua. It seems likely that the uniform east-to-west sequence of monument dedication and text ordering among the Platform 1A-1 program evokes the movement of the sun during the day.

The placement of the monuments at intercardinal points on Platform 1A-1 may also be a solar reference. These points are of widespread interest among ancient and modern Maya alike as the critical stations at which the sun pauses on the horizon at the summer and winter solstices.[16] Indeed, the solstice points form the basis of one of the most widely recognized of Maya cosmograms: the square divided into quadrants. In Yukatek cosmology, giant Pawatuns lift the sky from the earth at these four corners (Thompson 1970: 195). For the Ch'orti', four cosmic corner posts support the sky as the corner posts support the walls and roof of a house (Fought 1972: 433; Girard 1962: 45). The Ch'orti' also generate a cosmogram from stone markers placed at solstitial points.

A similar domestic metaphor is apparent in the Quirigua program, in the explicit references to cosmic architectural tripod-supports in the texts of Stela F and Stela C and in the images of cosmic measuring-cords on the obverse of Stelae A and C. In fact, among its many symbolisms, the Platform 1A-1 program may have been conceived as a great symbolic house, with a foundation tripod, stelae as corner posts, and the sky as a roof. Such a metaphorical significance is not far-fetched, especially as Stela J at neighboring Copan was originally capped by a trapezoidal stone effigy roof. The domestic symbolism of the Platform 1A-1 monuments also recalls the Creation narrative from the Cross Group at Palenque, which mentions the dedication of a house in the north in association with the date February 5, 3112 B.C. (Freidel, Schele, and Parker 1993: 71–73). In the interpretation offered here, the 1A-1 program at Quirigua, erected at the northern end of the site core, may represent this very structure. Indeed, the "Six Sky *ajaw*" appellative that appears on QRG Stela C (B15) may be a reference to this structure. In the Palenque Tablet of the Cross text (D10), the name of the cosmic house of the north includes a similar collocation. The six monuments of the 1A-1 program may therefore directly evoke the "Six Sky ajaw" as a personified cosmic dwelling.

From the subtropical point of view of the Maya, cosmograms such as the 1A-1 program represent the unification of space and time, in which the sun over the course of the year sweeps northward and then southward, encompassing the entire surface of the flat, square earth. On days of zenith passage, when the sun stands directly overhead at noon, the corners of the diagram frame the sun as if they were the four corners of the cosmos bracketing the center. The program of K'ak' Tiliw actually commemorates both zenith passages in its texts. The May 3 passage is commemorated by the decapitation of Waxaklajun Ub'ah K'awil cited prominently on Stelae F and E, while the zenith passage on August 11 corresponds to the date inscribed on Stela C north. In this latter instance, the association of zenith passage and cosmogenesis is clear, as the zenith passage date is paired with an image of the celestial umbilicus falling from heaven. In total, the stelae make permanent the configuration of four marked corners of the earth with the sun at the center, thereby identifying the program, and Quirigua itself, with the center of the cosmos. Marking off a k'atun of history in hotun intervals, the stelae suggest the symmetry between historic cycles and those of a much larger scale—the succession of cosmic manifestations. Adorned with huge royal portraits, the stelae identify the king's body with the corners of the cosmos, a spatial symbolism reinforced by textual and iconographic references to the king as a creator deity and cosmic architect.

Comparison with the use of cosmograms by the Ch'orti', in fact, suggests that the Quirigua program was also specifically adapted from a ritual procedure designed to control the weather (Looper 2003). As emphasized by Girard (1966, 1995), the Ch'orti' create diagrams of solar movement expressly for this purpose. In the shrine at Quetzaltepeque, the local saint is incorporated into this structure, framed by a quincunx of stones arranged on the altar beneath the image. Perhaps the most complex variant is documented at Chiquimula, in which a feast to the gods is arranged on the temple floor, extending in a long rectangle from the entry on the west to the altar in the east (Girard 1966: 137–138). This arrangement, identified as a diagram of the sun's path, features twelve gourds of chilate on the northern edge, reserved for the clouds, and twelve more on the south, assigned to the angels. A bowl of chilate at the center is designated for the "Center God," a personification of the forces of fertility located at the zenith.

Although their forms are extremely diverse, such Ch'orti' meteorological cosmograms always consist of multiple elements that are viewed as a symbolic totality. They include a cross and/or saint's image, a pit, and a designated zone, sometimes elevated on a table, for the display of food offerings. With the exceptions of Quetzaltepeque and Chiquimula, most shrines have permanent pits located in front of the altar. At Santa Rosalía the pit is called the "soul of the world," while at Quetzaltepeque the canoe substitutes for the pit (Girard 1966: 168). Girard (1966: 164) notes that the combination of altar, cross, and pit is called "the form" (la forma) by the Ch'orti'. While many altars feature arbors of saplings or canes arched over the cross or image, others enclose the entire "form" beneath a celestial arbor. This is documented at Tunucó, where a platform of poles is built over a spring, supported by four forked uprights (Girard 1966: 166). A cross clothed in leaves is located in the center, beneath two leaf-covered arches that connect opposite corners of the platform. Underneath is a pit for offerings. This structure is analogous to the ceremonial house at Cayur, in which the entire interior space is encompassed by flexible poles wrapped in foliage that connect the interior posts (Girard 1966: 163–164). In addition to representing the sky, these arbors constitute miniature houses (Fought 1972: 525). As such, they emphasize the significance of the "form" as a protective and geometrically ordered cosmographic construct that is activated by prayer, sacrifice, and feasting in order to draw beneficent forces from the periphery to the center.

The Ch'orti' are not alone in utilizing complex solar diagrams to manipulate the weather. In the Yucatan the ch'a chàak ceremony is conducted utilizing similar structures and for essentially the same purpose (Freidel, Schele, and Parker 1993: 29–33, 51–58; Sosa 1985: 341, 376–403). In this ritual a four-sided table, embodying the cosmos, is created out of lashed poles. Green boughs arc over the surface of the table, uniting opposite corners and establishing the center of the sky at their crossing point. From the crossing point of the arbor hangs a cord, which supports a ring hung with thirteen gourds. During the ceremony, the ring suspended by the cord at the center of the altar functions as an aperture through which food offerings placed on the table ascend to the rain-bringing Chàaks. Vines attached to the corners of the table are pulled like drawstrings, guiding the offerings toward the sky. Finally, when "the sacred sun is in the middle of the sky at twelve o'clock," the Chàaks assemble overhead, promising rain (Sosa 1985: 393–394). Although separated from the Classic period by over a millennium and performed by village priests rather than by kings, the Ch'orti' and Yukatek Maya rainmaking ceremonies illustrate the remarkable persistence of Maya cosmology, in which the zenith marks a fundamental portal through which fertility is brought to earth, borne on cords.

At Quirigua similar ritual procedures were manipulated during period-ending rites, celebrated by the Platform 1A-1 program. Integrating images of the cosmic rain-bringing cords (Stelae A, C, and F), references to rain deities (Stelae D and F), decapitation events (Stelae E and F), zenith passage dates (Stelae E, F, and C), and a ritual formula related to rainmaking (Stela F), through a cosmic diagram of solar movement, the Platform 1A-1 program implies the transformation of political actions by the ruler into the divine blessings of fertility through regular rainfall. Even the beards sported by the rulers on the Platform 1A-1 monuments could relate to the domain of fertility through control of the elements. They may be compared to the Ch'orti' conception of the wind gods at the four corners of the cosmos, the *aj yum ik'ar*, as bearded (Girard 1966: 27). The Yukatek Maya also associate these cosmic corner-posts with the winds, as recorded in the *Chilam Balam of Chumayel* (Roys 1967). Rainmaking ceremonies were part of the esoteric knowledge that made possible the transformation of K'ak' Tiliw into one of his most compelling ritual personae.

The association of the Platform 1A-1 monuments with meteorological control may also suggest a symbolic relationship between stela dedication and planting ritual. The laying out of the cosmos in a four-part diagram is analogous to the demarcation of a cornfield as practiced by contemporary Ch'orti' Maya. In this ceremony, lineage heads establish the four corners of the field and then proceed to deposit a liquid offering in the center (Girard 1966: 127). After this, seeds are planted using a digging stick. The stela may therefore relate either to the form of a digging stick or to a marking post used to lay out a square cornfield. Alternatively, the function of the Classic-period stela as a time-keeping device may suggest its derivation from a wooden gnomon or similar staff used to determine the proper time for planting. The possible relationship between the stela and planting ceremony suggests yet another way in which Classic-period elite ceremonies were related to popular traditions. The stela ceremony may have embodied the ruler's ritual identification with maize, symbolizing his control of food production and role as a provider for the community.

While the existence of monumental portraiture implies the presence of the ruler and his command of

ceremonies at Quirigua, the bounded spatial envelope formed by the monuments of Platform 1A-1 and their surrounding architecture seems strangely empty. The interpretation of the monuments would clearly benefit from a better understanding of how performances related to the inscribed texts and images. Unfortunately, without contemporary accounts or substantial material evidence, such reconstructions must remain speculative. It is obvious that the plaza area in which the monuments were set was a huge open space of a profoundly public character. Between the Ballcourt Plaza and Structure 1A-3, the Great Plaza seems to have been completely open to river view, with at least one dock allowing for the mooring of canoes. The plaza could easily have held the entire projected population of the Quirigua area with room to spare, suggesting that the space may have been designed to accommodate people from more distant regions, especially the lower Motagua valley (see Schortman 1993: 201). In fact, archaeological evidence attests to the presence of large crowds in the Great Plaza, for ceramic fragments were found ground into the plaza surface (Jones, Ashmore, and Sharer 1983: 10).[17]

The function of stelae as pathways of supernatural communication suggests that Platform 1A-1 was designed as a locus for sacrifice and prayer.[18] Large quantities of modeled effigy censer fragments found in the Great Plaza, often in association with the monuments, support this hypothesis (Ashmore 1981; Benyo 1979: 565). Other religious and dynastic ceremonies—such as the presentation of heirs, bloodletting ceremonies, sacrifice of captives, and dynastic anniversaries—were probably performed here as well. Like similar events in modern Maya towns, these religious ceremonies may also have involved economic activity. In addition to religious items, necessities such as food and drink would have been distributed to the multitudes that assembled for religious events. Evidence for feasting appears just south of Platform 1A-1, where a broken olla was recovered near a high-density area of Late Classic ceramic fragments (Jones, Ashmore, and Sharer 1983: 10).[19] Indeed, not only is the partaking of food and drink common in Maya religious ceremony, but modern rituals and festivals often extend several days, making the taking of sustenance a physical necessity.[20]

One type of performance that was likely to have taken place on Platform 1A-1 in the Classic period may have been similar to the contemporary dance-drama (Freidel, Schele, and Parker 1993: 257–292). In these performances, formal speeches alternate with dances accompanied by music as a means of communicating history and mythology but also as a sacrifice to spiritual beings. It is possible that the texts of K'ak' Tiliw's monuments served as the bases of such dramas and may have been read by actors performing the history and myths of the city among the monuments. It is probably in such a context that the political value of the monumental art programs achieved its maximum potency, enhanced by the affective qualities of live actors, the physiological effects of intoxicants, and mass excitement.

Of particular importance in establishing a theatrical nature for the 1A-1 program was its architectural backdrop, Structure 1A-3. This structure bounded the stage visually, providing a field of reference for viewing both monuments and performers. The six monoliths themselves likely served as stage properties, taking an active role in the generation of the theatrical environment. Notably, the diminished size of the monuments nearest to Structure 1A-3 (Stelae A, C, and D and Zoomorph B) relative to the two colossal stelae near the platform edge (E and F) generates a false perspective that enhances the sense of depth of the platform space, when viewed from the front (south). Ample space for the audience was provided on the south, east, and west sides of the platform, bounded by low mounds on the east and the river on the west. Viewers may also have been positioned on the stairway of Structure 1A-3, looking down upon the platform. The resulting frontal stage configuration recalls the raised, covered stages mentioned in reports of Maya dances from the sixteenth century to the present (Estrada Monroy 1979: 168; Ponce 1932: 328; Redfield and Villa Rojas 1962: 153–154; Tovilla 1960: 183).

The placement of monuments at four corners on Platform 1A-1 suggests that performers may have grouped themselves in circular formations, observing performers in the center. Such a configuration is common in early colonial-period descriptions of Maya dance, as in the Kolomche' of the Yukatek Maya:

> For playing it, a large circle of dancers is formed with their music, which gives them the rhythm, and two of them leap in to the centre of the wheel in time to it, one with a bundle of reeds, and he dances with these perfectly upright; while the other dances crouching down but both keeping within the limits of the circle. And he who has the sticks flings them with all his force at the second, who by the help of a little stick catches them with a great deal of skill. When they have finished the reeds, they return in their rhythm to the circle, and others go out to do the same. (Tozzer 1941: 93–94)

Sacrificial dances, in which victims were paraded in a circle around a court, are also known from this period (Palacio 1985: 40; Tozzer 1941: 117–118). Circumambula-

tion and circular dance are well documented at major Aztec festivals, such as the Izcalli festival, a commemoration of the five "empty days" that preceded the Aztec New Year, celebrated every fourth year (Sahagún 1951– 1970: bk. 2, 151–152). The "Lordly Dance" performed on this occasion by Moctezuma in the company of the highest Aztec lords consisted of the fourfold circling of the principal ritual plaza of Tenochtitlan, in front of the Templo Mayor. As suggested by Richard Townsend (1979: 47), this ritual movement within the cosmologically defined space adjacent to the Templo Mayor purified both city and empire in preparation for the ceremonies of year renewal. The analogies between cosmological symbolisms of the sacred precinct of Tenochtitlan and the Quirigua Platform 1A-1 sculpture program and between the Aztec New Year and Maya period ending suggest that circumambulatory dances similar to the "Lordly Dance" may have taken place upon the Quirigua platform, among the stelae.

In performances such as the Lordly Dance, the circularity of motion is semantically significant. It may be characterized as a cosmic movement, based on the perceived movement of the sun around the earth, that orders both space and time from the epicenter of a ceremonial precinct. Another example of the performative realization of circular time-space is observed in contemporary Chamula during the Festival of Games, a calendrical ceremonial cycle during which the moral Tzotzil Maya world is ritually destroyed and recreated (Gossen 1986). At the climax of the festival, the principal performers or "Passions," who are charged with caring for the head of the Sun/Christ, run into the ceremonial center and circle it counterclockwise three times. This motion has clear cosmological significance, as it maps out the movement of the sun on a horizontal plane.[21] Following this, the performers walk on burning coals, an act which represents the ascent of the Sun/Christ into the heavens and the reordering of the cosmos. Across Mesoamerica from ancient to contemporary times, circular performances establish the cosmological significance of calendar ceremony, through a patterning of human movements and timing onto a sacred landscape.

In the Platform 1A-1 program there are hints of similar patterns of movement, suggested by the narrative structures of the monuments and their order of dedication. For example, the consistent reading order of the monumental images from south to north suggests that a procession would enter the group from the south side, between the gatelike Stelae E and F. The placement of Zoomorph G directly on this pathway is particularly telling in this respect, for the monument served as the death memorial for the great king. The Maya frequently placed such funerary monuments in principal entryways of architectural groups in order to "terminate" the spaces within. The initiation of the monumental program at Quirigua with Stela F may suggest that the procession would execute a right-hand turn upon entering the platform space, in order to pass this monument first. Continuing to the north, the rigorous narrative ordering of the monuments' texts of east to west would indicate that, after passing by Stela D, the procession should move to the west toward Stela C. Finally, like the "Passions" of Chamula, the counterclockwise circuit would be completed adjacent to Stela E. The placement of texts on Zoomorph B reinforces this pattern, as a counterclockwise movement around the monument is required to read them.

Classic Maya kings such as K'ak' Tiliw would surely have been aware of the myriad benefits of festivals to both ruler and subject. The average farmer would have been attracted by the opportunity to experience the king's supernatural powers, satisfy religious desires, socialize and assert status, be entertained, and trade. The festival served the king as a way to renew charismatic bonds with his subjects, fulfill his sacred duties in grand fashion, and impress foreign visitors. Such compelling reasons seem to justify the immense expense of creating a public work such as Platform 1A-1 and its collection of finely carved stone sculptures. The presence of the monuments themselves attests to the success of such festivals as well as to the ability of the Quirigua elite to capitalize on the power of art and ritual to transform religious lore into political currency.

The Platform 1A-1 Program in Relation to Copan

The construction of K'ak' Tiliw's magnum opus between 761 and 780 occurred during a time of important political developments at Copan. Shortly after K'ak' Tiliw's actions in concert with K'in B'alam of Xkuy in 762, the king's rival at Copan, K'ak' Yipyaj, died; and a new ruler took the throne: Yax Pasaj (Fig. 5.33).[22] These events were reflected in a repositioning relative to the grand artistic tradition of Copan. Most apparent is the virtual absence of large-scale royal portraiture during this period. The first act of Yax Pasaj was the termination of the great ritual area of the Great Plaza at Copan and its cycle of stelae dedicated by Waxaklajun Ub'ah K'awil. This involved the placement of a small monument in the form of a supernatural serpent, CPN Altar GIII, between Stelae F and H. This dedication happened on the same date as K'ak' Tiliw's erection of QRG Stela D (A.D. 766).

5.33. Portrait of Yax Pasaj of Copan, from CPN Structure 10L-18. Photo by Thomas Tolles.

Following this act, two major architectural projects were begun at Copan: the final phase of Structure 10L-11 (dedicated in late 773) and Structure 10L-16 (dedicated on the same date as K'ak' Tiliw's Stelae A and C, in 775). Structure 10L-11 was a grand cosmic statement, which in many ways repeated and elaborated upon Waxaklajun Ub'ah K'awil's 10L-22 (Schele and Freidel 1990: 322–328). The two-story superstructure of 10L-11 revived the sculptural themes of the Creation mountain and Cosmic Monster found on the earlier temple. To the south of 10L-11, a terrace or reviewing stand marked with caimans and conch shells replicated the underworld in which the Creation mountain floats. Below this symbolic "water surface" lay the portal to the underworld and place of sacrifice, configured as a false ballcourt and reached by a stairway. Structure 10L-16, which faced the same court, likewise looked back to the reign of a previous king iconographically; but in this case it was to the art of K'ak' Yipyaj. Heavily laden with the imagery of Tlaloc-Venus warfare and accented by Altar Q, Structure 10L-16 eloquently evoked the ties of Yax Pasaj to the founder of Copan, Yax K'uk' Mo', whose actions are recorded in the altar text and who was closely associated with the imagery of Tlaloc-Venus war.[23]

As K'ak' Tiliw completed his own great cosmological statement with the dedication of Zoomorph B in late 780, Yax Pasaj began a series of monument dedications representing concessions to the power of lower-ranking nobility. First were dedications of benches in two of the major lineage compounds of Sepulturas, a densely populated and wealthy urban area to the east of the acropolis. Next, for the one-*k'atun* anniversary of his accession, Altar T was placed in the area of what is now Copan village. Such monument dedications, which continued after the death of K'ak' Tiliw, may represent attempts to garner support of powerful nobles for Yax Pasaj in order to but-

5.35. QRG Stela A, east text detail. Photo by Thomas Tolles.

5.34. QRG Stela C, south face, detail of headdress. Photo by Thomas Tolles.

tress the by now seriously ailing monarchy at Copan. These projects at Copan stand in dramatic contrast to the contemporary works of K'ak' Tiliw, which not only exaggerate the image of the king to an unprecedented degree, as in QRG Stela E, but convey a strong statement of the unique position of the king as center of mundane and supernatural power. The lord of Xkuy on QRG Stela E is the only nondynastic figure mentioned in the 1A-1 program; however, this person was an ally rather than a local lord. Likewise, while the stela form so favored by the predecessors of Yax Pasaj was suppressed at Copan, the ruler of Quirigua forged ahead with this monumental mode, stressing its most deeply rooted cosmological associations with celestial pillars.

The disjunction between monumental programs at Quirigua and Copan during the final years of K'ak' Tiliw's reign suggests that political tensions between the sites may have lessened after the death of K'ak' Yipyaj. This development would eventually culminate in a reestablishment of ritual ties between the two sites during the reign of Jade Sky, after the death of K'ak' Tiliw (see Chapter 6).

K'ak' Tiliw's stelae also remained stylistically conservative as he neared the end of his life, repeating in Stelae A and C many elements first fully realized in Stela E. These include the emphasis on four distinct sides, extreme flattening of relief, contrast of a flat figure with a deeply modeled face, and squaring of forms and glyph blocks (Figs. 5.34, 5.35, 5.36).[24] Such stylistic and programmatic considerations suggest that, as the new ruler took the throne at Copan, monumental projects at Quirigua became chiefly concerned with maintaining the unity of the 1A-1 program and the continuity of local tra-

ditions. In contrast to times past, when monuments such as Stelae H and J protested the pronouncements of Copan, the final years of K'ak' Tiliw's reign are characterized by a self-assurance that was built upon an impressive monumental tradition and sanctioned by the ruler's advanced age. At the end of the Classic period, as centers throughout the Maya lowlands were collapsing, art at Quirigua remained staunchly conservative, even fundamentalist. Its equation of king with polity and king with cosmos resonated through the valley as long as the ruler himself remained alive.

5.36. QRG Stela C, east text detail. Photo by Thomas Tolles.

6

IN HONOR OF A GREAT WARRIOR

The Legacy of K'ak' Tiliw

THE DEDICATION of Zoomorph B in the year 780 saw Quirigua at its apogee. Over the course of the eighth century the regional population had reached its peak, and extensive building projects both within the site core and in the surrounding valley attest to a robust economy. Zoomorph B and the other monuments of Platform 1A-1 seem to express this climate of growth and prosperity through their erection at a distance of almost a half-kilometer from the heart of the kingdom, the acropolis court. As a conceptual map of the realm, the widely distributed monuments suggest the expansive policies adopted by the ruler, for monuments served not only as a vehicle for a portrait image but as a means of personalizing spaces as well. They specifically inscribed the landscape with a recognizable body-image, drawing lines of power that converged on the ruler himself.

At almost eighty years of age, K'ak' Tiliw might have appeared to enjoy the endurance of his stone effigies. After over sixty years of rule, however, the king died on July 31, 785 (9.17.14.13.2; Fig. 6.1). Even as the body was interred in a yet undiscovered location, his successors were occupied with the reinvention of the ruler. Mainly through references in hieroglyphic texts, the spirit of K'ak' Tiliw remained vital at Quirigua, constituting a key source of political currency for the new kings, Sky Xul and Jade Sky. Even so, these rulers could not escape the general economic and political shifts in the Maya lowlands, for most of the rituals of divine kingship (including carved monuments and hieroglyphic inscriptions) did not survive more than twenty-five years after K'ak' Tiliw's death.

The most visible manifestation of the continued growth of Quirigua after the death of the king was the ar-

chitectural elaboration of the acropolis. In particular, the extensive final phase of the acropolis corresponds both to the reign of Jade Sky and to the unidentified lords who succeeded him. This phase is characterized by intense building activity on the north, south, and east sides of the acropolis, including the construction of the final phases of Structures 1B-1 and 1B-3, which feature marble masonry (Jones 1987; Jones, Ashmore, and Sharer 1983). Work at the acropolis probably continued beyond 10.0.0. 0.0 (A.D. 830), long after the cessation of the historical record at Quirigua (Jones 1987: 212). Even though the known dynasty of kings ended with Jade Sky, the site was occupied until about A.D. 900, as attested by plumbate ceramics, metalwork, and other features typical of the Postclassic period (Ashmore 1987: 221; Sharer 1978).

Sky Xul and the Reign of K'ak' Tiliw

The first steps in the appropriation of K'ak' Tiliw's personae after his death took place in the context of his funeral, the proceedings of which are recorded on Zoomorph G. The date chosen for this ceremony was ten days after his death, on August 10, 785 (9.17.14.13.12), which happens to be the day preceding the second solar zenith passage of the year. If this timing is not a coincidence, then it may suggest a symbolic relationship between funeral events and the decapitation of the Copan ruler Waxaklajun Ub'ah K'awil, a pivotal event in the reign of K'ak' Tiliw that took place on the first zenith passage in 738.[1] Carrying out the funerary rites for the deceased ruler was Sky Xul, who became the next king of Quirigua on October 15, 785 (9.17.14.16.18). The possible timing of the funeral to compare K'ak' Tiliw's burial with the famous victory suggests a commitment to the glorification of the martial prowess of his predecessor and, presumably, ancestor. This particular persona of K'ak' Tiliw as a great warrior would become a standard trope in the monuments and texts of Sky Xul and his successors alike.

The monument upon which the death and funeral events are recorded, Zoomorph G, presents K'ak' Tiliw in particularly martial terms (Fig. 6.2). The dedication of this sculpture on the 9.17.15.0.0 period ending (November 6, 785) follows shortly after the accession of Sky Xul. Placed on three huge slabs at the south edge of Platform 1A-1, the monument represents a "Waterlily Jaguar"

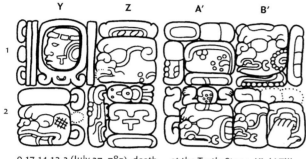

9.17.14.13.2 (July 27, 785), death   at the Turtle Stone, K'ak' Tiliw

6.1. Death of K'ak' Tiliw. Zoomorph G, Y1–B'2. Drawing by author.

facing northward, with human figures wearing skeletal headdresses emerging from both ends (Morley 1913: 340; Stone 1983, 1991). Although the image on the north face of Zoomorph G, a figure emerging out of the mouth of the jaguar, is analogous to the transformational imagery of Zoomorph B, the rear figure is highly unusual. Here it seems to issue from the birth canal of the jaguar, surrounded by blood scrolls. This image may suggest a process of ancestral rebirth, accomplished through rituals of veneration by Sky Xul. Given the formal and iconographic similarity of these figures to previous images of K'ak' Tiliw, it is possible that at least one of them represents the dead king and the other, perhaps, the new ruler. Lengthy texts occupy the east and west flanks of Zoomorph G. The dedication text that appears on the east side refers to the monument as a "jaguar platform/throne stone," thus evoking the form of the first stone of Creation mentioned and depicted on K'ak' Tiliw's Stela C (Fig. 6.3). The association of the first Creation stone with the male ancestor (discussed in the previous chapter) imbues Zoomorph G with special relevance to the reign of Sky Xul, suggesting a genealogical relationship between the two rulers. Moreover, the association of the mythological throne with warfare frames the monument as a

6.2. QRG Zoomorph G, west side. From Maudslay 1889–1902, *Archaeology*, vol. 2, Plate 42. From the facsimile edition of *Biologia Centrali-Americana* by Alfred Percival Maudslay. Published 1974 by Milpatron Publishing Corp., Stamford, Conn. Further reproduction prohibited.

celebration of the ancestral powers of warfare, bestowed upon the heir through his ceremonial seating on this throne.

The rendering of Zoomorph G as the jaguar platform or throne of Creation also echoes the martial tone of the monument's texts, which highlight the great military victories of K'ak' Tiliw. Prominently displayed on the west flank of the sculpture is a text recounting the crucial events of his reign. Following the formula established by K'ak' Tiliw's Stela J, the text notes the accession of K'ak' Tiliw (K'2–L'2) as the background event for the sacrifice of Waxaklajun Ub'ah K'awil (L'3–L'4).[2] Below this, in the basal text, appears a reference to K'in B'alam of Xkuy, the lord featured on K'ak' Tiliw's Stela E (Fig. 6.4). In fact, Xkuy is cited on two other monuments of Sky Xul, implying that at the close of the eighth century a continuing alliance with this site was even more politically significant than the sacrifice of the Copan king. Zoomorph G does not refer to Xkuy in association with the date of the capture of the palanquin in 762 but records that the Xkuy lord witnessed the death of K'ak' Tiliw. The text thus evokes the parallel event inscribed on Stela E, in which the Xkuy *ajaw* witnessed K'ak' Tiliw's period ending of 9.17.0.0.0. In the subsequent monuments of Sky Xul, the military victories of K'ak' Tiliw—but especially that involving the participation of the Xkuy *ajaw*—are presented as the models for his own military campaigns in order to amplify their political significance.

Although the exceedingly lengthy texts of Zoomorph G are an innovation of Sky Xul and typical of his monument programs, the throne form of the monument itself represents a second dimension of the continuity between his reign and that of K'ak' Tiliw. The throne emulates the tradition initiated with K'ak' Tiliw's Zoomorph B, with reference to size, dimensions, foundation, and low-relief

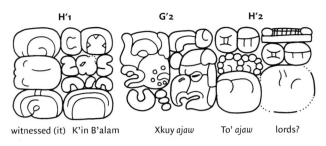

6.4. Citation of Xkuy ajaw on QRG Zoomorph G, H'1a–H'2. Drawing by author.

treatment. In addition, the placement of the monument elicits a strong association with the former ruler. Not only is its location on the axis of Platform 1A-1 (Fig. 1.23), just to the south of the line between Stelae F and E, near the monuments of K'ak' Tiliw, but its position at the front center of the group suggests that it "terminates" the 1A-1 program. Sky Xul's action is closely analogous to those of other Maya rulers, who often obstructed the entries to a previous ruler's ritual space through an architectural monument or stone marker. For example, after the death of K'inich Kan B'alam II of Palenque, his younger brother K'inich K'an Joy Chitam II erected Temple XIV in the processional route between the palace and the Cross Group erected by the former king (Schele 1988; Schele and Miller 1986: 65, 74).[3] A more contemporary and regional precedent was set by the Copan king Yax Pasaj, whose first monumental dedication, Altar GIII, marked the eastern entryway to the Great Plaza stela group of Waxaklajun Ub'ah K'awil. Such "terminations" represent both a means of paying homage to the previous ruler and a way of containing the supernatural powers focused by groups of monuments or buildings. The rituals enabled new kings to control the powers of their predecessors, thus enhancing the inauguration of their own reign.

The evocation of K'ak' Tiliw through Sky Xul's monuments continued in his next project, Zoomorph O, commissioned for the 9.18.0.0.0 period ending (A.D. 790; Fig. 6.5). Surviving only in fragmentary condition, this huge sculpture reinterprets Zoomorph B, representing the crocodilian Cosmic Monster with a personified mountain on its back (Stone 1983). With Zoomorph O, however, Sky Xul initiated the sculptural embellishment of a new architectural space, a court located to the northeast of the acropolis. Referred to as the Ballcourt Plaza, this court featured the east–west oriented ballcourt, Structure 1B-7. Unlike Zoomorph B, Zoomorph O was paired with a flat altar (Altar O'), placed on its north side (Fig. 6.6). This innovative monument portrays the half-

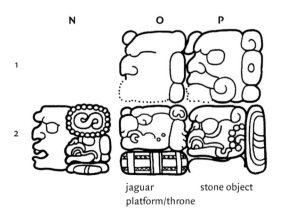

6.3. Name of QRG Zoomorph G, east text, N2–P2. Drawing by author.

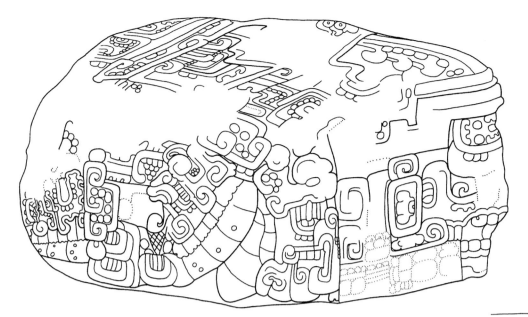

6.5. QRG Zoomorph O, west. Drawing by author.

quatrefoil-shaped opening in the Maya mountain of Creation, out of which dances a lightning god, enveloped in clouds (Coe 1978: 76; Taube 1986: 57). Placed adjacent to Zoomorph O, Altar O′ may be considered an extension of the iconographic theme stated by the zoomorph. A long text which adorns the quatrefoil frame of Altar O′ recounts numerous events in the early years of the reign of Sky Xul, beginning with his accession (M1–P1). The figure of K'ak' Tiliw is prominent in the text, his nominal glyphs appearing equal in size to those of Sky Xul and four times larger than the rest of the glyph-blocks in the text. Here is clear evidence of the attempt to compare the two rulers. The event attributed to K'ak' Tiliw is his military action in the company of K'in B'alam (the Xkuy *ajaw*), in 762 (Fig. 6.7), previously recorded on Stela E. For Sky Xul's purposes, this event serves as the backdrop for his own military victories in 786 (Looper 1999). Thus, in the text of Altar O′, Sky Xul invoked the military success of K'ak' Tiliw to enhance his own prestige.

To celebrate the 9.18.5.0.0 period ending (September 15, 795), a new set of monuments very similar to the previous one was placed just to the west of Zoomorph O and Altar O′. Zoomorph P, like Zoomorphs O and B, represents a Cosmic Monster with a mountain on its back (Figs. 6.8, 6.9), while Altar P′ recapitulates Altar O′, depicting a lightning deity emerging from a cave in the mountain (Fig. 6.10; Looper 2002b). Texts occupy analogous positions to those of Zoomorph O and Altar O′. In addition, Zoomorph P features a text written in car-

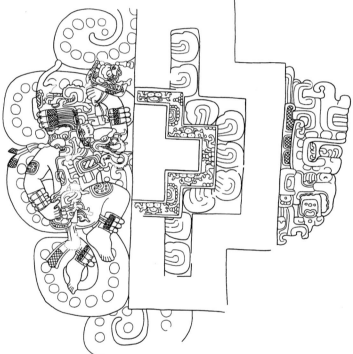

6.6. QRG Altar O′, text removed. Drawing by author.

touches surrounding the north-facing front muzzle of the Cosmic Monster. These muzzle cartouches have been of considerable interest to Mayanists, as they convey history relating to the founding of the Quirigua and Copan dynasties (see Chapter 1). In addition, cartouches 8–13 mention K'ak' Tiliw in association with Sky Xul, planting a stone to celebrate the 9.15.0.0.0 4 Ajaw 13 Yax period ending (Fig. 2.2a). This serves as a background event for the celebration of the current period ending, which also had a 4 Ajaw *tzolk'in* position, and echoes the 9.15.0.0.0 date cited on K'ak' Tiliw's Stela E (Fig. 2.2b). Seen from the Maya perspective of cyclic history, the citation of ritual performances of K'ak' Tiliw and Sky Xul on the 4 Ajaw period ending in 731 established the spiritual presence of both rulers during the 4 Ajaw period ending of 795. The rear (south) text of Zoomorph P also demonstrates a remarkably intense devotion to the legacy of K'ak' Tiliw. Following the initial series, the scattering rite for the period ending is stated as having taken place at "the throne? of K'ak' Tiliw and Waxaklajun Ub'ah K'awil" (Fig. 6.11; see Grube, Schele, and Fahsen 1991). As such ceremonies surely took place at the monument itself, this passage indicates that Zoomorph P was specially dedicated to the previous ruler of Quirigua and the lord from Copan whom he defeated.

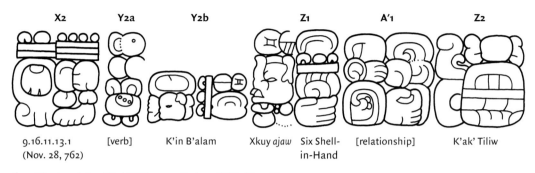

X2	Y2a	Y2b		Z1	A'1	Z2
9.16.11.13.1 (Nov. 28, 762)	[verb]	K'in B'alam	Xkuy *ajaw*	Six Shell-in-Hand	[relationship]	K'ak' Tiliw

6.7. War involving K'ak' Tiliw, as cited on QRG Altar O', X2–Z2. Drawing by author.

6.8. QRG Zoomorph P, north face. From Maudslay 1889–1902, *Archaeology*, vol. 2, Plate 57. From the facsimile edition of *Biologia Centrali-Americana* by Alfred Percival Maudslay. Published 1974 by Milpatron Publishing Corp., Stamford, Conn. Further reproduction prohibited.

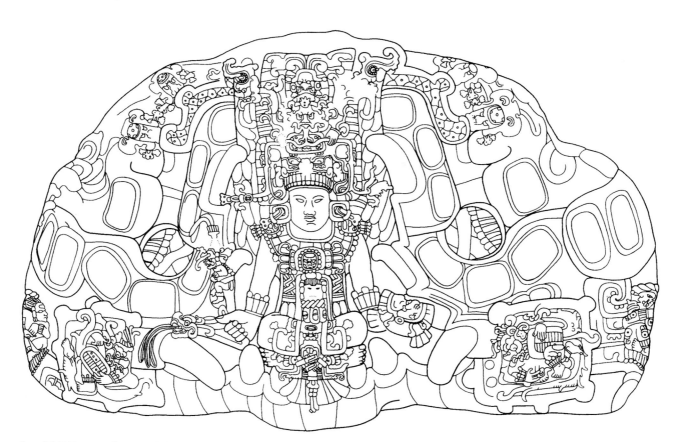

6.9. QRG Zoomorph P, north face, text removed. Drawing by author.

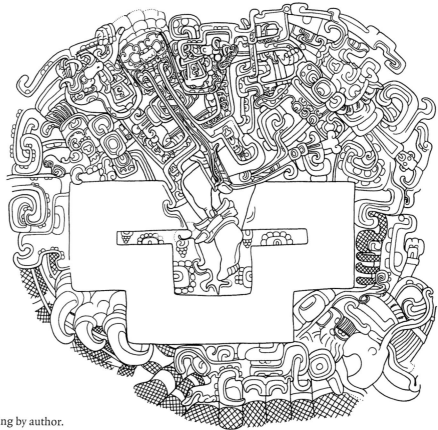

6.10. QRG Altar P′, text removed. Drawing by author.

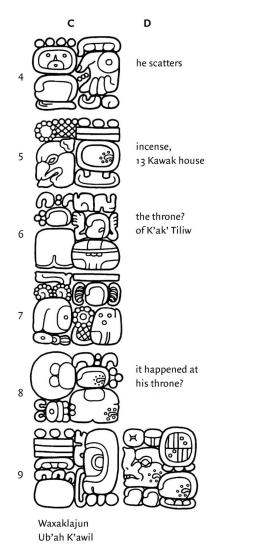

C   D

4   he scatters

5   incense,
     13 Kawak house

6   the throne?
     of K'ak' Tiliw

7

8   it happened at
     his throne?

9

Waxaklajun
Ub'ah K'awil

6.11. QRG Zoomorph P, south text, C4–D9. Drawing by author.

Sky Xul's strategy to connect his reign to that of an illustrious predecessor through comparisons of his own actions with the accomplishments of his ancestor is common in Classic Maya rhetoric. One well-known example is illustrated in the series of ballgame panels installed in the Yaxchilan Structure 33 stairway by K'ak' Tiliw's contemporary at Yaxchilan, Bird Jaguar IV. Flanking the large central scene of Bird Jaguar's own ballgame in A.D. 744 are scenes of ballgames played by the king's father and grandfather on previous occasions (Schele and Freidel 1990: 283). At Copan legitimacy was often traced to the founder of the local dynasty, K'inich Yax K'uk' Mo', who is cited, for example, on CPN Stela J and Altar Q. At Quirigua the text of Zoomorph P combines these two approaches, citing both his predecessor (K'ak' Tiliw) and the dynastic founder (Tok Casper) as royal

paragons whose actions of monument dedication set the precedent for Sky Xul.

The text of Altar P′ is considerably briefer than that of O′, though it repeats several of the events recorded on the earlier monument. Following the initial series, the period-ending ritual and Sky Xul's accession are given greater significance through an imbedded account of primordial Creation which appears as background information (L1b2–N2; see Looper 2002b). This passage draws attention to the identity of tzolk'in dates of Creation and the dedication date of the altar and zoomorph (4 Ajaw). It also provides additional grounds for identifying Zoomorph P as the third stone of Creation, a water throne. Further along in the text is new information, not recorded in the text of Altar O′. This includes various events probably of a military nature that involve a lord of an unknown site, the name of which is undeciphered but includes a bat head like that of Copan or Xkuy. As a precedent for these events, the historical occasion in 762 in which K'in B'alam of Xkuy acted in the company of K'ak' Tiliw is cited (Fig. 6.12). Thus, like Altar O′, the rhetoric of Altar P′ compares the victories of Sky Xul and K'ak' Tiliw, stressing the continuities between the reigns of the two kings.

In summary, the monuments of Sky Xul consistently draw upon one of the most productive ritual guises of K'ak' Tiliw in order to support the new ruler's aim of achieving prestige through warfare. Most of these references are conveyed through inscriptions, in which the military successes of K'ak' Tiliw are compared to those of Sky Xul. In iconography, the allusion is generally more indirect. Zoomorph G takes the form of the first platform or throne of Creation, which the Maya associated with the martial powers of male ancestors. One of the figures shown emerging from the end of the monument may represent K'ak' Tiliw, although the figure itself does not display specifically martial iconography.

The subsequent programs of Zoomorph O/Altar O′ and Zoomorph P/Altar P′ focus on more general themes of Creation. Even these images may contain a veiled reference to K'ak' Tiliw, however. Although it is not certain, the figures that dominate the compositions of Altars O′ and P′ may in fact have been interpreted as images of the great king apotheosized as a lightning deity (Fig. 6.13). There is precedent for such a ritual transformation, as illustrated by the Dumbarton Oaks tablet from Palenque, which shows the deceased ruler K'inich K'an Joy Chitam II dancing as a lightning deity named Ux B'olon Chaak (Schele and Miller 1986: 274–276).[4] Interestingly, a different lightning deity is shown on the Quirigua altars. At

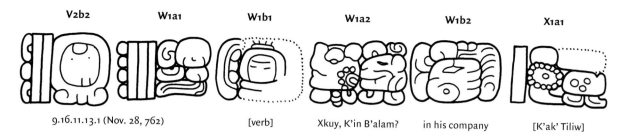

| V2b2 | W1a1 | W1b1 | W1a2 | W1b2 | X1a1 |

9.16.11.13.1 (Nov. 28, 762)   [verb]   Xkuy, K'in B'alam?   in his company   [K'ak' Tiliw]

6.12. War involving K'ak' Tiliw, as cited on QRG Altar P', V2b2–X1a1. Drawing by author.

least on O', the figure holds in his right hand the quatrefoil stone wielded by the Yo'at/Yo'pat spirit who assists in the resurrection of maize from the cosmic turtle. Thus, Altar O' may depict the deceased ruler in a guise consistent with that promoted during K'ak' Tiliw's own reign. If this interpretation is correct, then Sky Xul's monuments can be seen as presenting a contrast between the representation of K'ak' Tiliw in texts (as a human warrior) and in images (as a divine being). This differs from the representations of K'ak' Tiliw in his own monuments, whose divinity is only implied through association with supernatural emblems and performance of rituals. During his own reign, K'ak' Tiliw is consistently given a human face.

Jade Sky and the Reign of K'ak' Tiliw

Although no death date is preserved for Sky Xul, we know that the king did not live to see the next period ending, 9.18.10.0.0 (A.D. 800). The monument erected on this date was Stela I, a relatively modest shaft located a few meters north of K'ak' Tiliw's Stela J. The name of the patron of Stela I, written on the north face of the stela (A8–B8), has elements similar to those of the patron of the next two monuments at Quirigua, known as Jade Sky. There are enough differences, however, to consider the possibility that he was a distinct ruler with Stela I as his sole monument.[5]

In contrast to the monuments of Sky Xul, Stela I and the remaining monuments of Jade Sky suggest a policy of political reconciliation with Copan, despite the return to a format typical of the reign of K'ak' Tiliw. Stela I is slightly shorter than Stela J (4.1 m) but wider. Like Stela J, Stela I has a continuous text on its north and south faces which is read in the same order (north to south) and has the royal portrait facing toward the west (Fig. 6.14). Instead of having a text on the reverse (east) like Stela J, Stela I features an image of the back of the king's ceremonial costume (Fig. 6.15). It shows a human figure seated on a personified hill, surrounded by a skyband.

6.13. QRG Altar O', detail of figure. Photo by Thomas Tolles.

The Principal Bird Deity perches aloft, while (above and below) square-nosed serpents enclosing "sky" glyphs and crossed bands develop a celestial context for the figure. Although it has been suggested that this figure represents the current ruler upon his accession throne (by analogy with the Piedras Negras "niche" stelae; see Fig. 5.30), the mirror body-markings clearly identify him as a supernatural being (Fig. 6.16). In fact, the entire assemblage on the east face represents a backrack, akin to those worn by the personification of maize as the so-called Holmul Dancer (Reents-Budet 1985). Rather than

6.14. QRG Stela I, west face. Drawing by author.

6.15. QRG Stela I, east face. Drawing by author.

the Piedras Negras stelae, the inspiration for this iconography was probably Copan Stela H (west face), which depicts the ruler as a maize deity, complete with a backrack. The obverse (east face) of QRG Stela I shows the ruler wearing a costume seen repeatedly at Quirigua and holding a shield and God K scepter in the manner of the adjacent Stela J.

While the iconography of this monument is unremarkable, its text is of considerable interest, as it prominently features military actions of K'ak' Tiliw. In fact, almost the entire south text of the monument is devoted to

recounting the deeds of K'ak' Tiliw that led up to the decapitation of Waxaklajun Ub'ah K'awil, even though the sacrifice itself is not mentioned (Fig. 6.17). The story begins with an account of the 9.15.5.0.0 period ending celebrated by K'ak' Tiliw and a subsequent mention of the king of Calakmul, in an unclear context (Fig. 3.7). This is followed by a complex narrative of what may be the capture and burning of deity images of Copan, six days prior to the sacrifice of the Copan king (see Chapter 3; Fig. 3.4). The political significance of this inscription, however, is not entirely clear. By A.D. 800 the dynasty of Calakmul was no longer an important political force in the Maya world, and its elaborate alliance network was a thing of the past. Thus, these references may have been conceived as an attempt to blame the Quirigua-Copan conflict on a foreign power that no longer held sway over local affairs. This interpretation is supported by the fact that the Stela I text refrains from using the military actions of K'ak' Tiliw as a precedent for those of the current king of Quirigua, as had been common in the monuments of Sky Xul. Such distancing, however, is subverted somewhat by the siting of Stela I only a few meters from K'ak' Tiliw's Stela J—a monument laden with martial iconography—and oriented in the same direction, looking toward the west.

The treatment accorded to Stela S during the reign of the Stela I ruler suggests further distancing from K'ak' Tiliw. This monument had originally been dedicated by K'ak' Tiliw in 746, probably in the Great Plaza. Sometime around A.D. 800, however, it was transported to

6.17. QRG Stela I, south text. Photo by Thomas Tolles.

6.16. QRG Stela I, east face, detail of figure in niche. Photo by Thomas Tolles.

Group 7A-1 (Group B), to the north of the site core, where it was installed in a new foundation of the same type as Stela I (Fig. 1.1; Jones, Ashmore, and Sharer 1983: 19–20). While this act clearly shows the honor accorded to the earlier king, it may also have constituted a physical metaphor for the political difference between K'ak' Tiliw and the current king. Located approximately on the edge of the settlement, this new shrine might have diverted veneration of K'ak' Tiliw from the site core, in an attempt to appease visiting dignitaries from Copan. Wendy Ashmore (n.d.) notes that around the same time a similar treatment was accorded to Waxaklajun Ub'ah K'awil by Yax Pasaj through the construction of the memorial Group 8L-10 at Copan. At a time of regional political upheaval, the distancing from controversial former rulers may have been deemed conducive to the renewal of intersite alliances.

The next monument at Quirigua, Stela K (Fig. 6.18), conveys a political ambiguity akin to that expressed in

Stela I and the relocation of Stela S. This short but beautifully carved stela, dedicated by Jade Sky on 9.18.15.0.0 (A.D. 805) to the east of Stela I, contains not a single textual reference to K'ak' Tiliw but merely records the rites of the present king on its side texts, oriented to the north and south. Visually, however, the monument is related to several works of the past at Quirigua. In format Stela K closely approximates Stela F, with frontal portraits of the king on two sides (here east and west). Iconographically as well, Stela K quotes Stela F, with the king holding a double-headed serpent bar on the east (functionally equivalent to the celestial cords of Stela F) and displaying the *sak*-pectoral/God K/shield emblem complex on the west. If the movement of the sun provides a model for the reading order of this stela, then this imagery is ordered in the same sequence as Stela F. The representation of the double-headed serpent on Stela K is similar to that on Stela H, which is located on the opposite side of the plaza. Like the earlier monument, the mouths of the bar on Stela K disgorge God K images, with shields dangling below the snakes' lower jaws. Trapezoidal banners originally adorned the shields and also appear in the headdress, recalling the imagery of the nearby Stela J. Stela K thus preserves the forms associated with K'ak' Tiliw but none of the visionary personalized qualities or specific political references emphasized in the preceding monumental program.

A more radical change is seen upon the next period ending, which was celebrated not with a stela but with the dedication of an elaborately decorated building located on the south side of the acropolis court, Structure 1B-1. This structure had both a hieroglyphic cornice, which recorded the 9.19.0.0.0 *k'atun* ending (A.D. 810), and a hieroglyphic step or bench in each of its three rooms. As noted by William Fash (1984), the contemporary ruler of Copan (Yax Pasaj) is mentioned in these texts performing period-ending rituals (Fig. 6.19). Although the text does not specifically state that Jade Sky conducted the ritual *in the company of* the Copan king, the parallelism of their rituals suggests not only that Quirigua and Copan may finally have achieved some sort of accord but also that it was to Jade Sky's immediate political advantage to record the name of the king of the neighboring site. Despite these intriguing suggestions, a full understanding of the political significance of this structure must await the reconstruction of its cornice inscription, which today lies in stacks near the site warehouse. For on two of these blocks, disassociated from any event, the name of K'ak' Tiliw appears (Fig. 6.20). Thus, even at the end of recorded history at Quirigua, the legacy of

K'ak' Tiliw remained alive, transformed into a textual mode. Such references suggest that K'ak' Tiliw's monumental personae still influenced political events at Quirigua, just as his portrait stelae dominate the site today.

The Evolution of Personae at Quirigua

It is useful to summarize the transformation of personae at Quirigua in order to understand its relation to political history. The presence of K'ak' Tiliw is first felt in the years between his accession in 725 and the war with Copan in 738, through new architectural projects that associate him with sites of city-founding. During this early period, he also dedicated Altars M and N, which represent supernatural toponyms and function as stage properties to generate a sacred context for rituals. In these years K'ak' Tiliw's ritual guises were presumably generated by his *association* with stone monuments during performances. There is no inscription of his physical presence in the form of a portrait, suggesting that such a tangible embodiment of persona may have been prohibited to this vassal of Copan. Despite this display of subordination, the burst of creative energy that followed the accession of K'ak' Tiliw may actually have contributed to the outbreak of hostility between the two sites. At Quirigua public works enhanced the presence and spiritual potency of the ruler through performance, thus providing a forum for centralization of power. The Copan king Waxaklajun Ub'ah K'awil, who had recently sponsored K'ak' Tiliw's accession, may have felt threatened by this ostentatious display of wealth and power and either attacked Quirigua or instigated repressive measures that resulted in a revolt by K'ak' Tiliw. While the details of cause and effect are elusive, the monumental record at Quirigua clearly indicates local support for the position of the new ruler, prior to the war with Copan.

Following independence in 738, there is a short interlude in monumental commissions at Quirigua, probably attributable to economic consolidation and the opening of new sandstone quarries. Finally, by 746, the tradition of stela dedication is reestablished with Stela S. Although poor preservation of this monument precludes discussion of its presentation of persona, on the next stela (H, dedicated in 751) the image of the king is striking and complex, demonstrating the supernatural martial powers of K'ak' Tiliw. The grouping of stelae in an open plaza at Quirigua, to create foci for pilgrimage and ceremony, is a monumental arrangement specifically adapted from that of Waxaklajun Ub'ah K'awil, which personalizes space through a series of monumental personae. However, there are differences between the two

6.18. QRG Stela K, west face. From Maudslay 1889–1902, *Archaeology*, vol. 2, Plate 48a. From the facsimile edition of *Biologia Centrali-Americana* by Alfred Percival Maudslay. Published 1974 by Milpatron Publishing Corp., Stamford, Conn. Further reproduction prohibited.

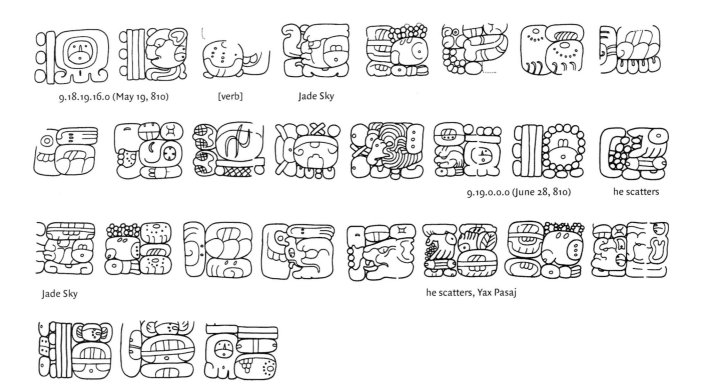

9.18.19.16.0 (May 19, 810) [verb] Jade Sky

9.19.0.0.0 (June 28, 810) he scatters

Jade Sky he scatters, Yax Pasaj

6.19. QRG Structure 1B-1 hieroglyphic step inscription. Drawing by author.

rulers' approaches. At Copan stelae pertaining to the previous ruler, Smoke Imix, peer from the east and west margins of the plaza toward those of Waxaklajun Ub'ah K'awil. As permanent embodiments of the former ruler, these monuments (Stelae I and E) literally "oversee" the works of his successor (and probably his son), lending them legitimacy. References to dynastic traditions and earlier rulers are also explicit in the texts of Waxaklajun Ub'ah K'awil's stelae. At Quirigua, in contrast, there were no standing ancestral monuments from which support could be drawn. Instead, Stela H and the associated radial pyramid 1A-11 served to *recreate* a local Early Classic ceremonial landscape. Despite these differences, both sites enlist a specific type of performance venue—the open plaza with clustered stelae—to foster political centralization. K'ak' Tiliw's adaptation of spatial concepts originally developed at Copan suggests an attempt to surpass and thereby claim political ascendancy of Quirigua over Copan, specifically through the victory over Waxaklajun Ub'ah K'awil.

With the accession of Copan's fifteenth king—K'ak' Yipyaj—shortly after the war, a pattern of competition over regional supremacy is expressed through monumental iconography commissioned by this king and K'ak' Tiliw. In particular, a similar complex of militarism

and sacrifice appears on the Hieroglyphic Stairway/Stela M group at Copan and on Stela J at Quirigua, both dedicated in 756. The rhetorical significance of the two programs varies, however. At Copan militarism is integrated into dynastic history in such a way as to suggest its continuity through a line of rulers as well as the ultimate origins of martial powers in the exotic ceremonies of Teotihuacan. In contrast, Quirigua Stela J emphasizes the unique role of K'ak' Tiliw in achieving the independence of Quirigua as an incarnation of the lightning deity Chaak. This persona dominates monumental sculpture

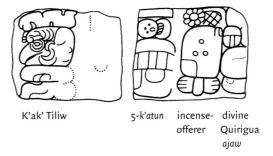

K'ak' Tiliw   5-k'atun   incense-   divine
                          offerer   Quirigua
                                     ajaw

6.20. QRG Structure 1B-1 cornice inscription, 29–32. Drawing by author.

at Quirigua through the dedication of Stela E in A.D. 771. In these programs, then, we have a case of distinct and competitive ritual personae presented at the two sites. Indeed, the development of the lightning-deity persona for K'ak' Tiliw at Quirigua may have been a specific response to the rhetoric of the Copan Hieroglyphic Stairway, which phrased the death of Waxaklajun Ub'ah K'awil in the context of the birth of the deity Yax Ha'al Chaak.

The discourse between K'ak' Tiliw and K'ak' Yipyaj hinges to a large degree on the issue of ancestral legitimation. At Copan the persona of K'ak' Yipyaj as warrior is transparently linked to those of his ancestors, passed on through successive rulers. He is presented essentially as a reincarnation of the founder, K'inich Yax K'uk' Mo', with whom Teotihuacan-derived iconography is most intimately associated. The association of Stela M with Structure 10L-26 adds to these ancestral comparisons, for within this structure was buried the twelfth king, Smoke Imix. In contrast, at Quirigua Stela J presents K'ak' Tiliw as an independent agent, whose supremacy is affirmed primarily through direct control of the spiritual forces that govern the conduct of warfare. The monument, like its predecessor, claims that through royal rituals of warfare and sacrifice the forces of fertility are manifested for human use. Through a recreation of the style and iconography of Early Classic monuments at Quirigua, K'ak' Tiliw's stelae claim that this was no usurpation but a legitimate reassertion of local autonomy.

The construction of Platform 1A-1 as a setting for subsequent monument dedications between 761 and 780 represents shifts both in spatial deportment of monuments and in the guises conveyed through the portraits. One of the most highly integrated monumental programs known from the ancient Maya, the 1A-1 group develops two major personae for K'ak' Tiliw in addition to his association with the domain of Chaak. Organized thematically into opposite corners of the platform, the king is shown as cosmic architect and creator and as traveler to the sacred times and places of the ancient past. Within each of these categories are more subtle distinctions, such as the representations of Stelae C and A, which show the ruler empowered with the complementary domains of two of the stone platforms of creation. Sexual dimensions of these personae are promulgated as well, in the role of the king as "mother" who gives birth to the gods and as masculine archetype, inscribed in phallic form and from whose loins emerge vital energies. Indeed, it can be argued that *all* of the monumental portraits of K'ak' Tiliw at Quirigua associate him with the powers of botanical growth and especially with the maize spirit, a principal embodiment of procreative potential. This is suggested by the triadic emblems (shield, God K, sak-pectoral) he manipulates on most of the stelae (J, F, D, and E). These icons imply both his supervision of cosmogenesis and ritual rebirth as the flower-bedecked spirit of maize. At the beginning and end of this series, Stela H and Zoomorph B depict the king as the essence of maize reborn from the mountain of Creation.

The emphasis on power through the metaphor of Creation embodied especially in the A-B-C program is evidence of a lessening of political tensions between Copan and Quirigua during the reign of Yax Pasaj. As the Copan ruler's monumental art focused increasingly on appeasing local nobility, K'ak' Tiliw's monuments were designed to appeal to a general audience through their "fundamentalist" message.

From this summary it is clear that "K'ak' Tiliw" is not a unified, stable identity but rather a collection of personae that were continually reinvented during the king's life. Two particular dimensions of monumental art permitted this process. First, as portraits, the monuments allowed the "dividuation" of the king into multiple manifestations, each expressing distinct political and religious meanings (see Strathern 1988). Second, as freestanding public objects, monuments became foci for the creation of communal values. Performance was the key to bridging these different dimensions, for it was through contact with these images that the meanings and associations of each persona were impressed upon the collective memory and condensed into a single "superpersona," an ideological talisman that served as the basis for political control. For K'ak' Tiliw, this composite persona is highly subjective, evoking the image of a superhuman who was able to access divine powers directly through ritual practice. It also seems to have converged to some extent with his name, identifying him with a manifestation of lightning. And yet interaction with each monument allows the viewer to contemplate successive guises. The consideration of K'ak' Tiliw's collective monumental commissions suggests the nature of ancient Maya personae as conventional masks that are revealed through performance. These masks were manipulated in direct response to historical requirements and often in competition with those developed by other rulers.

The richly personal vision embodied by K'ak' Tiliw's monuments stands in contrast to the transformation of his personae upon the ruler's death in 785. Principally through hieroglyphic inscriptions, his successors cast K'ak' Tiliw in the highly reductive mold of a warrior-ancestor. Such a persona had, in fact, been conveyed through certain aspects of the Stela C portrait during K'ak' Tiliw's lifetime; but after his death this image is converted into a rhetorical argument of secondary importance to the personae promulgated by his successors. This transformation of the king's identity again underscores the highly performative nature of persona, which is by definition *embodied*. As a conveyor of persona, the portrait is of key importance in establishing the bodily presence. Through associated costume, attributes, and texts, the body-image becomes a vehicle for presenting complex identities. The portrait monuments of K'ak' Tiliw, while not reproducing all aspects of ritual, did manipulate space and present the royal visage in a theatrical setting. In this way, personae were deployed in social contexts at Quirigua.

Domains of Power

A useful conclusion to the interpretations considered above is to place the concept of personae as defined at ancient Quirigua into the context of power, for in a profound sense power is the meaning of history. In particular, the legacy of texts, monuments, and architecture left by K'ak' Tiliw points to certain interrelated types of power that were considered crucial to his reign. One category of power could be defined as the control of supernatural forces through ritual, documented in elaborate detail in text and image on K'ak' Tiliw's monuments. This domain of power derived from the king's position as a mediator between the everyday world and the spirit world inhabited by the gods and ancestors. Featured events in hieroglyphic texts are acts of sacrifice, such as bloodletting, incense scattering, and human sacrifice, which cast the king as a sustainer of the gods. Also mentioned is the act of conjuration, whereby instruments such as the double-headed serpent bar allowed direct access to supernaturals through their "birth" into the human world. Many of these events were carried out in the context of public performance, captured in the monumental images of the king with their lavish displays of ritual costume. Several of the most common costume elements shown on the stelae, such as high-backed sandals and shell tinklers, are rhythmic musical instruments which were used in the ritual dances through which the king entered a trance and traveled to the spirit world.[6]

Many of the powers attributed to supernatural influence were expressed through rituals of cosmic renewal, modeled on the narrative of cosmogenesis which took place in 3114 B.C. The most direct and frequent evocation of this power is the literary trope which compares the king's ritual activities with those of supernatural beings in the far distant past. Nearly every public artistic form at Quirigua endows the ruler with powers of creation and renewal, from temples which represent the mountain of Creation to stelae which represent the pillars established at the corners and center of the nascent world. These symbolisms were explicitly developed in terms of the narrative of cosmogenesis at Quirigua, wherein royal monument dedications were likened to cosmic architecture. In addition, astrology constituted a highly potent elite technology, for the appearance and movement of celestial bodies were seen as an artifact of Creation, established and controlled by the king. K'ak' Tiliw frequently made reference to such eternal cycles in iconography and through his most grand architectural commission, the Great Plaza. Most importantly, the monumental images imply that it was the ruler himself who ritually conjured and reestablished the primordial forces of cosmic order at Quirigua. Such energies are prominently symbolized on monuments, as scrolls which emerge from the Creation platforms depicted on Stelae C and A. Thus, the cyclic conception of time cultivates the image of the king as a divine being whose ritual program guarantees access to the primordial powers of renewal. Rooted in the symbolism of agriculture and the change of seasons, the rituals of monument dedication claim power over food production and earthly fertility as well.

Monumental building enterprises constitute a second index of power, for the commissioning of masonry architecture and monumental sculpture was the traditional prerogative of Maya kings. Through their cosmological symbolisms, K'ak' Tiliw's sculptures were of major importance in promoting the polity as a powerful, independent entity. The fashioning of these monuments in the image of the king and their distribution in the ceremonial landscape generated a map of the "body-politic," impressing upon all who witnessed them the identity between king and state. Monuments and architecture also served as indexes of power in that they constituted evidence of an ability to mobilize human forces. Large-scale building and monumental activity implies the existence of an economy stable enough to support such specialized and costly labor. In particular, the elaboration of the sacred center of Quirigua promoted an image of economic prosperity for the polity, fostered by the king's leadership. The rituals by which these monuments were dedicated also served as a major forum for the display of power, as their erection and dedication entailed sacrificial bloodletting, the burning of offerings, the conjuration of spirit beings, and the display of power objects, war trophies, and sacred costume. The erection of monuments in an enormous public space at the center of the settlement charged the space with the powers signified by these objects and rituals. As memorials to the king and his rituals, the sculpture programs established a context for future pageants, festivals, and other gatherings which took place on the Great Plaza. The continued use of the Great Plaza for sacred ceremony ennobled these rituals and celebrations through a comparison with the sacred and historical acts of the powerful ruler represented on the monuments. In this way, access to the "king," a complex of personae sanctified by myth and ritual, was guaranteed.

The appearance of the monuments commissioned by K'ak' Tiliw held the potential for associative meanings that were equally important in the exercise of royal power at Quirigua. Specifically, the rapid improvement in sculptural quality seen, for example, over the fifteen years between Stela S and Stela J strongly suggests that high-quality craftsmanship was valued in the artistic culture of the eighth century. Such striving for sculptural excellence—that is, conforming to Classic Maya canons of design and finish—may be interpreted as a significant political tool.[7] Dorie Reents-Budet (1994: 97) discusses the social value attributed to high-quality painted ceramics in the Late Classic period, which were not only frequently signed by the artist but also prized as gifts. Similarly, the elaborateness and quality of carved monuments may have connoted the elite status of their patron as well as his precedence over a well-developed and cultured court, comparable to the other centers of the Maya world.

Of fundamental importance to the interpretation of style at Quirigua, however, was its capacity for expressing K'ak' Tiliw's links to the past. Because of the disruption of the stela tradition at Quirigua between the fifth and late seventh centuries, the choice to revive it was in part an archaizing move that invoked the authority of the ancient rulers of the site. By the Late Classic period, stelae, altars, and thrones were already ancient art forms, and this association enhanced the messages conveyed within these sculptural modes at Quirigua. More precisely, however, K'ak' Tiliw's monuments recalled styles characteristic of Early Classic Quirigua. His sculptors reinterpreted several Early Classic features of stelae, including the wrap-around compositional mode, frontal pose, registers, low relief, facial emphasis, squared forms, and emphasis on the stela block. A highly conservative and locally specific style served as an immediately intelligible and potent means for stressing the continuity between fifth- and eighth-century rulers at Quirigua. As such, it complemented the textual, iconographic, and programmatic meanings of K'ak' Tiliw's sculpture. While texts, imagery, and programming demonstrated the king's active and central role in cosmic and political organization, style established the precise locus for the cosmic center at Quirigua. It cultivated a history of artistic and dynastic greatness that served as a foundation upon which K'ak' Tiliw set his own stones of power.

At the juncture of these two sites of power—ritual practice and monumental works—and essential to the development of both was charisma, the king's power of persona. In its original sense, this term (from Greek *kharis* "favor, grace") referred to a gift of power thought to have been divinely bestowed. In modern sociological writings (e.g., Geertz 1985; Weber 1968), however, the meaning has shifted to encompass the special authority possessed by elites. In its function at ancient Quirigua, charisma was a form of personal agency of supernatural origin that legitimated the authority of kings. Furthermore, it was inherently performative, and ritual was its principal mode of expression. Ritual both symbolized and actuated through performance the supernatural sources of royal power. The divine personae embodied in monumental portraits were the means by which charisma could be perpetuated. Their principal function was to objectify the subjective state of psychological transformation and permanently link these spiritual identities to a specific historical person. Through contact with these great embodiments of royal presence in the Great Plaza, crowds of people could experience an effervescent state of collectivity that is the hallmark of the charismatic experience (see Durkheim 1965: 140; Lindholm 1990). Indeed, the multiplicity of monumental personae at Quirigua may embody the disintegration of individuality that occurs during an ecstatic state. As such, they may relate closely to the institution of shamanism, the crux of Maya religion, which is based on the control of fearful spirit forces that cause psychic fragmentation. Captured in aesthetic forms and interpreted through ritual and the language of imagery, these dangerous forces were "tamed" by the rulers, absorbed into their mystique, and made available to the audience/participant.

Crucial to the cultivation of royal charisma was the establishment of a symbolic center for Quirigua. As discussed by Edward Shils (1961: 117), such centers have "nothing to do with geometry and little with geography." Rather, they are loci of importance, where events crucial to the core value system of a society are carried out. Symbolic centers function as maps of power, diagramming the charismatic relationship between leader and follower. At Quirigua the geographical center was little more than a muddy riverbank. The principal ideological center, however, was marked by a complex of structures that we call the acropolis, built upon this riverbank. Its sacred nature was affirmed by its massive presence, signaling the ritual accumulation of several generations of kings, including key sacra, such as the entombed relics of an Early Classic ruler and precious offerings in caches. The center was also defined by performance (and by the memories of a history of performances) of the ritual events of highest importance within its confines, particularly those ceremonies aimed at controlling rain, agricultural abundance, and human fecundity. As a spiritual conduit, the king drew upon the most potent forces of the cosmos located at distant places and times, releasing them to the community through a ritual center. By living and performing rituals in this elevated compound, the rulers demonstrated their nearness to the sacred sources of their charisma, in the sky, underworld, and periphery of the cosmos.

The distribution of carved monuments throughout the site maintains a constant reference to this center. These portrait images are in fact aligned in accord with the master axis established by the layout of the acropolis, Great Plaza, and surrounding structures. Thus, even though each stela constitutes a center of power, it is subordinated to the group of monuments to which it belongs and the group in turn to the overall design of the site, established by the acropolis. In addition, the monuments of Platform 1A-1 face the acropolis, staring perpetually toward its north face. Through this spatial and visual correspondence, the stelae and zoomorphs maintain symbolic ties with the acropolis, which is the "true" center of the realm, where the king actually lived. This intimate dialogue between monumental portraits and the politico-religious center of Quirigua may be interpreted as a fundamental aspect of charisma which emanated from the king's performances in the acropolis and which was refracted and propagated through monument groups. Integrated into a public setting, the monuments mediated the charismatic bond between elite and non-elite. Following the death of K'ak' Tiliw, there is a noticeable contraction of power toward the center, evidenced by the shift of monumental activity during the reigns of the final two kings. First is the "termination" of the 1A-1 program by Zoomorph G, followed by the dedication of monuments in the Ballcourt Plaza and southern portion of the Great Plaza, and finally the elaboration of the acropolis alone.

The acropolis was not the only center of power, however. Indeed, charisma has a complex history at Quirigua, characterized by changing loci of ideological significance. Following the defeat of Copan, the center of power invoked by K'ak' Tiliw's political rhetoric was principally the sphere of Waxaklajun Ub'ah K'awil, although links are also established with the early elite center of Quirigua, Group 3C-7. During this period, the path to power lay both in local memory and in a claim to eclipse the nearby center. This view acknowledged the validity of distinctive centers of power in the Maya world, but with the provision that they could at any time be appropriated through military force, conducted in a ritual manner and drawing upon the will of the gods. In other words, the divine right of charisma permitted the restructuring of the political landscape through spiritual conquest. With Stelae J and F, the center shifted slightly, focusing on the power sphere of K'ak' Yipyaj. During this period, charisma was expressed as a direct competition between two politically equal centers. After the death of K'ak' Yipyaj, however, Quirigua again looked homeward, toward its roots in the Early Classic period and toward the universal Maya myths of centering embodied in the lore of cosmic renewal. Finally, following the death of K'ak' Tiliw, the ruler himself became a rhetorical center, characterized by his successors as an archetypal warrior. Thus, as in the process of substitution which permitted rulers to succeed each other, the power of K'ak' Tiliw was first legitimated by reference to external loci but later became a center itself. Such was the process of legitimization for the ancient Maya, in which hierarchies of power were continually restructured and recycled.

Yet another aspect of charisma is expressed through royal rituals and monumental art at Quirigua. The exaggerated sexualized personae portrayed in huge phallic monuments that represent the ruler manifesting forces of fertility strongly suggest that sexual power was a crucial dimension of their symbolism. This feature is not distinctive to Quirigua, for it is seen throughout the Maya lowlands during the Classic period, wherever rulers erected stelae with carved portraits. These images support the identification of the period ending and its stela ceremony with an ideology of procreation, focused on the ruler's powers over both male and female sexuality as an incarnation of the dual-gendered maize deity. This persona is of the utmost importance at Quirigua, where it is elaborated in a spectacular over-life-sized sculptural form and referenced in iconography and text. As such, the monuments created an object of desire for the members of the community, into which they could project their sexualities and likewise draw on the forces magically realized through the images. Such interchanges were likely specifically embodied in ceremonies in which blood offerings—for men, sometimes drawn from the genitals—were deposited at the base of the stela. These rituals provided a structure for the return promised by the monuments' imagery.

The sexual symbolism of stelae leads to further implications concerning their capacity to function as agents. Supported by rituals of world-renewal, the stela images afforded the king the possibility of literally and symbolically reproducing himself according to a regular temporal schedule. With the passing of each *hotun* of time, a new stone image of the king was born, swaddled in cloth wrappings, and given life through the shedding of royal blood. Vision serpents, symbolizing supernatural umbilici, were conjured, and the new being was purified through the offering of incense. Embodying the succession of Ajaw-days upon which they were dedicated, the sculptures were akin to a dynasty within a dynasty—a series of *ajaw*-rulers that reinforced the authority of the king who created them. Depicting the ruler in successive supernatural personae was an expressly dynastic representation, conveying the many ancestral faces that were reborn through royal art and ritual. The embodiment of these personae within the time frame of cosmic creation assured the divine continuity of K'ak' Tiliw through the universal cycles of birth, death, and rebirth.

And yet the monuments were only *secondary* agents, a fact underscored by the capacity of the Quirigua dynasty to sustain itself for less than twenty-five years after the death of K'ak' Tiliw (see Gell 1998). Without the charismatic presence of the ruler himself, the breath of life which animated the sculptures grew weaker, until finally the ritual feeding of the monuments ceased altogether, and they passed into a perpetual repose. Indeed, without the continued support of trade and alliance networks, which were rapidly collapsing throughout the southern lowlands in the late eighth century, the expensive rituals that typified the Classic-period culture of monumental art could not be maintained for long. Lacking support from allied nobles, the rulers of Quirigua were unable to defend the site from an intrusion of newcomers, who took over at Quirigua sometime during the ninth century.[8]

Although K'ak' Tiliw's stelae and thrones stand as icons of the success of a ruler over the short term, they also typify the political fragmentation which character-

ized the final decades of Classic Maya civilization. In fact, the program of K'ak' Tiliw may be interpreted as a prime example of a ritual complex designed to thwart change (see Bateson 1958; Blier 1996: 193). In their massive size, the stelae of K'ak' Tiliw assert with increasing intensity the fixity and permanence of kingship at the site. The staid conservatism of iconography and style typical of these monuments promotes the ideology of the regular cycling of time and the king's manipulation of these cycles to buttress a faltering political system. In the end, the paradox of these monument's inception in a break from the sphere of Copan to create a new center came full circle and contributed to the complete decentralization of the region. Abandoned to the encroaching jungle, Quirigua was to slumber in oblivion for almost a millennium until its rediscovery in the nineteenth century set modern scholars on the path to the recovery of its history.

The monuments and other material remains of Quirigua seem still to preserve additional secrets. The better we are able to read the inscriptions and decipher the complex iconography of K'ak' Tiliw's monuments, the more keenly we feel the pull of their rhetoric. In a manner similar to that which compelled Ernst Gombrich (1966: 40) "to feel something of Cosimo [de Medici's] spirit in the buildings he founded, something of his reticence and lucidity, his seriousness and restraint," we are captured by the aura of a personality that seems larger than life, endowed with superhuman heroic powers—the very essence of a lightning-warrior. But, of course, this is precisely the intention of the sculptures—to seduce the viewer with the spectacle of an active patron invested with divinity. And while the conceptual categories of Renaissance humanism prompted Gombrich to attempt to see the Medicis "in human and not in mythical terms" (Gombrich 1966: 35), such an approach to K'ak' Tiliw is fundamentally inconsistent with the nature of Maya lore, which holds the "mythological" to be as truthful as the "historical." In fact, the events usually taken by Mayanists to be purely historical are far from neutral, objective statements of fact but served to communicate supernatural identities, through the mythical resonances of actions and relationships. Even the likes of parentage statements should be seen not as genealogical documents per se but as a trope which conveyed the sacred identity of a person through his or her divine bloodlines.

From the secular, scientific viewpoint of contemporary Western scholarship, the inseparability of myth and history may be difficult to accept. Nevertheless, such is the foundation of the Mesoamerican view of the past, to which we must open our consciousness and adapt our frameworks of investigation. When K'ak' Tiliw took office as king and patriarch of Quirigua, he entered into a long series of transformations which, like a succession of masks, became symbolic of his changing social and spiritual roles. Unlike masks, however, the personae of K'ak' Tiliw are fixed, bound in the materiality and patterning of the remains he and his people left behind. Just as the tomb of the ruler has never been located, any attempt to remove his masks and discover the essential identity behind them will meet with failure. For the ancient Maya, personality was not fixed in a single body but was manifested in diverse forms in the landscape. The search for K'ak' Tiliw leads inevitably to the social world in which he lived—to the lives of the nobles and farmers who fostered the growth of his personae—and to the spirit world which gave him power and identity.

Appendix A

Rulers of Quirigua

Succession Number	Glyphic Name	Name (or Nickname)	Previous Names	Accession Date	Other Dates	Monuments
[1]		Tok Casper		8.19.10.11.0		
?		Tutum Yol K'inich			9.1.0.0.0	
?		Turtle Shell			9.2.5.11.0	U
3?		Basket Skull				
4?		Mih Toh		9.2.18.13.1 or 9.2.18.13.10	9.3.0.0.0	26
?		K'awil Yo'at/Yo'pat			9.11.0.11.11	L
14		K'ak' Tiliw Chan Yo'at/Yo'pat	Ruler 1 Two-Legged Sky Two-Armed Sky Kawak Sky B'utz' Tiliw	9.14.13.4.17	see App. B	M, N, S, H, J, F, D, E, C, A, B
[15]		Sky Xul	Ruler 2	9.17.14.16.18	see App. B	G, O, O', P, P'
16		Scroll Sky? (possibly same as Jade Sky)			9.18.10.0.0	I
[17]?		Jade Sky			9.18.15.0.0, 9.19.0.0.0	K, 1B-1

Appendix B

Historical Events Recorded in the Texts of Quirigua

Long Count	Calendar Round	Gregorian Date	Event	Protagonist	Monument
8.19.10.10.17	5 Kab'an 15 Yaxk'in	Sept. 6, 426	comes to the "founding house"	—	P
8.19.10.11.0	8 Ajaw 18 Yaxk'in	Sept. 9, 426	plants a stone; fastens headband (accession)	Tok Casper	P
9.1.0.0.0	6 Ajaw 13 Yaxk'in	Aug. 28, 455	plants a stone	Tutum Yol K'inich	C
9.2.5.0.0	10 Ajaw 8 Pop	Apr. 18, 480	—		U
9.2.5.11.0	9 Ajaw 8 Keh	Nov. 24, 480	"places"	Turtle Shell	U
9.2.18.13.1 or 9.2.18.13.10	11 Imix 4 Sak or 7 Ok 13 Sak	Oct. 28, 493, or Nov. 6, 493	is made *ajaw*	Mih Toh	26
9.3.0.0.0	2 Ajaw 3 Sotz'	Jan. 30, 495	—	—	26
9.5.7.0.0?	9 Ajaw 3 Sotz'	May 29, 541	plants a stone	supervised by "Yob'a B'alam"	P
9.11.0.0.0	12 Ajaw 8 Keh	Oct. 14, 652	arrive/witness?	Smoke Imix	L
9.11.0.11.11	9 Chuwen 14 Sek	June 2, 653	burns the structure (dedication); dances	K'awil Yo'at	L
9.13.0.0.0?	8 Ajaw 8 Wo	Mar. 18, 692	—	—	T
9.14.13.4.17	12 Kab'an 5 K'ayab'	Jan. 2, 725	receives K'awil; fastens headband; is seated in reign (accession)	K'ak' Tiliw	E, F J G
9.15.0.0.0	4 Ajaw 13 Yax	Aug. 22, 731	??; plants a stone; ??; tripod is manifested	Sky Xul — —	P E F
9.15.3.2.0	6 Ajaw 18 Sak	Sept. 15, 734	makes the throne?	?? supervised by K'ak' Tiliw	M
9.15.5.0.0	10 Ajaw 8 Ch'en	July 26, 736	plants a stela	K'ak' Tiliw	I
9.15.6.14.0	13 Ajaw 18 Sotz'	Apr. 27, 738	captures or pierces wood; drills fire	—	I
9.15.6.14.6	6 Kimi 4 Sek	May 3, 738	decapitates Waxaklajun Ub'ah K'awil	supervised by K'ak' Tiliw	E, F, G, J

Long Count	Calendar Round	Gregorian Date	Event	Protagonist	Monument
9.15.10.0.0	3 Ajaw 3 Mol	June 30, 741	"stela Copan"	—	F
9.15.15.0.0	9 Ajaw 18 Xul	June 4, 746	—	K'ak' Tiliw	S
9.15.17.9.5?	4 Chikchan 13 Muwan	Nov. 25, 748	—	—	H
9.16.0.0.0	2 Ajaw 13 Sek	May 9, 751	plants ??; scatters incense	K'ak' Tiliw	H
9.16.5.0.0	8 Ajaw 8 Sotz'	Apr. 12, 756	scatters incense; plants a monument	K'ak' Tiliw	J
9.16.10.0.0	1 Ajaw 3 Sip	Mar. 17, 761	scatters incense; plants a monument	K'ak' Tiliw	F
9.16.11.13.1	11 Imix 19 Muwan	Nov. 28, 762	receives "palanquin"	K'in B'alam, supervised by K'ak' Tiliw	E, O', P'
9.16.13.4.17	8 Kab'an 5 Yaxk'in	June 6, 764	completes two k'atuns	K'ak' Tiliw	D
9.16.15.0.0	7 Ajaw 18 Pop	Feb. 19, 766	plants monument; scatters incense; is made ajaw	K'ak' Tiliw; —	D
9.17.0.0.0	13 Ajaw 18 Kumk'u	Jan. 24, 771	plants monument; scatters incense; witnesses it	K'ak' Tiliw; Xkuy ajaw	E
9.17.4.10.12	1 Eb' 5 Yax	Aug. 3, 775	(stela event)	—	C
9.17.4.11.0	9 Ajaw 13 Yax	Aug. 11, 775	??	Jun Ajaw; Yax B'alam	C
9.17.5.0.0	6 Ajaw 13 K'ayab'	Dec. 29, 775	scatters drops; plants monument	K'ak' Tiliw	C, A
??	??	??	??	—	O'
9.17.7.8.7	9 Manik' 5 Yaxk'in	June 3, 778	??	??	O', P'
9.17.10.0.0	12 Ajaw 8 Pax	Dec. 2, 780	makes the monument	K'ak' Tiliw	B
9.17.12.7.8	9 Lamat 1 Sek	Apr. 19, 783	??	??	O', P'
9.17.14.13.0	9 Ajaw 3 Yax	July 29, 785	??	??	G
9.17.14.13.2	11 Ik' 5 Yax	July 31, 785	dies; witnesses it	K'ak' Tiliw; Xkuy ajaw	G
9.17.14.13.12	8 Eb' 15 Yax	Aug. 10, 785	buried	K'ak' Tiliw	G
9.17.14.16.18	9 Etz'nab' 1 K'ank'in	Oct. 15, 785	fastens headband; is seated (accession)	Sky Xul	G, O', P' O'
9.17.15.0.0	5 Ajaw 3 Muwan	Nov. 6, 785	bundles monument; scatters incense	Sky Xul	G G, O'
9.17.15.6.9	4 Muluk 7 Sip	Mar. 15, 786	??	—	O'
9.17.15.6.17	12 Kab'an 15 Sip	Mar. 23, 786	carries?	—	O'
9.17.15.6.18	13 Etz'nab' 16 Sip	Mar. 24, 786	??	in the company of Sky Xul	O', P'
9.17.15.6.19	1 Kawak 17 Sip	Mar. 25, 786	??	in the company of Sky Xul	O'
9.17.15.7.0	2 Ajaw 18 Sip	Mar. 26, 786	dies; takes possession of ??	Yi'h K'in At	O'
9.17.16.0.4 or 9.17.16.0.11	5 K'an 2 Muwan or 12 Chuwen 9 Muwan	Nov. 5, 786, or Nov. 12, 786	?? is captured; receives ??	Xkuy ajaw	O'

Long Count	Calendar Round	Gregorian Date	Event	Protagonist	Monument
9.17.16.7.4	2 K'an 17 Sip	Mar. 25, 787	dies	??	O'
9.17.19.9.15	2 Men 13 Sek	Apr. 29, 790	??	??	O'
9.18.0.0.0	11 Ajaw 18 Mak	Oct. 11, 790	[dedication]	—	O, O'
9.18.5.0.0	4 Ajaw 13 Keh	Sept. 15, 795	scatters incense; plants a stone	Sky Xul	P, P'
9.18.10.0.0	10 Ajaw 8 Sak	Aug. 19, 800	plants the stela	Jade Sky?	I
9.18.15.0.0	3 Ajaw 3 Yax	July 24, 805	scatters incense	Jade Sky	K
9.18.19.16.0	8 Ajaw 18 Xul	May 19, 810	??	Jade Sky	1B-1
9.19.0.0.0	9 Ajaw 18 Mol	June 28, 810	scatters incense; scatters incense	Jade Sky; Yax Pasaj	1B-1

Appendix C

Selected Historical Events from the Texts of Copan

Long Count	Calendar Round	Gregorian Date	Event	Protagonist	Monument
8.19.10.10.17	5 Kab'an 15 Yaxk'in	Sept. 6, 426	takes K'awil at the "founding house"	K'uk' Mo' Ajaw	Q
8.19.10.11.0	8 Ajaw 18 Yaxk'in	Sept. 9, 426	comes to the "founding house"	K'inich Yax K'uk' Mo'	Q
9.7.5.0.8	8 Lamat 6 Mak	Nov. 19, 578	accedes	B'utz' Chan	HS
9.9.14.17.5	6 Chikchan 18 K'ayab'	Feb. 8, 628	accedes	Smoke Imix	J, HS
9.10.19.15.0	12 Ajaw 13 K'ayab'	Aug. 15, 692	scatters incense	Smoke Imix	3
9.12.3.14.0	5 Ajaw 8 Wo	Mar. 22, 676	dedicates Stela I	Smoke Imix	I
9.13.3.6.8	7 Lamat 1 Mol	July 9, 695	accedes	Waxaklajun Ub'ah K'awil	J
9.13.10.0.0	7 Ajaw 8 Kumk'u	Jan. 26, 702	dedicates Stela J	Waxaklajun Ub'ah K'awil	J
9.13.18.17.9	12 Muluk 7 Muwan	Nov. 29, 710	dedicates 10L-26 stair	Waxaklajun Ub'ah K'awil	HS
9.14.0.0.0	6 Ajaw 13 Muwan	Dec. 5, 711	dedicates Stela C	Waxaklajun Ub'ah K'awil	C
9.14.3.6.8	5 Lamat 1 Sip	Mar. 27, 715	dedicates 10L-22	Waxaklajun Ub'ah K'awil	10L-22
9.14.6.5.9	13 Muluk 7 Pop	Feb. 20, 718	burns Xkuy	Waxaklajun Ub'ah K'awil	Cylinder
9.14.10.0.0	5 Ajaw 3 Mak	Oct. 13, 721	dedicates Stela F	Waxaklajun Ub'ah K'awil	F
9.14.15.0.0	11 Ajaw 18 Sak	Sept. 17, 726	sets up Stela 4	Waxaklajun Ub'ah K'awil	4
9.14.19.5.0	4 Ajaw 18 Muwan	Dec. 5, 730	sets up Stela H	Waxaklajun Ub'ah K'awil	H
9.14.19.8.0	12 Ajaw 18 Kumk'u	Feb. 3, 731	sets up Stela A	Waxaklajun Ub'ah K'awil	A
9.15.0.0.0	4 Ajaw 13 Yax	Aug. 22, 731	sets up Stela B	Waxaklajun Ub'ah K'awil	B
9.15.5.0.0	10 Ajaw 8 Ch'en	July 26, 736	sets up Stela D	Waxaklajun Ub'ah K'awil	D
9.15.6.8.13	10 B'en 16 K'ayab'	Jan. 10, 738	dedicates Ballcourt III	Waxaklajun Ub'ah K'awil	BC III
9.15.6.14.6	6 Kimi 4 Sek	May 3, 738	death	Waxaklajun Ub'ah K'awil	HS
9.15.6.16.5	6 Chikchan 3 Yaxk'in	June 11, 738	accedes	K'ak' Joplaj Chan K'awil	HS
9.15.15.0.0	9 Ajaw 18 Xul	June 4, 746	dedicates 10L-22A	K'ak' Joplaj Chan K'awil	10L-22A
9.15.17.13.10	11 Ok 13 Pop	Feb. 18, 749	accedes	K'ak' Yipyaj Chan K'awil	N, HS
9.16.4.1.0	6 Ajaw 13 Sek	May 8, 755	dedicates 10L-26 and HS	K'ak' Yipyaj Chan K'awil	HS
9.16.5.0.0	8 Ajaw 8 Sotz'	Apr. 12, 756	sets up Stela M	K'ak' Yipyaj Chan K'awil	M
9.16.10.0.0	1 Ajaw 3 Sip	Mar. 17, 761	sets up Stela N	K'ak' Yipyaj Chan K'awil	N

Long Count	Calendar Round	Gregorian Date	Event	Protagonist	Monument
9.16.12.5.17	6 Kab'an 10 Mol	July 2, 763	accedes	Yax Pasaj Chan Yo'at	10L-11
9.16.15.0.0	7 Ajaw 18 Pop	Feb. 19, 766	makes Altar GIII	Yax Pasaj Chan Yo'at	GIII
9.16.18.2.12	8 Eb' 15 Sip	Mar. 27, 769	makes structure	Yax Pasaj Chan Yo'at	10L-11
9.16.18.9.18	11 Etz'nab' 1 Sak	Aug. 20, 769	dedicates Altar Z	Yax Pasaj Chan Yo'at	Z
9.17.0.0.0	13 Ajaw 18 Kumk'u	Jan. 24, 771	dedicates 10L-21A; Altar 41	Yax Pasaj Chan Yo'at	10L-21A; 41
9.17.2.12.16	1 Kib' 19 Keh	Sept. 26, 773	dedicates 10L-11	Yax Pasaj Chan Yo'at	10L-11
9.17.5.0.0	6 Ajaw 13 K'ayab'	Dec. 29, 775	dedicates Altar Q; 10L-16	Yax Pasaj Chan Yo'at	Q
9.17.10.0.0	12 Ajaw 8 Pax	Dec. 2, 780	dedicates 9M-27	Yax Pasaj Chan Yo'at	9M-27
9.17.10.11.0	11 Ajaw 3 Ch'en	July 10, 781	dedicates 9N-82	Yax Pasaj Chan Yo'at	9N-82
9.17.12.5.17	4 Kab'an 10 Sip	Mar. 19, 783	dedicates Altar T	Yax Pasaj Chan Yo'at	T
9.17.12.6.2	9 Ik' 15 Sip	Mar. 24, 783	conjures *k'awil*	Yax Pasaj Chan Yo'at	8

Appendix D

Transcriptions and Translations of the Monumental Inscriptions Commissioned by K'ak' Tiliw

ALTAR M

Coordinate	Block Transcription	Block Maya	Block English
A01	oo o2 winal hi ya	mix? cha' winikjiy	o [k'ins] 2 winals
B01	03 hab' ya	ux hab'iy	3 tuns
A02	tzutz _ 04 ajaw	tzutzjiy chan ajaw	(since) 4 Ajaw (9.15.0.0.0) was completed
B02	13 yax	uxlajun yax	13 Yax
A03	i u ti o6 ajaw	i ut wak ajaw	and then 6 Ajaw (9.15.3.2.0) happens
B03	18 sak	waxaklajun sak	18 Sak
A04	i pat ta wi	i pataw	and then [he] makes
B04	u kuch? tun ni	ukuchtun?	his throne?
A05	u _	u-_	his _
B05	_	_	_
C01	_ chi pi xi	_	_
D01	o5 winik hab' pi tzi la	ho' winik hab' pitzal	five-k'atun ballplayer
C02	u kab' hi _	ukab'jiy?	under his supervision
D02	k'ak' ti li	k'ak' tiliw	K'ak' Tiliw
C03	wi chan na	chan	Chan
D03	yo'at/yo'pat ti	yo'at/yo'pat	Yo'at/Yo'pat
C04	ik' xu ku pi _	ik' xukpi _	black Copan [ajaw]
D04	no noh la	nohol	south
C05	_	[kalomte']	[kalomte']
D05	_ ajaw ?? wa	_ ?? ajaw	_ Quirigua ajaw

Paraphrase:

It was o [k'ins] 2 winals, 3 tuns since 4 Ajaw 13 Yax (9.15.0.0.0; August 22, 731) was completed, and then 6 Ajaw 18 Sak (9.15.3.2.0; September 15, 734) happens.

And then . . . the five-k'atun ballplayer makes his seat-stone?, his . . . , under the supervision of K'ak' Tiliw, black Copan [ajaw], south [kalomte'], . . . Quirigua ajaw.

Coordinate	Block Transcription	Block Maya	Block English
A01–B02	–	–	[ISIG]
A03–B04	09 pih	b'olon pih	9 b'aktuns
A05–B06	15 winik hab'	ho'lajun winik hab'	15 k'atuns
A07–B08	15 hab'	ho'lajun hab'	15 tuns
A09–B10	00 winal _	mix? winal	0 winals
A11–B12	00 k'in	mix? k'in	0 k'ins
C01	–	–	[9 Ajaw]
D01	–	–	[G9]
C02	–	–	[F]
D02	05 hu? li? ya	ho' huliy	five since it arrived
C03	04 _ k'al ja	k'alaj chan _	is closed, 4 _ lunation
D03	–	–	[X]
C04	u k'ab'a' ch'o _	uch'ok k'ab'a'	its young name
D04	20 10	k'al lajun	30
C05	08/18 10/te	waxaklajun (te?)	18
D05	chichin? ni	chichin?	Xul
C06	u _ k'al? _	uk'al? _	he bundles/closes? _
D06	–	–	–
C07	–	–	–
D07	yo? _	–	–
C08	–	–	–
D08	u? _	–	–
C09	–	–	–
D09	u? k'uhul? k'ab'a'	uk'uhul? k'ab'a'	its divine? name
C10	–	–	–
D10	tun? ni?	tunil?	stone?
(left)			
E01	k'ak' ti li wi	k'ak' tiliw	K'ak' Tiliw
F01	chan na	chan	Chan
E02	yo/yop at ti	yo'at/yo'pat	Yo'at/Yo'pat
F02	u chok?	uchok?	he scatters
E03	–	–	–
F03	–	–	–
E04	–	–	–
F04	–	–	–
E05	u k'uhul? k'ab'a'	uk'uhul k'ab'a'	its divine name
F05	u lakam ma	ulakam	his huge
E06	tun ni?	tunil	stone
F06	09 ajaw	b'olon ajaw	9 Ajaw

STELA S (continued)

Coordinate	Block Transcription	Block Maya	Block English
E07	–	ukab'jiy?	under his supervision
F07	–	–	–
E08	–	–	–
F08	k'uhul? ajaw? ?? _	k'uhul ?? ajaw?	divine Quirigua *ajaw*?
(right)			
G01–H08	–	–	–

Paraphrase:

. . . 9 *b'aktuns*, 15 *k'atuns*, 15 *tuns*, 0 *winals*, 0 *k'ins*, . . . (June 4, 746) 5 days since it arrives, 4 _ lunation is closed, [X] is its young name, 30, 18 Xul, he bundles/closes? . . . is the divine name of the . . . stone? of K'ak' Tiliw Chan Yo'at/Yo'pat.

He scatters . . . the divine name of the stela of 9 Ajaw, supervised by? . . . divine Quirigua *ajaw*?.

STELA H

Coordinate	Block Transcription	Block Maya	Block English
A01–B02	tzi ka kab' hab'	tzik? kab' hab'	count? of the earth *hab'*
C01	09 pih	b'olon pih	9 *b'aktuns*
D01	16 winik hab'	waklajun winik hab'	16 *k'atuns*
C02	00 hab'	mix? hab'	0 *tuns*
D02	00 winal	mix? winal	0 *winals*
E01	00 k'in	mix? k'in	0 *k'ins*
F01	02 ajaw	cha' ajaw	2 Ajaw
E02	13 ka se wa	uxlajun kasew	13 Sek
F02	nal ?? yi	??	G9
G01	u ?? hun na	u-?? hun	its ?? book/headband
H01	05 hu _	ho' huliy?	5 since it arrives
G02	–	–	[C]
H02	–	–	[X]
I01	u ch'o k'ab'a'	uch'ok k'ab'a'	its young name
J01	20 _ 10	k'al lajun	30
I02	–	–	[verb]
J02	tun? ni	tunil?	stone?
K01	–	–	–
L01	_ chan na	_ chan	_ sky
K02	–	–	–
L02	u? k'ab'a' k'uhul	uk'uhul k'ab'a'	its divine name
M01	u _	u-_	its _
N01	tz'a pa? ja	tz'apaj	is set up
M02	ik' nahb'?	ik' nahb'?	Black Lake?
N02	chan ch'e'en? na	chan ch'e'en?	celestial cave?
O01	–	–	[scatters]

Coordinate	Block Transcription	Block Maya	Block English
P01	ch'a hi	ch'ah	incense
O02	k'a _	k'ak'	K'ak'
P02	ti li wi	tiliw	Tiliw
Q01	chan yo'at/yo'pat ti	chan yo'at/yo'pat	Chan Yo'at/Yo'pat
R01	k'uhul ajaw ?? _	k'uhul ?? ajaw	divine Quirigua *ajaw*
Q02	_ no _ _	[nohol kalomte']	[south *kalomte'*]
R02	ch'a ho ma	ch'ahom(a)	incense-offerer
S01	no noh tan na	nohol tan	south center
T01	_ ni	_	_
S02	15? ??	ho'lajun? ??	15? days
T02	_	_	[8? *winals*]
U01	02 hab' ya	cha' hab'iy	2 tuns
V01	u? ti ya	utiy	since it happened
U02	04 chikchan?	chan chikchan?	4 Chikchan? (9.15.17.9.5?)
V02–B'02	_	_	[13 Muwan?]

Paraphrase:

Count? of the earth *hab'*, 9 *b'aktuns*, 16 *k'atuns*, 0 tuns, 0 *winals*, 0 *k'ins* 2 Ajaw (May 9, 751) 13 Sek, G9 is its ?? book/headband, 5 since it arrives, [C and X] is its young name 30, . . . a stone . . . sky . . . is its divine name, its. . . .

It is set up at Black Lake celestial cave?

K'ak' Tiliw Chan Yo'at/Yo'pat, divine Quirigua *ajaw*, [south *kalomte'*], incense-offerer, south center . . . [scatters] incense.

15? days, [8? *winals*], 2 tuns since 4 Chikchan? [13 Muwan? (9.15.17.9.5; November 25, 748)] . . . happened.

STELA J

Coordinate	Block Transcription	Block Maya	Block English
(east)			
A01–D05	tzi ka nahb'? hab'	tzik? nahb'? hab'	count? of the lake? *hab'*
A06	09	b'olon	9
B06	pih	pih	*b'aktuns*
A07	16	waklajun	16
B07	winik hab'	winik hab'	*k'atuns*
A08	05	ho'	5
B08	hab'	hab'	tuns
A09	00	??	0
B09	winal	winal	*winals*
A10	00	??	0
B10	k'in	k'in	*k'ins*
A11	08	waxak	8
B11	ajaw	ajaw	Ajaw
A12	k'in ?? yi	??	G9

STELA J (continued)

Coordinate	Block Transcription	Block Maya	Block English
B12	?? hun	?? hun	?? book/headband (F)
A13	04 hul li ya	chan huliy	4 days since it arrives (4D)
B13	06 uh? k'al li	k'al wak uh?	closure of sixth of the (skull) lunation (6CS)
A14	?? ?? och? ch'ahb'	??	X
B14	u k'ab'a' ch'o ko	uch'ok k'ab'a'	its young name (B)
A15	20 09	k'al b'olon	29
B15	08 sotz'	waxak sotz'	8 Sotz'
A16	nah 05 tun ni	nah ho'tun	first five stone
B16	u chok? hi?	uchok? ch'ah?	he scatters incense?
A17	u tz'a pa wa	utz'apaw	he plants
B17	yax u _	yax u- _	first its? _
A18	chan nu	chan?	sky?
B18	u _ k'ab'a' k'uhul	uk'uhul k'ab'a'	its divine name
C06	08 ajaw tun ni	waxak ajaw tun	8 Ajaw stone
D06	u hi b'a	ub'ahil?	his image?
C07	u ch'ahb'	uch'ahb'	his penance
D07	ya ak'	yak'il	his offering
C08	?? ha'? ek'?	??	?? (vision serpent event)
D08	yax chit? ta	yax chit?	first ??
C09	01 ??	jun ??	1 ??
D09	nah chan	nah chan	first snake
C10	u yo ok te'	uyokte'?	the pillar-tree? of
D10	chan na	chan	sky
C11	u yo ok te'	uyokte'?	the pillar-tree? of
D11	kab'	kab'	earth
C12	k'ak' til li wi	k'ak' tiliw	K'ak' Tiliw
D12	chan na	chan	Chan
C13	yo'at/yo'pat	yo'at/yo'pat	Yo'at/Yo'pat
D13	ch'ahom(a) ma	ch'ahom(a)	incense-offerer
C14	no noh la	nohol	south
D14	kalomte'	kalomte'	*kalomte'*
C15	ik' xu ku pi	ik' xukpi	black Copan
D15	ajaw	ajaw	*ajaw*
C16	u 14 tz'ak b'u li	uchanlajun tz'akb'uil	fourteenth in succession
D16	wi' te nah	?? nah	?? building (founding house)
C17	[ch'a] ho ma	ch'ahom(a)	incense-offerer
D17	nal ?? ik' la	ik' ?? nal	Black Hole place
C18	yo ok te'	yokte'?	pillar-tree?
D18	b'a ka b'a	b'akab'	*b'akab'*

STELA J (continued)

Coordinate	Block Transcription	Block Maya	Block English
(north)			
E01	a ?? ya	??	(focus marker)
F01	03 13 winal ji ya	ux uxlajun winaljiy	3 [k'ins] 13 winals
E02	11 hab' ya	b'uluch hab'iy	11 tuns
F02	00 winik hab' ya	mix? winik hab'iy	0 [1] k'atuns
E03	u ti ya	utiy	since it happened
F03	12 kab'an	lajchan kab'an	12 Kab'an (9.14.13.4.17)
E04	05 k'an a si ya	ho' k'anasiy	5 K'ayab'
F04	k'al ja ya	k'alajiy	was fastened
E05	09 tzak ja	b'olon tzakaj	9/many-conjured
F05	k'ak' xok ki	k'ak' xok	fire-shark
E06	hun	hun	headband
F06	tu hi b'a	tub'ah	for him/on his head
E07	k'ak' til li wi	k'ak' tiliw	K'ak' Tiliw
F07	chan na yo/yop at ti	chan yo'at/yo'pat	Chan Yo'at/Yo'pat
E08	ch'a ho ma	ch'ahom(a)	incense-offerer
F08	k'uhul ajaw ?? wa	k'uhul ?? ajaw	divine Quirigua ajaw
(south)			
G01	a ?? ya	??	(focus marker)
H01	14 03 winal hi ya	chanlajun ux winaljiy	14 [k'ins] 3 winals
G02	18 hab' ya	waxaklajun hab'iy	18 tuns
H02	06 kimi	wak kimi	6 Kimi (9.15.6.14.6)
G03	04 ka? se wa	chan kasew	4 Sek
H03	ch'ak b'a hi ya	ch'akb'ahiy	decapitated
G04	18 u b'a	waxaklajun ub'ah	Waxaklajun Ub'ah
H04	k'awil	k'awil	K'awil
G05	k'uhul ajaw xu [ku] pi	k'uhul xukpi ajaw	divine Copan ajaw
H05	u ch'am wa	uch'amaw	he receives
G06	k'awil	k'awil	K'awil/God K
H06	k'ak' ti li wi	k'ak' tiliw	K'ak' Tiliw
G07	chan na	chan	Chan
H07	yo'at/yo'pat	yo'at/yo'pat	Yo'at/Yo'pat
G08	04 te ch'o tzu ko	chante ch'ok tzuk	four sprout? province?
H08	04 te ch'a ho ma	chante ch'ahom(a)	four incense-offerer

Paraphrase:

Count? of the lake? hab', 9 b'aktuns, 16 k'atuns, 5 tuns, 0 winals, 0 k'ins, 8 Ajaw (April 12, 756), G9 is the ?? book/headband, 4 days since it arrives, closure of 6 of the (skull) lunation, X is its young name, 29, 8 Sotz', first five stone.

He scatters incense?.

He plants first its? . . .-sky, the divine name of the 8 Ajaw stone.

It is the image? of his penance, his offering.

?? first ?? 1 ?? first snake, pillar-tree? of the sky, pillar-tree? of the earth, K'ak' Tiliw Chan Yo'at/Yo'pat, incense-offerer, south *kalomte'*, black Copan *ajaw*, fourteenth in succession of the ?? building (founding house), incense-offerer, Black Hole place pillar-tree?, *b'akab'*.

It is? 3 [*k'ins*], 13 *winals*, 11 *tuns*, 0 [1] *k'atuns* since it happened, 12 Kab'an 5 K'ayab' (January 2, 725), since the 9/many-conjured-fire-shark headband was fastened for/on K'ak' Tiliw Chan Yo'at/Yo'pat, incense-offerer, divine Quirigua *ajaw*.

It is? 14 [*k'ins*], 3 *winals*, 18 *tuns* since 6 Kimi 4 Sek (May 3, 738), since Waxaklajun Ub'ah K'awil, divine Copan *ajaw*, was decapitated.

K'ak' Tiliw Chan Yo'at/Yo'pat, four sprout? province?, four incense-offerer, receives K'awil/God K.

STELA F

Coordinate	Block Transcription	Block Maya	Block English
(east)			
C01–D02	tzi ka ?? hab'	tzik? ?? hab'	count? of the ?? *hab'*
C03	09 pih	b'olon pih	9 b'aktuns
D03	16 winik hab'	waklajun winik hab'	16 k'atuns
C04	10 hab'	lajun hab'	10 tuns
D04	00 winal	?? winal	0 winals
C05	00 k'in	?? k'in	0 k'ins
D05	01 ajaw	jun ajaw	1 Ajaw
C06	?? k'in ?? hun	?? hun	G9 is the ?? book/headband (F)
D06	?? ya ju li ya	?? huliy	o since it arrived (0D)
C07	u 06 ?? k'al	k'al uwak ??	closure of the sixth of the (moon goddess) lunation (6CF)
D07	chan kab' ?? si	chan kab' ??	X
C08	20 10	k'al lajun	30 (10A)
D08	03 chak k'at	ux chak k'at	3 Sip
C09	cho? ka ja ch'a hi	chokaj? ch'ah	incense is scattered
D09	ti pi hi? witz? yi	ti ?? ??	on ?? ??
C10	tun ni li u k'uhul lu	tunil uk'uhul	stone object its divine
D10	k'ab'a' a a 01 ajaw wa	k'ab'a' jun ajaw	name 1 Ajaw
C11	tun ni u tz'a pa wa	tun utz'apaw	stone he plants
D11	u mam? pi	u-??	its/his ??
C12	chan k'ak' til chan	chan k'ak' tiliw chan	sky K'ak' Tiliw Chan
D12	yo/yop at ch'ahom(a)	yo'at/yo'pat ch'ahom(a)	Yo'at/Yo'pat incense-offerer
C13	03 11 pih ajaw	ux b'uluch pih ajaw	3-11 bundle/cycle? *ajaw*
D13	00 li nal 05 k'an hab'	?? ??	o *alawtuns*
C14	tzutz hi ya 19 nal ?? hab'	tzutzjiy b'olonlajun ??	completed 19 x 20⁷ tuns
D14	ti 01 ajaw 13 mo lo	ti jun ajaw uxlajun mol	on 1 Ajaw 13 Mol (LC?)
C15	u ti hi ya ti yax tzi pi	utiy ti yax ??	it happened at/on first/green ??
D15	01 ?? u ti ya	jun ?? utiy	1 ?? it happened
C16	ik' nal nahb'? 00 li ?? to pi	ik' nahb'? nal ?? ??	Black Lake? place o *piktuns*
D16	13 nu tzutz pi ti 01 ajaw	uxlajun ?? ti jun ajaw	13 *kalab'tuns*? since 1 Ajaw (LC?)
C17	13 yax k'in ni ch'ak u b'a	uxlajun yaxk'in ch'ak ub'ah	13 Yaxk'in is decapitated

Coordinate	Block Transcription	Block Maya	Block English
D17	ya? _ chi k'in ni la	_ k'inichal	_ sun-faced
C18	ajaw wa lakam tun ni	ajaw lakamtun	*ajaw* stela
D18	_ u kab' hi ya	_ ukab'jiy?	_ under his supervision
C19	k'uhul _	k'uhul _	divine _
D19	_ nal _	_ nal	_ place?
(west)			
A01–B02	tzi ka ?? hab'	tzik? ?? hab'	count? of the ?? *hab'*
A03	09 pih	b'olon pih	9 *b'aktuns*
B03	14 winik hab'	chanlajun winik hab'	14 *k'atuns*
A04	13 tun	uxlajun tun	13 *tuns*
B04	04 winal	chan winal	4 *winals*
A05	17 k'in	wuklajun k'in	17 *k'ins*
B05	12 kab'an	lacha' kab'an	12 Kab'an
A06	05 k'an a si ya	ho' k'anasiy	5 K'ayab'
B06	k'awil ch'am wi	ch'amaw k'awil	receives K'awil/God K
A07	k'ak' til chan yo/yop at ti	k'ak' tiliw chan yo'at/yo'pat	K'ak' Tiliw Chan Yo'at/Yo'pat
B07	u 14 tz'ak b'u wi nah te	uchanlajun tz'akb'uil ?? nah	fourteenth in succession of the ?? building (founding house)
A08	ch'ahom(a) 04 te	ch'ahom(a) chante	incense-offerer four
B08	ik' ?? u ?? na?	ik' ?? ??	black ?? ??
A09	16 xu? k'in? 09 ok k'in ni	waklajun ?? b'olon ??	16 ?? 9 ??
B09	ik' xu ku pi ajaw	ik' xukpi ajaw	black Copan *ajaw*
A10	k'uhul ajaw ?? _ b'a ka b'a	k'uhul ?? ajaw b'akab'	divine Quirigua *ajaw b'akab'*
B10	09 09 winal hi ya 13 hab' ya	b'olon b'olon winaljiy uxlajun hab'iy	9 [*k'ins*], 9 *winals*, 13 *tuns*
A11	u ti ya 12 kab'an	utiy lacha' kab'an	since it happened 12 Kab'an
B11	i u ti 06 kimi	i ut wak kimi	and then it happens 6 Kimi (9.15.6.14.6)
A12	04 ka? se? wa ch'ak hi ya u b'a	chan kasew ch'akjiy ub'ah	4 Sek decapitated
B12	18 u b'a k'awil	waxaklajun ub'ah k'awil	Waxaklajun Ub'ah K'awil
A13	ajaw xu ku pi u kab' hi ya	xukpi ajaw ukab'jiy?	Copan *ajaw* under his supervision
B13	ajaw kuch? ab'ak? nah k'ak' til chan wi	kuch? ab'ak? nah ajaw k'ak' tiliw chan	ink-pot? building *ajaw* K'ak' Tiliw Chan
A14	yo/yop at ti u ti ya	yo'at/yo'pat utiy	Yo'at/Yo'pat it happened at
B14	nal na ik' way? la u nah _	ik' way? nal unah_	Black Hole place its? first? _
A15	03 ajaw 03 mo lo	ux ajaw ux mol	3 Ajaw 3 Mol (9.15.10.0.0)
B15	lakam? tun ni xu ku pi	lakamtun xukpi	stela Copan
A16	10 sak? tun/ku? lam tan ja	lajun sak? tun? tanlamaj	10 pure/white? ?? is half-diminished
B16	04 wi ti _ ku? hal ja k'o b'a	chan witik? halaj k'ob'	four roots? the tripod? is manifested
A17	ti 04 ajaw 13 yax	ti chan ajaw uxlajun yax	on 4 Ajaw 13 Yax (9.15.0.0.0)

Coordinate	Block Transcription	Block Maya	Block English
B17	03 13 winal hi ya 16 hab' ya	ux uxlajun winaljiy waklajun hab'iy	3 [k'ins] 13 winals 16 tuns
A18	01 winik hab' ya 12 kab'an	jun winik hab'iy lacha' kab'an	1 k'atun [since] 12 Kab'an (9.14.13.4.17)
B18	05 k'an a si ya i u ti	ho' k'anasiy i ut	5 K'ayab' and then it happens
A19	01 ajaw 03 chak k'at	jun ajaw ux chakk'at	1 Ajaw 3 Sip (9.16.10.0.0)
B19	ti tan lam ti 13 ajaw	ti tan lam ti uxlajun ajaw	on the half-diminishing of 13 Ajaw (9.17.0.0.0)

Paraphrase:

(east)

Count? of the ?? hab', 9 b'aktuns, 16 k'atuns, 10 tuns, 0 winals, 0 k'ins, 1 Ajaw (March 17, 761), G9 is the ?? book/headband, 0 since it arrived, closure of the sixth of the (moon goddess) lunation, X, 30, 3 Sip.

Incense is scattered on ?? stone object, the divine name of the 1 Ajaw stone.

K'ak' Tiliw Chan Yo'at/Yo'pat, incense-offerer, 3-11 bundle/cycle? ajaw plants its/his ?? sky.

0 alawtuns, completed 19 x 20⁷ tuns on 1 Ajaw 13 Mol (LC?), it happened at/on first/green ?? 1 ??, it happened at Black Lake? place.

0 piktuns, 13 kalab'tuns? since 1 Ajaw 13 Yaxk'in (LC?), . . . sun-faced ajaw stela is decapitated, under the supervision of divine . . . place?

(west)

Count of the ?? hab', 9 b'aktuns, 14 k'atuns, 13 tuns, 4 winals, 17 k'ins, 12 Kab'an 5 K'ayab' (January 2, 725), receives K'awil/God K, K'ak' Tiliw Chan Yo'at/Yo'pat, fourteenth in succession of the ?? building (founding house), incense-offerer, four black ?? ??, 16 ?? 9 ??, black Copan ajaw, divine Quirigua ajaw b'akab'.

9 [k'ins], 9 winals, 13 tuns since 12 Kab'an (9.14.13.4.17; January 2, 725) happened, and then 6 Kimi 4 Sek (9.15.6.14.6; May 3, 738) happens; Waxaklajun Ub'ah K'awil Copan ajaw is decapitated, under the supervision of ink-pot? building ajaw, K'ak' Tiliw Chan Yo'at/Yo'pat, it happened at Black Hole place its? first?. . . .

On 3 Ajaw 3 Mol (9.15.10.0.0; June 30, 741) stela Copan 10 pure/white? ?? is half-diminished four roots?

The tripod? is manifested on 4 Ajaw 13 Yax (9.15.0.0.0; August 22, 731).

3 [k'ins], 13 winals, 16 tuns, 1 k'atun since 12 Kab'an 5 K'ayab' (9.14.13.4.17; January 2, 725), and then 1 Ajaw 3 Sip (9.16.10.0.0; March 17, 761) happens, on the half-diminishing of 13 Ajaw (9.17.0.0.0; January 24, 771).

STELA D

Coordinate	Block Transcription	Block Maya	Block English
(east)			
C01–D02	tzi ka b'alam hab'	tzik? b'alam hab'	count? of the jaguar hab'
C03–D04	09 pi	b'olon pih	9 b'aktuns
C05–D06	16 winik hab'	waklajun winik hab'	16 k'atuns
C07–D08	15 hab'	ho'lajun hab'	15 tuns
C09–D10	00 winal	?? winal	0 winals
C11–D12	00 k'in	?? k'in	0 k'ins
C13–D14	07 ajaw	wuk ajaw	7 Ajaw
C15	?? k'in yi ni	??	G9
D15	?? hun	?? hun	?? book/headband (F)
C16	tan na chapat nah ?? k'al	tan chapat k'al nah ??	center of the centipede (0D) closure of the first of (skull) lunation (1CS)

Coordinate	Block Transcription	Block Maya	Block English
D16	?? ?? k'uhul u k'ab'a' ch'o ko	?? uch'ok k'ab'a'	X is its young name
C17	20 10 18 k'an jal wa	k'al lajun waxaklajun k'anjalaw	30 18 Pop
D17	tz'a pa ja k'an te' nah chan	tz'apaj k'an te' nah chan	is planted yellow tree first/structure sky
C18	yo'at/yo'pat u k'uhul k'ab'a'	yo'at/yo'pat uk'uhul k'ab'a'	yo'at/yo'pat its divine name
D18	07 ajaw tun ni u chok? wa ch'a hi	wuk ajaw tun uchokaw? ch'ah	7 Ajaw stone he scatters incense
C19	k'ak' til chan na yo'at/yo'pat ti ch'ahom(a)	k'ak' tiliw chan yo'at/yo'pat ch'ahom(a)	K'ak' Tiliw Chan Yo'at/Yo'pat incense-offerer
D19	ik' xu ku pi ajaw k'uhul ajaw ?? wa b'a ka b'a	ik' xukpi ajaw k'uhul ?? ajaw b'akab'	black Copan *ajaw* divine Quirigua *ajaw b'akab'*
C20	13 nu tzutz pi hi yi 07 ajaw 03 k'an jal wa	uxlajun ?? pihiy wuk ajaw ux k'anjalaw	13 k'inchiltuns (since) 7 Ajaw 3 Pop (LC?)
D20	yi li hi ya a ku li k'an nu	yilijiy ahkul k'an nun?	he witnessed turtle yellow ??
C21	kuch? ab'ak? nah ajaw u ti ya	kuch? ab'ak? nah ajaw utiy	ink-pot? structure *ajaw* it happened at
D21	yax ?? nal ch'e'en? na i u ti	yax ?? nal ch'e'en? i ut	first/green ?? cave? and then it happens
C22	07 ajaw 13 k'an jal wa wi'il 05 tun ni il hi	wuk ajaw uxlajun k'anjalaw wi'il ho' tun ilaj	7 Ajaw 13 Pop (9.16.15.0.0) lacking five stone, it is witnessed
D22	k'ak' til chan yo/yop at ti 04 ik' te ?? b'a ka b'a	k'ak' tiliw chan yo'at/yo'pat chante ik' ?? b'akab'	K'ak' Tiliw Chan Yo'at/Yo'pat four black ?? *b'akab'*
(west)			
A01–B02	tzi ka k'in hab'	tzik? k'in hab'	count? of the sun/day *hab'*
A03–B04	09 pih	b'olon pih	9 b'aktuns
A05–B06	16 winik hab'	waklajun winik hab'	16 k'atuns
A07–B08	13 hab'	uxlajun hab'	13 tuns
A09–B10	04 winal	chan winal	4 *winals*
A11–B12	17 k'in	wuklajun k'in	17 k'ins
A13–B14	08 kab'an	waxak kab'an	8 Kab'an
A15	na sak	??	G7
B15	?? hun na	?? hun	?? book/headband (F)
A16	04 hul li ya 04 ?? k'al	chan huliy k'al chan ??	4 since it arrives (4D) closure of 4 (jaguar god) lunation (4CY)
B16	?? u k'ab'a' ch'o ko	?? uch'ok k'ab'a'	X is its young name
A17	20 09 05 yax k'in ni	k'al b'olon ho' yaxk'in	29 (9A) 5 Yaxk'in
B17	tzutz yi u 02 winik hab' ti ajaw le?	tzutzuy ucha' winik hab' ti ajawlel	completes the second *k'atun* in reign
A18	k'ak' til chan yo'at/yo'pat	k'ak' tiliw chan yo'at/yo'pat	K'ak' Tiliw Chan Yo'at/Yo'pat
B18	ch'ahom(a) 04 te ik' ??	ch'ahom(a) chante ik' ??	incense-offerer four black ??
A19	ik' xu ku pi ajaw k'uhul ?? wa b'a ka b'a	ik' xukpi ajaw k'uhul ?? ajaw b'akab'	black Copan *ajaw* divine Quirigua *ajaw b'akab'*
B19	u ti ya e hi? _ muwan?	utiy ??	it happened at ??
A20	ye te te winal ya 01 pih k'uh	???? jun pih k'uh	?? ?? one-bundle? god
B20	u ti ya ma ?? la nal tu ma _ ni	utiy ?? nal _	it happened at ?? place _

STELA D (continued)

Coordinate	Block Transcription	Block Maya	Block English
A21	?? o1 ?? na chan u tz'ak 'a	?? jun ?? nah chan utz'aka'	?? Jun ?? first snake it is exchanged
B21	o3 13 winal hi ya o1 hab' ya _ tu? _	ux uxlajun winaljiy jun hab'iy _	3 [k'ins] 13 winals 1 tun _
A22	i u ti _ ajaw 13 _ _	i ut _ ajaw uxlajun _	and then it happens [7 Ajaw] 13 [Pop] (9.16.15.0.0) _
B22	i ajaw ja u b'a? hi? _ ch'o? ko	i ajawaj ub'ahil? _ ch'ok?	and then the image of _ young? is made *ajaw*
A23	tun ni li u cho? ko wa ch'a hi u _	tunil uchokow? ch'ah uti?	stone object he scatters incense it happened at?
B23	o4 nal tun? lakam ma k'ak' til chan yo'at/yo'pat	chan ?? nal lakam k'ak' tiliw chan yo'at/yo'pat	four ?? place huge/banner K'ak' Tiliw Chan Yo'at/Yo'pat
A24	ch'a ho ma k'uhul ajaw ?? wa b'a ka b'a yi ta hi	ch'ahom(a) k'uhul ?? ajaw b'akab' yitaj	incense-offerer divine Quirigua *ajaw* b'akab' ??
B24	ja k'a/k'i ta k'ak' k'in? te xu?	?? k'ak' k'in? ??	?? K'ak' K'in? ??

Paraphrase:

(east)

Count? of the jaguar *hab'*, 9 *b'aktuns*, 16 *k'atuns*, 15 *tuns*, o *winals*, o *k'ins* 7 Ajaw (February 19, 766), G9 ?? book/headband, center of the centipede, closure of the first of the skull lunation, X is its young name, 30, 18 Pop.

The yellow tree first/structure sky Yo'at/Yo'pat is planted; it is the divine name of the 7 Ajaw stone.

K'ak' Tiliw Chan Yo'at/Yo'pat, incense-offerer, black Copan *ajaw*, divine Quirigua *ajaw*, b'akab' scatters incense.

13 *k'inchiltuns* since 7 Ajaw 3 Pop (LC?), the ink-pot? structure *ajaw* witnessed turtle yellow ??; it happened at first/green ?? cave?.

And then 7 Ajaw 13 Pop (9.16.15.0.0; February 19, 766) happens, lacking five stone; it is witnessed by K'ak' Tiliw Chan Yo'at/Yo'pat, four black ??, b'akab'.

(west)

Count? of the sun/day *hab'*, 9 *b'aktuns*, 16 *k'atuns*, 13 *tuns*, 4 *winals*, 17 *k'ins*, 8 Kab'an (June 6, 764), G7 is the ?? book/headband, 4 since it arrives, closure of 4 (jaguar god) lunation, X is its young name, 29, 5 Yaxk'in.

K'ak' Tiliw Chan Yo'at/Yo'pat, incense-offerer, four black ??, black Copan *ajaw*, divine Quirigua *ajaw*, b'akab' completes the second *k'atun* in reign; it happened at . . . one-bundle? god; it happened at . . . place. . . .

. . . Jun ?? first snake.

3 [k'ins], 13 *winals*, 1 tun are exchanged . . . and then [7 Ajaw] 13 [Pop] (9.16.15.0.0; February 19, 766) happens.

And then the image? of the _ young? stone object is made *ajaw*.

K'ak' Tiliw Chan Yo'at/Yo'pat, incense-offerer, divine Quirigua *ajaw*, b'akab' scatters incense; it happened at? four ?? place huge/banner, ?? K'ak' K'in? ??.

STELA E

Coordinate	Block Transcription	Block Maya	Block English
(east)			
Co1–Do2	tzi ka ?? hab'	tzik ?? hab'	count? of the ?? *hab'*
Co3	o9 pih	b'olon pih	9 *b'aktuns*
Do3	17 winik hab'	wuklajun winik hab'	17 *k'atuns*
Co4	oo hab'	mix? hab'	o *tuns*
Do4	oo winal	mix? winal	o *winals*
Co5	oo k'in	mix? k'in	o *k'ins*
Do5	nal k'in ?? yi ?? hun	?? ?? hun	G9 is the ?? book/headband (F)

Coordinate	Block Transcription	Block Maya	Block English
C06	13 ajaw	uxlajun ajaw	13 Ajaw
D06	?? ya chan na	?? chan	?? sky
C07	u 02 ?? k'al li	k'al ucha' ??	closure of the second of the (moon goddess) lunation (2CF)
D07	na? po k'a/k'i	??	X
C08	u k'ab'a' ch'o ko 'a	uch'ok k'ab'a'	its young name
D08	20 09	k'al b'olon	29
C09	18 ol la	waxaklajun ol	18 Kumk'u
D09	tz'a pa ja	tz'apaj	is planted
C10	yax chit? ti	yax chit?	first/green ??
D10	?? yi nik? sak ik'	?? sak nik? ik'	?? white flower? breath/spirit
C11	13 ajaw tun ni	uxlajun ajaw tun	13 Ajaw stone
D11	u kab' hi ya	ukab'jiy?	under his supervision
C12	ch'a 04 ho ma	chan ch'ahom(a)	four incense-offerer
D12	tzutz hi ya 19 05 nal?	tzutzjiy b'olonlajun ??	completed 19 ??
C13	u ti ya	uti	since it happened
D13	13 ajaw 18 sa ku	uxlajun ajaw waxaklajun sak	13 Ajaw 18 Sak (LC?)
C14	yi li a hi ya ik' ma 'a	yilajiy ik' ma'	he witnessed it, Ik' Ma'
D14	nal sa tzu?	??	??
C15	u ti ya nal lo? ??	utiy ?? nal	it happened at ?? place
D15	tzutz hi ya 06 nal ik' nahb'	tzutzjiy wak ik' nahb'? nal	completed 6 ??
C16	13 ajaw 13 ik' k'at	uxlajun ajaw uxlajun ik' k'at	13 Ajaw 13 Wo (LC?)
D16	u kab' ya nal mi xi?	ukab'jiy? mixnal?	under the supervision of Mixnal?
C17	u ti ya yax hi chi li	utiy yax hichil?	it happened at First Harvest?
D17	wi witz ha i	witz ja'i'	Mountain this is
C18	u kab' ya hi u hi b'a li	ukab'jiy? ub'ahil	under the supervision of his image
D18	k'an te' nah nal ?? hun ek'	k'an te' nah nal ?? hun ek'	yellow tree first/building place ?? headdress star?
C19	k'ak' til chan yo'at/yo'pat	k'ak' tiliw chan yo'at/yo'pat	K'ak' Tiliw Chan Yo'at/Yo'pat
D19	u chok? ch'a wa? 13 ajaw	uchokow? ch'ah uxlajun ajaw	he scatters incense 13 Ajaw
C20	18 ol u b'u t'u	waxaklajun ol ub'ut'	18 Kumk'u (9.17.0.0.0) they cover
D20	?? le ?? 'a ajaw tak?	?? ajawtak?	?? *ajaw* (pl.)?
(west)			
A01–B02	tzi ka ixik? hab'	tzik ikik? hab'	count? of the (moon goddess?) *hab'*
A03	09 pih	b'olon pih	9 *b'aktuns*
B03	14 winik hab'	chanlajun winik hab'	14 *k'atuns*
A04	12 tun	lajcha' hab'	12 [13] *tuns*
B04	04 winal	chan winal	4 *winals*
A05	17 k'in	wuklajun k'in	17 *k'ins*
B05	12 kab'an	lajcha' kab'an	12 Kab'an

Coordinate	Block Transcription	Block Maya	Block English
A06	u ?? _ li	_ ?? hun	_ (G) is the ?? book/headband (F)
B06	07 _ hul li 03 ?? k'al li	wuk huliy k'al ux ??	7 since it arrives (7D) closure of 3 (jaguar god) lunation (3CY)
A07	?? u k'ab'a' ch'o ko ja	?? uch'ok k'ab'a'	X is its young name (B)
B07	20 10 05 k'an a si _	k'al lajun ho' k'anasiy	30 (10A) 5 K'ayab'
A08	u k'awil ch'am k'ak' til chan	uch'am k'awil k'ak' tiliw chan	he receives K'awil/God K K'ak' Tiliw Chan
B08	yo'at/yo'pat ch'a ho ma	yo'at/yo'pat ch'ahom(a)	Yo'at/Yo'pat incense-offerer
A09	u [kab'] hi ya 18 u b'a k'awil	ukab'jiy? waxaklajun ub'ah k'awil	under the supervision of Waxaklajun Ub'ah K'awil
B09	ajaw xu ku pi 13 03 winal hi ya	xukpi ajaw uxlajun ux winaljiy	Copan *ajaw* 13 [k'ins] 3 *winals*
A10	06 hab' ya i u ti	wak hab'iy i ut	6 *tuns* and then it happens
B10	04 ajaw 13 yax	chan ajaw uxlajun yax	4 Ajaw 13 Yax (9.15.0.0.0)
A11	i? ajaw ?? ja ja _ ta	i? ?? ajaw ??	and then? ?? *ajaw* ??
B11	06 14 winal ya 01 hab' ya	wak chanlajun winaljiy jun hab'iy	6 [k'ins] 14 *winals* 1 [6] *tun*
A12	i u ti 06 kimi	i ut wak kimi	and then it happens 6 Kimi (9.15.6.14.6)
B12	04 ka se wa u ch'ak b'a hi	chan kasew ch'ak ub'ah	4 Sek decapitates
A13	18 u b'a k'awil 16 15 winal ya	waxaklajun ub'ah k'awil waklajun ho'lajun winaljiy	Waxaklajun Ub'ah K'awil 16 [k'ins] 15 *winals*
B13	01 hab' ya 01 winik hab' ya	jun hab'iy jun winik hab'iy	1 [4] *tun* 1 *k'atun*
A14	i u ti 11 imix	i ut b'uluch imix	and then it happens 11 Imix (9.16.11.13.1)
B14	19 muwan ni ch'am? wa ajaw? ??	b'olonlajun muwan ch'amaw ?? ajaw?	19 Muwan receives ?? *ajaw?*
A15	k'in ni kuch? b'alam	k'in kuch? b'alam	K'in Kuch? B'alam
B15	ajaw xu ku ya wa u kab' hi ya	xkuy? ajaw ukab'jiy?	Xkuy? *ajaw* under his supervision
A16	ch'a ho ma 14 04 winal ya	ch'ahom(a) chanlajun chan winaljiy	incense-offerer 14 [k'ins] 4 *winals*
B16	08 hab' ya i u ti	waxak hab'iy i ut	8 *tuns* and then it happens
A17	13 ajaw 18 ol la	uxlajun ajaw waxaklajun ol	13 Ajaw 18 Kumk'u (9.17.0.0.0)
B17	17 winik hab' chok? wa ch'a hi	wuklajun winik hab' chokow? ch'ah	17 *k'atuns* scatters incense
A18	?? wo chan na	?? chan	?? sky
B18	k'awil la k'ak' til chan	k'awil k'ak' tiliw chan	K'awil/God K K'ak' Tiliw Chan
A19	yo'at/yo'pat ik' ajaw xu ku pi	yo'at/yo'pat ik' xukpi ajaw	Yo'at/Yo'pat black Copan *ajaw*
B19	u chan nu 18 u b'a k'awil	ukanun? waxaklajun ub'ah k'awil	guardian? of Waxaklajun Ub'ah K'awil
A20	ajaw xu ku pi yi il hi	xukpi ajaw yilaj	Copan *ajaw* he witnesses
B20	ajaw xu ku ya wa 06 nal ??	xkuy ajaw wak ?? nal	Xkuy *ajaw* 6 ?? place

Paraphrase:

(east)

Count? of the ?? hab', 9 b'aktuns, 17 k'atuns, o tuns, o winals, o k'ins, G9 is the ?? book/headband, 13 Ajaw (January 24, 771), ?? sky, closure of the second of the (moon goddess) lunation, X is its young name, 29, 18 Kumk'u, the first/green ?? white flower? breath/spirit 13 Ajaw stone is planted under the supervision of the four incense-offerer.

19 ?? were completed since 13 Ajaw 18 Sak (LC?) happened; Ik' Ma' ?? witnessed it; it happened at ?? place.

6 ?? were completed since 13 Ajaw 13 Wo (LC?) under the supervision of Mixnal?, it happened at First Harvest? Mountain; this is under the supervision of the image of yellow tree first/building place ?? headdress star, K'ak' Tiliw Chan Yo'at/Yo'pat.

He scatters incense [on] 13 Ajaw 18 Kumk'u (9.17.0.0.0; January 24, 771). The ?? ajaw (pl.) cover it.

(west)

Count? of the (moon goddess) hab', 9 b'aktuns, 14 k'atuns, 12 [13] tuns, 4 winals, 17 k'ins, 12 Kab'an (January 2, 725) . . . is the ?? book/headband, 7 since it arrives, closure of 3 of the (jaguar god) lunation, X is its young name, 30, 5 K'ayab', K'ak' Tiliw Chan Yo'at/Yo'pat, incense-offerer, receives K'awil/God K, under the supervision of Waxaklajun Ub'ah K'awil, Copan ajaw.

13 [k'ins], 3 winals, 6 tuns, and then 4 Ajaw 13 Yax (9.15.0.0.0; August 22, 731) happens and then? ?? ajaw ??.

6 [k'ins], 14 winals, 1 [6] tun, and then 6 Kimi 4 Sek (9.15.6.14.6; May 3, 738) happens, Waxaklajun Ub'ah K'awil is decapitated.

16 [k'ins], 15 winals, 1 [4] tun, 1 k'atun and then 11 Imix 19 Muwan (9.16.11.13.1; November 28, 762) happens; K'in Kuch? B'alam, Xkuy ajaw receives ?? ajaw?, under the supervision of the incense-offerer.

14 [k'ins], 4 winals, 8 tuns and then 13 Ajaw 18 Kumk'u (9.17.0.0.0; January 24, 771) happens, 17 k'atuns; ?? sky K'awil/God K K'ak' Tiliw Chan Yo'at/Yo'pat, black Copan ajaw, guardian? of Waxaklajun Ub'ah K'awil, Copan ajaw, scatters incense. Xkuy ajaw 6 ?? place witnesses it.

STELA C

Coordinate	Block Transcription	Block Maya	Block English
(east)			
A01–B02	tzi ka ?? hab'	tzik? ?? hab'	count? of the ?? hab'
A03	13 pih	uxlajun pih	13 b'aktuns
B03	oo li winik hab'	?? winik hab'	o k'atuns
A04	oo li hab'	?? hab'	o tuns
B04	oo winal	mix? winal	o winals
A05	oo li k'in	?? k'in	o k'ins
B05	04 ajaw	chan ajaw	4 Ajaw
A06	08 ol la	waxak ol	8 Kumk'u
B06	hal la ja k'o b'a	halaj k'ob'	the tripod? is manifested
A07	03 tun k'al ja	k'alaj ux tun	three stones are bundled
B07	u tz'a pa wa	utz'apaw	they plant
A08	tun ni ??	tun ??	a stone Jaguar Paddler
B08	??	??	Stingray Paddler
A09	u ti ya nah 05 chan	utiy nah ho' chan	it happened at First Five Sky
B09	hix ?? tun 'a	hix ?? tun?	jaguar platform/throne stone
A10	u tz'a pa wa tun ni	utz'apaw tun	he plants a stone
B10	ik' nah chak ??	ik' nah chak ??	Ik' Nah Chak ??
A11	u ti ya lakam ka? hi/ma	utiy lakam kah?	it happened at Large Town?
B11	chan ?? tun ni	chan ?? tun	snake platform/throne stone
A12	i u ti ya tun ni k'al	i utiy k'al tun	and then it happened, bundled a stone
B12	na itzam hi	itzamnah	Itzamnah (God D)
A13	ha' ?? tun ni	ha' ?? tun	water platform/throne stone

Coordinate	Block Transcription	Block Maya	Block English
B13	u ti ya ?? chan na	utiy ?? chan	it happened at ?? Sky
A14	yax nal ??	yax ?? nal	First Three-Stone place
B14	tzutz ya 13 pih	tzutzuy uxlajun pih	are completed 13 b'aktuns
A15	u kab' ya	ukab'jiy?	under his supervision
B15	06 ajaw chan wa	wak chan ajaw	Six Sky ajaw
(west)			
C01–D02	tzi ka k'in hab'	tzik? k'in hab'	count? of the day/sun hab'
C03	09 pih	b'olon pih	9 b'aktuns
D03	01 winik hab'	jun winik hab'	1 k'atun
C04	00 hab'	mix? hab'	0 tuns
D04	00 winal la	mix? winal	0 winals
C05	00 k'in ni	mix? k'in	0 k'ins
D05	i u ti	i uht	and then it happens
C06	06 ajaw	wak ajaw	6 Ajaw
D06	13 yax k'in ni	uxlajun yaxk'in	13 Yaxk'in
C07	u tz'a pa wa	utz'apaw	he plants
D07	tun ni tu tu ma	tun tutum	a stone Tutum
C08	yo ol k'inich	yol k'inich	Yol K'inich
D08	k'uhul ajaw ?? wa	k'uhul ?? ajaw	divine Quirigua ajaw
C09	u ti ya	utiy	it happened at
D09	tza? chak ku?	?? chak ??	?? Great/Red ??
C10	tz'u nu	tz'unun	Hummingbird
D10	00 00 winal ya	mix? mix? winaljiy	0 [k'ins] 0 winals
C11	05 hab' ya 17 winik hab'	ho' hab'iy wuklajun winik hab'iy	5 tuns 17 k'atuns
D11	i u ti 06 ajaw	i ut wak ajaw	and then it happens 6 Ajaw (9.17.5.0.0)
C12	13 k'an a si ya	uxlajun k'anasiy	13 K'ayab'
D12	nah 05 tun ni	nah ho' tun	first five stone
C13	u chok? wa	uchokow?	he scatters
D13	k'ak' til chan	k'ak' tiliw chan	K'ak' Tiliw Chan (Yo'at/Yo'pat)
C14	05 winik hab'	ho' winik hab'	five-k'atun
D14	ch'a ho ma	ch'ahom(a)	incense-offerer
(south)			
E01	01 eb'	jun eb'	1 Eb' (9.17.4.10.12)
F01	05 yax	ho' yax	5 Yax
G01	?? ho? ja	??	?? (verb)
H01	06 ajaw tun ni	wak ajaw tun	6 Ajaw stone
(north)			
I01	08 la ta	waxak lat	8 [k'ins] until

STELA C (continued)

Coordinate	Block Transcription	Block Maya	Block English
J01	09 ajaw	b'olon ajaw	9 Ajaw (9.17.4.11.0)
K01	u? tu ho?	??	?? (verb)
L01	01 ajaw wa yax b'alam	jun ajaw yax b'alam	Jun Ajaw Yax B'alam

Paraphrase:

(east)

Count? of the ?? hab', 13 b'aktuns, o k'atuns, o tuns, o winals, o k'ins, 4 Ajaw 8 K'umk'u (August 13, 3114 B.C.), the tripod? is manifested.

Three stones are bundled.

Jaguar Paddler and Stingray Paddler plant a stone; it happened at First Five Sky; [it was a] jaguar platform/throne stone.

Ik' Nah Chak ?? plants a stone; it happened at Large Town?, [it was a] snake platform/throne stone.

And then it happened, Itzamnah bundled a stone, it is a water platform/throne stone, it happened at ?? Sky, First Three-Stone place.

13 b'aktuns are completed under the supervision of the Six Sky ajaw.

(west)

Count? of the day/sun hab', 9 b'aktuns, 1 k'atun, o tuns, o winals, o k'ins, and then 6 Ajaw 13 Yaxk'in (August 28, 455) happens; Tutum Yol K'inich, divine Quirigua ajaw, plants a stone; it happened at ?? Great/Red ?? Hummingbird.

o [k'ins], o winals, 5 tuns, 17 k'atuns, and then 6 Ajaw 13 K'ayab' (9.17.5.0.0; December 29, 775) happens, first five stone; K'ak' Tiliw Chan Yo'at/Yo'pat, five-k'atun incense-offerer, scatters.

(south)

1 Eb' 5 Yax (9.17.4.10.12; August 3, 775), ?? the 6 Ajaw stone.

(north)

8 [k'ins] until 9 Ajaw (9.17.4.11.0; August 11, 775) ?? Jun Ajaw, Yax B'alam.

STELA A

Coordinate	Block Transcription	Block Maya	Block English
(east)			
A01–B02	tzi ka ixik? hab'	tzik? ixik? hab'	count of the (moon goddess) hab'
A03	09 pih	b'olon pih	9 b'aktuns
B03	17 winik hab'	wuklajun winik hab'	17 k'atuns
A04	05 hab'	ho' hab'	5 tuns
B04	oo li winal	?? winal	o winals
A05	oo li k'in	?? k'in	o k'ins
B05	06 ajaw	wak ajaw	6 Ajaw
A06	nah 05 tun ni	nah ho' tun	first five stone
B06	nal k'in ?? ni ?? hun na	?? ?? hun	G9 ?? book/headband (F)
A07	06 20 hi ya	wak k'aljiy	26 (6E)
B07	hul li ya	huliy	since it arrives (D)
A08	u 02 ?? k'al ja	k'al ucha' ??	closure of the second of the (jaguar god) lunation (2CY)
B08	mi k'u ??	??	X
A09	20 10 na	k'al lajun	30
B09	13 k'an a si ya	uxlajun k'anasiy	13 K'ayab'
A10	tz'a pa ja	tz'apaj	is planted

Coordinate	Block Transcription	Block Maya	Block English
B10	06 ajaw	wak ajaw	6 Ajaw
A11	tun ni	tun	stone
B11	nah 05 tun ni	nah ho' tun	first five stone
(west)			
C01	tzutz hi ya	tzutzjiy	completed
D01	19 o hab'	b'olonlajun ??	19 ??
C02	06 ajaw	wak ajaw	6 Ajaw (CR?)
D02	13 yax?	uxlajun yax?	13 Yax?
C03	u kab' hi ya	ukab'jiy?	under his supervision
D03	ik' hun	ik' hun	Ik' Hun
C04	u ya ti	utiy	it happened at
D04	ik' kab' nal ??	ik' kab' ?? nal	Black Earth ?? place
C05	a ?? ya	??	(focus marker)
D05	u chok? ch'a	uchok? ch'ah	he scatters incense
C06	05 winik hab' ch'a ho ma	ho' winik hab' ch'ahom(a)	five-k'atun incense-offerer
D06	k'ak' til chan wi	k'ak' tiliw chan	K'ak' Tiliw Chan
C07	yo'at/yo'pat	yo'at/yo'pat	Yo'at/Yo'pat
D07	04 ch'a ho la	chan ch'ahom(a)	four incense-offerer
C08	04 te ik' ??	chante ik' ??	four black ??
D08	ik' ajaw xu ku wa pi	ik' xukpi ajaw	black Copan *ajaw*
C09	ajaw ik' nal way? la	ik' way? nal ajaw	Black Hole place *ajaw*
D09	k'uhul ajaw ?? wa	k'uhul ?? ajaw	divine Quirigua *ajaw*
C10	u chan na	ukanun?	his guardian?
D10	18 u b'a k'awil la	waxaklajun ub'ah k'awil	Waxaklajun Ub'ah K'awil
C11	no noh chan yo ok? k'in ni	nohol chan ?? k'in	south sky ?? sun
D11	b'a ka b'a	b'akab'	*b'akab'*

Paraphrase:

(east)

Count? of the (moon goddess) *hab'*, 9 *b'aktuns*, 17 *k'atuns*, 5 *tuns*, o *winals*, o *k'ins*, 6 Ajaw (December 29, 775), first five stone, G9 is the ?? book/headband, 26 days since it arrives, closure of the second of the (jaguar god) lunation, X, 30, 13 K'ayab', the 6 Ajaw stone is planted, first five stone.

(west)

19 ?? were completed on 6 Ajaw 13 Yax? (CR?), under the supervision of Ik' Hun; it happened at Black Earth ?? place.

It is? (9.17.5.0.0; December 29, 775), the five-*k'atun* incense-offerer, K'ak' Tiliw Chan Yo'at/Yo'pat, four incense-offerer, four black ??, black Copan *ajaw*, Black Hole place *ajaw*, divine Quirigua *ajaw*, the guardian? of Waxaklajun Ub'ah K'awil, south sky ?? sun, *b'akab'*, scatters incense.

Coordinate	Block Transcription	Block Maya	Block English
00	tzi ka te' hab'	tzik? te' hab'	count? of the tree *hab'*
01	09 pih	b'olon pih	9 *b'aktuns*
02	17 winik hab'	wuklajun winik hab'	17 *k'atuns*
03	10 tun	lajun tun	10 *tuns*
04	00 winal	?? winal	0 *winals*
05	00 k'in	?? k'in	0 *k'ins*
06	12 ajaw	lajchan ajaw	12 Ajaw
07	k'in ?? ?? hun	?? ?? hun	G9 is the ?? book/headband (F)
08	20 07 hul	k'al wuk huliy	27 since it arrives (27D)
09	u 02 k'al ??	k'al ucha' ??	bundling of the second of the (skull) lunation (2CS)
10	?? k'uhul u ch'o ko k'ab'a' 'a	?? uch'ok k'ab'a'	X is its young name (B)
11	20 09 08 te pax	k'al b'olon waxakte pax	29 (9A) 8 Pax
12	pat ni ?? 'a e/hu	patwan? ??	made ??
13	?? ?? ahin? ??	?? ?? ahin? ??	?? crocodile? ??
14	_ u chahk/ku? ni 04 ??	_ chan ?? ??	_ 4 ?? ??
15	ju? nal? 'a nu ni	??	??
16	k'ak' ti li chan yo'at/yo'pat	k'ak' tiliw chan yo'at/yo'pat	K'ak' Tiliw Chan Yo'at/Yo'pat
17	ch'ahom(a) ik' ajaw xu?	ch'ahom(a) ik' xukpi ajaw	incense-offerer black Copan *ajaw*

Paraphrase:

Count? of the tree *hab'*, 9 *b'aktuns*, 17 *k'atuns*, 10 *tuns*, 0 *winals*, 0 *k'ins*, 12 Ajaw (December 2, 780), G9 is the ?? book/headband, 27 since it arrives, bundling of the second of the (skull) lunation, X is its young name, 29, 8 Pax, made ?? crocodile? ?? . . . 4 ?? ??, K'ak' Tiliw Chan Yo'at/Yo'pat, incense-offerer, black Copan *ajaw*.

Notes

Preface

1. In the present work, I refer to rulers in a manner consistent with Martin and Grube (2000). The orthography for all words of Mayan derivation employed in this study is adapted from the Academia de Lenguas Mayas de Guatemala system (López Raquec 1989). Some scholars have recently begun to render vowel length in transcriptions of ancient Maya texts based on patterns of disharmonic spelling (see Houston, Robertson, and Stuart 1998). As these patterns have yet to be systematically explored within the entire corpus of inscriptions, this practice is not followed in the present work. Instead, complex vowels are rendered when reconstructible based on historical linguistics (see Kaufman and Norman 1984; Macri and Looper 2003). In addition, as it is evident that Quirigua inscriptions are generally based on Eastern Ch'olan languages, Ch'olan renderings are used for ambiguous spellings (e.g., "black" is ik').

2. Grube, Schele, and Fahsen (1991); Jones and Sharer (1980); Kelley (1962); Looper (1995b, 1999, n.d.); Proskouriakoff (1973, 1993); Stuart (1987a, 1992b).

3. Hatch (1975) offered an alternative dynastic sequence that differs radically from those put forward by other authors. Many of the nominals Hatch proposed are now generally accepted as titular in nature. For a summary of arguments against Hatch's sequence, see Stone (1983).

4. Monumental designations in this book follow the original system of Maudslay (1889–1902) and Morley (1935, 1937–1938). The monuments discovered by the University of Pennsylvania Quirigua Project are numbered according to the schema of that project (Coe and Sharer 1979: Table 2; Sharer 1990). Structure designations at Quirigua follow the system of the Pennsylvania Quirigua Project (Coe and Sharer 1979: Table 1).

5. Hewett (1911, 1912, 1913, 1915, 1916); Morley (1935, 1937–1938).

6. Ashmore (1979, n.d.); Schortman (1993); Schortman and Urban (1983); Sharer (n.d.).

7. Grube, Schele, and Fahsen (1991); Kelley (1962); Looper (1995a, 1999); Martin and Grube (2000: 214–225); Riese (1986); Schele and Looper (1996); Sharer (1978, 1988).

8. For a comprehensive bibliography of archaeological research at Copan, see Fash and Andrews (n.d.).

9. The most important studies include Baudez (1994); Baudez and Riese (1990); Gordon (1902); Maudslay (1889–1902); Morley (1920); Newsome (2001); and Schele and Mathews (1993: 133–174).

Introduction

1. On the emblem glyph and its political significance, see Marcus (1976); Martin and Grube (2000: 17–20); and Mathews (1984, 1988).

2. Bricker (1986); Houston and Mathews (1985); Martin and Grube (2000); Mathews and Justeson (1984); Stuart (n.d.a).

3. On the history of intersite political relationships in the Classic period, see Grube (1996); Houston (1993); Houston, in Chase (1991); Marcus (1973, 1976); Martin and Grube (1995, 2000); Molloy and Rathje (1974: 435–442); Schele and Freidel (1990); Schele and Grube (1994); and Schele and Mathews (1991).

4. On the role of warfare in the formation of Maya kingdoms, see Webster (1977).

5. This ruler has also been known as "Two-Legged Sky" (Kelley 1962); "Two-Armed Sky" (Marcus 1976); "Cauac Sky" (Jones and Sharer 1980); and Butz' Tiliw (Chan Yoat) (Grube, Schele, and Fahsen 1991; Looper 1995a, 1999).

6. Both the reading and etymology of the name of this deity are in question. The decipherments offered might be related to various Yukatek terms, including oatlil "erección" and yo'pat "una manera de coroza o mitra que usaban los indios antiguos" (Barrera Vásquez 1980: 593, 980). Martin and Grube (2000: 231) credit David Stuart with a "yopaat" reading for this glyph.

7. On these stelae, Monuments 25/26, 27, 88, and 89, see González Lauck (1997); Reilly (1994); Tate (1999); and Taube (1996: 50).

8. See Stuart (1996). This reading of the glyph for "stela" supersedes a previous erroneous decipherment as te' tun "tree stone" by Schele and Stuart (1985).

9. For examples of world trees in the Maya ethnographic record, see Núñez de la Vega (1702: 9); Tozzer (1907: 154); and Alfonso Villa Rojas, in León-Portilla (1988). The concept of the world tree in ancient Maya art is discussed by Schele and Miller (1986: 76–77, 108–109) and by Newsome (2001).

10. These temporal units are conventional labels. They do not necessarily reflect the terminology that would have been used in the Classic period.

11. The *tzolk'in* consists of a cycle of 20 days combined with coefficients from 1 to 13, thus returning to 4 Ajaw every 260 days. The *hab'* is a cycle of 18 months of 20 days each, counted 0–19, plus a period of 5 days. This cycle returns to 8 Kumk'u every 365 days.

12. Other zoomorphic sculptures are referred to using T174 compounds, which may incorporate the term *kuch* "contain, carry." See MacLeod (n.d.).

13. Freidel, Schele, and Parker (1993: 173–207) cite several examples of modern Maya belief in stones and images inhabited by spirits and give evidence for the same concepts in the Classic period.

14. Note Yukatek *ch'ah* "gota de cualquier licor o resina de árbol" (Barrera Vásquez 1980: 121); *ch'áah* "drip; drop" (Bricker, Po'ot Yah, and Dzul de Po'ot 1998: 78).

15. The offering of blood is strongly suggested by images such as La Pasadita Lintel 2 (Schele and Miller 1986: Pl. 76), which show penitents in a "scattering" ritual dressed in costume associated with bloodletting, such as the triple-knot motif (see Joralemon 1974; Schele and Miller 1986; Stuart 1984, 1988).

16. Nikolai Grube (personal communication, 1994) has posited the phonetic value of the "lu-bat" collocation as *yuxul* "it is the sculpture of," based on a colonial Tzeltal gloss of *ux* as "raspar como ladrillos" (Ara 1986: 414).

17. See Madrid Codex, pp. 95d, 96d, 97b, 98b, 98c, 101b.

18. On the physical properties of sandstone, see Rich (1947: 220–222).

19. These titles do not include the standard scribal title *aj tz'ib'* "writer" (Stuart 1987b: 1–11) but rather a title reading *aj nab'il* "painter" and one which may read *aj b'ik'al*. The latter may relate to the Yukatek term *bik'yah tz'ib*, meaning "to scribble on paper" ("escarabajear papel"; Barrera Vásquez 1980:53), and therefore be translated "scribbler, sketcher." *Aj nab'il* appears in sculptors' signatures on Yaxchilan Lintel 45 and on a stela of unknown provenance (Coe and Kerr 1997: Pl. 88). *Aj b'ik'al* titles appear on Piedras Negras Throne 1, Lintel 3, Stelae 12 and 15, and the Cleveland Panel. On the role of scribes and writing in Classic Maya culture, see Coe and Kerr (1997) and Reents-Budet (1994: 36–71).

20. On the supernatural patronage of Classic Maya artists, see Coe (1977) and Coe and Kerr (1997: 101–110).

21. The conformation of Maya sculpture to the aesthetics of painting may also have to do with sculptors' following of master drawings. Master drawings are documented on two stone sculptures at Palenque: the Palace Tablet and the Sarcophagus of the Temple of Inscriptions (Schele and Miller 1986: 39–40).

22. The theory that Quirigua was a colony of Copan is usually attributed to Morley (1920, 1935).

23. See the discussions of Bloch (1974); Galaty (1983); Gluckman (1965); Jackson (1983); Kapferer (1979a); and Schieffelin (1985).

24. On the nature of Maya spiritual forces, see Freidel, Schele, and Parker (1993); Houston and Stuart (1996); Houston and Taube (2000); Looper and Kappelman (2001); Marcus (1978); and Ringle (1988).

25. The expression appears on the Palenque Tablet of the Cross, E3, and Quirigua Stela J, C7–D7. Maya metaphors of birth are discussed by Taube (1994) and Looper and Kappelman (2001). On the deity conjuration as "birth," see Stuart (1984: 14–15).

26. It is likely that these developments occurred long before the Late Formative period, as Olmec art seems to express similar concepts (e.g., see Kappelman and Reilly 2001).

27. The small text located in the lower left part of the panel is a record of the dedication of the lintel by the artist, which also serves as a commemoration of the making and use of the sculpture.

28. The apparent contradiction of monuments as gifts is even seen in the contrast between the public (given) space of the plaza and the private (kept) space of the royal palace.

29. See the discussion in Chapter 4.

30. The verb *ajawaj* is a passive form derived from the noun *ajaw* "lord." In Maya inscriptions, this verb is usually given the positional suffix *-yan* rather than the passive. See Palenque Temple of the Inscriptions, west panel, H2.

31. Tate (1992: 37) suggests that the emphasis on the head and upper register on many Maya stelae indicates a focusing of ritual heat in these areas.

32. Interestingly, these two fields consider the relation between persona and "reality" in exactly opposite ways. While literary critics see persona as "the sum of the author's conscious choices in a realized and more complete self as 'artist'" (Fowler 1987: 177), Jung (1953) sees the persona as something essentially false and illusory.

33. In employing the distinction between myth and history in the ancient Maya context, I follow such scholars as Lounsbury (1976, 1985) and Schele and Freidel (1990).

34. On this approach to Maya iconography, see Freidel and Schele (1988b) and Schele and Miller (1986: 15).

35. Important studies of Maya sculptural style include McHargue (1995) and Proskouriakoff (1950).

Chapter 1. Life at the Crossroads

1. The earliest definable ceramic complex at Quirigua, designated Catherwood, does not correspond to the Late Formative period but to the Protoclassic/Early Classic period (Ashmore 1987: 219).

2. These early artifacts were not excavated under controlled conditions. See Ashmore (1987: 219) and Jones, Ashmore, and Sharer (1983: 12).

3. In the warehouse at the Quirigua site is located a drain trough carved in the form of a serpent head. Although this sculpture may not be of Late Formative date, it is related to Late Formative forms found in the Guatemalan highlands and Pacific slope. Similar drain troughs are known from Kaminaljuyu (Parsons 1986: Fig. 49) and Izapa (Norman 1976: Fig. 5.28). It is possible that the Quirigua pedestal sculptures are an Early Classic continuation from the more ancient highland traditions.

4. The dating of this phase of the acropolis is approximate, based on ceramic typologies and comparisons with data from Early Classic Copan. See Sharer (1997).

5. Morley (1935: 43–44; 1937–1938, vol. 4: 241) identified Locus 011 (his Group C) as early, based partly on the presence of Monument 25 there. The monument is a plain round column of schist, measuring about 2.5 m long and 0.6 m in diameter. The material is consistent with that used for the other early monuments at Quirigua, including Monument 26, Stela U, and the pedestal sculptures, Monuments 29 and 30. On these and other Early Classic groups, see Ashmore (1984, 1987, n.d.) and Jones (1987: 211).

6. The Copan acropolis was begun around A.D. 420. See Fash and Sharer (1991); W. Fash et al. (1992); Sharer (1999); Sharer, Miller, and Traxler (1992); and Sharer et al. (n.d.). On early architecture of Copan, see also Andrews (n.d.); Andrews and Fash (1992); Schele and Freidel (1990: Chap. 8); Sharer, Fash, et al. (1999); Sharer, Traxler, et al. (1999); and Stuart (1992b). See also discussion in Fahsen, Schele, and Grube (1995) and Grube, Schele, and Fahsen (1995).

7. Peter Mathews was the first to interpret the Stela C inscription as naming a founder (Jones and Sharer 1980). Looper and Schele (1994) suggest that Stela C and Zoomorph P refer to the same person, which, in my present view, remains a viable option. Martin and Grube (2000: 216–217) identify Tok Casper and Tutum Yol K'inich as two different rulers.

8. The *kalomte'* title was originally identified as "batab" by Berlin (1958). See Stuart, Grube, and Schele (1989).

9. Martin and Grube (2000); Schele (1990c); Schele and Grube (1992a); Schele and Villela (1992, 1994); Stuart (2000).

10. The "west *kalomte'*" title has been identified in the title sequences of the following Copan rulers: K'inich Yax K'uk' Mo' (Stela 15), Stela 32 ruler, Waterlily Jaguar (Stela E), B'utz' Chan (Altar Y), and K'ak' Joplaj Chan K'awil (Hieroglyphic Stairway).

11. Group 3C-8, located less than 150 m northwest of Group 3C-7, also has round-faced masonry typical of the Early Classic period. The group included a platform (3C-2) and Structures 3C-17 and 3C-18 and is described as an elaborate patio group or ballcourt like Copan Ballcourt I (Ashmore 1987: 219).

12. The association of this person, nicknamed "Basket Skull," with the "third successor" title introduces a problem in the dynastic count of Quirigua, as three previous rulers (instead of two) are elsewhere documented. This suggests that the "succession" referred to here may not have been a dynastic count. Alternatively, it suggests that the Stela U ruler Turtle Shell may have not been counted or that Tutum Yol K'inich, mentioned on Stela C, might have been an alternative name for the founder or second ruler.

13. The most important of these Venus-timed events were the founding events of K'inich Yax K'uk' Mo' on maximum altitude and elongation of the Morning Star (Schele 1989a; Schele and Larios 1991). The accession of Smoke Imix took place on the elongation date of the Morning Star (Schele and Fash 1991). Waxaklajun Ub'ah K'awil undertook rituals on dates of important Evening Star positions, and K'ak' Joplaj Chan K'awil's accession took place on a date of Morning Star elongation (Schele and Fash 1991). See also Schele (1991b).

14. Miller (1999: 101) suggests that the beading around the ruler's face on Monument 26 derived from a style of figural incense burner having the same feature. This style of incense burner is unknown at Quirigua, however.

15. A metaphor for death in the Classic period was probably *och ha'* "enter water" (Stuart 1998: 388). Death was also conceived through the metaphor of a sinking canoe (Freidel, Schele, and Parker 1993: 89–91). Conversely, resurrection is often shown as emergence out of water, as, for example, on the panel of Palenque Temple XIV or the many vases which depict the emergence of the maize deity out of the waterlily-marked turtle (Freidel, Schele, and Parker 1993: Fig. 3.27).

16. On stylistic grounds, Schele originally placed Stela 53 between 9.1.0.0.0 and 9.1.10.0.0 and Stela 60 between 9.2.10.0.0 and 9.3.10.0.0 but more recently (personal communication, 1994) suggested that Stela 53 dates later than 9.1.10.0.0 and that both stelae were likely carved before 9.3.10.0.0.

17. On the date of this monument, see Baudez (1983, vol. 2: 186–187, 190).

18. Unfortunately for the purposes of comparison, none of the frontally represented faces of rulers survive from early Copan.

19. The stelae of Waxaklajun Ub'ah K'awil and K'ak' Yipyaj are commonly thought to be or to approach "in-the-round" sculptures. Nevertheless, in each example, sculptors are careful to preserve a sense of the block from which the figure emerges.

20. There is one possible record of monument erection dating to the mid-sixth century at Quirigua, recorded on Zoomorph P, associated with the calendar round date 9 Ajaw 3 Sotz', appearing in cartouches 1 and 2 of the muzzle text. The same date appears on the south inscription of Zoomorph P and with a long distance number which makes probable a placement in the Early Classic period. For the corresponding Long Count, Grube, Schele, and Fahsen (1991) offered a solution of 9.2.14.5.0; however, because erection of monuments occurs only on *tun*-endings at Quirigua—with the exception of the actions of the founder on 8.19.10.11.0—an alternative date is 9.5.7.0.0 (A.D. 541).

21. The seventh-century ceramic complex (Maudslay, late facet) includes some shallow polychrome dishes and plates reportedly similar to Tepeu 1 of the northeastern Peten (Ashmore 1984: 378; Willey et al. 1980).

22. An alternative interpretation is that Monument 26 was ritually "killed" through its defacement in local dedication and termination rituals. According to Schele and Miller (1986: 74), objects were often intentionally defaced after a ruler's death in order to release accumulated supernatural powers. Without a precise ar-

chaeological context for Monument 26, we cannot be sure which interpretation is correct.

23. On Altar L, see Fash and Stuart (1991); Morley (1937–1938, vol. 4: 94); Satterthwaite (1979); and Schele (1989d).

24. On this ritual, see Stuart (1998: 389–393).

25. The same *tzak hul* combination seen on Altar L appears at Yaxchilan in the context of sites that had recently experienced wars (Martin and Grube 2000: 201).

26. For political interpretations of Smoke Imix's 9.11.0.0.0 stela program, see Baudez (1986: 20); Fash (1983); Marcus (1976: 129); Newsome (1991: 172–199); Proskouriakoff (1973); Schele and Freidel (1990); and Schele and Grube (1988).

27. Giant Ajaw altars are also known from Tikal (Altar 14) and Tonina, but these are of later date than QRG Altar L. See Satterthwaite (1951, 1979).

28. Regarding the relative dates of Sub.4 and 1B-2, Jones and Sharer (1980: 17) note: "We can detect some time depth for Construction Stage 3, with 1B-2 appearing to be later in masonry style than the ballcourt itself." In addition, the Sub.4 ballcourt was in poor condition when 1B-2 was built, implying that some years had intervened between the construction of these two buildings. On the acropolis architecture of this phase, see Jones, Ashmore, and Sharer (1983: 4–5).

29. On the relationships of maize and moon deities, see Joyce (1992); Looper (2002a); Schele and Mathews (1998: 348); Stross (1994); and Taube (1992: 64–69).

Chapter 2. A Restive Vassal

1. Additional evidence in favor of a local origin of K'ak' Tiliw is found in his name, which includes a *chan yo'at/yo'pat* element that is seen frequently in the Southeast. In the past, some scholars proposed that K'ak' Tiliw was a member of a "Sky Dynasty" having branches in a number of sites, including Tikal and Copan (Kelley 1962; Sharer 1978). This notion, however, is no longer tenable, as it takes as a family name the *chan* "sky" component of the proper name of K'ak' Tiliw and other Quirigua rulers. Further, the "sky" element in Tikal ruler names is part of their proper names as well. For example, the proper name of "Stormy Sky" of Tikal is Siyaj Chan K'awil (see Coggins 1975; Schele and Grube 1994: 92).

2. This technique of determining the age of the ruler follows the methodology outlined by Proskouriakoff (1963–1964). The earliest *k'atun* title occurs on the two monuments erected on 9.17.5.0.0, Stela A (C6) and Stela C (C14–D14). Here the king is a *ho' winik hab' ch'om(a)* "five-k'atun incense-offerer," suggesting that at this time he would have been between eighty and one hundred *tuns* in age. He is given the same *k'atun* number at his death on 9.17.14.13.2 (Zoomorph G, Y1–C'1), so it follows that at 9.17.5.0.0 he could not have been much more than ninety 360-day years in age. Given the difference between the Stela A and C dedication date and the accession date of 2.11.13.3, or just under fifty-two years, his age upon accession would have been between about twenty-eight and thirty-eight years old. Riese (1980: 164) calculated K'ak' Tiliw's accession age as twenty-eight. Kelley

(1962) erroneously interpreted the accession as the birth date ("initial date") of the ruler. Proskouriakoff (1973: 168) first identified the date of K'ak' Tiliw's accession.

3. Cohodas (1991: 276) identifies the image of Altar M as a variant of the rabbit hand-protector shown on the Copan Ballcourt II-B center marker. The hand-protector, however, has no spots on the ear and lacks the *imix* eyelid and ophidian features seen on Altar M. The "Vase of the Seven Gods" is illustrated in Reents-Budet (1994: 64).

4. See also Smith and Kidder (1943: 117–118, Fig. 60) and Villacorta (1927: 246).

5. On Ani, see Sharer, Fash, et al. (1999: 234–238). Linda Schele (personal communication, 1994) first noted the correspondence between the iconography of Ani and QRG Structure 1B-2. The design of the Quirigua temple based on a structure commissioned by Ruler 8 of Copan recalls the close connection between the two sites during the mid-sixth century. We are reminded specifically of the large number of ceramic vessels of Quirigua manufacture that were deposited in the Copan ruler's tomb (see Reents-Budet et al. n.d.). For some unknown reason, it appears that Structure 1B-2 was designed specifically as a tribute to Ruler 8.

6. These include CPN Stela C, QRG Stela A, the Cosmic Plate, the "Vomit Pot" in the Museum of the American Indian, and Step 34 of the Copan Hieroglyphic Stairway (Schele and Grube 1990b).

7. On possible readings of the "flower" logographs, see Boot, Looper, and Wagner (1996).

Chapter 3. Rebellion and Revival

1. The date 9.15.6.14.6 6 Kimi 4 Sek was first noted by Morley (1915: 221) at Quirigua, who also identified the "axe" verb associated with it. Kelley (1962: 328) suggested that the date recorded an interaction between Quirigua and Copan, perhaps the conquest of Quirigua or the accession of a ruler from Copan at Quirigua. Proskouriakoff (1973: 168), however, noted the prominence of the event at Quirigua and assumed that the "axe" verb associated with the date recorded an event in which Quirigua "had the upper hand" over Copan. Marcus (1976: 134–140) confirmed Proskouriakoff's suggestion by identifying on various Quirigua monuments a title of K'ak' Tiliw that refers to him as the "captor of" Waxaklajun Ub'ah K'awil, the ruler of Copan. Although Marcus interpreted the "axe" verb as a record of battle, its decipherment as *ch'ak* "chop, cut" suggests other meanings (Orejel 1990). While the "axe" verb is sometimes used with reference to the destruction of places, it is also clearly associated with decapitation (Looper and Schele 1991; Stuart 1992b). For example, on a polychrome vase from Altar de Sacrificios (Fig. 3.1), the glyph appears in a text accompanying a self-decapitating God A', suggesting that the verb refers to this action. On the vase the passage is nominal, identifying the adjacent deity as *ch'ak b'a(h)* "self-chopping" (Houston and Stuart 1996: 295). At Quirigua, however, the "axe" glyph is clearly used in a verbal construction, reading *ch'ak ub'ah*, which probably refers to the severing of the head (Houston and Stuart 1998).

2. This passage is discussed in detail by Grube, Schele, and Fahsen (1991) and Looper (1999: 268). Interestingly, this date

also corresponds to a solar eclipse station (Grube, Schele, and Fahsen 1991). That is, it is a day of the new moon on which an eclipse would be visible somewhere on earth, although in this case not in the Maya area.

3. More precisely, this person is said to be a divine lord of Chik Nahb', a toponym which may refer to the region surrounding Calakmul. See discussion in Looper (1999); Martin and Grube (2000); and Stuart and Houston (1994).

4. New epigraphic evidence from Dos Pilas suggests that Calakmul strongly coerced Dos Pilas to make war against Tikal. Recently discovered sections of Dos Pilas Hieroglyphic Stairway 2 indicate that Calakmul actually attacked Dos Pilas in order to make an ally of its king (Fahsen 2002).

5. On the archaeology of the Great Plaza, see Jones, Ashmore, and Sharer (1983: 8–11).

6. This is the so-called batab title, discussed by Berlin (1958: 114); Schele and Grube (1992a: 4); and Stuart, Grube, and Schele (1989).

7. Linda Schele (personal communication, 1994) first brought this fact to my attention.

8. On the glyph for "hill/mountain," see Stuart (1987b).

9. This term does not survive in Ch'olan languages, but in Yukatek it means "alimento" (Barrera Vásquez 1980: 387).

10. Aztec art exhibits examples of both survivals and revivals, although in this case the revivals are imitations of art belonging to earlier civilizations, especially the visual cultures of Tula, Teotihuacan, and Xochicalco (Umberger 1981, 1987).

11. On the debate concerning the stylistic sources of the QRG Stela H text format, see Grube, Schele, and Fahsen (1991); Jones and Sharer (1980); Miller (1983); and Riese (1986).

12. The frame for the inscription of CPN Stela J east is rendered as an illusion of a plaited textile strip, in which the reading order of the glyphs follows the length of the strip (Maudslay 1889–1902, vol. 1: 54). In contrast, the QRG Stela H text frame consists of a series of staggered, diagonally oriented rectangles, with the glyphs reading in a normal double-column fashion proceeding from the topmost rectangle downward. The arrangement of the QRG Stela H text is more similar to that of the cylindrical fragment from Copan shown in Fig. 4.19, which may have partly inspired it. It is not certain, however, that the Copan cylindrical monument was publicly known at the time that QRG Stela H was designed.

13. The process of hardening of sandstone to which Morley refers is due to the presence of dissolved minerals in the quarry water—the moisture that permeates the living rock. As this water evaporates, the minerals are deposited on the walls of the pore cavities, lending the stone greater hardness (Rich 1947: 221).

14. See also the important concept of "technological style," as developed by Lechtman (1977).

15. See Schele (1989b) for structurally related visionary events recorded at Pomona and Yaxchilan.

16. On the jaguar as a symbol of warfare, see Freidel (1989); Freidel, Schele, and Parker (1993: 310–317); Schele and Miller (1986: 213–214); and Thompson (1970: 291).

17. The Jaguar War Deity is alternatively interpreted as a Venus symbol (Schele and Grube 1988).

18. Proskouriakoff's (1950: 66) designation for the motif was "medallion ornament."

19. Proskouriakoff (1950: 66) termed this pectoral the "bar ornament."

20. These include Aguateca Stelae 3 and 7; Dos Pilas Stelae 11, 14, and 15; Jimbal Stela 1; Machaquila Stela 2; Naranjo Stelae 13 and 28; Quirigua Stelae D, E, F, I, J, and K and Zoomorph P; Tikal Temple 1, Lintel 3, and the Structure 4D-52 lintel; and Tzum Stela 3. Itzimte Lintel 1 and Yaxchilan Lintel 58 also feature this imagery but are of uncertain date. On Yaxchilan Lintels 1, 3, 52, and 54 this iconographic complex is associated with period endings, while 32, 42, and 53 show the imagery in association with non-period-ending dates.

21. The Jester God infix is most clearly visible on the pectoral on Stela F north but can also be seen on Stela E south. Elsewhere the infix is eroded beyond recognition. Certain examples from Dos Pilas depict a deity with hands replacing the lower mandible.

22. Usually termed a "skeletal serpent," the creature to which these jaws pertain is identified as a centipede by comparison with a scene from a polychrome vase. In the glyphic caption of this scene, a bicephalic variant of this creature is termed *chapat* "centipede." In the Maya system, centipedes belong to the same class as snakes (Grube and Nahm 1994: 702).

23. On CPN Structure 10L-22A and its antecedents, see B. Fash (1996); B. Fash et al. (1992); W. Fash (1998, 2001: 130–135); Fash and Fash (1990); Freidel, Schele, and Parker (1993); Ringle (1990); Schele (1998); Schele, Stuart, and Grube (1991); and Stomper (2001).

24. On the archaeology, iconography, and texts of Copan Structure 10L-26, see B. Fash (1992); W. Fash (1988, 2001); Fash and Fash (1990, 2000); W. Fash et al. (1992); Fash and Stuart (1991); Schele and Freidel (1990); Stuart (1992b, 2000, n.d.b); and Stuart and Schele (1986a).

25. Coggins (1988b) suggests that the K'inich Ahaw Wall imagery indicates the importance of sun-related ceremonies at Quirigua, an interpretation that is consistent with the one developed here.

Chapter 4. Dreams of Power

1. The archaeology of Platform 1A-1 and Structure 1A-3 is described in Coe and Sharer (1979: 15) and Jones, Ashmore, and Sharer (1983: 9).

2. Of the Platform 1A-1 stelae, only the foundations of Stelae A and E were investigated by Strömsvik (1941). Strömsvik's (1941: Fig. 9) drawings of the below-ground portions of these two stelae indicate that they were rounded on the south sides, a design that would have facilitated their raising to the north. The only dedication cache among the Platform 1A-1 stelae recovered by

Strömsvik (1941: 81) was that of Stela E, an empty rectangular, lidded ceramic box found east of the stela, crushed in the plaza fill.

3. A "sunwise" reading order for Maya stelae was first suggested by Tate (1991).

4. Among K'ak' Tiliw's titles on Stela F east is the 3-11-pih ajaw title in its unique appearance at Quirigua. This title is also found in early texts at Copan (Stela 49; Papagayo Step) and Naranjo (Altar 1). This usage at Quirigua may represent an attempt at legitimation through a reference to an archaic title from Copan. In addition, the 3-11-pih ajaw title may suggest a relationship between the ruler and cosmogenesis. On Tikal MT26 are listed three intervals of 1.4.1.0 (8,660 days) after 13.0.0.0.0 4 Ajaw 8 Kumk'u. These intervals are referenced using compounds of 11-pih. The third 11-pih interval after this date is recorded as 10 Ajaw 8 Sip (13.3.12.3.0).

5. This suffix, -jiy, was termed a "backgrounding marker" by Josserand (1991) and may function as a marker for completive aspect (Stuart, Houston, and Robertson 1999: 28) or a perfect tense (Barbara MacLeod, personal communication, 2002).

6. Janis Indrikis (1997) calculated the most recent past period ending that satisfies the criteria as 13.13.11.18.9.19.0.0.0.0.0.0.0. 0.0. The distance between completions is 2.7.9.0.0.0.0.0.0.0.0.0. 0.0.

7. As observed by Newsome (2001: 85–86), the association of the supernatural decapitation with a 1 Ajaw date seen on Stela F also occurs on the Yaxchilan Structure 33 Hieroglyphic Stairway, Step 7. It is possible that the Maya considered each period-ending date to commemorate a particular supernatural event. As in the case of Stela F, this association may have contributed to the decision to emphasize the political and religious connotations of decapitation sacrifice in its texts and images.

8. One of these titles, at A9, is probably a variant of the "9.16.9" title that occurs at other sites, such as Palenque (Temple of Inscriptions, middle panel, B9–C1) and Chichen Itza (Temple of the Four Lintels, Lintel 3, H1–H3).

9. This argument was presented by Stuart (1992a) and elaborated by Freidel, Schele, and Parker (1993). See also Looper and Kappelman (2001).

10. On Maya celestial cords, see Looper and Kappelman (2001); Miller (1974); Sosa (1985: 341); and Taube (1994: 659).

11. The provenience of this vase was identified by Reents-Budet and Bishop (2000).

12. The manifestation of the cosmic umbilicus on 4 Ajaw 8 Kumk'u is described on QRG Altar P' (see Looper 2002b).

13. The sequencing of double-headed serpent imagery before triadic imagery appearing on Stela F is analogous to the ordering of imagery on Quirigua Stela K. On this monument of Jade Sky, the eastern image shows the king holding the double-headed serpent bar; the west shows the king with the pectoral/God K/shield triad.

14. On events involving Xkuy, see Looper (1999); Schele (1987); and Schele and Looper (1996).

15. This site could well have been located very close to Quirigua, possibly one of numerous small sites on the upper reaches of the Morjá River. These sites have been shown to have close contacts with Copan in the eighth century, through their use of Copador ceramics (Fash 2001: 151).

16. On the interpretation of these Copan toponyms, see Looper (1991c) and Schele and Grube (1990b). Xkuy may have meant "owl."

17. In their analysis of the text of Stela N, Baudez and Riese (1990, vol. 2: 150) suggest that the name of the monument includes the name of the sixteenth Copan king, Yax Pasaj Chan Yo'at/Yo'pat. Only the first half of this name is included at A17, however, and the "Chan Yo'at/Yo'pat" element is missing, suggesting that the reference is not to a historical person.

18. Structurally similar headdresses with descending serpent-cords appear on Itzimte Stela 1 and Stela 7 (Von Euw 1977: Figs. 9, 19).

19. The final clause of the monument (A24b2–B24) names an additional entity, who is connected to K'ak' Tiliw by a yitaj expression. Various identifications of this character have been offered, including the ruler of Copan, K'ak' Joplaj; a local noble (Looper 1994); and a Venus deity (Looper 1997b). While the name of the Stela D entity does not match that of K'ak' Joplaj (who was deceased by the time of the Stela D dedication), the significance of this reference is still uncertain.

20. The Principal Bird Deity may refer to a circumpolar constellation visible on this evening, such as the Big Dipper, rising in the northeast, or Cassiopeia, which was high in the sky.

21. The record of the dark moon appears at C16, citing the moon's location as tan "in the center of," the centipede which represents the maw of the underworld.

22. The glyph (D6) that follows the tzolk'in in this text was identified by Kelley (1977b) as a record of a solar eclipse. Although this eclipse was not visible at Quirigua, it was confirmed fifteen days later by a total lunar eclipse (see Schele and Looper 1994).

23. A compound that is parallel to the name for the being in the QRG Stela E south-face headdress appears in the text of Palenque Temple of the Inscriptions, west panel, J4 (yax-chit? "shell-in-hand").

24. The name of this location includes the term hichil or chihil, which may be related to Yukatek hich "coger fruta o frijoles" or hi-ich't "deshojar" (Barrera Vásquez 1980: 208).

25. See Stone (1983) and Freidel and Schele (1988b). The personification of the number nine wears this same headdress on Zoomorph B, glyph 1. The same headdress may also be worn by the personification of ch'ahom(a) "censer" (Zoomorph B, glyph 17) and by the supernatural who represents completion or zero (Stela D, C9–D10).

26. Miller (1983: 133–134) and Proskouriakoff (1950: 129–130) also argue for a stylistic relationship between Late Classic Quirigua and Salinas de los Nueve Cerros, a site located near the upper Chixoy River, just south of Altar de Sacrificios. The comparison is specifically with Salinas Monument 1 (illustrated by Seler 1902–

1923, vol. 3: Pl. 1), a sandstone sculpture representing a human face surrounded by an elaborate headdress and with glyphs on the sides. The face and the personification heads above and below it are carved three-dimensionally, projecting from the rest of the block. The remainder of the carving, consisting of earflare assemblages placed to the sides of the face and heads, is executed in very low relief, conforming to the planar face of the block. In Miller's (1983: 134) opinion, the projection of the face from the rest of the block is similar to Late Classic Quirigua sculptures. As discussed in Chapter 3, however, at Quirigua the faces do not project from the main sculptural mass. Instead, facial planes are carved back into the stone itself. Miller also compares the headdress band of the Salinas monument to Quirigua Stela D; but this element is fairly widely distributed in the Maya area, seen, for example, at Aguateca (Stela 3), Dos Pilas (Stela 14), Tikal (Stela 25), Naranjo (Stelae 6 and 13), and Tonina (Monument 26). This trait cannot be taken as evidence of stylistic influence between Quirigua and Salinas. Similarly, the framing of the face by vertical design elements on the Salinas monument—considered by Miller to be another feature connecting the two sites—is also common at Tonina (e.g., Monument 26) and cannot therefore be said to constitute a specific stylistic association between Salinas and Quirigua.

In summary, I see no clear evidence of a meaningful stylistic connection between Salinas de los Nueve Cerros Monument 1 and Late Classic Quirigua sculptures. Nor is there any other monument at Salinas that suggests specific ties to Quirigua (see Dillon 1977). The projection of the face and headdress personifications from the sculptural mass and the generally curvilinear drawing of the design of Salinas Monument 1 suggest a much stronger relationship with the Tonina tradition. In fact, Salinas Monument 1 is probably not a fragment of a full-figural representation at all, as Miller thought, but is of a class of stone sculptures related to the flanged incensarios of the western region (see Rands 1968; Rands and Rands 1959; Schmidt, de la Garza, and Nalda 1998: Cat. 131).

Chapter 5. Foundation of the Cosmic House

1. The name of Zoomorph G includes the logograph for "platform, throne" at O2; and Zoomorph P is named at C6a with a sign that includes the T174 affix read by MacLeod (n.d.) as *kuch* "seat, container."

2. Freidel, Schele, and Parker (1993: 140, 433) and Taube (1998) discuss the symbolism of the three Creation stones by triadic architectural design. For other interpretations of this architectural configuration, see Ashmore (1989); Cohodas (1985: 58–59); Freidel (1979); Hansen (1992: 54–56, 1998: 77–81); Looper (2002a); and Reese (1996).

3. On stereotypical gender roles in Maya ritual, see Freidel (1989); Joyce (1996, 2000); Looper (2000, 2002a); Proskouriakoff (1961); and Stone (1988).

4. These monuments include Lintels 13, 14, 15, 17, 24, 25, 38, 40, 43, 51, and 55 and a number of the Structure 33 stairs (see Tate 1992: Figs. 68, 90, 93, 111, 148, 157, 159).

5. Lounsbury (1980) designated the progenitor deity at Palenque as "GI senior," later GI′ ("god one prime") (Schele and Freidel 1990: 245). Lounsbury (1985) identified this figure as equivalent to Jun Junajpu in the *Popol Vuh*, while Taube (1985) associated the latter with the Classic "Tonsured Maize God." Freidel, Schele, and Parker (1993: 59–122) synthesized and elaborated on these interpretations in their discussion of the Maize God as "First Father."

6. The focus marker (D5) used to introduce the Calendar Round of this text suggests that the text of Stela C reads continuously from east to west and supports like interpretations for reading continuity on previous stelae.

7. Tikal Temple 4 Lintel 2 A11 (Jones and Satterthwaite 1982: Fig. 73).

8. Cohodas (1991: 278) connects the reference to the "Headband Twins" (Jun Ajaw and Yax B'alam) on the Stela C north text to the paired gods that occupy the main visual field on the north faces of Stelae C and A and suggests that there is an underlying symbolic complex in this program that relates to the ballgame. There is, however, no specific reference to the ballgame in these images and texts that confirms this hypothesis.

9. In Maudslay's (1889–1902, vol. 2: Pl. 8) drawing, the eye is misdrawn with an axe pupil.

10. Cohodas (1991: 278) identifies the deities on the reverse of Stelae C and A as pertaining to a complex of "paired sacrificer imagery."

11. See Freidel, Schele, and Parker (1993: 257–292); Grube (1992); and Looper (1991a).

12. The cache of Zoomorph B consisted of a set of seven flint blades, varying from 14 to 46 cm in length, interred in a pit under the south foundation slab (Strömsvik 1941: 80).

13. Further, House E at Palenque was decorated with a stucco image of the Cosmic Monster, at the midpoint of which was placed an image of the Principal Bird Deity holding the celestial umbilicus in its beak. Not only does this celestial umbilicus mark House E as a symbolic place of birth, but the Cosmic Monster labels it as a place of accession, a function also indicated by the presence of a accession monuments within the building. The Oval Palace Tablet and its associated throne were installed in House E. As noted by Schele (1985), the Tablet of the 96 Glyphs also records accession in a white building, identified as the white-painted House E. Baudez (1988: 140) associated QRG Zoomorphs O and P (which depict Cosmic Monsters, like Zoomorph B) with themes of rebirth and accession.

14. On *tzuk* as "partition," see Grube and Schele (1991). In Yukatek, *tzuk* is glossed "barbas de mazorca de maíz" (Barrera Vásquez 1980: 866). Kaufman and Norman (1984: 134) reconstruct proto-Ch'olan *tzuk ti'* for "beard."

15. One might even speculate that the youthful visages of the ruler depicted at Quirigua relate to a persona associated with growing maize. This association, however, is general throughout most Classic-period elite portraiture.

16. The most pervasive ancient Maya observatory form is probably the "E Group," a solstice observatory first identified at Uaxac-

tun by Ricketson (1928). On the observation of solstice positions among the modern Maya, see Milbrath (1999: 14–15, 19–20).

17. For additional discussion of the public use of the Great Plaza, see Sanchez (1997: 102–112).

18. The use of stelae as pilgrimage shrines at Quirigua was likely inspired by the precedent of the stelae of Waxaklajun Ub'ah K'awil at Copan (Newsome 1991, 2001).

19. See also Ashmore and Sharer (1978) for interpretations of this part of the plaza as a market.

20. See, for example, the lengthy festivals documented in Chichicastenango by Bunzel (1952). In modern ceremonies, ritual drinking is often conceived as a sacrifice.

21. Similar concepts are documented in Mam (Mayan) grammar, in which space and world directions are modeled on the circular movement of the sun (Watanabe 1983).

22. The art and politics during the reign of Yax Pasaj have been discussed at length by Fash (2001: 153–172) and Schele and Freidel (1990: 306–345).

23. Yax Pasaj undertook other minor architectural projects early in his reign and commissioned several small altars, including Z and 41, at this time.

24. It should be noted that even though Stelae A and C are each of relatively uniform style, the monuments are not stylistically identical. Differences are especially apparent in the well-preserved glyphs, showing not only higher quality in Stela A but also slight differences in sculptural execution. The Stela C glyphs are characterized by lack of modeling, frequently incised details, rarity of head-variant glyphs, tight closure, and stasis of form, while the Stela A glyphs are interpenetrating and are characterized by more interest in modeling and planar variety, dynamism, and common use of head-variants. Compare, for instance, the K'ayab' and "scattering" verbs on the two monuments.

Chapter 6. In Honor of a Great Warrior

1. Generally, Maya rulers seem to have been buried within a few days of their death. For example, Itzamnaj K'awil of Dos Pilas was buried four days after his death; Piedras Negras Ruler 4, three days; and Smoke Imix of Copan, two days.

2. For illustrations of these texts, see Figures 2.1 and 3.2. A second reference to the thirteenth Copan ruler appears at S5–T5, unfortunately in an eroded context.

3. See also Schele and Freidel's (1990: 464) discussion of the placement of Temple 5D-33-1st at the southern edge of the Tikal North Acropolis.

4. Schele and Miller (1986) mistakenly identify the deity as "Chac-Xib-Chac."

5. Sharer (1978) distinguishes the Stela I ruler, whom he termed "Scroll Sky," from Jade Sky. Grube, Schele, and Fahsen (1991) conflate the two, suggesting that the names of Jade Sky and Scroll Sky are merely variant spellings of the same name.

6. Vogt (1976: 136) documents the Tzotzil conceptualization of slapping sandals and feet during dance as percussive music. These sandals are similar to those depicted on Classic lowland Maya monuments. On the relation of these costumes to dance performance, see Looper (1997a, 2001).

7. On the meanings of artistic quality among the ancient Maya, see Stuart (1989c).

8. The presence of these foreign invaders is attested by artifacts such as the chacmool found at the site as well as new types of ceramics. See Ashmore (1987: 221) and Sharer (1978).

Bibliography

Altman, Patricia B., and Caroline D. West

1992 *Threads of Identity: Maya Costume of the 1960's in Highland Guatemala.* Los Angeles: Fowler Museum of Cultural History.

Andrews, E. Wyllys, V

n.d. The Organization of a Royal Maya Residential Compound at the Center of Copan. In *Copan: The Rise and Fall of a Classic Maya Kingdom,* ed. William L. Fash and E. Wyllys Andrews V. Santa Fe: School of American Research Press.

Andrews, E. Wyllys, V, and Barbara W. Fash

1992 Continuity and Change in a Royal Maya Residential Complex at Copan. *Ancient Mesoamerica* 3: 63–88.

Ara, Domingo de

1986 *Vocabulario de lengua tzeltal según orden de Copanabastla.* Mexico City: Universidad Nacional Autónoma de México.

Ashmore, Wendy

1980a The Classic Maya Settlement at Quirigua. *Expedition* 23 (3): 20–27.

1980b Discovering Early Classic Quirigua. *Expedition* 23 (3): 35–44.

1981 Precolumbian Occupation at Quirigua, Guatemala: Settlement Patterns in a Classic Maya Center. Ph.D. diss., University of Pennsylvania.

1984 Quirigua Archaeology and History Revisited. *Journal of Field Archaeology* 11: 365–386.

1986 Peten Cosmology in the Maya Southeast: An Analysis of Architecture and Settlement Patterns at Classic Quirigua. In *The Southeast Maya Periphery,* ed. Patricia A. Urban and Edward M. Schortman, pp. 35–49. Austin: University of Texas Press.

1987 Research at Quirigua, Guatemala: The Site-Periphery Program. In *The Periphery of the Southeastern Maya Realm,* ed. Gary Pahl, pp. 217–225. Los Angeles: Latin American Center, University of California at Los Angeles.

1989 Construction and Cosmology: Politics and Ideology in Lowland Maya Settlement Patterns. In *Word and Image in Maya Culture,* ed. William F. Hanks and Donald S. Rice, pp. 272–286. Salt Lake City: University of Utah Press.

1991 Site-Planning Principles and Concepts of Directionality among the Ancient Maya. *Latin American Antiquity* 2: 199–226.

n.d. Settlement Archaeology at Quirigua. In *Quirigua Reports: Volume 4.* Gen. ed. Robert J. Sharer. Philadelphia: University Museum Publications, University of Pennsylvania.

Ashmore, Wendy, ed.

1979 *Quirigua Reports: Volume 1.* Gen. ed. Robert J. Sharer. University Museum Monograph 37. Philadelphia: University Museum Publications, University of Pennsylvania.

Ashmore, Wendy, Edward M. Schortman, and Robert Sharer

1983 The Quirigua Project: 1979 Season, with an Appendix by Bruce Bevan. In *Quirigua Reports: Volume 2,* ed. Edward M. Schortman and Patricia A. Urban, pp. 55–78. University Museum Monograph 49. Philadelphia: University Museum Publications, University of Pennsylvania.

Ashmore, Wendy, and Robert J. Sharer

1978 Excavations at Quirigua, Guatemala: The Ascent of a Maya Elite Center. *Archaeology* 31 (6): 10–19.

Attinasi, John Joseph

1973 Lak T'an: A Grammar of the Chol (Mayan) Word. Ph.D. diss., University of Chicago.

Aulie, H. Wilbur, and Evelyn W. de Aulie

1978 *Diccionario Ch'ol-Español, Español-Ch'ol.* Serie de Vocabulario y Diccionarios Indígenas "Mariano Silva y Aceves" 21. Mexico City: Instituto Lingüístico de Verano.

Barrera Vásquez, Alfredo

1980 *Diccionario Maya Cordemex: Maya-Español, Español-Maya.* Mérida: Ediciones Cordemex.

Barthes, Roland

1977 *Image-Music-Text.* Trans. Stephen Heath. New York: Noonday Press.

Bateson, Gregory

1958 *Naven.* 2nd ed. Stanford: Stanford University Press.

Baudez, Claude-François

1986 Iconography and History at Copan. In *The Southeast Maya Periphery,* ed. Patricia A. Urban and Edward M. Schortman, pp. 17–26. Austin: University of Texas Press.

1988   Solar Cycle and Dynastic Succession in the Southeast Maya Zone. In *The Southeast Classic Maya Zone*, ed. Elizabeth H. Boone and Gordon R. Willey, pp. 125–148. Washington, D.C.: Dumbarton Oaks.

1992   The Maya Snake Dance: Ritual and Cosmology. *RES: Anthropology and Aesthetics* 21 (Spring): 37–52.

1994   *Maya Sculpture of Copán: The Iconography*. Norman: University of Oklahoma Press.

Baudez, Claude-François, ed.

1983   *Introducción a la arqueología de Copán, Honduras.* 3 vols. Proyecto Arqueológico Copán. Tegucigalpa, Honduras: Instituto Hondureño de Antropología e Historia.

Baudez, Claude-François, and Berthold Riese

1990   *The Sculpture from Copán.* Microfilm Collection of Manuscripts on Cultural Anthropology 381, series 73. Chicago: University of Chicago Library.

Baxandall, Michael

1985   *Patterns of Intention: On the Historical Explanation of Pictures.* New Haven: Yale University Press.

Becker, Marshall J.

1972   Plaza Plans at Quirigua, Guatemala. *Katunob* 8: 47–62.

Beetz, Carl P., and Linton Satterthwaite

1981   *The Monuments and Inscriptions of Caracol, Belize.* Philadelphia: University Museum Publications, University of Pennsylvania.

Bell, Catherine

1992   *Ritual Theory, Ritual Practice.* New York: Oxford University Press.

Benyo, Julie

1979   The Pottery Censers of Quirigua, Izabal, Guatemala. Master's thesis, State University of New York, Albany.

Berlin, Heinrich

1958   El glifo "emblema" en las inscripciones mayas. *Journal de la Société des Américanistes* 47: 111–119.

1963   The Palenque Triad. *Journal de la Société des Américanistes* (Paris) n.s. 52: 91–99.

Berlo, Janet Catherine

1983   Conceptual Categories for the Study of Texts and Images in Mesoamerica. In *Text and Image in Pre-Columbian Art: Essays on the Interrelationship of the Verbal and Visual Arts*, ed. Janet Catherine Berlo, pp. 1–39. British Archaeological Reports, International Series 180. Oxford: BAR.

1984   *Teotihuacan Art Abroad: A Study of Metropolitan Style and Provincial Transformation in Incensario Workshops.* British Archaeological Reports, International Series 199. Oxford: BAR.

Blier, Suzanne Preston

1996   Ritual. In *Critical Terms for Art History*, ed. Robert S. Nelson and Richard Schiff, pp. 187–196. Chicago: University of Chicago Press.

Bloch, Maurice

1974   Symbols, Song, Dance, and Features of Articulation. *European Journal of Sociology* 15: 55–81.

Boas, Franz

1925   *Contributions to the Ethnology of the Kwakiutl.* Columbia University Contributions to Anthropology, 3. New York: Columbia University Press.

Boot, Erik, Matthew Looper, and Elisabeth Wagner

1996   *A New k'a Syllable: T627a/T538/T583.* Texas Notes on Precolumbian Art, Writing, and Culture 77. Austin: Center for the History of Art and Ancient American Culture, Art Department, University of Texas.

Borhegyi, S. F. de

1965   Archaeological Synthesis of the Guatemalan Highlands. In *Handbook of Middle American Indians: Volume 2*, ed. R. Wauchope and Gordon R. Willey, pp. 3–58. Austin: University of Texas Press.

Bricker, Harvey M., and Victoria R. Bricker

1992   Zodiacal References in the Maya Codices. In *The Sky in Mayan Literature*, ed. Anthony F. Aveni, pp. 148–183. New York: Oxford University Press.

Bricker, Victoria R.

1981   *The Indian Christ, the Indian King.* Austin: University of Texas Press.

1986   *A Grammar of Mayan Hieroglyphs.* Middle American Research Institute, Publication 56. New Orleans: Tulane University.

Bricker, Victoria R., Eleuterio Po'ot Yah, and Ofelia Dzul de Po'ot

1998   *A Dictionary of the Maya Language: As Spoken in Hocabá Yucatán.* Salt Lake City: University of Utah Press.

Broda, Johanna

1987   Templo Mayor as Ritual Space. In *The Great Temple of Tenochtitlan: Center and Periphery in the Aztec World*, ed. Johanna Broda, Davíd Carrasco, and Eduardo Matos Moctezuma, pp. 61–123. Berkeley: University of California Press.

Buikstra, Jane

1997   The Bones Speak: High-Tech Approach to the Study of Our Ancestors. Lecture presented for the Loren Eisley Associates, University of Pennsylvania Museum, Philadelphia.

Bunzel, Ruth

1952   *Chichicastenango, a Guatemalan Village.* Publications of the American Ethnological Society 22. Locust Valley, N.Y.: J. J. Augustin.

Carlson, John B., and Linda Landis

1985   Bands, Bicephalic Dragons and Other Beasts: The Skyband in Maya Art and Iconography. In *Fourth Palenque Round Table, 1980*, ed. Merle Greene Robertson and Elizabeth P. Benson, pp. 115–140. San Francisco: Pre-Columbian Art Research Institute.

Chase, Arlen F.

1991   Cycles of Time: Caracol and the Maya Realm, with an Appendix on Caracol Altar 21 by Stephen D. Houston. In *Sixth Palenque Round Table, 1986*, ed. Virginia M. Fields, pp. 32–42. Norman: University of Oklahoma Press.

Cheek, Charles D.

1986   Construction Activity as a Measurement of Change at Copan, Honduras. In *The Southeast Maya Periphery*, ed. Patricia Urban and Edward Schortman, pp. 50–71. Austin: University of Texas Press.

Cheek, Charles D., and Daniel E. Milla Villeda

1983   La Estructura 10L-4. In *Introducción a la arqueología de Copán, Honduras*, vol. 2, ed. Claude-François Baudez, pp. 37–91. 3 vols. Tegucigalpa, Honduras: Instituto Hondureño de Antropología e Historia.

Christie, Jessica

1995 Maya Period Ending Ceremonies: Restarting Time and Rebuilding the Cosmos to Assure Survival of the Maya World. Ph.D. diss., University of Texas at Austin.

Clancy, Flora

1986 Text and Image in the Tablets of the Cross Group at Palenque. *RES: Anthropology and Aesthetics* 11 (Spring): 17–32.

1988 The Compositions and Contexts of the Classic Stelae at Copan and Quirigua. In *The Southeast Classic Maya Zone*, ed. Elizabeth H. Boone and Gordon R. Willey, pp. 195–222. Washington, D.C.: Dumbarton Oaks.

1990 A Genealogy for Freestanding Maya Monuments. In *Vision and Revision in Maya Studies*, ed. Flora S. Clancy and Peter D. Harrison, pp. 21–32. Albuquerque: University of New Mexico Press.

1999 *Sculpture in the Ancient Maya Plaza: The Early Classic Period.* Albuquerque: University of New Mexico Press.

Clark, John E., and Michael Blake

1994 The Power of Prestige: Competitive Generosity and the Emergence of Rank Societies in Lowland Mesoamerica. In *Factional Competition and Political Development in the New World*, ed. Elizabeth M. Brumfiel and John W. Fox, pp. 17–30. Cambridge: Cambridge University Press.

Codex Dresdensis Maya

1880 Introduction by Ernst Förstemann. Leipzig: A. Naumann.

Codex Peresianus: Manuscrit hiératique des anciens Indiens de l'Amérique Central, conservé à la Bibliothèque Nationale de Paris

1888 Introduction by Léon de Rosny. Paris: Bureau de la Société Américaine.

Coe, Michael D.

1973 *The Maya Scribe and His World.* New York: Grolier Club.

1977 Supernatural Patrons of Maya Scribes and Artists. In *Social Process in Maya Prehistory: Studies in Honour of Sir Eric Thompson*, ed. Norman Hammond, pp. 327–347. New York: Academic Press.

1978 *Lords of the Underworld: Masterpieces of Classic Maya Ceramics.* Princeton: Art Museum, Princeton University.

Coe, Michael D., and Justin Kerr

1997 *The Art of the Maya Scribe.* New York: Harry N. Abrams.

Coe, William R., and Robert J. Sharer

1979 The Quirigua Project: 1975 Season. In *Quirigua Reports: Volume 1*, ed. Wendy Ashmore and Robert J. Sharer, pp. 13–32. University Museum Monograph 37. Philadelphia: University Museum Publications, University of Pennsylvania.

Coggins, Clemency C.

1975 Painting and Drawing Styles at Tikal: An Historical and Iconographic Reconstruction. Ph.D. diss., Harvard University. Ann Arbor: University Microfilms.

1988a The Manikin Scepter: Emblem of Lineage. *Estudios de Cultura Maya* 17: 123–158.

1988b On the Historical Significance of Decorated Ceramics at Copan and Quirigua Related Classic Maya Sites. In *The Southeast Classic Maya Zone*, ed. Elizabeth Boone and Gordon R. Willey, pp. 95–123. Washington, D.C.: Dumbarton Oaks.

Cohodas, Marvin

1985 Public Architecture of the Maya Lowlands (Arquitectura pública de las tierras bajas mayas). *Cuadernos de Arquitectura Mesoamericana* 6: 51–68.

1991 Ballgame Imagery of the Maya Lowlands: History and Iconography. In *The Mesoamerican Ballgame*, ed. Vernon L. Scarborough and David R. Wilcox, pp. 251–288. Tucson: University of Arizona Press.

Davis, Whitney

1990 Style and History in Art History. In *The Uses of Style in Archaeology*, ed. by Margaret W. Conkey and Christine A. Hastorf, pp. 18–31. Cambridge: Cambridge University Press.

Dillon, Brian D.

1977 *Salinas de los Nueve Cerros, Guatemala: Preliminary Archaeological Investigations.* Socorro, N.Mex.: Ballena.

Drucker, Philip

1952 *La Venta, Tabasco: A Study of Olmec Ceramics and Art.* Bureau of American Ethnology, Bulletin 153. Washington, D.C.: U.S. Government Printing Office.

Durkheim, Emile

1965 *The Elementary Forms of the Religious Life.* New York: Free Press.

Earle, Timothy

1990 Style and Iconography as Legitimization of Complex Chiefdoms. In *The Uses of Style in Archaeology*, ed. Margaret W. Conkey and Christine A. Hastorf, pp. 73–81. Cambridge: Cambridge University Press.

Eggebrecht, Eva, Arne Eggebrecht, Nikolai Grube, and Wilfried Seipel, eds.

1993 *Die Welt der Maya.* Mainz am Rhein: Verlag Philipp von Zabern.

Eliade, Mircea

1964 *Shamanism: Archaic Techniques of Ecstasy.* Translated from the French by Willard R. Trask. Bollingen Series 76. Princeton, N.J.: Princeton University Press.

Estrada Monroy, Agustín

1979 *El Mundo K'ekchi' de la Vera-Paz.* Guatemala City: Editorial del Ejército.

Fahsen, Federico

2002 Rescuing the Origins of Dos Pilas Dynasty: A Salvage of Hieroglyphic Stairway #2, Structure L5-49. Online: http://www.famsi.org/reports/01098/index.html.

Fahsen, Federico, Linda Schele, and Nikolai Grube

1995 *The Tikal-Copan Connection: Shared Features.* Copán Note 123. Copán, Honduras: Copán Mosaics Project and the Instituto Hondureño de Antropología e Historia.

Fash, Barbara W.

1992 Late Classic Architectural Sculpture Themes in Copan. *Ancient Mesoamerica* 3: 89–104.

1996 Copan's House of Lords. *Natural History* 105 (4): 30–31.

n.d. Iconographic Evidence for Water Management at Copan. In *Copan: The Rise and Fall of a Classic Maya Kingdom*, ed. William L. Fash and E. Wyllys Andrews V. Santa Fe: School of American Research Press.

Fash, Barbara, William Fash, Sheree Lane, Rudy Larios, Linda Schele, Jeffrey Stomper, and David Stuart

1992   Investigations of a Classic Maya Council House at Copán, Honduras. *Journal of Field Archaeology* 19 (4): 419–442.

Fash, William L.

1983   Maya State Formation: A Case Study and Its Implications. Ph.D. diss., Harvard University. Ann Arbor: University Microfilms.

1984   Regional Interaction in the Southeast Maya Area: An Epigraphic Approach. Paper presented at the Annual Meeting of the American Anthropological Association, Denver.

1986   History and Characteristics of Settlement in the Copan Valley, and Some Comparisons with Quirigua. In *The Southeast Maya Periphery*, ed. Patricia A. Urban and Edward M. Schortman, pp. 72–93. Austin: University of Texas Press.

1988   A New Look at Maya Statecraft from Copan, Honduras. *Antiquity* 62:157–159.

1998   Dynastic Architectural Programs: Intention and Design in Classic Maya Buildings at Copan and Other Sites. In *Function and Meaning in Classic Maya Architecture*, ed. Stephen D. Houston, pp. 223–270. Washington, D.C.: Dumbarton Oaks.

2001   *Scribes, Warriors, and Kings: The City of Copán and the Ancient Maya*. Rev. ed. London: Thames & Hudson.

Fash, William L., and E. Wyllys Andrews V, eds.

n.d.   *Copan: The Rise and Fall of a Classic Maya Kingdom*. Santa Fe: School of American Research Press.

Fash, William L., and Barbara W. Fash

1990   Scribes, Warriors, and Kings: Ancient Lives of the Copan Maya. *Archaeology* 45 (3): 26–35.

2000   Teotihuacan and the Maya: A Classic Heritage. In *Mesoamerica's Classic Heritage: From Teotihuacan to the Aztecs*, ed. Davíd Carrasco, Lindsay Jones, and Scott Sessions, pp. 433–463. Niwot: University Press of Colorado.

Fash, William L., and Robert J. Sharer

1991   Sociopolitical Developments and Methodological Issues at Copan, Honduras: A Conjunctive Perspective. *Latin American Antiquity* 2: 166–187.

Fash, William L., and David Stuart

1991   Dynastic History and Cultural Evolution at Copan, Honduras. In *Classic Maya Political History: Hieroglyphic and Archaeological Evidence*, ed. T. Patrick Culbert, pp. 147–179. Cambridge: Cambridge University Press.

Fash, William L., Richard V. Williamson, Carlos Rudy Larios, and Joel Palka

1992   The Hieroglyphic Stairway and Its Ancestors: Investigations of Copan Structure 10L-26. *Ancient Mesoamerica* 3: 105–116.

Fields, Virginia M.

1989   The Origins of Divine Kingship among the Lowland Classic Maya. Ph.D. diss., University of Texas at Austin.

Fought, John G.

1972   *Chorti (Mayan) Texts*, 1. Ed. Sarah S. Fought. Philadelphia: University of Pennsylvania Press.

Fowler, Roger

1987   *A Dictionary of Modern Critical Terms*. Revised ed. London:
[1973]   Routledge & Kegan Paul.

Fox, John W.

1991   The Lords of Light Versus the Lords of Dark: The Postclassic Highland Maya Ballgame. In *The Mesoamerican Ballgame*, ed. Vernon L. Scarborough and David R. Wilcox, pp. 213–238. Tucson: University of Arizona Press.

Freidel, David A.

1979   Cultural Areas and Interaction Spheres: Contrasting Approaches to the Emergence of Civilization in the Maya Lowlands. *American Antiquity* 44: 6–54.

1989   The Maya War Jaguar: Historical Invention and Structural Transformation. Paper presented at the Society for American Archaeology meeting, Atlanta, Georgia.

Freidel, David, and Barbara MacLeod

2000   Creation Redux: New Thoughts on Maya Cosmology from Epigraphy, Iconography, and Archaeology. *PARI Journal* 1 (2): 1–8, 18.

Freidel, David, and Linda Schele

1988a   Kingship in the Late Preclassic Lowlands: The Instruments and Places of Ritual Power. *American Anthropologist* 90 (3): 547–567.

1988b   Symbol and Power: A History of the Lowland Maya Cosmogram. In *Maya Iconography*, ed. Elizabeth P. Benson and Gillett G. Griffin, pp. 44–93. Princeton, N.J.: Princeton University Press.

Freidel, David, Linda Schele, and Joy Parker

1993   *Maya Cosmos: Three Thousand Years on the Shaman's Path*. New York: William Morrow.

Fuente, Beatriz de la

1973   *Escultura monumental olmeca: Catálogo*. Cuadernos de la Historia del Arte 1. Mexico City: Instituto de Investigaciones Estéticas, Universidad Nacional Autónoma de México.

Galaty, John G.

1983   Ceremony and Society: The Poetics of Maasai Ritual. *Man* n.s. 18: 361–382.

Geertz, Clifford

1966   Religion as a Cultural System. In *Anthropological Approaches to the Study of Religion*, ed. Michael Banton, pp. 1–46. London: Tavistock.

1985   Centers, Kings, and Charisma: Reflections on the Symbolics of Power. In *Rites of Power: Symbolism, Ritual, and Politics since the Middle Ages*, ed. Sean Wilentz, pp. 13–38. Philadelphia: University of Pennsylvania Press.

Gell, Alfred

1998   *Art and Agency: An Anthropological Theory*. Oxford: Oxford University Press.

1999   The Technology of Enchantment and the Enchantment of Technology. In *The Art of Anthropology: Essays and Diagrams*, ed. E. Hirsch, pp. 159–186. London School of Economics Monographs on Social Anthropology 67. London and New Brunswick, N.J.: Athlone. (First published in *Anthropology, Art, and Aesthetics*, ed. J. Coote and A. Shelton, pp. 40–67. Oxford: Oxford University Press, 1992.)

Gillespie, Susan D.

1991 Ballgames and Boundaries. In *The Mesoamerican Ballgame*, ed. Vernon L. Scarborough and David R. Wilcox, pp. 317–345. Tucson: University of Arizona Press.

Girard, Rafael

1962 *Los Mayas eternos.* Mexico City: Antigua Librería Robredo.

1966 *Los Mayas: Su civilización, su historia, sus vinculaciones continentales.* Mexico City: Libro Mexicano.

1995 *People of the Chan.* Trans. Bennett Preble. Chino Valley, Ariz.: Continuum Foundation.

Gluckman, Max

1965 *Politics, Law and Ritual in Tribal Society.* Chicago: Aldine.

Gombrich, Ernst H.

1966 *Norm and Form: Studies in the Art of the Renaissance.* London: Phaidon.

1972 Introduction: Aims and Limits of Iconology. In *Symbolic Images*, pp. 1–22. London: Phaidon.

González Lauck, Rebecca B.

1997 Acerca de pirámides de tierra y seres sobrenaturales: Observaciones preliminares en torno al Edificio C-1, La Venta, Tabasco. *Arqueología* 17: 79–98.

Gordon, George Byron

1902 The Hieroglyphic Stairway, Ruins of Copan: Report on Explorations by the Museum. Memoirs of the Peabody Museum of American Archaeology and Ethnology, vol. 1 (6). Cambridge, Mass.: Harvard University.

1913 An Unpublished Inscription from Quirigua, Guatemala. In *Proceedings of the Eighteenth International Congress of Americanists*, Part 1, pp. 238–240. London: Harrison & Sons.

Gossen, Gary H.

1986 The Chamula Festival of Games: Native Macroanalysis and Social Commentary in a Maya Carnival. In *Symbol and Meaning beyond the Closed Community*, ed. Gary H. Gossen, pp. 227–254. Albany: Institute for Mesoamerican Studies, State University of New York.

Greenhalgh, Michael

1987 *The Classical Tradition in Art.* New York: Harper & Row.

Griffin, Gillett G.

1976 Portraiture in Palenque. In *The Art, Iconography, and Dynastic History of Palenque Part III*, ed. Merle Greene Robertson, pp. 137–147. Pebble Beach, Calif.: Pre-Columbian Art Research, Robert Louis Stevenson School.

Grove, David C.

1984 *Chalcatzingo: Excavations on the Olmec Frontier.* London: Thames & Hudson.

Grube, Nikolai

1990a Caracol's Impact on the Tikal Hiatus. Paper presented at the Sixth Texas Symposium, University of Texas at Austin.

1990b *A Reference to Water-Lily Jaguar on Caracol Stela 16.* Copán Note 68. Copán, Honduras: Copán Mosaics Project and the Instituto Hondureño de Antropología e Historia.

1992 Classic Maya Dance: Evidence from Hieroglyphs and Iconography. *Ancient Mesoamerica* 3: 201–218.

1994 Epigraphic Research at Caracol, Belize. In *Studies in the Archaeology of Caracol, Belize*, ed. Arlen Chase and Diane Chase, pp. 83–122. San Francisco: Pre-Columbian Art Research Institute.

1996 Palenque in the Maya World. In *Eighth Palenque Round Table, 1993*, ed. Martha J. Macri and Jan McHargue, pp. 1–13. San Francisco: Pre-Columbian Art Research Institute.

Grube, Nikolai, and Werner Nahm

1994 A Census of Xibalba: A Complete Inventory of 'Way' Characters on Maya Ceramics. In *The Maya Vase Book: Volume 4*, ed. Justin Kerr and Barbara Kerr, pp. 686–715. New York: Kerr & Associates.

Grube, Nikolai, and Linda Schele

1988 *A Quadrant Tree at Copán.* Copán Note 43. Copán, Honduras: Copán Mosaics Project and the Instituto Hondureño de Antropología e Historia.

1991 *Tzuk in the Classic Maya Inscriptions.* Texas Notes on Precolumbian Art, Writing, and Culture 14. Austin: Center for the History of Art and Ancient American Culture, Art Department, University of Texas.

1992 *Yet Another Look at Stela 11.* Copán Note 106. Copán, Honduras: Copán Mosaics Project and the Instituto Hondureño de Antropología e Historia.

Grube, Nikolai, Linda Schele, and Federico Fahsen

1991 Odds and Ends from the Inscriptions of Quirigua. *Mexicon* 13 (6): 106–112.

1995 *The Tikal-Copan Connection: Evidence from External Relations.* Copán Note 121. Copán, Honduras: Copán Mosaics Project and the Instituto Hondureño de Antropología e Historia.

Grube, Nikolai, Linda Schele, David Stuart, and William Fash

1989 *The Date of Dedication of Ballcourt III at Copán.* Copán Note 59. Copán, Honduras: Copán Mosaics Project and the Instituto Hondureño de Antropología e Historia.

Hanks, William F.

1989 Word and Image in a Semiotic Perspective. In *Word and Image in Maya Culture*, ed. William F. Hanks and Don S. Rice, pp. 8–21. Salt Lake City: University of Utah Press.

2000 *Intertexts: Writings on Language, Utterance, and Context.* Lanham, Md.: Rowman & Littlefield.

Hansen, Richard

1989 Las investigaciones del sitio Nakbé, Petén, Guatemala Temporada 1989. Paper presented at the Tercer Simposio de Arqueología Guatemalteca, Museo Nacional de Arqueología y Etnología, Guatemala City, July.

1992 The Archaeology Ideology: A Study of Maya Preclassic Architectural Sculpture at Nakbe, Guatemala. Ph.D. dissertation, University of California at Los Angeles.

1998 Continuity and Disjunction: The Pre-Classic Antecedents of Classic Maya Architecture. In *Function and Meaning in Classic Maya Architecture*, ed. Stephen D. Houston, pp. 49–122. Washington, D.C.: Dumbarton Oaks.

Harrison, Peter D.

1999 *The Lords of Tikal: Rulers of an Ancient Maya City.* London: Thames & Hudson.

Hassig, Ross

1988 *Aztec Warfare, Imperial Expansion and Political Control.* Norman: University of Oklahoma Press.

Hatch, Marion Popenoe de

1975 A Study of Hieroglyphic Texts at the Classic Maya Site of Quirigua, Guatemala. Ph.D. diss., University of California at Berkeley.

Hays-Gilpin, Kelley, and Jane H. Hill

1999 The Flower World In Material Culture: An Iconographic Complex in the Southwest and Mesoamerica. *Journal of Anthropological Research* 55 (1): 1–37.

Hellmuth, Nicholas M.

1987 *Monster und Menschen in der Maya-Kunst.* Graz: Akademische Druck- u. Verlagsanstalt.

Hewett, Edgar L.

1911 Two Seasons' Work in Guatemala. *Bulletin of the Archaeological Institute of America* 2 (3): 117–134.

1912 The Third Season's Work in Guatemala. *Bulletin of the Archaeological Institute of America* 3: 163–171.

1913 The Excavation of Quirigua, Guatemala, by the School of American Archaeology. In *Proceedings of the Eighteenth International Congress of Americanists, 1912, Part 1,* pp. 241–248. London: Harrison & Sons.

1915 Ancient America at the Panama-California Exposition. *Art and Archaeology* 2 (3): 64–102.

1916 Latest Work of the School of American Archaeology at Quirigua. In *Holmes Anniversary Volume, Anthropological Essays,* ed. E. W. Hodge, pp. 157–162. Washington, D.C.: J. W. Bryan Press.

Hill, Jane H.

1992 The Flower World of Old Uto-Aztecan. *Journal of Anthropological Research* 48: 117–144.

Hohmann, Hasso, and Annegrete Vogrin

1982 *Die Architektur von Copan.* Graz, Austria: Akademische Druck- u. Verlagsanstalt.

Houston, Stephen D.

1989 Archaeology and Maya Writing. *Journal of World Prehistory* 3(1): 1–32.

1993 *Hieroglyphs and History at Dos Pilas: Dynastic Politics of the Classic Maya.* Austin: University of Texas Press.

1994 Literacy among the Pre-Columbian Maya: A Comparative Perspective. In *Writing without Words: Alternative Literacies in Mesoamerica and the Andes,* ed. Elizabeth H. Boone and Walter D. Mignolo, pp. 27–49. Durham, N.C.: Duke University Press.

1996 Symbolic Sweatbaths of the Maya: Architectural Meaning in the Cross Group at Palenque, Mexico. *Latin American Antiquity* 7 (2): 132–151.

Houston, Stephen D., and Peter Mathews

1985 *The Dynastic Sequence of Dos Pilas, Guatemala.* Pre-Columbian Art Research Institute, Monograph 1. San Francisco: Pre-Columbian Art Research Institute.

Houston, Stephen D., John Robertson, and David Stuart

1998 Disharmony in Maya Hieroglyphic Writing: Linguistic Change and Continuity in Classic Society. In *Anatomía de una civilización: Aproximaciones interdisciplinarias a la cultura maya,* ed. A. Ciudad, Y. Fernández, J. M. García, María J. Iglesias, A. Lacadena, and L. T. Sanz, pp. 275–296. Madrid: Sociedad Española de Estudios Mayas.

Houston, Stephen D., and David Stuart

1989 *The Way Glyph: Evidence for "Co-essences" among the Classic Maya.* Research Reports on Ancient Maya Writing 30. Washington, D.C.: Center for Maya Research.

1996 Of Gods, Glyphs and Kings: Divinity and Rulership among the Classic Maya. *Antiquity* 70: 289–312.

1998 The Ancient Maya Self: Personhood and Portraiture in the Classic Period. *RES: Anthropology and Aesthetics* 33: 73–101.

Houston, Stephen D., and Karl A. Taube

2000 An Archaeology of the Senses: Perception and Cultural Expression in Ancient Mesoamerica. *Cambridge Archaeological Journal* 10 (2): 261–294.

Indrikis, Janis

1997 In Search of a Myth: Enigmatic Calendric Glyphs at Quiriguá. In *Proceedings of the 1995 and 1996 Latin American Symposia,* ed. Alana Cordy-Collins and Grace Johnson, pp. 101–111. San Diego Museum of Man Paper 34. San Diego: San Diego Museum of Man.

Jackson, Michael

1983 Knowledge of the Body. *Man* n.s. 18: 327–345.

Jonaitis, Aldona, ed.

1991 *Chiefly Feasts: The Enduring Kwakiutl Potlatch.* New York: American Museum of Natural History.

Jones, Christopher

1977 Inauguration Dates of Three Late Classic Rulers of Tikal, Guatemala. *American Antiquity* 42: 28–60.

1983a Monument 26, Quirigua, Guatemala. In *Quirigua Reports: Volume 2,* ed. Edward M. Schortman and Patricia A. Urban, pp. 118–128, University Museum Monograph 49. Philadelphia: University Museum Publications, University of Pennsylvania.

1983b New Drawings of Monuments 23 and 24, Quirigua, Guatemala. In *Quirigua Reports: Volume 2,* ed. Edward M. Schortman and Patricia A. Urban, pp. 137–140, University Museum Monograph 49. Philadelphia: University Museum Publications, University of Pennsylvania.

1987 The Stratigraphic Sequence of the Acropolis at Quirigua and Its Possible Correlation to Dynastic Rules. In *The Periphery of the Southeastern Maya Realm,* ed. Gary Pahl, pp. 211–213. Los Angeles: Latin American Center, University of California at Los Angeles.

Jones, Christopher, Wendy Ashmore, and Robert J. Sharer

1983 The Quirigua Project: 1977 Season. In *Quirigua Reports: Volume 2,* ed. Edward M. Schortman and Patricia A. Urban, pp. 1–38. University Museum Monograph 49. Philadelphia: University Museum Publications, University of Pennsylvania.

Jones, Christopher, and Linton Satterthwaite

1982 *The Monuments and Inscriptions of Tikal: The Carved Monuments.* Tikal Report 33, Part A, University Museum Monograph 44. Philadelphia: University Museum Publications, University of Pennsylvania.

Jones, Christopher, and Robert Sharer

1980 Archaeological Investigations in the Site Core of Quirigua. *Expedition* 23 (3): 11–19.

1986 Archaeological Investigations in the Site Core of Quirigua, Guatemala. In *The Southeast Maya Periphery,* ed. Patricia A.

Urban and Edward M. Schortman, pp. 27–34. Austin: University of Texas Press.

Joralemon, P. David

1974   Ritual Blood Sacrifice among the Ancient Maya: Part I. In *Primera Mesa Redonda de Palenque, Part 2*, ed. Merle Greene Robertson, pp. 59–75. Pebble Beach, Calif.: Robert Louis Stevenson School.

Josserand, J. Kathryn

1991   The Narrative Structure of Hieroglyphic Texts at Palenque. In *Sixth Palenque Round Table, 1986*, ed. Virginia M. Fields, pp. 12–31. Norman: University of Oklahoma Press.

Joyce, Rosemary A.

1992   Dimensiones simbólicas del traje en monumentos clásicos mayas: La construcción del género a través del vestido. In *La indumentaria y el tejido mayas a través del tiempo*, ed. Linda Asturias de Barrios and Dina Fernández García, pp. 29–38. Guatemala City: Ediciones del Museo Ixchel.

1996   The Construction of Gender in Classic Maya Monuments. In *Gender and Archaeology*, ed. Rita P. Wright, pp. 167–195. Philadelphia: University of Pennsylvania Press.

2000   *Gender and Power in Prehispanic Mesoamerica*. Austin: University of Texas Press.

Joyce, T. A., T. Gann, E. L. Gruning, and R. C. E. Long

1928   Report of the British Museum Expedition to British Honduras, 1928. *Journal of the Royal Anthropological Institute* 58 (London): 323–350.

Jung, Carl G.

1953   Two Essays on Analytical Psychology. In *Collected Works: Volume 7*, trans. R. F. C. Hull, Second Essay, pars. 202–295, Bollingen Series 20. Princeton, N.J.: Princeton University Press.

Kapferer, Bruce

1979a   Entertaining Demons: Comedy, Interaction and Meaning in a Sinhalese Healing Ritual. *Social Analysis* 1: 108–152.

1979b   Introduction: Ritual Process and the Transformation of Context. *Social Analysis* 1: 3–19.

Kappelman, Julia Guernsey, and F. Kent Reilly III

2001   Paths to Heaven, Ropes to Earth: Birds, Jaguars, and Cosmic Cords in Formative Period Mesoamerica. *Ancient America* 3: 33–52.

Kaufman, Terrence S., and William M. Norman

1984   An Outline of Proto-Cholan Phonology, Morphology, and Vocabulary. In *Phoneticism in Mayan Hieroglyphic Writing*, ed. John S. Justeson and Lyle Campbell, pp. 77–167. Institute for Mesoamerican Studies Publication No. 9. Albany: Institute for Mesoamerican Studies, State University of New York.

Kelley, David

1962   Glyphic Evidence for a Dynastic Sequence at Quiriguá, Guatemala. *American Antiquity* 27: 323–335.

1977a   Maya Astronomical Tables and Inscriptions. In *Native American Astronomy*, ed. Anthony F. Aveni, pp. 57–73. Austin: University of Texas Press.

1977b   A Possible Maya Eclipse Record. In *Social Process in Maya Prehistory: Studies in Honour of Sir Eric Thompson*, ed. Norman Hammond, pp. 405–408. New York: Academic Press.

Kidder, Alfred V., Jesse D. Jennings, and Edwin M. Shook

1946   *Excavations at Kaminaljuyu, Guatemala*. Carnegie Institution of Washington Publication 561. Washington, D.C.: Carnegie Institution of Washington.

Koontz, Rex

1994   The Iconography of El Tajín, Veracruz. Ph.D. diss., University of Texas at Austin.

Kubler, George

1969   *Studies in Classic Maya Iconography*. Memoirs of the Connecticut Academy of Arts and Sciences 18. New Haven: Connecticut Academy of Arts and Sciences.

1984   *The Art and Architecture of Ancient America: The Mexican, Maya,*
[1962] *and Andean Peoples*. 3rd ed. Baltimore, Md.: Pelican.

La Ruta Maya Conservation Foundation

n.d.   *Preservando el pasado para un mejor mañana*. Undated pamphlet.

Laude, Jean

1973   *African Art of the Dogon: The Myths of the Cliff Dwellers*. New York: Brooklyn Museum and Viking.

Laughlin, Robert M.

1988   *The Great Tzotzil Dictionary of Santo Domingo Zinacantán*. Smithsonian Contributions to Anthropology 31. Washington, D.C.: Smithsonian Institution Press.

Lechtman, Heather

1977   Style in Technology—Some Early Thoughts. In *Material Culture: Styles, Organization, and Dynamics of Technology*, ed. H. Lechtman and R. S. Merrill, pp. 3–20. 1975 Proceedings of the American Ethnological Society. St. Paul, Minn.: West.

León-Portilla, Miguel

1988   *Time and Reality in the Thought of the Maya*. 2nd ed. Introduction by A. Villa Rojas. Norman: University of Oklahoma Press.

Lindholm, Charles

1990   *Charisma*. Cambridge: Basil Blackwell.

Looper, Matthew G.

1991a   The Dances of the Classic Maya Gods Chak and Hun Nal Ye. M.A. thesis, University of Texas at Austin.

1991b   *The Name of Copan and of a Dance at Yaxchilan*. Copán Note 95. Copán, Honduras: Copán Mosaics Project and the Instituto Hondureño de Antropología e Historia.

1991c   Sublords and Sages at Tortuguero. Paper presented at the Ninetieth Annual Meeting of the American Anthropological Association, Chicago, Illinois.

1994   Un título para nobles en Quiriguá. Paper presented at the Octavo Simposio de Arqueología Guatemalteca, Museo Nacional de Arqueología y Etnología, Guatemala.

1995a   The Sculpture Programs of Butz'-Tiliw, an Eighth-Century Maya King of Quiriguá, Guatemala. Ph.D. diss., University of Texas at Austin.

1995b   The Three Stones of Maya Creation Mythology at Quiriguá. *Mexicon* 17 (2): 24–30.

1997a   Sculpture and Performance at Quiriguá. In *Proceedings of the 1995 and 1996 Latin American Symposia*, ed. Alana Cordy-Collins and Grace Johnson, pp. 35–48. San Diego Museum of Man Paper 34. San Diego: San Diego Museum of Man.

1997b *A Venus God as Patron of Quiriguá.* Glyph Dwellers 1. Davis: Maya Hieroglyphic Database Project, Department of Native American Studies, University of California at Davis.

1999 New Perspectives on the Late Classic Political History of Quirigua, Guatemala. *Ancient Mesoamerica* 10: 263–280.

2000 *Gifts of the Moon: Huipil Designs of the Ancient Maya.* San Diego Museum Papers 38. San Diego, Calif.: San Diego Museum of Man.

2001 Dance Performances at Quiriguá. In *Landscape and Power in Ancient Mesoamerica,* ed. Rex Koontz, Kathryn Reese-Taylor, and Annabeth Headrick, pp. 113–135. Boulder, Colo.: Westview.

2002a Ancient Maya Women-Men (and Men-Women): Classic Rulers and the Third Gender. In *Ancient Maya Women,* ed. Traci Ardren, pp. 171–202. Walnut Creek, Calif.: Altamira.

2002b Quiriguá Zoomorph P: A Water-Throne and Mountain of Creation. In *Heart of Creation: Linda Schele and the Mesoamerican World,* ed. Andrea Stone, pp. 185–200. Tuscaloosa: University of Alabama Press.

2003 Wind, Rain, and Stone: Ancient and Contemporary Maya Meteorology. In *Shamanism, Mesas, and Cosmology in Mesoamerica,* ed. Douglas Sharon. San Diego, Calif.: San Diego Museum of Man.

n.d. The Monuments and Inscriptions of Quirigua. In *Quirigua Reports: Volume 5,* ed. Robert Sharer. Philadelphia: University Museum Publications, University of Pennsylvania.

Looper, Matthew G., and Julia Guernsey Kappelman

2001 The Cosmic Umbilicus in Mesoamerica: A Floral Metaphor for the Source of Life. *Journal of Latin American Lore* 21 (1): 3–53.

Looper, Matthew G., and Linda Schele

1991 *A War at Palenque during the Reign of Ah-K'an.* Texas Notes on Precolumbian Art, Writing, and Culture 25. Austin: Center for the History of Art and Ancient American Culture, Art Department, University of Texas.

1994 *The Founder of Quiriguá, Tutum-Yol-K'inich.* Copán Note 119. Copán, Honduras: Copán Mosaics Project and the Instituto Hondureño de Antropología e Historia.

López Raquec, Margarita

1989 *Acerca de los alfabetos para escribir los idiomas mayas de Guatemala.* Colección Literatura Guatemalteca Siglo XX, no. 2. Guatemala City: Proyecto Lingüístico Francisco Marroquín.

Lounsbury, Floyd

1976 A Rationale for the Initial Date of the Temple of the Cross at Palenque. In *The Art, Iconography, and Dynastic History of Palenque, Part III,* ed. Merle Greene Robertson, pp. 211–224. Pebble Beach, Calif.: Robert Louis Stevenson School, Pre-Columbian Art Research.

1980 Some Problems in the Interpretation of the Mythological Portion of the Hieroglyphic Text of the Temple of the Cross at Palenque. In *Third Palenque Round Table, 1978, Part 2,* ed. Merle Greene Robertson, pp. 99–115. Austin: University of Texas Press.

1985 The Identities of the Mythological Figures in the "Cross Group" of Inscriptions at Palenque. In *Fourth Round Table of Palenque, 1980: Volume 6,* ed. Merle Greene Robertson and Elizabeth P. Benson, pp. 45–58. San Francisco: Pre-Columbian Art Research Institute.

Love, Bruce

1987 *Glyph T93 and Maya "Hand-Scattering" Events.* Research Reports on Ancient Maya Writing 5. Washington, D.C.: Center for Maya Research.

MacLeod, Barbara

1991 *Maya Genesis: The First Steps.* North Austin Hieroglyphic Hunches 5. Note distributed to epigraphers.

n.d. The Affix T174 as *kuch* "seat, carry, (storage) place." Unpublished note distributed to epigraphers, dated March 1993.

Macri, Martha J., and Matthew G. Looper

2003 *The New Catalog of Maya Hieroglyphs, Vol. 1: The Classic Period Inscriptions.* Norman: University of Oklahoma Press.

The Madrid Maya Codex

1933 With an introduction by Wiliam Gates. Baltimore, Md.: Maya Society.

Marcus, Joyce

1973 Territorial Organization of the Lowland Classic Maya. *Science* 180 (4089): 911–916.

1976 *Emblem and State in the Classic Maya Lowlands: An Epigraphic Approach to Territorial Organization.* Washington, D.C.: Dumbarton Oaks.

1978 Archaeology and Religion: A Comparison of the Zapotec and Maya. *World Archaeology* 10: 172–191.

1992 *Mesoamerican Writing Systems: Propaganda, Myth, and History in Four Ancient Civilizations.* Princeton, N.J.: Princeton University Press.

Martin, Simon

1996 Tikal's "Star War" against Naranjo. In *Eighth Palenque Round Table, 1993,* ed. Martha J. Macri and Jan McHargue, pp. 223–236. San Francisco: Pre-Columbian Art Research Institute.

Martin, Simon, and Nikolai Grube

1995 Maya Superstates. *Archaeology* 48 (6): 41–46.

2000 *Chronicle of the Maya Kings and Queens.* London: Thames & Hudson.

Matheny, Ray T.

1987 El Mirador: An Early Maya Metropolis Uncovered. *National Geographic* 172 (3): 317–339.

Mathews, Peter

1979 Notes on the Inscriptions of "Site Q." Manuscript on file, Department of Archaeology, University of Calgary, Alberta.

1980 Notes on the Dynastic Sequence of Bonampak, Part 1. In *Third Palenque Round Table, 1978, Part 2,* ed. Merle Greene Robertson, pp. 60–73. Austin: University of Texas Press.

1984 Emblem Glyphs in Classic Maya Inscriptions. Paper presented at the Eighty-third Annual Meeting of the American Anthropological Association, Denver.

1985 Maya Early Classic Monuments and Inscriptions. In *A Consideration of the Early Classic Period in the Maya Lowlands,* ed. Gordon R. Willey and Peter Mathews, pp. 5–54. Albany: Institute for Mesoamerican Studies, State University of New York at Albany.

1988   The Sculptures of Yaxchilán. Ph.D. diss., Yale University.

Mathews, Peter, and John Justeson

1984   Patterns of Sign Substitution in Mayan Hieroglyphic Writing: The "Affix Cluster." In *Phoneticism in Mayan Hieroglyphic Writing*, ed. John S. Justeson and Lyle Campbell, pp. 185–231. Institute for Mesoamerican Studies Publication 9. Albany: Institute for Mesoamerican Studies, State University of New York.

Matos Moctezuma, Eduardo

1984   The Templo Mayor of Tenochtitlan: Economics and Ideology. In *Ritual Human Sacrifice in Mesoamerica*, ed. Elizabeth H. Boone, pp. 133–164. Washington, D.C.: Dumbarton Oaks.

1987   The Templo Mayor of Tenochtitlan: History and Interpretation. In *The Great Temple of Tenochtitlan: Center and Periphery in the Aztec World*, ed. Johanna Broda, Davíd Carrasco, and Eduardo Matos Moctezuma, pp. 15–60. Berkeley: University of California Press.

Maudslay, Alfred P.

1889–   Archaeology. 5 vols. *Biologia Centrali-Americana*. London:
1902   Porter, Dulau & Co.

Mauss, Marcel

1985   A Category of the Human Mind: The Notion of the Person; the Notion of the Self. In *The Category of the Person: Anthropology, Philosophy, History*, ed. Michael Carrithers, Steven Collins, and Steven Lukes, pp. 1–25. Cambridge: Cambridge University Press.

McHargue, Janise Y.

1995   Maya Relief Sculpture: Regional Styles and Community Identity at Copán, Palenque, and Yaxchilán. Ph.D. diss., University of California at Berkeley.

Milbrath, Susan

1979   *A Study of Olmec Sculptural Chronology*. Studies in Pre-Columbian Art and Archaeology, 23. Washington, D.C.: Dumbarton Oaks.

1999   *Star Gods of the Maya: Astronomy in Art, Folklore, and Calendars*. Austin: University of Texas Press.

Miles, Susan W.

1965   Sculpture of Guatemalan-Chiapas Highlands and Pacific Slopes, and Associated Hieroglyphs. In *Handbook of Middle American Indians: Volume 2*, ed. Robert Wauchope and Gordon R. Willey, pp. 237–275. Austin: University of Texas Press.

Miller, Arthur G.

1974   The Iconography of the Painting in the Temple of the Diving God, Tulum, Quintana Roo, Mexico: The Twisted Cords. In *Mesoamerican Archaeology: New Approaches*, ed. Norman Hammond, pp. 167–186. London: Duckworth.

1983   Stylistic Implications of Monument Carving at Quirigua and Copan. In *Quirigua Reports: Volume 2*, ed. Edward M. Schortman and Patricia A. Urban, pp. 129–136. University Museum Monograph 49. Philadelphia: University Museum Publications, University of Pennsylvania.

Miller, Mary Ellen

1999   *Maya Art and Architecture*. London: Thames & Hudson.

Miller, Mary Ellen, and Stephen D. Houston

1987   The Classic Maya Ballgame and Its Architectural Context:

A Study of Relations between Text and Image. *RES: Anthropology and Aesthetics* 14: 47–66.

Molloy, John P., and William L. Rathje

1974   Sexploitation among the Late Classic Maya. In *Mesoamerican Archaeology: New Approaches*, ed. Norman Hammond, pp. 431–444. London: Duckworth.

Montejo, Victor Dionicio

1984   *El Kanil, Man of Lightning*. English version by Wallace Kaufman. Carrboro, N.C.: Signal.

Montgomery, John

1995   Sculptors of the Realm: Classic Maya Artists' Signatures and Sculptural Style during the Reign of Piedras Negras Ruler 7. M.A. thesis, University of New Mexico, Albuquerque.

Moran, Pedro

1935   *Arte y diccionario en lengua Choltí*. Baltimore, Md.: Maya Society.

Morley, Sylvanus G.

1912   Quirigua, an American Town 1400 Years Old. *Scientific American* 107 (5): 96.

1913   Excavations at Quirigua, Guatemala. *National Geographic* 24 (3): 339–361.

1915   *An Introduction to the Study of Maya Hieroglyphics*. New York:
[1975] Dover.

1920   *The Inscriptions at Copan*. Carnegie Institution of Washington Publication 219. Washington, D.C.: Carnegie Institution of Washington.

1923   Archaeology. In *Carnegie Institution of Washington Year Book* 22, p. 264. Washington, D.C.: Carnegie Institution of Washington.

1935   *Guide Book to the Ruins of Quirigua*. Carnegie Institution of Washington, Supplementary Publication 16. Washington, D.C.: Carnegie Institution of Washington.

1937–   *The Inscriptions of Petén*. 5 vols. Carnegie Institution of
1938   Washington, Publication 437. Washington, D.C.: Carnegie Institution of Washington.

Newsome, Elizabeth

1991   The Trees of Paradise and Pillars of the World: Vision Quest and Creation in the Stelae Cycle of 18-Rabbit-God K, Copan, Honduras. Ph.D. diss., University of Texas at Austin.

2001   *Trees of Paradise and Pillars of the World: The Serial Stelae Cycle of "18-Rabbit-God K," King of Copan*. Austin: University of Texas Press.

Norman, V. Garth

1976   *Izapa Sculpture, Part 2: Text*. Papers of the New World Archaeological Foundation 30. Provo: New World Archaeological Foundation, Brigham Young University.

Núñez de la Vega, Fray Francisco

1702   *Constituciones dioecesanos del obispado de Chiapas*. Rome: Caietano Zenobi.

Orejel, Jorge

1990   The "Axe/Comb" Glyph as ch'ak. Research Reports on Ancient Maya Writing 31. Washington, D.C.: Center for Maya Research.

Orozco, Rebecca, Richard Bronson, Elsa Chang, Donaldo Castillo, Clive Carruthers, and Mario Flores

n.d.   Proyecto Arqueológico Izabal: Fase II. Report on file at the Centro de Investigaciones Regionales en Mesoamérica, La Antigua, Guatemala, dated 1991.

Ortner, Sherry

1978   *Sherpas through Their Rituals.* Cambridge: Cambridge University Press.

Palacio, Diego García de

1985   *Letter to the King of Spain.* Trans. Ephraim G. Squier. Culver City, Calif.: Labyrinthos.

Parsons, Lee Allen

1986   *The Origins of Maya Art: Monumental Stone Sculpture of Kaminaljuyu, Guatemala, and the Southern Pacific Coast.* Studies in Pre-Columbian Art and Archaeology, 28. Washington, D.C.: Dumbarton Oaks.

Ponce, Fray Alonso

1932   *Fray Alonso Ponce in Yucatán 1588.* Trans. Ernest Noyes. Middle American Research Series Publication 4. New Orleans: Department of Middle American Research, Tulane University.

Pope, Elizabeth

1999   The Place of Creation in the Maya Madrid Codex. Paper presented at the College Art Association annual meeting, Los Angeles, California.

Porter, James B.

1996   Celtiform Stelae: A New Olmec Sculpture Type and its Implication for Epigraphers. In *Beyond Indigenous Voices: LAILA/ALILA Eleventh International Symposium on Latin American Indian Literatures (1994),* ed. Mary H. Preuss, pp. 65–72. Lancaster, Calif.: Labyrinthos.

Proskouriakoff, Tatiana

1946   *An Album of Maya Architecture.* Carnegie Institution of Washington Publication 558. Washington, D.C.: Carnegie Institution of Washington.

1950   *A Study of Classic Maya Sculpture.* Carnegie Institution of Washington Publication 593. Washington, D.C.: Carnegie Institution of Washington.

1961   Portraits of Women in Maya Art. In *Essays in Pre-Columbian Art and Archaeology,* ed. Samuel K. Lothrop et al., pp. 81–99. Cambridge, Mass.: Harvard University Press.

1963–   Historical Data in the Inscriptions of Yaxchilán, Parts I and
1964   II. *Estudios de Cultura Maya* 3: 149–167; and 4: 177–201.

1965   Sculpture and Major Arts of the Maya Lowlands. In *Archaeology of Southern Mesoamerica, Part 1,* ed. Gordon R. Willey, pp. 469–497. *Handbook of Middle American Indians,* vol. 2. Gen. ed. Robert Wauchope. Austin: University of Texas Press.

1973   The Hand-Grasping-Fish and Associated Glyphs on Classic Maya Monuments. In *Mesoamerican Writing Systems,* ed. Elizabeth P. Benson, pp. 165–178. Washington, D.C.: Dumbarton Oaks.

1978   Olmec Gods and Maya God-Glyphs. In *Codex Wauchope: A Tribute Roll,* ed. Marco Giardino, Barbara Edmonson, and Winifred Creamer, pp. 113–117. New Orleans: Bureau of Administrative Services, Tulane University.

1993   *Maya History.* Ed. Rosemary Joyce. Austin: University of Texas Press.

Rands, Robert L.

1968   Relationship of Monumental Stone Sculpture of Copán with the Maya Lowlands. In *Verhandlungen des XXXVIII. International Amerikanistenkongresses, Stuttgart-München 12. bis 18. August 1968,* vol. 1, pp. 518–529. 4 vols. Munich: Klaus Renner.

Rands, Robert L., and Barbara C. Rands

1959   The Incensario Complex at Palenque, Chiapas. *American Antiquity* 25 (2): 225–236.

Rappaport, Roy

1999   *Ritual and Religion in the Making of Humanity.* Cambridge: Cambridge University Press.

Recinos, Adrián

1957   Títulos de la casa Ixquín-Nehaib, señora del territorio de Otzoya. In *Crónicas indígenas de Guatemala,* ed. Adrián Recinos, pp. 71–94. Guatemala City: Editorial Universitaria.

Redfield, Robert, and Alfonso Villa Rojas

1962   *Chan Kom: A Maya Village.* Chicago: University of Chicago Press.

Reents-Budet, Dorie

1985   The Late Classic Maya Holmul Style Polychrome Pottery. Ph.D. diss., University of Texas at Austin.

1994   *Painting the Maya Universe: Royal Ceramics of the Classic Period.* Durham, N.C.: Duke University Press.

Reents-Budet, Dorie, Ellen E. Bell, Loa P. Traxler, and Ronald L. Bishop

n.d.   Early Classic Ceramic Offerings at Copán: A Comparison of the Hunal, Margarita, and Sub-Jaguar Tombs. Unpublished manuscript.

Reents-Budet, Dorie, and Ronald Bishop

2000   War and Feasts: Ceramic Styles of the Ik' Polity, Guatemala. Paper presented at the Thirty-third Annual Chacmool Conference, Calgary, November.

Reents-Budet, Dorie, Ronald L. Bishop, Jennifer T. Taschek, and Joseph W. Ball

2000   Out of the Palace Dumps: Ceramic Production and Use at Buenavista del Cayo. *Ancient Mesoamerica* 11 (1): 99–121.

Reese, Kathryn V.

1996   Narratives of Power: Late Formative Public Architecture and Civic Center Design at Cerros, Belize. Ph.D. diss., University of Texas at Austin.

Reilly, F. Kent, III

1989   Enclosed Ritual Space and the Watery Underworld in Formative Period Architecture: New Observations on the Function of La Venta Complex A. Paper presented at the Séptima Mesa Redonda, Palenque, Chiapas.

1994   Visions to Another World: Art, Shamanism, and Political Power in Middle Formative Mesoamerica. Ph.D. diss., University of Texas at Austin.

Rich, Jack C.

1947   *The Materials and Methods of Sculpture.* New York: Oxford University Press.

Ricketson, Oliver G., Jr.

1928 Astronomical Observations in the Maya Area. *Geographical Review* 18: 215–225.

1933 Unpublished fieldnotes, on file at the Peabody Museum, Harvard University.

1935 Maya Pottery Well from Quiriguá Farm, Guatemala. *Maya Research* 2: 103–105.

Ricketson, Oliver G., and Edith B. Ricketson

1937 *Uaxactún, Guatemala: Group E 1926-1931.* Carnegie Institution of Washington Publication 477. Washington, D.C.: Carnegie Institution of Washington.

Riese, Berthold

1980 Katun-Altersangaben in klassischen Maya-Inschriften. *Baessler-Archiv: Beiträge zur Völkerkunde* 28: 155–180.

1984 Hel Hieroglyphs. In *Phoneticism in Maya Hieroglyphic Writing*, ed. John S. Justeson and Lyle Campbell, pp. 263–286. Institute for Mesoamerican Studies Publication 9. Albany: Institute for Mesoamerican Studies, State University of New York.

1986 Late Classic Relationship between Copan and Quirigua: Some Epigraphic Evidence. In *The Southeast Maya Periphery*, ed. Patricia A. Urban and Edward M. Schortman, pp. 94–101. Austin: University of Texas Press.

1988 Epigraphy of the Southeast Zone in Relation to Other Parts of the Maya Realm. In *The Southeast Classic Maya Zone*, ed. Elizabeth Boone and Gordon R. Willey, pp. 67–94. Washington, D.C.: Dumbarton Oaks.

Ringle, William M.

1988 *Of Mice and Monkeys: The Value and Meaning of T1016, the God C Hieroglyph.* Research Reports on Ancient Maya Writing 18. Washington, D.C.: Center for Maya Research.

1990 Who Was Who in Ninth-Century Chichen Itza. *Ancient Mesoamerica* 1: 233–243.

Robicsek, Francis, and Donald Hales

1981 *The Maya Book of the Dead: The Ceramic Codex.* Charlottesville: University of Virginia Museum. Distributed by the University of Oklahoma Press.

Roys, Ralph L.

1949 *The Prophesies for the Maya tuns or Years in the Books of Chilam Balam of Tizimin and Mani.* Carnegie Institution of Washington Publication 585, Contribution 51. Washington, D.C.: Carnegie Institution of Washington.

1965 *Ritual of the Bacabs.* Norman: University of Oklahoma Press.

1967 *The Book of the Chilam Balam of Chumayel.* Norman: University of Oklahoma Press.

Sahagún, Bernardino de

1950– *The Florentine Codex.* Trans. Arthur J. O. Anderson and
1982 Charles E. Dibble. 12 books in 13 vols. Santa Fe: Monographs of the School of American Research and University of Utah Press.

Sanchez, Julia L.

1997 Royal Strategies and Audience: An Analysis of Classic Maya Monumental Art. Ph.D. diss., University of California at Los Angeles.

Satterthwaite, Linton

1951 Reconnaissance in British Honduras. *Bulletin of the University Museum* 16 (1): 21–37.

1952 *Piedras Negras Archaeology: Architecture, Part V: Sweathouses.* Philadelphia: University Museum Publications, University of Pennsylvania.

1979 Quirigua Altar L (Monument 12). In *Quirigua Reports: Volume 1*, ed. Wendy Ashmore, pp. 39–43. University Museum Monograph 37. Philadelphia: University Museum Publications, University of Pennsylvania.

Sauerländer, Willibald

1983 From Stilus to Style: Reflections on the Fate of a Notion. *Art History* 6: 253–270.

Saville, Marshall H.

1919 Bibliographic Notes on Quirigua, Guatemala. *Indian Notes and Monographs* 4 (1): 5–22. New York: Museum of the American Indian, Heye Foundation.

Scarborough, Vernon L.

1991 Courting in the Southern Maya Lowlands: A Study in Pre-Hispanic Ballgame Architecture. In *The Mesoamerican Ballgame*, ed. Vernon L. Scarborough and David R. Wilcox, pp. 129–144. Tucson: University of Arizona Press.

Schapiro, Meyer

1953 Style. In *Anthropology Today*, ed. A. L. Kroeber, pp. 287–312. Chicago: University of Chicago.

Schele, Linda

1976 Accession Iconography of Chan-Bahlum in the Group of the Cross at Palenque. In *The Art, Iconography and Dynastic History of Palenque, Part III*, ed. Merle Greene Robertson, pp. 9–34. Pebble Beach, Calif.: Pre-Columbian Art Research, Robert Louis Stevenson School.

1979 Genealogical Documentation in the Tri-Figure Panels at Palenque. In *Tercera Mesa Redonda de Palenque, vol. 4*, ed. Merle Greene Robertson, pp. 41–70. Palenque: Pre-Columbian Art Research and Monterey: Herald Printers.

1982 *Maya Glyphs: The Verbs.* Austin: University of Texas Press.

1985 *Notebook for the IXth Maya Hieroglyphic Workshop at Texas.* Austin: University of Texas at Austin.

1987 *A Brief Commentary on a Hieroglyphic Cylinder from Copan.* Copán Note 27. Copán, Honduras: Copán Mosaics Project and the Instituto Hondureño de Antropología e Historia.

1988 The Xibalba Shuffle: A Dance after Death. In *Maya Iconography*, ed. Elizabeth Benson and Gillett Griffin, pp. 294–317. Princeton, N.J.: Princeton University Press.

1989a *A Brief Commentary on the Top of Altar Q.* Copán Note 66. Copán, Honduras: Copán Mosaics Project and the Instituto Hondureño de Antropología e Historia.

1989b A Brief Note on the Name of a Vision Serpent. In *The Maya Vase Book: Volume 1*, ed. Justin Kerr, pp. 146–148. New York: Kerr & Associates.

1989c *A New Glyph for "Five" on Stela E.* Copán Note 53. Copán, Honduras: Copán Mosaics Project and the Instituto Hondureño de Antropología e Historia.

1989d *Some Further Thoughts on the Quiriguá-Copán Connection.* Copán Note 67. Copán, Honduras: Copán Mosaics Project and the Instituto Hondureño de Antropología e Historia.

1990a *The Early Classic Dynastic History of Copán: Interim Report 1989.* Copán Note 70. Copán, Honduras: Copán Mosaics Project and the Instituto Hondureño de Antropología e Historia.

1990b *Early Quiriguá and the Kings of Copán.* Copán Note 75. Copán, Honduras: Copán Mosaics Project and the Instituto Hondureño de Antropología e Historia.

1990c *Further Comments on Stela 6.* Copán Note 73. Copán, Honduras: Copán Mosaics Project and the Instituto Hondureño de Antropología e Historia.

1990d *Speculations from an Epigrapher on Things Archaeological in the Acropolis at Copán.* Copán Note 80. Copán, Honduras: Copán Mosaics Project and the Instituto Hondureño de Antropología e Historia.

1991a *Notebook for the XVth Maya Hieroglyphic Workshop at Texas.* Austin: University of Texas at Austin.

1991b *Venus and the Monuments of Smoke-Imix-God K and Others in the Great Plaza.* Copán Note 101. Copán, Honduras: Copán Mosaics Project and the Instituto Hondureño de Antropología e Historia.

1992a *The Founders of Lineages at Copan and Other Maya Sites.* Ancient Mesoamerica 3 (1): 135–144.

1992b *Notebook for the XVIth Maya Hieroglyphic Workshop at Texas.* Austin: University of Texas at Austin.

1998 The Iconography of Maya Architectural Façades during the Late Classic Period. In *Function and Meaning in Classic Maya Architecture,* ed. Stephen D. Houston, pp. 479–517. Washington, D.C.: Dumbarton Oaks.

Schele, Linda, and Barbara Fash

1991 *Venus and the Reign of Smoke-Monkey.* Copán Note 100. Copán, Honduras: Copán Mosaics Project and the Instituto Hondureño de Antropología e Historia.

Schele, Linda, and David Freidel

1990 *A Forest of Kings: The Untold Story of the Ancient Maya.* New York: William Morrow.

1991 The Courts of Creation: Ballcourts, Ballgames, and Portals to the Maya Otherworld. In *The Mesoamerican Ballgame,* ed. Vernon L. Scarborough and David R. Wilcox, pp. 289–315. Tucson: University of Arizona Press.

Schele, Linda, and Nikolai Grube

1988 *A Venus Title on Copán Stela F.* Copán Note 41. Copán, Honduras: Copán Mosaics Project and the Instituto Hondureño de Antropología e Historia.

1990a *The Glyph for Plaza or Court.* Copán Note 86. Copán, Honduras: Copán Mosaics Project and the Instituto Hondureño de Antropología e Historia.

1990b *A Preliminary Inventory of Place Names in the Copán Inscriptions.* Copán Note 93. Copán, Honduras: Copán Mosaics Project and the Instituto Hondureño de Antropología e Historia.

1992a *The Founding Events at Copán.* Copán Note 107. Copán, Honduras: Copán Mosaics Project and the Instituto Hondureño de Antropología e Historia.

1992b *Venus, the Great Plaza, and Recalling the Dead.* Copán Note 108. Copán, Honduras: Copán Mosaics Project and the Instituto Hondureño de Antropología e Historia.

1994 *Notebook for the XVIIIth Maya Hieroglyphic Workshop.* Austin: University of Texas at Austin.

Schele, Linda, Nikolai Grube, and Federico Fahsen

1992 *The Lunar Series in Classic Maya Inscriptions: New Observations and Interpretations.* Texas Notes on Precolumbian Art, Writing, and Culture 29. Austin: Center for the History of Art and Ancient American Culture, Art Department, University of Texas.

1993 *The Tikal-Copan Connection: The Copan Evidence.* Copán Note 122. Copán, Honduras: Copán Mosaics Project and the Instituto Hondureño de Antropología e Historia.

1994a *The Floor Marker from Motmot.* Copán Note 117. Copán, Honduras: Copán Mosaics Project and the Instituto Hondureño de Antropología e Historia.

1994b *The Xukpi Stone: A Newly Discovered Early Classic Inscription from the Copan Acropolis, Part II: Commentary on the Text.* Copán Note 114. Copán, Honduras: Copán Mosaics Project and the Instituto Hondureño de Antropología e Historia.

Schele, Linda, Nikolai Grube, and David Stuart

1989 *The Date of Dedication of Ballcourt III at Copán.* Copán Note 59. Copán, Honduras: Copán Mosaics Project and the Instituto Hondureño de Antropología e Historia.

Schele, Linda, and Julia Guernsey Kappelman

2001 What the Heck's Coatépec?: The Formative Roots of an Enduring Mythology. In *Landscape and Power in Ancient Mesoamerica,* ed. Rex Koontz, Kathryn Reese-Taylor, and Annabeth Headrick, pp. 29–53. Boulder, Colo.: Westview.

Schele, Linda, and Rudy Larios

1991 *Some Venus Dates on the Hieroglyphic Stair at Copán.* Copán Note 99. Copán, Honduras: Copán Mosaics Project and the Instituto Hondureño de Antropología e Historia.

Schele, Linda, and Matthew G. Looper

1994 *The 9.17.0.0.0 Eclipse at Quiriguá and Copán.* Copán Note 115. Copán, Honduras: Copán Mosaics Project and the Instituto Hondureño de Antropología e Historia.

1996 *Workbook for the XXth Maya Hieroglyphic Forum.* Austin: Department of Art and Art History, College of Fine Arts, and Institute of Latin American Studies, University of Texas at Austin.

Schele, Linda, and Peter Mathews

1991 Royal Visits and Other Intersite Relationships among the Classic Maya. In *Classic Maya Political History: Hieroglyphic and Archaeological Evidence,* ed. T. Patrick Culbert, pp. 226–252. Cambridge: Cambridge University Press.

1993 *Notebook for the XVIIth Maya Hieroglyphic Workshop at Texas.* Austin: University of Texas at Austin.

1998 *The Code of Kings: The Language of Seven Sacred Maya Temples and Tombs.* New York: Scribner.

Schele, Linda, and Mary Ellen Miller

1986 *The Blood of Kings: Dynasty and Ritual in Maya Art.* Fort Worth: Kimbell Art Museum.

Schele, Linda, and David Stuart

1985 *Te-Tun as the Glyph for "Stela."* Copán Note 1. Copán, Honduras: Copán Mosaics Project and the Instituto Hondureño de Antropología e Historia.

Schele, Linda, David Stuart, and Nikolai Grube

1991 *A Commentary on the Inscriptions of Structure 22A at Copán.* Copán Note 98. Copán, Honduras: Copán Mosaics Project and the Instituto Hondureño de Antropología e Historia.

Schele, Linda, and Khristaan Villela

1992   *Some New Ideas about the T713-757 "Accession" Phrases.* Texas Notes on Precolumbian Art, Writing, and Culture 27. Austin: Center for the History of Art and Ancient American Culture, Art Department, University of Texas.

1994   *The Helmet of the Chakte'.* Texas Notes on Precolumbian Art, Writing, and Culture 63. Austin: Center for the History of Art and Ancient American Culture, Art Department, University of Texas.

1996   Creation, Cosmos, and the Imagery of Palenque and Copan. In *Eighth Palenque Round Table, 1993,* ed. Martha J. Macri and Jan McHargue, pp. 15–30. San Francisco: Pre-Columbian Art Research Institute.

Schieffelin, Edward L.

1985   Performance and the Cultural Construction of Reality. *American Ethnologist* 12 (4): 707–724.

Schmidt, Peter, Mercedes de la Garza, and Enrique Nalda, eds.

1998   *Maya.* New York: Rizzoli.

Schortman, Edward M.

1980   Archaeological Investigation in the Lower Motagua Valley. *Expedition* 23 (3): 28–34.

1993   Archaeological Investigations in the Lower Motagua Valley, Izabal, Guatemala: A Study in Monumental Site Function and Interaction. *Quirigua Reports: Volume 3.* Gen. ed. Robert J. Sharer. University Museum Monograph 80. Philadelphia: University Museum Publications, University of Pennsylvania.

Schortman, Edward M., and Patricia A. Urban, eds.

1983   *Quirigua Reports: Volume 2.* Gen. ed. Robert J. Sharer. University Museum Monograph 49. Philadelphia: University Museum Publications, University of Pennsylvania.

Sedat, David W., and Fernando López

1999   Tunneling into the Heart of the Copan Acropolis. *Expedition* 41 (2): 16–21.

Seler, Eduard

1899   Die Monumente von Copán und Quiriguá und die Altarplaten von Palenque. *Zeitschrift für Ethnologie* 31: 670–738.

1900   Einiges mehr über die Monumente von Copán und Quiriguá. *Zeitschrift für Ethnologie* 32: 188–227.

1902–   *Gesammelte Abhandlungen zur Amerikanischen Sprach- und Alter-*
1923   *thumskunde.* 5 vols. Berlin: A. Asher

Sharer, Robert J.

1978   Archaeology and History at Quirigua, Guatemala. *Journal of Field Archaeology* 5: 51–70.

1980   The Quirigua Project, 1974–1979. *Expedition* 23 (3): 5–10.

1988   Quirigua as a Classic Maya Center. In *The Southeast Classic Maya Zone,* ed. Elizabeth H. Boone and Gordon R. Willey, pp. 31–65. Washington, D.C.: Dumbarton Oaks.

1990   *Quirigua: A Classic Maya Center and Its Sculptures.* Durham, N.C.: Carolina Academic Press.

1997   *The Tombs of Copan and Quirigua Founders.* Early Copan Acropolis Paper 9. Philadelphia: University of Pennsylvania.

1999   Archaeology and History in the Royal Acropolis, Copan, Honduras. *Expedition* 41 (2): 8–15.

Sharer, Robert J., ed.

n.d.   *Quirigua Reports: Volume 5.* Philadelphia: University Museum Publications, University of Pennsylvania.

Sharer, Robert J., Wendy Ashmore, Edward M. Schortman, Patricia A. Urban, John L. Seidel, and David W. Sedat

1983   The Quirigua Project: 1978 Season. In *Quirigua Reports: Volume 2,* ed. Edward M. Schortman and Patricia A. Urban, pp. 39–54. University Museum Monograph 49. Philadelphia: University Museum Publications, University of Pennsylvania.

Sharer, Robert J., William L. Fash, David W. Sedat, Loa P. Traxler, and Richard Williamson

1999   Continuities and Contrasts in Early Classic Architecture of Central Copan. In *Mesoamerican Architecture as a Cultural Symbol,* ed. Jeff K. Kowalski, pp. 220–249. Oxford: Oxford University Press.

Sharer, Robert J., Christopher Jones, Wendy Ashmore, and Edward M. Schortman

1979   The Quirigua Project: 1976 Season. In *Quirigua Reports: Volume 1,* ed. Wendy Ashmore, pp. 45–73. University Museum Monograph 37. Philadelphia: University Museum Publications, University of Pennsylvania.

Sharer, Robert J., Julia C. Miller, and Loa P. Traxler

1992   Evolution of Classic Period Architecture in the Eastern Acropolis, Copan: A Progress Report. *Ancient Mesoamerica* 3: 145–159.

Sharer, Robert J., David W. Sedat, Loa P. Traxler, and Julia C. Miller

n.d.   Early Classic Royal Power in Copan: The Origins and Development of the Acropolis. In *Copan: The Rise and Fall of a Classic Maya Kingdom,* ed. William L. Fash and E. Wyllys Andrews V. Santa Fe: School of American Research Press.

Sharer, Robert J., Loa P. Traxler, David W. Sedat, Ellen E. Bell, Marcello A. Canuto, and Christopher Powell

1999   Early Classic Architecture beneath the Copan Acropolis: A Research Update. *Ancient Mesoamerica* 10: 3–23.

Shaw, Thomas J.

1976   Notes on Historical Data in the Inscriptions of Quirigua and Palenque. *Katunob* 9 (1): 8–15.

Sheets, Payson D.

1983   Guatemalan Obsidian: A Preliminary Study of Sources and Quirigua Artifacts. In *Quirigua Reports: Volume 2,* ed. Edward M. Schortman and Patricia A. Urban, pp. 87–101. University Museum Monograph 49. Philadelphia: University Museum Publications, University of Pennsylvania.

Shils, Edward A.

1961   Centre and Periphery. In *The Logic of Personal Knowledge: Essays Presented to Michal Polanyi on His Seventieth Birthday, 11th March 1961,* ed. Michael Polanyi, pp. 117–130. London: Routledge & Kegan Paul.

Smith, A. Ledyard, and Alfred V. Kidder

1943   *Explorations in the Motagua Valley, Guatemala.* Carnegie Institution of Washington Publication 546, Contributions to American Anthropology and History 41. Washington, D.C.: Carnegie Institution of Washington.

Sosa, John R.

1985 The Maya Sky, the Maya World: A Symbolic Analysis of Yucatec Maya Cosmology. Ph.D. diss., State University of New York at Albany.

Spero, Joanne Marie

1987 Lightning Men and Water Serpents: A Comparison of Mayan and Mixe-Zoquean Beliefs. M.A. thesis, University of Texas at Austin.

Spinden, Herbert J.

1913 A Study of Maya Art, Its Subject Matter and Historical Development. Memoirs of the Peabody Museum of American Archaeology and Ethnology, Harvard University, vol. 6. Cambridge, Mass.: Peabody Museum of American Archaeology and Ethnology.

Stephens, John Lloyd

1841 Incidents of Travel in Central America, Chiapas, and Yucatan. 2 vols. New York: Harper & Brothers.

Stomper, Jeffrey A.

2001 A Model for Late Classic Community Structure at Copán, Honduras. In Landscape and Power in Ancient Mesoamerica, ed. Rex Koontz, Kathryn Reese-Taylor, and Annabeth Headrick, pp. 197–229. Boulder, Colo.: Westview.

Stone, Andrea

1983 The Zoomorphs of Quirigua. Ph.D. diss., University of Texas at Austin.

1985 Variety and Transformation in the Cosmic Monster Theme at Quirigua, Guatemala. In Fifth Palenque Round Table, 1983, ed. Virginia Fields, pp. 39–48. Palenque Round Table Series 7. San Francisco: Pre-Columbian Art Research Institute.

1986 Paper presented at the Primer Simposio Mundial sobre Epigrafía Maya, Guatemala City.

1988 Sacrifice and Sexuality: Some Structural Relationships in Classic Maya Art. In The Role of Gender in Precolumbian Art and Architecture, ed. Virginia E. Miller, pp. 75–103. Lanham, Md.: University Press of America.

1989 Disconnection, Foreign Insignia, and Political Expansion: Teotihuacan and the Warrior Stelae of Piedras Negras. In Mesoamerica after the Decline of Teotihuacan A.D. 700–900, ed. Richard A. Diehl and Janet Catherine Berlo, pp. 153–172. Washington, D.C.: Dumbarton Oaks.

1991 Quirigua Zoomorph G: The Waterlily Jaguar and the Dead Maya King. Paper presented at the Ninetieth Annual Meeting of the American Anthropological Association, Chicago, Illinois, November.

Strathern, Marilyn

1988 The Gender of the Gift: Problems with Women and Problems with Society in Melanesia. Berkeley: University of California Press.

Strömsvik, Gustav

1941 Substela Caches and Stela Foundations at Copán and Quiriguá. Carnegie Institution of Washington Publication 528, Contribution to American Anthropology and History 37. Washington, D.C.: Carnegie Institution of Washington.

1952 The Ballcourts at Copan, with Notes on Courts at La Unión, Quirigua, San Pedro Pinula and Asunción Mita. Carnegie Institution of Washington Publication 596, Contributions to American Anthropology and History 55. Washington, D.C.: Carnegie Institution of Washington.

Stross, Brian

1994 Maize and Fish: The Iconography of Power in Late Formative Mesoamerica. RES: Anthropology and Aesthetics 25: 10–25.

Stuart, David

1984 Royal Auto-Sacrifice among the Maya: A Study of Image and Meaning. RES: Anthropology and Aesthetics 7 (8): 6–20.

1986 The Chronology of Stela 4. Copán Note 12. Copán, Honduras: Copán Mosaics Project and the Instituto Hondureño de Antropología e Historia.

1987a Nuevas interpretaciones de la historia dinástica de Copán. A paper presented at El Seminario de Arqueología Hondureña, La Ceiba, Atlántida, Honduras.

1987b Ten Phonetic Syllables. Research Reports on Ancient Maya Writing 14. Washington, D.C.: Center for Maya Research.

1988 Blood Symbolism in Maya Iconography. In Maya Iconography, ed. Elizabeth P. Benson and Gillett G. Griffin, pp. 175–221. Princeton, N.J.: Princeton University Press.

1989a Comments on the Temple 22 Inscription. Copán Note 63. Copán, Honduras: Copán Mosaics Project and the Instituto Hondureño de Antropología e Historia.

1989b Hieroglyphs on Maya Vessels. In The Maya Vase Book: Volume 1, ed. Justin Kerr, pp. 149–160. New York: Kerr & Associates.

1989c The Maya Artist: An Epigraphic and Iconographic Study. Honors thesis, Princeton University.

1990 A New Carved Panel from the Palenque Area. Research Reports on Ancient Maya Writing 32. Washington, D.C.: Center for Maya Research.

1992a Flower Symbolism in Maya Iconography. Paper presented at the Eighth Symposium of the Maya Meetings at Texas, "Origins: Creation and Continuity, Mythology and History in Mesoamerica," University of Texas at Austin.

1992b Hieroglyphs and Archaeology at Copan. Ancient Mesoamerica 3: 169–184.

1995 A Study of Maya Inscriptions. Ph.D. diss., Vanderbilt University. Ann Arbor: University Microfilms.

1996 Kings of Stone: A Consideration of Stelae in Ancient Maya Ritual and Representation. RES: Anthropology and Aesthetics 29/30: 149–171.

1998 "The Fire Enters His House": Architecture and Ritual in Classic Maya Texts. In Function and Meaning in Classic Maya Architecture, ed. Stephen D. Houston, pp. 373–425. Washington, D.C.: Dumbarton Oaks.

2000 "The Arrival of Strangers": Teotihuacan and Tollan in Classic Maya History. In Mesoamerica's Classic Heritage: From Teotihuacan to the Aztecs, ed. Davíd Carrasco, Lindsay Jones, and Scott Sessions, pp. 465–513. Niwot: University Press of Colorado.

n.d.a Epigraphic Evidence of Political Organization in the Western Maya Lowlands. Unpublished manuscript circulated by the author, dated 1986.

n.d.b The Texts of Temple 26: The Presentation of History at a Maya Dynastic Shrine. In Copan: The Rise and Fall of a Classic

Maya Kingdom, ed. William L. Fash and E. Wyllys Andrews V. Santa Fe: School of American Research Press.

Stuart, David, Nikolai Grube, and Linda Schele

1989 A Substitution Set for the "Macuch/Batab" Title. Copán Note 58. Copán, Honduras: Copán Mosaics Project and the Instituto Hondureño de Antropología e Historia.

Stuart, David, and Stephen D. Houston

1994 *Classic Maya Place Names*. Studies in Pre-Columbian Art and Archaeology 33. Washington, D.C.: Dumbarton Oaks.

Stuart, David, Stephen Houston, and John Robertson

1999 *Recovering the Past: Classic Mayan Language and Classic Maya Gods*. Workbook for the Twenty-third Linda Schele Forum on Maya Hieroglyphic Writing, University of Texas, Austin.

Stuart, David, and Linda Schele

1986a *Interim Report on the Hieroglyphic Stair of Structure 26*. Copán Note 17. Copán, Honduras: Copán Mosaics Project and the Instituto Hondureño de Antropología e Historia.

1986b *Yax-K'uk'-Mo', the Founder of the Lineage of Copán*. Copán Note 6. Copán, Honduras: Copán Mosaics Project and the Instituto Hondureño de Antropología e Historia.

Tate, Carolyn

1991 The Cosmological Stelae of Yaxchilán. In *Sixth Palenque Round Table, 1986*, ed. Merle Greene Robertson and Virginia M. Fields, pp. 171–181. San Francisco: Pre-Columbian Art Research Institute.

1992 *Yaxchilan: The Design of a Maya Ceremonial City*. Austin: University of Texas Press.

1999 Patrons of Shamanic Power: La Venta's Supernatural Entities in Light of Mixe Beliefs. *Ancient Mesoamerica* 10: 169–188.

2001a Art. In *Archaeology of Ancient Mexico and Central America: An Encyclopedia*, ed. Susan Toby Evans and David L. Webster, pp. 41–51. New York and London: Garland Publishing.

2001b Sculpture. In *The Oxford Encyclopedia of Mesoamerican Cultures: The Civilizations of Mexico and Central America*, ed. Davíd Carrasco, vol. 3, pp. 125–130. 3 vols. Oxford: Oxford University Press.

Taube, Karl A.

1985 The Classic Maya Maize God: A Reappraisal. In *Fifth Palenque Round Table, 1983*, ed. Virginia M. Fields, pp. 171–181. San Francisco: Pre-Columbian Art Research Institute.

1986 The Teotihuacan Cave of Origin: The Iconography and Architecture of Emergence Mythology in Mesoamerica and the American Southwest. *RES: Anthropology and Aesthetics* 12: 51–82.

1989 *Itzam Cab Ain: Caimans, Cosmology, and Calendrics in Postclassic Yucatán*. Research Reports on Ancient Maya Writing 26. Washington D.C.: Center for Maya Research.

1992 *The Major Gods of Ancient Yucatan*. Studies in Pre-Columbian Art and Archaeology 32. Washington, D.C.: Dumbarton Oaks.

1994 The Birth Vase: Natal Imagery in Ancient Maya Myth and Ritual. In *The Maya Vase Book: Volume 4*, ed. Justin Kerr and Barbara Kerr, pp. 652–685. New York: Kerr & Associates.

1996 The Olmec Maize God: The Face of Corn in Formative Mesoamerica. *RES: Anthropology and Aesthetics* 29/30: 39–81.

1998 The Jade Hearth: Centrality, Rulership, and the Classic Maya Temple. In *Function and Meaning in Classic Maya Architecture*, ed. Stephen D. Houston, pp. 427–478. Washington, D.C.: Dumbarton Oaks.

2000 The Turquoise Hearth: Fire, Self-Sacrifice, and the Central Mexican Cult of War. In *Mesoamerica's Classic Heritage: From Teotihuacan to the Aztecs*, ed. Davíd Carrasco, Lindsay Jones, and Scott Sessions, pp. 269–340. Niwot: University Press of Colorado.

Tedlock, Dennis

1983 *The Spoken Word and the Work of Interpretation*. Philadelphia: University of Pennsylvania Press.

1985 *Popol Vuh: The Definitive Edition of the Mayan Book of the Dawn of Life and the Glories of Gods and Kings*. New York: Simon & Schuster.

Tezozomoc, Hernando Alvarado

1944 *Crónica mexicana*. Mexico City: Editorial Leyenda.

Thompson, J. Eric S.

1950 *Maya Hieroglyphic Writing: An Introduction*. Carnegie Institution of Washington Publication 589. Washington, D.C.: Carnegie Institution of Washington.

1970 *Maya History and Religion*. Norman: University of Oklahoma Press.

1972 *A Commentary on the Dresden Codex: A Maya Hieroglyphic Book*. Philadelphia: American Philosophical Society.

Tovilla, Martín Alfonso

1960 *Relaciones histórico-descriptivas de la Verapaz, el Manché y Lacandón, en Guatemala*. Guatemala City: Editorial Universitaria.

Townsend, Richard F.

1979 *State and Cosmos in the Art of Tenochtitlan*. Studies in Pre-Columbian Art and Archaeology 20. Washington, D.C.: Dumbarton Oaks.

1982 Pyramid and Sacred Mountain. In *Ethnoastronomy and Archaeoastronomy in the American Tropics*, ed. Anthony F. Aveni and Gary Urton, pp. 37–62. Annals of the New York Academy of Sciences, vol. 385. New York: New York Academy of Sciences.

Tozzer, Alfred M.

1907 *A Comparative Study of the Mayas and the Lacandones*. London: Macmillan & Co.

1941 *Landa's Relación de las Cosas de Yucatán*. Papers of the Peabody Museum of American Archaeology and Ethnology 18. Cambridge, Mass.: Harvard University.

Traxler, Loa P.

2001 The Royal Court of Early Classic Copan. In *Royal Courts of the Ancient Maya, Volume 2: Data and Case Studies*, ed. Takeshi Inomata and Stephen D. Houston, pp. 44–73. Boulder, Colo.: Westview.

Turner, Victor

1967 *The Forest of Symbols*. Ithaca, N.Y.: Cornell University Press.

Umberger, Emily

1981 *Aztec Sculptures, Hieroglyphs, and History*. Ph.D. diss., Columbia University.

1987   Antiquities, Revivals and References to the Past in Aztec Art. *RES: Anthropology and Aesthetics* 13: 63–106.

Vail, Gabrielle

2000   Pre-hispanic Maya Religion: Conceptions of Divinity in the Postclassic Maya Codices. *Ancient Mesoamerica* 11 (1): 123–147.

Villacorta, Antonio J.

1927   *Quiriguá. Anales de la Sociedad de Geografía e Historia de Guatemala* 3 (3): 244–270.

Vogt, Evon Z.

1970   *The Zinacantecos of Mexico: A Modern Maya Way of Life.* Case Studies in Cultural Anthropology. New York: Holt, Rinehart & Winston.

1976   *Tortillas for the Gods: A Symbolic Analysis of Zinacanteco Rituals.* Cambridge, Mass.: Harvard University Press.

Von Euw, Eric

1977   *Corpus of Maya Hieroglyphic Inscriptions.* Vol. 4, Part 1. Cambridge, Mass.: Peabody Museum of Archaeology and Ethnology, Harvard University.

von Simson, Otto

1988   *The Gothic Cathedral: Origins of Gothic Architecture and the Me-*
[1956] *dieval Concept of Order.* 3rd ed. Bollingen Series 48. Princeton, N.J.: Princeton University Press.

Wagley, Charles

1957   *Santiago Chimaltenango.* Guatemala City: Seminario de Integración Social Guatemalteca.

Wagner, Elisabeth

n.d.   Locating Mo' Witz. Unpublished manuscript in possession of the author, dated November 1993.

Watanabe, John M.

1983   In the World of the Sun: A Cognitive Model of Mayan Cosmology. *Man* 18 (4): 710–728.

Weber, Max

1968   *Max Weber on Charisma and Institution Building.* Ed. and with an introduction by S. N. Eisenstadt. Chicago: University of Chicago Press.

Webster, David L.

1977   Warfare and the Evolution of Maya Civilization. In *The Origins of Maya Civilization,* ed. Richard E. W. Adams, pp. 335–372. Albuquerque: University of New Mexico Press.

Webster, David L., William T. Sanders, and Peter van Rossum

1992   A Simulation of Copan Population History and Its Implications. *Ancient Mesoamerica* 3: 185–198.

Weiner, Annette B.

1992   *Inalienable Possessions: The Paradox of Keeping-While-Giving.* Berkeley: University of California Press.

Willey, Gordon R., Robert J. Sharer, Rene Viel, Arthur A. Demarest, Richard M. Leventhal, and Edward M. Schortman

1980   A Study of Ceramic Interaction in the Southeastern Maya Periphery. Paper presented at the Forty-fifth Annual Meeting of the Society for American Archaeology, Philadelphia.

Wisdom, Charles

1940   *The Chorti Indians of Guatemala.* Chicago: University of Chicago.

1950   *Materials on the Chortí Language.* Microfilm Collection of Manuscripts on Cultural Anthropology 28. Chicago: University of Chicago Library.

Index

10L-26, 73, 109, 114–117, 118, 199, figs.
3.50, 3.51; titles used at, 60; toponyms
of, 135, 154; village, 184; war with Quirigua, 5, 59, 75, 76–81, 87, 88, 93, 107,
114, 117, 119, 120, 135, 194–195, 196, 198,
202, 203; Yax platform, 37; zoomorphic
altars of, 63
Cosmic Monster, 32, 63, 118, 159, 172, 174,
175, 176, 183, 188, 189, 237n. 13
Cosmic Plate, 69, 83, 85, 234n. 6, figs.
2.25, 3.10
cosmic umbilici, 32, 130–132, 133, 136, 141,
147, 168–170, 172, 176, 180, 203, 237n.
13, figs. 4.13, 5.20
cosmograms, 122–123, 170, 179–180. See
also landscape, sacred; quincunx
creation of cosmos, 10–11, 31–32, 126, 128,
138, 200; and accession, 177; and Altar
P', 192; and Ch'orti', 127, 170; day of creation (Aug. 13, 3114 BC), 10, 31; and
monuments at Palenque, 11, 179; and
monuments at Quirigua, 19, 34, 178,
199; and period ending, 10, 177; and rebirth of maize, 140; and Stela C, 11, 158,
160, 164, 172, 175, 176, 187; and Stela D,
140; and Stela F, 132, 133; three stones
of, 40, 106, 158–163, 164, 165, 166, 177,
237n. 2; and triadic emblems, 133; and
zenith passage of sun, 170; and Zoomorph G, 188–189, 192. See also mountain
of Creation; Popol Vuh
crocodiles, 32, 61, 118, 159, 172, 175, 176,
188. See also caimans; Cosmic Monster
crosses, 12, 15, 17, 85–86, 128, 180. See also
cross shrines
Cross of May, 85
cross shrines, 12–13

Dallas Art Museum, 152
dance-drama, 181
dances, 172, 182; of deities, 54, 87, 168,
172, 178, 189; of rulers, 23, 51, 114, 200,
238n. 6; sacrificial, 172, 182. See also
dance-drama; Holmul Dancer; Kolomche'; Lordly Dance
Davis, Whitney, 33, 34
death: and burial, 238n. 1; gods of, 28, 29,
87, 143; memorials of, 183, 187; metaphors for, 44, 54, 85, 175, 176, 179, 203,
233n. 15; ritual, 2, 105, 106; of rulers, 2;.
See also individual rulers; sacrifice; Xi-
b'alb'ans
decapitation, 127, 128, 234n. 3.1; and ballgame, 55; and Chaak, 83, 92; and rainmaking, 85–87; of turkeys, 86; of Xib'al-
b'ans, 31. See also Waxaklajun Ub'ah
K'awil, capture and sacrifice
deer ear, 62

directions: cardinal, 29, 36, 40, 179; disease, 31, 128; dismemberment, 31, 55;
gods of, 128; intercardinal, 179
Dos Pilas, 6, 17, 79, 81, 111, 235n. 4; El
Duende group, 6; Hieroglyphic Stairway
2, 235n. 4; Panel 18, 11; Panel 19, 17; stelae of, 235nn. 20, 21; Stela 14, 237n. 26;
Stela 15, 105
drain troughs, 233n. 3
dreams, 26, 140–141, 143
Dresden Codex, 13, 83, 84, 86, figs. I.16,
3.10d
dry season, 29, 32, 104, 136
Dumbarton Oaks Panel, 104, 192

earth gods, 41, 86. See also mountains; Pawatuns
eclipses: ecliptic, 130, 131, 132, 169; lunar,
143, 236n. 22; solar, 236n. 22; stations,
234n. 3.2. See also cosmic umbilici
E group, 237n. 16
18-Rabbit. See Waxaklajun Ub'ah K'awil
El Baúl, 8; Stela 1, 8, fig. I.8
El Cayo, 4
Eliade, Mircea, 8
El K'anil, 84
El Mirador, 7
El Orégano, 127, 128
El Tajin, 45
emblem glyphs: of Copan, 52–53, 59, 135;
definition of, 4; of Quirigua, 4, 52–53,
56, 57, 60, 118, fig. I.2
Emiliano Zapata panel, 15, fig. I.20
equinox, vernal, 86

farmers, 15, 183, 204
Fash, William L., 196
Festival of Games, 182
fire drilling, 78, 86–87, fig. 3.12
First Father, 71, 237n. 5. See also Jun Junajpu
First Five Sky, 11, 130, 158
fish, 86, 175
Five-Flower place, 69–71, 170, figs. 2.23,
2.24
flapstaffs, 46
flint, 15, 35, 76, 77, 90, 91, 99, 107, 118,
164, 237n. 12
flood, primordial, 32
floods at Quirigua, 50
flowers, 12, 32, fig. 2.22; birth from, 69–71;
glyphs for, 67–69, 168, 172, 234n. 7; regalia symbolizing, 41, 42, 105, 129, 130,
132, 147, 152, 167, 170, 199; white flower
spirit, 22, 42, 147, 168. See also Black
Earth Flower place; Five-Flower place;
Flower World; K'uy Nik? Ajaw
Flower World, 68
founding house, 36, 101, 127
fourteenth successor, vii, 101

Zoomorph G: dedication of, 187; iconography of, fig. 6.2; as jaguar platform/throne of Creation, 188, 192, fig. 6.3; location of, 182, 188, 202; royal portraits on, 187; text of, 11, 57, 77, 186, 187, 188, 234n. 2.2, figs. 6.1, 6.3, 6.4; as Waterlily Jaguar, 187

Zoomorph O: as Cosmic Monster, 176, 188, 189, 237n. 13; dedication of, 188; iconography of, 6.5; location of, 188–189, text of, 189

Zoomorph P: as Cosmic Monster, 176, 189, 237n. 13; dedication of, 189; iconography of, figs. 5.31b, 6.8, 6.9; location of, 189; paint on, 17; period ending records on, 233n. 20, figs. 2.2a, 6.11; text of, 36, 41, 58, 101, 118, 189–192, 233n. 7; as water platform/throne of Creation, 192

zoomorphs, viii, x, 6, 10, 19, 62, 63, 202, 232n. 12; as platforms/thrones, 11; at Pusilha, 60